Ministry of Defence

(NAVY)

WAR WITH JAPAN

VOLUME III

THE CAMPAIGNS IN THE
SOLOMONS AND NEW GUINEA

London: HMSO

© Crown copyright 1995

Applications for reproduction should be made to HMSO
First published 1995

ISBN 0 11 772819 5

Contents

APPENDICES

ILLUSTRATIONS

FIGURES

PLANS

(at end of text)

1. Indian Ocean and Pacific
2. Capture of Diego Suarez
3. Japanese submarine attack on Cape route, June–July 1942
4. Midget submarine attack on Sydney Harbour, 31st May/1st June 1942
5. Strategic situation in South and South-West Pacific, July 1942
6. Coast watching teleradio stations, 1941–1943
7. Cruises of German raiders in the Indian Ocean, 1942
8. The Solomon Islands and Bismarcks
9. Battle of Savo Island
10. Port Jackson, 31st May 1942
11. Battle of the Eastern Solomons, 23rd–25th August 1942
12. Naval operations, 1st–13th November 1942
13. Battle of Tassafaronga (Lunga Point) 30th November–1st December 1942
14. New Guinea.
15. Engagement in Kula Gulf, 6th March 1943
16. New Georgia
17. Battle of Kula Gulf, 5th–6th July, 1943
18. Battle of Kolombangara, 12th–13th July 1943
19. Battle of Vella Lavella, 6th/7th October 1943
20. Battle of Empress Augusta Bay, night of 1st–2nd November 1943
21. Battle of Cape St. George, 25th November 1943
22. Pacific Ocean, operating limits of Japanese area forces, August 1943
23. Principal air bases on the southern perimeter, September 1943
24. The Solomon Islands
25. Battle of Santa Cruz, 24th–27th October 1942
26. Battle of Guadalcanal, Battleship action, 14th–15th November 1942
27. Signatures of midget submarines off Sydney Harbour
28. The Netherlands East Indies and Philippine Islands
29. Bougainville and adjacent islands
30. The Pacific.

vi

LIST OF ABBREVIATIONS USED

ACNB	Australian Commonwealth Naval Board
A.I.B.	Allied Intelligence Bureau
AMC	Armed merchant cruiser
A.M/S	Auxiliary minesweeper
APc	Coastal transport (small)
ASV	Airborne search radar
A/T	Anti torpedo
A.T.I.S.	Allied Translator and Intelligence Section
B 17	Heavy bomber aircraft ('Fortress')
B 24	Heavy bomber aircraft ('Liberator')
B 25	Medium bomber aircraft ('Mitchell')
B 26	Medium bomber aircraft ('Marauder')
B 29	Very heavy bomber aircraft ('Superfortress')
BAD	British Admiralty Delegation
BB	Battleship
BIOS	British Intelligence Objectives Sub-Committee
CA	Heavy cruiser
Cincpac	Commander in Chief Pacific
CL	Light cruiser
Cominch	Commander in Chief US Fleet
Comsopac	Commander South Pacific
CV	Aircraft carrier
CVE	Escort aircraft carrier
CVL	Light aircraft carrier
CXAM	Radar for detecting both surface craft and aircraft at medium ranges
DD	Destroyer
DE	Destroyer escort
DEMS	Defensively equipped merchant ship
D/F	Direction finder (radio)
DRT	Dead reckoning tracer
DUKW	Amphibious truck
FEC	Far Eastern Command
FOIC	Flag Officer in Charge
HDML	Harbour defence motor launch
IFF	Challenge (' Interrogative, friend, foe ? ')

vii

LCA	Landing Craft, Assault
LCI	Landing Craft, Infantry
LCM	Landing Craft, Mechanised
LCP	Landing Craft, Personnel
LCP(R)	Landing Craft, Personnel (Ramp)
LCS	Landing Craft, Support
LCT	Landing Craft, Tank
LCV	Landing Craft, Vehicle
LST	Landing Ship, Tank
LVT	Landing Vehicle, Tracked
M	*Maru* (ship)
ML	Motor launch
M/S	Minesweeper
M/T Ship	Motor Transportation Ship
MTB	Motor torpedo boat
OTC	Officer in Tactical Command
PT	Patrol Vessel, Motor Torpedo Boat
RAAF	Royal Australian Air Force
RAN	Royal Australian Navy
RCT	Regimental Combat Team
RIN	Royal Indian Navy
SAAF	South African Air Force
SBD	Single engine naval scout bomber ('Dauntless')
SC–1	Radar for detecting both surface craft and aircraft at medium ranges
SG	Surface Search Radar (designed for installation in large vessels and used primarily for detection of surface craft)
S.I.B.	Secret Intelligence Bureau
SIO	Superintending Intelligence Officer
SNO	Senior Naval Officer
SWPA	South-west Pacific Area
TBR	Torpedo bomber reconnaissance aircraft
USMC	United States Marine Corps
USSBS	United States Strategic Bombing Survey
WIR	Admiralty Weekly Intelligence Report

Preface

THIS is the third of the six volumes of the Naval Staff History covering the war against Japan. It describes the operations in the Solomon Islands between August 1942 and February 1944 which stopped the Japanese advance southward, and the campaign in New Guinea between July 1942 and July 1944 which furnished the Allies with a main base in the Admiralty Islands, 1,500 miles closer to Japan than their previous South Seas base at Espiritu Santo in the New Hebrides. The volume also deals with the operations for the protection of our Indian Ocean shipping, from the date of the Japanese carrier raid at Easter 1942 until the U-boats were temporarily mastered in November 1943.

The Battle of Midway in June 1942, which was described in Volume II of this History, conferred on the Americans the initiative in the Pacific. Our Allies were not slow to profit by the rewards of their victory. Two months later, by attacking in the Solomon Islands they began the first of the campaigns which three years later brought them to the threshold of Japan. Simultaneously, a counter-attack by American and Australian forces undertaken for the protection of Port Moresby, our last remaining foothold in Papua, developed into an offensive for the clearance of New Guinea. Both of these began as slow, laborious campaigns, but in their later stages were characterised by rapidity resulting from a new strategic conception of by-passing and blockading all positions not required as Allied bases, a technique rendered possible by the growing power of the Americans at sea.

In the Indian Ocean, the many calls on our resources saw the Eastern Fleet reduced for a time to the status of a trade protection force. Madagascar was occupied in order to facilitate measures against enemy submarines attracted to the Mozambique Channel by the valuable shipping passing to the Middle East via the Cape of Good Hope. Despite the incursion of German U-boats and raiders into the Indian Ocean and the shortage of escort and anti-submarine vessels in the Eastern Fleet towards the end of the period the submarine menace was much reduced and a relaxation of convoy became possible. As will be recounted in Volume IV of this History, the respite was only temporary and the German and Japanese submarine menace was not finally mastered until general convoy was in operation on all routes, with air protection and the employment of anti-submarine escort carrier groups.

The principal sources used in compiling this volume are given in the Bibliography. Sources used in describing individual operations are given in footnotes to the text.

The spelling of place names is in accordance with the Admiralty sailing Directions, unless general custom prescribes some other spelling.

The complete list of volumes of the Naval Staff History, *War with Japan*, is as follows :—

Volume   I.   Background to the War.

Volume II.   Defensive Phase : Pearl Harbour and the Battle of Midway, with the Aleutian Operations.

Volume III.   The Campaigns in the Solomons and New Guinea.

Volume IV.   The South-East Asia Operations and the Central Pacific advance.

Volume V.   Blockade of Japan.

Volume VI.   Liberation of the Philippines and the final operations.

CHAPTER I

Madagascar

(*See* Plans 1, 2, 3)

1

THE withdrawal of the Eastern Fleet to Kilindini in April 1942 on account of the insecurity of its bases, Colombo and Trincomalee, came at a time when the closing of the Mediterranean to British shipping had enhanced the importance of the Cape route to the East. The strategic importance of Madagascar, which lay on this route roughly equidistant from Capetown and Aden, thus became emphasised. A fuelling base in the island would have been of great value to Japan in operations to interfere with our supply route to the Middle East, and there was the possibility that she might try to establish one with the connivance of the French. To prevent Germany and Japan from joining hands in Madagascar was recognised as one of the main defensive tasks of the Allies,[1] and an expedition to forestall its possible occupation by the enemy was already in process of being organised, now that it had at length become possible to make adequate resources available. The final decision to carry out the operation was delayed until the last possible moment, in the hope, which in the event was not fulfilled, that General de Gaulle might be successful in rallying the island to the Free French.

The best harbour in the island was the French naval and air base of Diego Suarez, a capacious port with a large dry dock and repair facilities, at the north end of Madagascar ; and the decision was taken to occupy it. Conduct of the expedition was entrusted to Rear-Admiral E. N. Syfret, Flag Officer, Force H, who was appointed Combined Commander-in-Chief of the operation, to which the code name ' Ironclad ' was given.[2] No political or other considerations were to restrict his actions in achieving the object of the expedition.[3] Force H had been constituted after the entry of Italy into the war and the fall of France in June 1940. It was based at Gibraltar, and its tasks included keeping the Italian Fleet shut in the Mediterranean and taking offensive action against that fleet and the Italian coasts. Its composition varied from time to time, and it formed the basis of Force F as the naval forces for Operation ' Ironclad ' were

---

[1] J.S.M. No. 155, 1905Q/1/4.

[2] The operation is described in detail in Naval Staff History Battle Summary No. 16, *Naval Operations at the capture of Diego Suarez* (*Operation ' Ironclad '*), May 1942, B.R. 1736 (9).

[3] The directive to the Combined Commander-in-Chief is in C.O.S. (42) 69 (O), 18th March 1942.

termed. As finally constituted, these consisted of the battleship *Ramillies,* flagship of the Commander-in-Chief, the carrier *Illustrious* (21 fighter aircraft, 20 Swordfish T.S.R.), the cruisers *Devonshire* and *Hermione,* eleven destroyers, six corvettes and six minesweepers : the latter had never swept in formation as a flotilla, and one ship had never yet swept at all. The carrier *Indomitable* (21 fighters, 24 Albacore T.S.R.) from the Eastern Fleet took the place of the *Hermes* which had been sunk in the recent raid on Trincomalee. Gathered from areas as far apart as the Western Approaches to the United Kingdom, the Atlantic seaboard of the U.S.A., the west coast of Africa, Capetown, Socotra and the Maldives the ships were ordered to concentrate at Durban which was selected as the advanced base.

The rank of the military commander was equivalent to that of the Commander-in-Chief, though at no time during the operation was any difficulty experienced on that account. The military forces were under the command of Major-General R. G. Sturges, Royal Marines, and consisted of three Infantry Brigade groups and a Commando. The 29th Infantry Brigade Group and No. 5 Commando which were to carry out the assault, and the 17th Infantry Brigade Group as floating reserve sailed from the United Kingdom in Convoy W.S.17, escorted by the *Illustrious,* their motor transport and stores coming out in Convoys O.S.22 and O.S.23. The 13th Infantry Brigade group, then on passage to India, was diverted and joined at Durban as additional floating reserve. In all, five assault ships, three personnel ships, six M.T. ships, one tank landing ship, two Royal Fleet auxiliaries, and a hospital ship conveyed and serviced the landing forces.

Rear-Admiral Syfret, at Gibraltar, had been represented on the planning staff in London by a naval captain of whom, however, circumstances deprived him before the operation began. He found this a considerable handicap. Definite orders from the Admiralty to carry out the assault landing were not received until the night 1st–2nd May, six days after the sailing of the expedition from Durban, consequently the operation orders could not be generally released until the 2nd, leaving only three days for study before the landings on the 5th. Rear-Admiral D. W. Boyd, R.A.(A), Eastern Fleet, whose flagship, the *Indomitable,* did not join the expedition until 0835 on 3rd May, had less than 48 hours to study and arrange the many complicated air commitments.

The attitude of the French could not be foreseen, but full resistance was provided against. Little naval opposition was expected other than by the four French submarines thought to be based on the island, but Diego Suarez was known to be defended by eight or nine coast batteries and had a considerable garrison, and there were fighter aircraft at the air base and a few bombers at Ivato (18° 27′ S., 47° 29′ E.) (*Figure 1,* p. 3).

The possibility of interference by the Japanese could not be ignored, and a proportion of the air striking force of Force F was held in readiness for this eventuality. During the operation, the available ships of the Eastern Fleet— two battleships, the carrier *Formidable,* cruisers and destroyers—provided cover from a position between 130 and 220 miles to the eastward of Diego Suarez ; and the Commander-in-Chief, Eastern Fleet, Admiral Somerville, arranged for Catalina patrols between 30th April and 9th May to the north-eastward.

Diego Suarez Bay (*See Plan 2*), cuts deeply into the northern tip of Madagascar, from which it is separated by a narrow isthmus. On the Antsirana Peninsula which thrusts into the south side of the Bay, was the naval base,

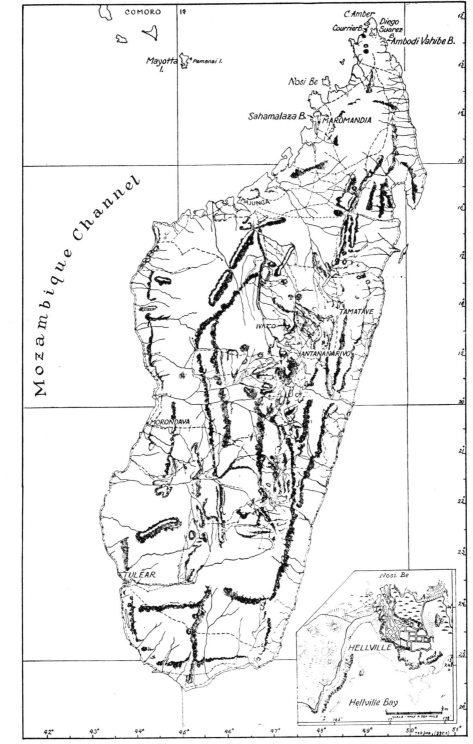

FIG. 1. MADAGASCAR

3

with the airfield 5 miles south of it. The bay is entered by Oronjia Pass ¾ mile wide, which was heavily defended. On the west coast of Madagascar, opposite Diego Suarez Bay, there are several bays, difficult of access, but capable of accommodating a considerable fleet.

The approach to Diego Suarez from Durban was made via the Mozambique Channel in two convoys, the slow (Convoy Y) sailing ten days ahead of the fast (Convoy Z). The landings were to be carried out on the west side of Madagascar, opposite Diego Suarez Bay. No. 5 Commando troops were to land in Courrier Bay, capture the two coast defence batteries there, advance eastward and secure Andrakaka Peninsula, over against Antsirana. Four battalions of the 29th Brigade were to land simultaneously in Ambararata Bay, secure a bridgehead, and advance towards Antsirana. Subsequent unloading of the transports was to take place in Ambararata Bay. The *Hermione* was to stage a simultaneous diversion off Ambodi Vahibe, 10 miles south of Oronjia Pass, on the east coast. Zero hour was provisionally fixed for 0430 on 5th May, an hour and twenty minutes before sunrise and two hours and twenty minutes before high water at Courrier Bay (8 feet).

Despite the noise of explosions of mines, two of which exploded in the sweeps in the small hours, surprise was achieved due largely to the belief held by the French authorities that the approach to the anchorage in Ambararata Bay was impossible at night ; there were consequently no arrangements for night firing by the batteries. Despite the navigational difficulties, Captain R. D. Oliver of the *Devonshire* brought the 34 ships of the combined convoys ' Y ' and ' Z ' safely to their anchorage, and the landings were made by the troops exactly as planned, opposition being encountered at only one of the four landing beaches.

Half an hour later, the carrier aircraft began to attack French shipping in Diego Suarez harbour and the Antsirana airfield, operating from a position 35 miles west of Cape Amber, screened by four destroyers. All the airfield hangars, which were full of aircraft, were left burning. In the harbour the A.M.C. *Bougainville* was hit by a torpedo and the submarine *Beveziers* was sunk by depth charges.

Despite unpleasant conditions in the anchorage, with wind up to force 8 and a heavy sea, landing operations continued throughout daylight on the 5th. Before nightfall No. 5 Commando had occupied Andrakaka Peninsula but the 29th Brigade was held up by heavy opposition on a line about 3 miles to 5 miles south of Antsirana. The only naval casualty was the minesweeper *Auricula* which struck a mine in Ambararata Bay, broke her back, and became a total loss. An ultimatum addressed to the Governor of Diego Suarez by instructions from the Admiralty was answered by the Military Commander who stated that he would defend to the last, followed by a message in a similar strain from the Governor-General at Antananarivo.

The 29th Brigade continued to be held up during the 6th. The *Devonshire* and *Hermione* had been sent round to the east side of the island to give supporting fire, but the enemy position was outside the range of ships' guns. The sloop *D'Entrecasteaux* which was firing on No. 5 Commando was set on fire by the *Indomitable's* fighters. French bombers appeared over Diego Suarez but were driven off by fighters from the *Illustrious*. Matters were not progressing.

At 1430 the suggestion was made that a small party should be put ashore on Antsirana Peninsula to create a diversion in the enemy's rear. It was acted upon with all speed. Within an hour a landing party of fifty Marines of the

Ramillies, under Captain M. Price, R.M. had embarked in the destroyer *Anthony* (Lieut.-Commander J. M. Hodges) in Ambararata Bay, and proceeded at high speed through a heavy sea towards Diego Suarez. The *Anthony* passed through Oronjia Pass at 22 knots soon after 2000. The batteries opened fire but failed to hit her. There was a strong off-shore wind, but her Captain, with fine seamanship, kept his ship's stern against the jetty long enough for the Marines to scramble ashore whilst the fire of all his ships' automatic quick-firing guns kept down the fire of the snipers on the jetty and in the woods nearby. The destroyer, having done her part, left at high speed, again passing safely through the Oronjia Pass ; and the small party of Marines was left to their own devices. Groping their way through the unknown dockyard in the dark they soon reached what proved to be the naval depot. A few hand grenades sufficed to silence the feeble fire which was opened on them and secured the surrender of the Commandant in person, followed by that of the artillery depot. Captain Price sent up the success signal, the 17th and 29th Brigades then pressed forward the attack which they had begun at 2030 ; and by 0300 on 7th May Brigadier F. W. Festing who commanded the 29th Brigade, was able to report that he was in complete possession of the town of Antsirana and its defences, and had received the personal surrender of the naval and military commanders and their staffs. The G.O.C. reported that the diversion by the *Anthony* and the Marines was the determining factor in the enemy's collapse.

At early dawn on 7th May a Swordfish from the *Illustrious* sank the submarine *Le Héros* at the entrance to Courrier Bay in 12° 3′ 45″ S., 49° 3′ 50″ E. Another, subsequently identified as the *Monge*, unsuccessfully attacked the *Indomitable* with torpedoes seven miles east of Oronjia Pass on the morning of the 8th and was sunk by counter-attack by the *Active* and *Panther*. During the early hours of the 7th, in response to a request from General Sturges for ship and air support of an assault on Oronjia Peninsula, which had yet to be subdued, the *Ramillies* joined the *Devonshire* and *Hermione* east of the peninsula. A short bombardment ' to encourage the enemy to surrender,' had the desired effect ; and that evening, a channel having been swept, the *Ramillies*, *Hermione*, *Paladin* and *Panther* entered Diego Suarez Harbour. The operation of capturing the place had taken barely 60 hours in all.

The capture of Diego Suarez was the first landing operation of the war on any scale to be undertaken by us, and although the attack was made by no more than one brigade group we learnt from it much that was valuable. In addition to the usual host of minor points that crop up time after time because there had been no previous specialisation in the type of operation being undertaken, three major lessons were learnt. The first was the importance of the L.S.T. as the carrier of guns, vehicles, ammunition and stores for the initial advance. The second was the need for landing craft to unload the transports anchored off the beaches. The third was the importance of building and training an organisation to receive, dump and issue the stores, vehicles and men as they arrived on a beach following a landing.

Pending a decision as to the use to be made of Diego Suarez, administration and planning proceeded on the basis that the port would be used as a repair base for cruisers, destroyers and light craft to the extent of the existing docking facilities, as a fuel and refuge port for all classes of ships, and as a convoy assembly port. For the time being, no further protection was available other than that normally provided for the occupation forces with the addition of certain minor under-water defences.

2

West Longitude Dates

As early as 12th March 1942 Admiral Raeder had reported to the Fuehrer that his information was the Japanese were planning to establish bases in Madagascar, though Hitler felt this was more than the French would stomach. Actually, the Japanese had no intention of going to such lengths, at least at that time ; but they were not deaf to the urging of the German Naval Staff that they should cooperate with the German spring offensive in the East by attacking the Cape route. Accordingly, five submarines, with two supply ships, were sent to operate in the Mozambique Channel.[1] Japanese submarines were accustomed in peace time to practising the operation of refuelling and transferring ammunition, torpedoes and supplies at sea.

The opportunity of sending ocean-going submarines was taken to convey one or more midgets to attack Diego Suarez, where the Japanese believed they would find the Eastern Fleet. The parent boats employed were part of the 8th Submarine Flotilla, which consisted at this date of 14 submarines, six of which were, however, earmarked for an expedition to Port Moresby at the beginning of May and the attack on Sydney harbour at the end of the month which was to be synchronised with the raid on Diego Suarez.

East Longitude Dates

Either the submarines found few ships to attack during the long passage from their station at Kwajalein in the Marshall Islands to their patrol positions in the Mozambique Channel, or else they were ordered not to reveal their presence in the Indian Ocean. The s.s. *Clan Murdoch* reported that the track of a torpedo passed 150 yards ahead of her on the night 7th/8th April in the Chagos Archipelago in 6° 50′ S., 76° 37′ E., about 250 miles east of Diego Garcia, but that was the only sign of them. It was otherwise with their supply ships, the converted light cruisers *Aikoku Maru* and *Hokoku Maru* which constituted the 24th Squadron of the Combined Fleet. These ships carried aircraft and worked together as commerce raiders as well as submarine supply ships. After operating from the beginning of December 1941 to the middle of January 1942 in the southern Pacific near the Tuamotu Islands where they sank the American s.s. *Malama* on 2nd January in 26° 39′ S., 151° 24′ W., they proceeded to the western side of the Indian Ocean, having called at Singapore or Penang or some East Indies port about the end of April. On 9th May they captured the Dutch tanker *Genota* (7,987 tons) in approximately 15° S., 75° E. They then proceeded to the Mozambique Channel approaches, where on 5th June both ships attacked with gunfire the s.s. *Elysia* (6,757 tons) in 27° 33′ S., 37° 5′ E. One of the raiders also catapulted off a small seaplane which bombed the *Elysia*, but the ship was not finally sunk until 9th June, when a torpedo from one of the enemy ships sent her to the bottom. The Japanese made no attempt to take any prisoners, but Allied ships later rescued most of the survivors. Less fortunate were the crew of the m.s. *Hauraki* (7,113 tons) the only other victim of the raiders, sunk without trace on 14th July in 17° 32′ S., 80° 25′ E., whilst the raiders were on their way home after acting as supply ships for the 8th Submarine Flotilla.

---

[1] *I–10, I–16, I–18, I–20*, and *I–30*. The latter submarine departed from position 28° 30′ S., 51° 00′ E. on 17th June, for Lorient, where she arrived on 6th August. She was sunk in the following October by a British mine in 1° N., 105° E. (Rhio Strait approaches) whilst returning to Yokosuka.

3

Times, Z — 3

Though the presence of Japanese submarines in the Mozambique Channel had long been reported these did not begin active operations until 30th May. On the previous night an unidentified monoplane with two floats had flown over Diego Suarez harbour. The aircraft was flown off the submarine *I–10* which with an aircraft from *I–30* had already reconnoitred Durban, Zanzibar, Aden and Dar es Salaam.[1] It was thought at the time that it might have come from a raider, though until the attack on the *Elysia* six days later there was no definite information that raiders were in the area. But the battleship *Ramillies*, which was in harbour, got under way at five o'clock next morning and steamed round the bay as a precaution against a dawn submarine or air attack. *I–10's* aircraft reconnoitred Diego Suarez again that day, however, unobserved, and evidently noted the change of berth by the *Ramillies*.

There was a great shortage of anti-submarine craft at Diego Suarez, the only vessels available for patrols being the corvettes *Thyme* and *Genista*, the former of which was on patrol. The night of 30th–31st May was clear and bright with a full moon. At 2025 the *Ramillies* was struck by a torpedo, and at 2120, in the midst of explosions of depth charges dropped by the two corvettes, the tanker *British Loyalty* (6,993 tons) was also torpedoed and sank rapidly. The *Ramillies*, though holed, was able to sail for Durban on 3rd June for repairs. The *British Loyalty* was raised six months later and put in service again.

The torpedoes had been fired by midget submarines launched from submarines *I–16* and *I–20* of the 8th Flotilla.[2] No midget was sighted and there was no indication that more than one was employed, for each carried two torpedoes. But on 2nd June a patrol on the north-west coast of Madagascar reported having killed two Japanese in 12° 0′ S., 49° 12′ E.[3] The clothing and effects of the dead men left little doubt that they belonged to a midget submarine which attacked Diego Suarez, for amongst them was a rough log of a successful torpedo attack at 2328 on 30th May enclosed in an envelope addressed to the Captain of Submarine *I–20*.[4] It appeared from the notes that the midget submarine grounded on Diego Suarez outer reef half an hour after the attack as the result of a rudder defect, but nothing is known of her ultimate fate. The Japanese believed they had torpedoed a battleship of the *Queen Elizabeth* class and a light cruiser of the *Arethusa* class.

4

East Longitude Dates

After the attack, four of the submarines[5] proceeded to operate in the Mozambique Channel and its approaches. The offensive began on 5th June with simultaneous sinkings at both ends of the Channel (*see* Plan 3). At the time,

---

[1] *Japanese Military and Naval Intelligence Division.*—U.S. Strategic Bombing Survey (Pacific).

[2] The Japanese report does not state how many midgets were used, but I. Hasimoto, in his book *Sunk* says that *I–16* and *I–20* each launched a midget, and that *I–18* was to have launched one but was prevented by a breakdown.

[3] *I–10's* aircraft searched the coast of Diego Suarez on 1st June, doubtless seeking these men and their midget submarine.

[4] Commander-in-Chief, East Indies *War Diary, 1st May–18th June 1942*, T.S.D. 3483/42, gives the time as 0228 G.M.T. on 31st May (= 2328Z–3 on 30th May). The only known attack on Diego Suarez took place, however, three hours earlier than this.

[5] *I–18* had engine trouble.

there was only one troop convoy in the Channel, C.M.28, consisting of three ships for East Africa and India, escorted by the *Frobisher*. But others were due to arrive shortly. The *Queen Mary*, unescorted, with troops for the Middle East, was about 200 miles north-west of Table Bay ; and convoy W.S.19 consisting of 15 ships with troops and supplies for the East escorted by the *Mauritius*, two destroyers and a sloop was about 130 miles closer, and other W.S. convoys were on the way. In addition to the troop convoys a number of merchant ships sailed independently through the Channel daily. The vastness of the area involved, which extended from the Cape to the Equator and was bounded for much of its length by neutral and potential enemy territory, with bases few and far between, made the task of organising intensive search and hunts almost impossible. The Mozambique Channel is 250 miles wide at its narrowest point, and for the most part of its length it is double this width.

It was not until 6th June, the day following the sinking of the *Elysia* in the southern approaches to the Mozambique Channel, that it became known that a raider was responsible. The attack had at first been attributed to a submarine, but on the 6th the *Abdiel*, which had been sent to pick up survivors, reported that the hospital ship *Dorsetshire* had rescued 119, and that the sinking was the work of a raider. The twofold offensive, by raiders and submarines, was difficult to counter with the few vessels available. Against the raiders the *Dorsetshire*, two old light cruisers and two armed merchant cruisers could be made available.[1] But ten of the Eastern Fleet destroyers were in the Eastern Mediterranean escorting a convoy to Malta. Many of those remaining were repairing defects whilst there was a severe shortage of other types of vessels suitable for escort duty. In addition to the Mozambique Channel, trade in the India–Ceylon area also required protection ; and A/S vessels, as well as three minesweepers temporarily on the Station, were employed in escorting merchant ships in and out of the main harbour at Kilindini and supplementing the inadequate A/S protection of the port.

Admiral Sir Geoffrey Arbuthnot, Commander-in-Chief East Indies, was responsible for the routeing of merchant shipping on the Station, for his appointment was not due to lapse and be merged with that of Commander-in-Chief Eastern Fleet until 18th June. When the news arrived of the attack on the *Elysia*, at first assumed to be the work of a submarine, Admiral Arbuthnot ordered all ships to close the coast with the object of taking advantage of any air or surface protection that could be provided by the Deputy Commander-in-Chief Eastern Fleet, Rear-Admiral V. D. Danckwerts. The latter had taken over his appointment on 27th May from Admiral Arbuthnot who held it simultaneously with the command of the East Indies Station. Admiral Danckwerts flew his flag ashore at Kilindini and was consequently well placed

---

[1] On 5th June the distribution of the Eastern Fleet ships in the western part of the East Indies Station was as follows :—

Indomitable at Kilindini with engine defects.
Devonshire nearing Kilindini from Bombay.
Danae, Caledon at Kilindini.
Dragon on distant patrol from Kilindini.
Dauntless, Anthony on passage to Diego Suarez.
Emerald, with Force F, on passage to Durban. (Force F consisted of *Ramillies, Duncan, Active, Decoy*, tug *Thames* and s.s. *Greystoke* in company ; it left Diego Suarez on 3rd June for Durban.)
Canton in 34° 55′ S., 19° 30′ E.
Chitral at Mauritius.
Abdiel at Durban.
Frobisher with convoy C.M.28 in the Mozambique Channel.

for the control and protection of shipping on the east coast of Africa.[1] Admiral Danckwerts was of the opinion that the raider would enter the Mozambique Channel, and he disposed his cruisers accordingly (*see* Section 6).

As further reports of attacks in the Mozambique Channel came in Admiral Somerville appreciated that submarines and not raiders were responsible. In view of the shortage of escort vessels he considered it impracticable to put trade into convoy for passage through the Channel.[2] The U-boats soon discovered that shipping was being concentrated near the coast and the system proved a death trap as it had done in the First World War and as more recently had a similar system organised on the east coast of the United States at the beginning of the U-boat offensive on their shipping in January 1942 when losses, prior to the adoption of convoy in the area, mounted to an unendurable figure. On 10th June, consequently, Admiral Danckwerts decided to adopt evasive routeing over the whole navigable width of the Mozambique Channel, and to route to the eastward of Madagascar all troop convoys and all large fast unescorted ships, the raider risk to the latter being accepted. Ships of 10 knots and above were ordered to zigzag during daylight hours and moonlight nights, and navigation lights were prohibited. No suggestion was made that merchant ships with sufficient speed should join troop convoys in order to take advantage of the protection of their escorts.

Though sinkings continued in the Mozambique Channel no ship diverted east of Madagascar was attacked.

5

Times, Z — 3

It appeared to the Commander-in-Chief that the submarine attacks in the Mozambique Channel were in the nature of waves lasting about ten days with an inactive period in between during which the submarines proceeded to the south-east of Madagascar, probably to replenish. It was expected that further destroyers would become available during the first half of July, and he proposed to send a force to operate in the Channel in conjunction with Catalina aircraft at the date when it was anticipated that the attacks would recommence. The operation was facilitated by the capture of Mayotta, an island in the Mozambique Channel, which took place on 22nd July 1942 (Operation ' Throat '). In the early morning of that day a military commando force convoyed by the cruiser *Dauntless* was landed. Although the corvette *Genista* (Lieut.-Commander R. M. Pattinson, R.N.R.) with the minesweeping trawler *Shapinsay* and an R-boat had a few days previously cut out from the harbour the s.s. *Général Duchesne*, a Greek ship seized by the French,[3] the local authorities were taking no precautions against surprise. The Government Commissioner, Police Commissioner and sixty policemen were captured in bed without bloodshed. The preparation of a forward operating base for Catalinas and the clearing of a runway for flying fighters from Tanganyika to Madagascar were begun without delay. An airfield was also established on Pamanzi Island, close by, which was occupied on the same day.

---

[1] On 13th June Admiral Danckwerts assumed control of the routeing of all merchant shipping off the coasts of East Africa and Madagascar between the latitudes of Durban and the Equator.

[2] What the Commander-in-Chief said was that he considered it impracticable either to put trade into convoy for passage through the Mozambique Channel, or to institute group sailings with escorts. Actually these are one and the same thing. *See* note 2, page 11.

[3] Operation ' Cut.' M.012907/42.

Though it was known that the Germans had asked the Japanese to increase their offensive against the Aden–Capetown route the requirements of a forth-coming diversion by the Eastern Fleet in the Bay of Bengal which our American allies had asked us to undertake in connection with the offensive about to be opened in the Solomon Islands rendered it impossible to reinforce the two destroyers which were all that were available for the anti-submarine operation arranged in the Mozambique Channel. The plan was based on destroyers and Catalina aircraft working together from Mayotta Island, ready to operate in the threatened area as a combined air and surface striking force. The *Albatross* was sailed to act as parent ship for four Catalinas, with the *Griffin* and *Foxhound* as the striking force. But by the time it was possible to undertake the operation the enemy submarine offensive had ended, and though the Germans continued to put pressure on the Japanese to do more to interfere with our Middle East and Persian Gulf traffic the Japanese were non-committal.

6

East Longitude Dates

As the best way of putting an end to the operations of the enemy submarines the Admiralty suggested to the Commander-in-Chief, Eastern Fleet that search should be made for the supply ships on which it seemed clear they relied, and which, as we know now, were the aforementioned raiders *Aikohu* and *Hokoku*. The Admiralty proposed that one of the two available carriers should be used to hunt down the supply ships, whilst the other was employed on the proposed diversion in the Bay of Bengal. Admiral Somerville rejected the proposal on the grounds that it would restrict too severely a diversionary operation which he intended to undertake to assist the Americans. In any case the search would need two carriers working in co-operation.

It seemed to Admiral Somerville that the attacks suggested the raiders would endeavour to intercept ships diverted from the Mozambique Channel as the result of submarine operations. As he was badly placed in Ceylon, where he had arrived with Force ' A ' (the fast ships of the Eastern Fleet)[1] to make a demonstration in response to a request from the Commander-in-Chief, United States Pacific Fleet, Admiral C. W. Nimitz, who had been forced to denude the South and Southwest Pacific areas to meet the Japanese threat to Midway, he directed Rear-Admiral Danckwerts to take all necessary measures. The dispositions made by the latter indicated that he strongly suspected the Japanese raiders would move north to attack the dense shipping route betweenMadagascar and Aden, though this Admiral Somerville considered unlikely. With the Commander-in-Chief's permission Admiral Danckwerts ended the *Indomitable's* self-refit, and sent her with the *Frobisher* to search in the approaches to Cape Guardafui. He guarded both ends of the Mozambique Channel using in the north the *Danae*, the *Devonshire* which was approaching Kilindini from Bombay, and the *Dragon* which had been on patrol south-east of Kilindini ; whilst to guard the south the *Emerald* was taken from the escort to Capetown of the damaged *Ramillies*, the *Canton* from patrol in the Agulhas Bank area, and the *Chitral* from Mauritius. The nearest long distance flying boats were in Ceylon, and pending the arrival of reinforcements from home three Catalinas were sent from Kogalla to patrol between the Seychelles and Farquhar Islands (north of Madagascar) ; daylight patrols being flown from Kilindini and night patrols

---

[1] *Warspite* (Flag), *Illustrious, Formidable, Gambia, Laforey, Lookout, Lightning.*

10

from Dar es Salaam. Three Catalinas were all that could be spared, for of the fifteen British and nine Dutch in Ceylon, seventeen in all, were either unserviceable or shortly due for major inspection. Patrols by the South African Air Force were also instituted over the north end of the Mozambique Channel, though the whole of the Force's coastal aircraft numbered but five, of which only two were serviceable. The strain on the five aircraft available soon made itself felt in the numbers of aircraft laid up with maintenance troubles. The *Aikoku* and *Hokoku* had no intention, however, of entering the Mozambique Channel. They remained in the south Indian Ocean, acting as fuelling and supply vessels for the submarines, and as there was no further evidence of raiders Admiral Danckwerts on 9th June redisposed his patrols on the supposition that the raiders might go north outside Madagascar and attack shipping between Mombasa and Guardafui or the concentration in the approaches to Durban.

The *Emerald* was sent to patrol 80 miles to the eastward of Durban ; the *Chitral* and *Canton* south of Madagascar ; the *Danae* and *Dauntless* between Diego Suarez and Farquhar Islands and the *Caledon* off Mombasa whilst the Catalinas were sent to Mombasa to act as A/S patrols from Lindi to the Mozambique Channel. By the middle of July however, the cruisers and armed merchant cruisers were no longer spread over wide ocean areas looking for raiders, ' a complete waste of effort ' as was pointed out at the Admiralty,[1] but were employed in providing escorts for troop convoys. As there was no prospect of being able in the near future to make the requisite number of escorts available for a general convoy system on the Cape to Suez route the Admiralty suggested to the Commander-in-Chief, Eastern Fleet that such anti-submarine vessels as there were should be used to protect escorted groups of ships[2] ; but Admiral Somerville held out no hope of being able to do this until the late autumn when a number of A/S vessels would be arriving.

Between 5th June and 8th July the submarines sank twenty ships, aggregating 93,960 tons (*see* Plan 3). All were sailing independently. No vessel was attacked in convoy. The offensive ended with an unsuccessful attack on 15th July on the Norwegian s.s. *Theima* to the east of Cape Corrientes, at the south entrance to the Mozambique Channel. The enemy then left for a raid on the Gulf of Aden before crossing the Indian Ocean to their base at Penang from which they worked for the next two years.

---

[1] *Protection of Trade in Indian Ocean*, minute by D.T.D. 14/7/42. M.013416/42.

[2] In referring to a ' general convoy system,' the Admiralty no doubt had in mind a regular schedule of convoys of the kind then in operation in the Atlantic. In both the *Naval War Manual*, 1947 and *Naval Control of Shipping in War*, C.B. 04498 of 1948, the definition of ' convoy,' though differently worded, is an ' organised group of merchant vessels sailing in formation, usually (but not necessarily) escorted by combatant forces.' In the view of the Historical Section, in the conditions of the Second World War, such groups only constituted ' convoys ' when sailing under the protection of one or more warships.

What the Admiralty were in effect suggesting, was that Admiral Somerville should introduce such a convoy system as was possible, for limited and extremely ill protected as it would necessarily be, experience had shown that it nevertheless would result in a diminution in the number of sinkings of ships.

CHAPTER II

Japanese Submarine Offensive off Australia

March–July 1942

(*See* Plans 4, 5, 10, 27)

7

DURING the first days of March two or three Japanese submarines appeared off Western Australia. On the 2nd the Dutch m.s. *Siantar* (8,667 tons) was sunk by torpedo and gunfire in 21° 20′ S., 108° 45′ E., some 300 miles west of Exmouth Gulf, and on the same day the SS. *Narbada* was unsuccessfully attacked 250 miles north-west of Fremantle by a submarine which after being engaged by the ship's gun broke off the action by disappearing. The s.s. *Tongariro*, from Fremantle to East London, was attacked next day in 33° 48′ S., 113° 30′ E., 80 miles north-west of Cape Leeuwin, by a submarine which she too drove off by gunfire without suffering damage herself.

It is not known what submarines were responsible for these attacks which were no doubt carried out by boats engaged on reconnaissance.

8

In the following month a much more serious threat occurred when part of the Japanese 1st and 8th Submarine Flotillas based on the Marshall Islands began operating against shipping off the east coast of Australia and between Fiji and Samoa. This was part of the South Pacific island routes from San Francisco and Hawaii to Brisbane, the integrity of which was vital to the build-up of American military strength, particularly air power, in Australia (*see* Section 24 and *Plan 5*). Heavy bombers staged through the islands and freighters carried to Australia fighter aircraft and other war material and supplies. Army, naval and air forces moved to their stations along the island chain, involving considerable movements of men and materials (*see* Section 30). Four months earlier, at the Arcadia Conference in Washington in December 1941–January 1942 the Prime Minister, Mr. Winston Churchill, had drawn attention to the need for better naval protection of the route. Fortunately, the attack, when it came, was neither heavy nor prolonged : indeed throughout the war Japanese submarine offensives were marked by an absence of sustained weight.

There had for some weeks been reports of submarines in the area, including one from the Panamanian m.s. *Firethorn* which reported being attacked on 16th April 650 miles south-east of Wellington in 45° 38′ S., 174° 10′ W. No further attacks took place until 7th May when the s.s. *John Adams* (7,180 tons) was torpedoed and sunk south-west of Numea in 23° 30′ S., 164° 35′ E., the Greek s.s. *Chloe* (4,641 tons) being sunk in the same area on the following day.

On the 7th also there were sightings in the Coral Sea to which the Japanese had despatched submarines of the 8th Flotilla to co-operate with the expedition to Port Moresby (*see* Volume II). On 16th May the Russian s.s. *Wellen* reported being shelled and slightly damaged off the east coast of Australia, 30 miles east of Newcastle, in 33° 0' S., 152° 30' E. : the submarine responsible, *I–29*, reported receiving one hit from the *Wellen's* fire. Next day the U.S. submarine *Tautog* sank *I–28* south of New Britain in 6° 30' N., 152° E. whilst the latter was returning to Truk. These attacks were carried out by five submarines of the 8th Submarine Flotilla (*I–21, I–22, I–24, I–27, I–29*), the force being termed the Eastern Advance Detachment. As the result of its observations the Japanese decided to carry out an attack on shipping in Sydney Harbour with midget submarines.

9

Times, Z — 10

On 29th May after nearly a fortnight without incident there were D/F indications of an enemy unit, probably a submarine, in 34° 10' S., 151° 50' E., approximately 40 miles east-south-east of Sydney. The Japanese had planned to raid Sydney harbour with midget submarines at the end of May simultaneously with the raid on Diego Suarez, following this up, as at Diego Suarez, by a campaign undertaken by the parent submarines in neighbouring waters. At Sydney, the Japanese hoped to find and put out of action important units of the Allied Fleet, but in actual fact, on the night of the attack, 31st May–1st June, there were in Sydney harbour no units heavier than the Australian cruisers *Canberra* and *Adelaide*, and the U.S.S. *Chicago*.

The raid was made by midget submarines carried by boats of the 8th Submarine Flotilla. Two of the midgets employed were numbered *14* and *21* respectively ; the numbers of the other one or two are not known. The parent submarines were *I–21* (S.O.), *I–22, I–24, I–27,* and *I–29*, three or four of which each carried one midget submarine, whilst *I–21* carried a floatplane which made reconnaissance flights over Sydney harbour on 28th May, over the Sydney area two days later, and again over Sydney harbour after the raid, on 2nd June.[1] The midget submarines were of a larger type than those employed in the raid on Pearl Harbour six months previously, being over 80 feet long. They could remain submerged for at least twelve hours ; and provided they could lie concealed on the surface at night in order to give the crew exercise and to ventilate the vessels it should have been possible for them to operate in a suitable harbour for a period up to one week. A/S craft equipped with asdics were able to establish contact with these craft.

The midgets were released from the parent submarines about 1800 hours on 31st May, off Port Jackson, at distances varying from 7 to 1½ miles to seaward, outside the loop area ; and from examination of a captured Japanese chart it seems that subsequent picking up positions were established on a line of bearing off Broken Bay 110° from a position 170° First Point 4 miles (*see* Plan 4).[2]

On the night of 31st May–1st June 1942, two of the six outer indicator loops at Port Jackson were out of action, but both the inner loops were in operation :

---

[1] Examination of captured documents showed that a call-sign was allocated to a floatplane for *I–29* also.

[2] On the other hand, a member of the crew of *I–24* who was subsequently taken prisoner of war stated that on account of their limited range return to the parent ship was not planned and the crews were expected to scuttle their boats after carrying out their missions, and save themselves if possible. (U.S. Pacific Fleet *Weekly Intelligence*, Vol. I, No. 48.)

signatures were obtained on only one of them. A fixed beam oscillator was in operation but failed to give any indication of the passage of the midgets. An anti-torpedo boom was in course of erection, but only the central portion was completed. The boom defence was floodlit by searchlight from 2200 onwards. The Australian A/S vessel *Yandra* was on duty in the loops area, the patrol boat *Yarroma* was on station at West Gate, and four naval auxiliary patrol boats were on duty in the harbour. There was a great deal of traffic on the night of the attack, and though four loop crossings were registered, none of them were connected at the time with midget submarines ; they were marked down as ferry, tug with barge, and the like. One midget was destroyed before crossing the loop, and the best expert opinion subsequently pronounced that one of the four signatures was an outward crossing. (Plan 27.)[1]

The moon was full and rose at 1813, illuminating the harbour when the sky cleared during the middle watch. Outside the harbour there was a rough sea and a moderate swell, with wind Force 4. High tide was at 2125 on 31st. The first midget, *No. 14*, crossed the loop at 2001. At 2015 a Maritime Services watchman sighted an object in the boom net defence. The *Yarroma* investigated and discovered a small submarine. At 2235 an explosion in the net defences was heard ; *No. 14* had been unable to get free and had blown herself up. The crew of two perished with the vessel, the wreck of which was subsequently recovered.

The second midget submarine crossed the loop at 2148 and entered the harbour unobserved. At 2252, the U.S.S. *Chicago*, lying at No. 2 Buoy (Plan 10), sighted a submarine some 200 yards off the Ferry Wharf at Garden Island proceeding towards the Harbour Bridge. The submarine was also sighted from Ferry Wharf and by a dockyard motor boat. The *Chicago* opened fire with 4-inch guns and Oerlikons ; and the A. M/S vessel *Whyalla*, which was near by and had also sighted the submarine, opened fire with machine guns. The midget then apparently turned towards the North Shore, instead of continuing up harbour ; she was sighted in the direction of Bradley's Head and fired on at 2310 by the *Whyalla* and the A. M/S vessel *Geelong* at Garden Island, which kept the area under observation with searchlights for half an hour. At 0030 on 1st June the submarine fired two torpedoes from the direction of Bradley's Head, apparently at the *Chicago*, which was about to slip from the buoy. The dock flood-lights which would have silhouetted the cruiser when under way were extinguished just before the torpedoes were fired. One of these ran ashore on Garden Island and failed to explode. The other passed under the Dutch submarine *K–9* which was lying alongside the depot ship *Kuttabul* at Garden Island, hit the sea bottom and exploded. The explosion sank the *Kuttabul*, with the loss of 21 killed and missing and 10 wounded. The enemy then apparently escaped out of the harbour, passing over the loop outward bound at 0158.

The third midget was unsuccessful in her attempt to enter the harbour. She was sighted about 2254 on the 31st between the outer and inner loops and outside the A/T boom by the *Yandra* and the patrol boat *Lauriana*. The latter illuminated her and at 2258 the *Yandra* intercepted and attempted to ram the vessel. At 2307 the *Yandra* dropped a full pattern of six depth charges in position 023° 3·6 cables from Hornby Light (near the extremity of Inner

---

[1] Presumably all the crossings were made at a point where the outer loop was not in operation, otherwise it should have been possible to establish whether the signature at the inner loop was that of an inward or outward bound vessel.

In the War Diary of the Sixth Fleet for 1942 it is stated that only three submarines, *I–22*, *I–24* and *I–27* launched midgets. I. Hasimoto, in his book *Sunk*, also says that only three midgets were launched.

South Head), and it was considered this destroyed the enemy vessel, but since the wreck was not discovered it seems probable that this midget was identical with one of the other three.

At 0250 1st June the *Chicago*, which was now proceeding out of harbour sighted another midget submarine passing through the Heads. This was *No. 21* ; she crossed the loop at 0301 and was lost to sight as she proceeded up harbour until near Bradley's Head where the *Kanimbla* sighted and opened fire on her at 0350. For the next hour or more the enemy remained undetected, but about 0500 she was sighted in Taylor Bay where she was attacked at intervals until 0827 with depth charges by the patrol boats *Sea Mist*, *Steady Hour* and *Yarroma*, and was considerably damaged and finally sunk. When salved, it was found that she had fired both torpedo tubes and the officer and rating forming her crew had committed suicide.

10

Until 3rd June there was no further enemy activity, but at 2110 that day the s.s. *Iron Age* was shelled but not hit by a submarine (*I–24*) off Sydney harbour in 33° 45' S., 151° 59' E., and about an hour and a half later s.s. *Iron Chieftain* (4,812 tons) was sunk some 10 miles to the southward, in 33° 55' S., 151° 50' E. The s.s. *Barwon* reported that a torpedo exploded near her at 0543 on the 4th, in 38° 5' S., 150° 14' E. ; and s.s. *Iron Crown* (3,353 tons) was torpedoed and sunk at 2000 that day in 38° 17' S., 149° 44' E., the submarine responsible (*I–27*) being unsuccessfully attacked by the R.A.A.F. A medium bomber aircraft flown by a Dutch pilot attacked a submarine at 1310 on the 5th in 35° 22' S., 152° 36' E. It was estimated that either three or four submarines were operating between Newcastle and Wilson's Promontory, three ships in all having been attacked by gunfire but escaped, in addition to the two sunk. Actually, three submarines were concerned, namely *I–24*, *I–27* and *I–21*. Australian aircraft carried out a number of attacks or had contacts over a wide area, but no attacks were successful. Sailings of merchant vessels of less than 12 knots speed from ports between Melbourne and Brisbane inclusive were temporarily suspended and navigation lights were ordered to be burned only to avoid collision. Coastal convoys were instituted on the 8th. At 0015 that day *I–24* shelled Sydney. Five of the seven shells fired failed to explode. An unidentified aircraft flew over the city a few minutes later. It came, no doubt, from *I–21*, which fired 25 shells at Newcastle about 0200, here also many of the shells being blind. Coastal batteries drove the enemy off. In neither case were any casualties or damage caused. On the 8th, too, the s.s. *Orestes* was unsuccessfully attacked with gunfire and torpedoes off Jervis Bay, 100 miles south of Sydney. The last sinking during this raid occurred on 12th June when the Panamanian s.s. *Guatemala* (5,527 tons), a straggler from convoy, was sunk outside Sydney harbour in 33° 52' S., 151° 58' E.

The Japanese report that at the end of June the seven boats of the 3rd Flotilla[1] relieved those of the 1st and 8th Flotillas. It was nearly a month before they began active operations, though submarines were reported on 2nd July off the New Hebrides, on the 3rd off New Caledonia, close inshore in the Townsville area next day, and off Sydney and on the Sydney–Townsville route on the 6th. Two submarines, *I–11* and *I–175* worked off the east coast of Australia and *I–169* off New Caledonia. On 20th July they sank one Greek and two American ships off Jervis Bay, the s.s. *G. S. Livanos* (4,835 tons) in 35° 00' S., 151° 00' E.,

---

[1] *I–168, I–169, I–171, I–172, I–174, I–175, I–11*.

15

the s.s. *Coast Farmer* (3,290 tons) in 35° 23′ S., 151° 00′ E. and the s.s. *William Dawes* (7,176 tons) in 35° 45′ S., 150° 20′ E. The s.s. *Allara* was attacked and damaged off Newcastle in 33° 3′ S., 152° 22′ E. two days later, and next day the s.s. *Murada* was unsuccessfully attacked with a torpedo some 90 miles north-east of the same position. The s.s. *Coolana* was shelled by a submarine off Cape Howe on the 26th and the s.s. *Katoomba* east-south-east of Albany on 4th August, but both escaped without damage. On 6th August the small m.v. *Mamutu* (300 tons) was sunk in Torres Strait. In all, *I–11*, *I–169* and *I–175* claimed to have sunk ten ships. The submarines left soon after to assist in the defence of the Solomon Islands where the Allies on 7th August began the long advance that ended with the surrender of Japan.

11

The U-boat raid on the Allied communications in the South Pacific, which the Japanese had conducted during a period of nearly four months, from 16th April to 7th August, had never much likelihood of success. Its description by the Japanese as a raid rather than a campaign, and the switching of the U-boats taking part to the defence of the Solomons directly Guadalcanal was attacked reveals the Japanese attitude to the attack on trade, which was considered to be merely one, and not the most important, of the functions of the submarine (*see* p. 23). The number of U-boats allotted by the Admiral Commanding the Sixth Fleet to Australian waters was far too small for the size of the area involved. During the thirty-one days from 16th April to 16th May six submarines (supposing all to have been on patrol simultaneously) operated in an area extending from latitude 23° S. to 45° S. and from longitude 152° E. to 174° W. They sank no more than two ships. One Japanese submarine was lost.

The second phase, from 31st May to 12th June, included the midget submarine raid on Sydney in which five U-boats were concerned, three of which, after the raid, operated for ten days in a much more restricted area off the east coast of Australia. In the Sydney area were at the time only two A/S vessels equipped with asdics, and four at Brisbane. The Australian naval authorities suspended coastwise sailings of ships with less than 12 knots speed pending the organisation of a system of coastal convoys which was put into operation on 8th June. Only three ships were sunk. No ship was attacked in convoy throughout the operations from April to August, though *I–11* and *I–175* each sighted a convoy on 31st July near Tasmania.

In the third phase, from 2nd July to 7th August, the Japanese report that no more than three submarines of a flotilla of seven were active in the huge area Sydney–Bass Strait–New Caledonia–New Hebrides–Torres Strait, where they sank four ships.

The Japanese professed to be content with the operations of the ' Eastern Advance Detachment,' describing them as brilliant. They took at their face value the reports of their submarine commanders.[1] These were distinguished not only by exaggeration of the number of ships sunk, but also of their tonnage. Though the largest ship sunk was one of 7,176 tons, the claims of the submarine commanders averaged 10,000 tons per ship. All this contributed to the Japanese mood of complacency with the progress of the war which continued for nearly two years and hindered until too late the adoption of many essential measures.

---

[1] Interrogation of Admiral Miwa, Commander-in-Chief, Sixth (Submarine) Fleet.

CHAPTER III

Diversive Operations for Guadalcanal

(*See* Plans 1, 22 and Figure 1)

12

THE Allied attack on the South Solomons, which developed into so great an undertaking, began as a limited offensive operation to secure the defences of the South and South-West Pacific. By June 1942, the Japanese Navy had sustained its initial defeats at the battles of the Coral Sea and Midway ; but their Army had as yet suffered no reverse. The successful termination of the Japanese invasions of Burma and the Philippines, for no other result could be hoped for, would obviously release additional forces for the enemy's use. Some limited action by the Allies was called for, and the decision was taken to attack in the late summer the South Solomons.

At the instigation of Admiral E. J. King, Commander-in-Chief, U.S. Fleet and Chief of Naval Operations, diversionary operations were undertaken both in the Pacific and Indian Ocean, in connection with the Solomons' offensive. The Pacific diversion consisted of a raid on Makin Island, in the Gilbert Islands which the enemy had occupied shortly after the outbreak of war. Small forces only were employed, for few were available after the claims of the Solomons' operations were satisfied. In particular, no naval surface forces could be spared and the raiders were conveyed in submarines. The operation was compromised by hurried planning. The Americans estimated that the garrison of the island numbered some 250, possibly supported by seaplanes and a few surface craft. At 0900 on 8th August (Hawaiian time) Captain J. M. Haines took out from Pearl Harbour two of the largest American submarines, the *Nautilus* (senior officer) and *Argonaut*, with 222 officers and men of the 2nd Marine Raider Battalion under Lieut.-Col. E. F. Carlson, U.S.M.C.R. on the 2,000 mile passage to Makin Island. The tactical objects of the raid were to create a diversion for the Guadalcanal operation and secondly to destroy the enemy forces and installations and gain information. After being escorted out of harbour the submarines separated, the *Nautilus* going ahead in order to reconnoitre the objective. Both submarines were air conditioned, but the temperature inside was usually above 90° F. and the humidity about 85 per cent. On the outward passage scarcely any water was allowed for washing, and each meal in the crowded *Argonaut* required three and a half hours to serve. But due to the fact that the submarines were able to proceed on the surface for the most part and that frequent disembarkation exercises were possible the crews suffered nothing worse than discomfort.

The two submarines made rendezvous off Little Makin Island at 0300 on 16th August and conducted a periscope reconnaissance. The landing on Makin Island was made at 0500 next day, half an hour before dawn, in such of the 18 rubber boats whose outboard motors could be induced to start ; the Japanese offered no opposition and the natives were friendly. The roar of the surf and wash of the swell through the submarines' limber holes drowned the shouted orders necessary for the assembling of the unmanageable rubber boats. The submarines sank by gunfire two ships at the wharf, one a patrol vessel, the other a transport used as barracks. Enemy air attacks began during the afternoon, but caused no losses, and one four-engined bomber, reported by the natives to be bringing thirty-five men to reinforce the garrison, was shot down. But the tenacious Japanese defence caused many losses to the Marines as they advanced, and when the Americans withdrew in the evening according to plan they believed they were still being strongly opposed. The attempt to re-embark proved costly, not through enemy opposition, for as was later discovered, practically the entire Japanese garrison had been killed in the day's fighting and opposition was being continued by no more than a few resolute men. The frail rubber boats could make no headway against the surf. Weapons, clothing and some lives were lost ; little more than a third of the raiders reached the submarines, and about 120 Marines were compelled to remain all night on the beach, in the rain, exhausted, half-clothed, and almost entirely unarmed. Renewed attempts to embark next morning were made under Japanese air attacks which caused some casualties and drove the Marines to keep under cover during most of the day. Eventually, it was decided to re-embark from the lee side of the atoll. Meanwhile, however, eighty-three enemy dead had been discovered, and it was revealed that the garrison had been annihilated almost to a man. Embarkation was easily effected from the west side of the island in the evening, after the tactical objects of the operation had been carried out.

The casualties were 30 Marines dead or missing and 14 wounded.

The Japanese did not attach great importance to the operation, which they correctly evaluated as a raid to destroy material.[1] They did, however, begin occupying such of the Gilbert Islands as they needed for their perimeter defence ; unopposed landing by naval parties brought from the Mandated Islands in destroyers, taking place from 22nd August onwards.

13

The possibility of a diversion by the Eastern Fleet was not overlooked. The first suggestion was that the fleet should cooperate with General MacArthur in a contemplated attack on Timor. After the Japanese landings in Timor

---

[1] Interrogation of Vice-Admiral S. Fukudome, Chief First Section, Naval General Staff, Tokyo. The Commander-in-Chief, U.S. Pacific Fleet believed at the time that the object of the expedition was achieved, and that at a crucial moment in the Solomon Islands operations the Japanese were forced to divert men, ships and aircraft to the relief of Makin Island. (*Report of Commander-in-Chief, Pacific. Reports of Actions and Campaigns, February 1942 to February 1943*, A.16–3/F.F.12, serial 034372.)

in February 1942 remnants of the Australian Imperial Force, Dutch troops, and the Australian 2nd Independent Company which had been sent to Dili in December 1941, a total of some 400 men, continued to resist in the mountains. After being isolated for two months, on 19th April 1942 they managed to make contact with Darwin by means of a wireless transmitter built from scraps gathered from different parts of the island and operated by means of fuel raided from Japanese dumps. On learning of their plight, supplies were dropped by air from Darwin or run in and the sick and wounded secretly evacuated by Australian and Dutch destroyers and other light naval craft. In September 1942 reinforcements were despatched in the Australian destroyer *Voyager*. On the 23rd whilst engaged in landing these reinforcements in Betano Bay (approximately 9° 11' S., 125° 42' E.) the *Voyager* grounded. She was later attacked by Japanese aircraft, and had finally to be destroyed by her crew, owing to the impossibility of salving her. The ship's company returned to Darwin with seven minor casualties. On 28th November 1942 the Australian motor patrol boat *Kuru* sailed from Darwin to evacuate women and children and others from Betano Bay where she was to rendezvous on the night 30th November–1st December with the Minesweepers *Castlemaine* and *Armidale*, carrying relief personnel and D/F equipment. The *Castlemaine* was unsuccessfully bombed during the afternoon and evening of the 30th, and the two ships arrived late at the rendezvous, after the *Kuru* had sailed. Receiving no reply from shore to their signals, they left without landing their passengers. After being bombed the *Kuru* met the minesweepers early next day. She transferred her refugee passengers to the *Castlemaine*, and with the *Armidale* returned to Betano Bay with the troops. The *Kalgoorlie* left Darwin late that afternoon to support the two ships, but did not make contact. Soon after parting company the *Armidale* (Lieut.-Commander D. H. Richards, R.A.N.R. (S)) was attacked by dive bombers, without success. During the afternoon, however, when about 350 miles from the Australian coast a second force of bombers and fighters appeared. The *Armidale* was struck by two torpedoes and sank in three minutes, during which time she shot down at least two of her attackers. Twenty survivors, including the captain, were saved after suffering at sea the tortures of thirst under a burning sun for several days ; but one officer and twenty-seven sailors on a raft, though sighted twice by Allied aircraft, were never located by rescue ships, and perished.

The last of the guerilla fighters were withdrawn in January and February 1943, by the *Arunta* and Dutch destroyers.

14

The Timor project referred to above was found on examination to be unsound. The nearest air base, Darwin, was beyond fighter range, and air cover would consequently have had to be given by carriers operating within range of strong enemy shore based air forces. The intention to attack the island was soon abandoned, and in its place on 10th July Admiral King asked that the Eastern Fleet should carry out a diversion in the Indian Ocean. He suggested action against the Andamans, where the Japanese had a flying boat base at Port Blair, or the Nicobars, objectives which the Chiefs of Staff in London extended to include Java or Sumatra at the Commander-in-Chief's discretion. At the time, all the ships of the Eastern Fleet, far from lying idle as the Americans believed, were so fully occupied that only a week previously Admiral Somerville had represented to the Admiralty the weakness of his available fleet, which was reduced to the *Warspite*, *Illustrious* and *Formidable*, one or two cruisers and

19

possibly five destroyers.[1] The fast portion of the Fleet (Force A) had just returned from a demonstration in the Bay of Bengal at the request of the Americans. The *Nelson, Rodney* and *Indomitable* were employed in fighting a convoy through to Malta, whilst the *Valiant* was working up after refitting at Durban, and would not be ready for service for another month or more. The *Ramillies* had been damaged at Diego Suarez by midget submarine attack a few days earlier, the *Revenge* was refitting at Durban, the *Resolution*, which had been escorting Convoy C.M.28 to Bombay was returning to Kilindini via the Seychelles, and the *Royal Sovereign* was 400 miles east-south-east of Mombasa escorting Convoy C.M.29, comprising six ships and the landing ship *Sobieski* with troops and supplies for the Middle East and Bombay. The escort of military convoys claimed all the available cruisers except the *Birmingham* and *Newcastle*, though in point of fact ' all ' is somewhat of a misnomer, for no less than nine of the cruisers, many of which were very old, were either refitting or proceeding to refit. The *Mauritius*, with the fast portion of Convoy W.S.19P containing ten ships with troops and supplies from the United Kingdom for the Middle East, was about 150 miles south-east of Tamatave. The slow portion of the convoy, twelve ships escorted by the Dutch A.A. ship (ex light cruiser) *Heemskerck* and the A.M.C. *Chitral* was a hundred miles south-east of Madagascar. The s.s. *Queen Elizabeth*, which had come out from the United Kingdom unescorted with troops for the Middle East was some 350 miles north-north-east of Diego Suarez, and the *Devonshire* also with troops for the Middle East, was on the other side of the Indian Ocean, about 550 miles west-south-west of Bombay, escorting the *Orizaba* to Aden and Suez. The *Enterprise* was escorting the *Monarch of Bermuda* from Aden to Kilindini. Three cruisers were off the station ; the *Gambia* which had not yet come out from Home Waters, the *Dauntless* which was returning home, and the *Hawkins* which was detailed to bring out Convoy W.S.21 from the United Kingdom.

The shortage of destroyers in the Eastern Fleet was serious, the more so because there was as yet no indication that the Japanese submarine offensive in the Mozambique Channel, which began on 5th June, had come to an end, though actually as we have seen no further sinkings occurred after 8th July. It was known that the Germans were putting pressure on the Japanese to do more to interfere with our Middle East and Persian Gulf traffic, but the Japanese were being non-committal as usual. Out of twenty-six destroyers only seven were available. Many were worn out. Four were in the Mediterranean, five had not yet joined, five were under repair, and five were away escorting the *Ramillies, Valiant* and *Queen Elizabeth*, the last of which was on her way to Kilindini since the mining and air threat to the main Mediterranean Fleet base at Alexandria had necessitated the withdrawal of important units south of the Suez Canal. Of the seven destroyers available, five were needed for screening Force A, and two were engaged on the work of anti-submarine escort in the Mozambique Channel.

15

Times, Z — 3

From the Mozambique Channel the Japanese submarines proceeded to the Gulf of Aden. The Gulf had remained part of the East Indies Command when the Commander-in-Chief, Mediterranean, took over the Red Sea on 21st October 1941, the western-boundary of the East Indies Station being fixed at longitude 45° 05′ E., thus excluding Aden itself.

---

[1] Commander-in-Chief, E.F. 1453/3/7/42.

On 23rd July a Japanese unit, thought in all probability to be a submarine, was plotted by D/F in position 400 miles east-south-east of Cape Guardafui. This same unit was again plotted on the following day in position 700 miles south-east of Cape Guardafui. For a month there was no further evidence of the enemy. But the probable threat of enemy submarines in the Gulf of Aden precipitated the execution of a plan already prepared, for instituting convoy in the Arabian Sea by transferring thither bodily the organisation from the India–Ceylon area ; and on 7th August the Commander-in-Chief directed that no further Bay of Bengal convoys should be run after the diversion operation (*see* Section 17). The first military convoy from Aden to the Persian Gulf, A.P.1, with troops for Iraq, was taken out by the *Frobisher* on 20th August.

On 24th and 25th August shore patrols reported a submarine close inshore off Singara, 20 miles east of Berbera ; and on the 28th strong W/T signals from a Japanese unit identified as the Senior Officer of the 8th Submarine Flotilla (*I-20*), were heard by Aden W/T bearing not very reliably 195°. Air reconnaissance patrols were sent out from Aden and a warship was sent to search, but nothing was found. Convoys were ordered to close the Aden shore. At 1155 on 1st September an independent ship the s.s. *Palma* sighted a submarine 30 miles south-east of Cape Guardafui, but shook her off by increasing speed to 10 knots. At 0215 next day what was probably the same submarine torpedoed and sank the s.s. *Gazcon* (4,224 tons) sailing independently in the Gulf, in 13° 01' N., 50° 30' E., 60 miles north of Cape Guardafui. On the 3rd the tanker *British Genius* was twice unsuccessfully attacked in the same area, the s.s. *Exhibitor* sighted a submarine next day but was not attacked, and on the 6th an aircraft on patrol unsuccessfully bombed a submarine in the Gulf in 14° 8' N., 49° 46' E.

At this date the Gulf of Aden was crowded with oilers from the Persian Gulf for the Middle East and with ships going up to Egypt with troops, equipment and supplies to build up the Eighth Army for its forthcoming advance from El Alamein. Admiral Somerville had anticipated that a submarine offensive would probably develop against this traffic, but the shortage of A/S vessels in all areas and the fact that the Eastern Fleet was engaged at the time in preparing for extensive fresh operations against Madagascar (*see* Sections 19, 20), had prevented him from despatching A/S vessels to the Gulf of Aden. On 25th August he sent three A/S whalers from Kilindini, and in response to his request the Commander-in-Chief, Mediterranean, on 5th September sent the destroyers *Hero* and *Tetcott* to reinforce the three vessels constituting the A/S forces in the Gulf ; to strengthen the air forces covering the Gulf Ceylon sent three Catalina aircraft two days later for employment as A/S escorts to important ships and convoys or in organised A/S hunts in co-operation with surface forces.

As the result of the sinking of the *Gazcon* on 2nd September important ships bound northward through the Guardafui Channel were diverted east of Socotra. Soon, however, the danger of crowding independent shipping in an area remote from our patrols in the Gulf of Aden caused convoys and independent ships to be routed through the Guardafui Channel again. To facilitate the work of air and surface patrols in the Gulf routes for important shipping were established, which differentiated between traffic to or from different areas. Shipping to and from the Persian Gulf, Karachi and Bombay was confined to a narrow lane close to the northern shore of the Gulf of Aden over which air cover could be provided from coastal airfields, whilst shipping to and from Ceylon and the south was confined to a similar lane close to the southern shore of the Gulf and extending to the eastern point of Socotra. As soon as they could be spared, which was not however until 27th September, the minesweepers *Cromer, Cromarty* and *Romney* which it had been thought would have an important part to play in the Madagascar operations, went up to Aden to strengthen the A/S forces there.

On 10th September the s.s. *Haresfield* (5,299 tons) was sunk sailing independently in the lane 30 miles north of Socotra and on the 16th the s.s. *Ocean Honour* (7,173 tons) was sunk in the Gulf. Though it was not evident at the time, these sinkings marked the end of the offensive, in which the Commander-in-Chief, Eastern Fleet, estimated that three submarines had taken part. He was of the opinion that the air patrols in the Gulf were probably partly responsible for the indifferent results obtained by the enemy. It will be seen that the losses were confined to independent ships and the immunity of the convoys fully justified Admiral Somerville's action in instituting them.

16

In October, there was some evidence of a possible submarine threat in the Persian Gulf, where the Japanese were apparently carrying out the reconnaissance which was the usual prelude to an offensive. The protection of the 600 mile long trade route, through waters where navigational difficulties forced shipping to pass along defined lanes and through focal points, all suitable for U-boat operations, presented a considerable problem. Not enough A/S vessels were available to run adequately escorted convoys.[1] The security of the Persian Gulf was important to the Allies on account of the oil supplies which were piped to Abadan. It also afforded a route by which a small quantity of supplies was sent to Russia.[2] The Anglo-Persian Oil Company's areas had been occupied by British forces in July 1941 (Operation 'Acquisition') owing to the danger of violation of Persian neutrality by the Germans who were infiltrating into the country. In August, a small naval force under Commodore C. M. Graham, S.N.O. Persian Gulf, in the armed merchant cruiser *Kanimbla*,[3] transported and covered troops which landed and captured the oil refinery at Abadan undamaged and occupied the town and the naval base at Khorramshahr and the southern terminus of the Trans-Iranian railway, Bandar Shahpur (Operation 'Countenance'). The expedition immobilised the Persian Navy,[4] and captured five German and three Italian merchant ships which had been sheltering at Bandar Shahpur.

On account of the possible threat in the Persian Gulf and the cessation of sinkings in the Gulf of Aden the Catalinas in the Gulf were transferred in October 1942 to the Persian Gulf, but here nothing came of the threat. One ship, the tanker *Ocean Vintage* (7,174 tons) was however sunk, on 22nd October, off Ras el Hadd, at the entrance to the Gulf of Oman, before the submarines withdrew to Penang.

From Penang, Japanese, and later also German submarines, worked in the Indian Ocean for the next two years. On the admission of the Japanese themselves one of the reasons why their submarines continued to operate in the

---

[1] There were 12 A/S vessels in the Gulf.

[2] During the war 87 ships carried to the Persian Gulf for Russia 160,965 tons of supplies, principally stores. In addition, 3,941 vehicles, 564 tanks, 823 aircraft, as well as guns, locomotives and other equipment were sent by this route.

[3] The remaining ships were : R.I.N. sloop *Lawrence*, sloop *Shoreham*, corvette *Snapdragon*, gunboat *Cockchafer*, armed trawler *Arthur Cavanagh*, M.S. trawler *Lilac*, two Anglo-Iranian Oil Co.'s tugs, a dhow and an R.A.F. picket boat.

[4] The sloops *Palang* and *Bahr* were sunk, and four gunboats, a depot ship, two tugs and a floating dock were captured.

Indian Ocean was that due to the shortage of A/S and escort vessels operating conditions were safer there than in other areas. The desire to husband their submarines for what they believed to be their true role, operations with the fleet, was always in the minds of the Japanese Naval Staff, who did not subscribe to the belief held both by the Allies and by the Germans that the correct function of the submarine was to attack merchant shipping.[1]

17

Times, Z — 6

In discussing with the Commander-in-Chief, Eastern Fleet, how best to aid the Americans the Admiralty voiced once more the apprehension they had felt after the Battle of the Coral Sea when Admiral King asked them to send an aircraft carrier to the South-West Pacific. The Admiralty's anxiety in this respect was that the carrier in such an area would be exposed to heavy shore-based air attacks. An opportunity of experiencing the way in which carriers could stand up to such attacks was about to occur for the *Victorious* and *Indomitable* were to be employed between 10th and 14th August in fighting a convoy through to Malta, within range of German and Italian airfields ; and the Admiralty wished to see how these ships fared before exposing the *Illustrious* and *Formidable* to similar conditions. This in effect limited the proposed diversion to carrier-based air raids on Port Blair or Sabang. The Dutch Commander-in-Chief, Vice-Admiral C. E. L. Helfrich, who after the Allies were driven out of the Java Sea had repaired to Ceylon to take charge of his few remaining ships under the British Commander-in-Chief, advised the latter that an attack on Sabang was unlikely to be productive as the jungle lent itself to effective dispersal of aircraft. At Port Blair the main target would be flying boats which would best be attacked by fighters. The maximum combat radius of these was such that a close approach of the carriers to the objective would have to be made and to the Japanese airfields thus exposing the carriers to attack by shore-based air forces. It was therefore decided to substitute a diversion towards the Andamans which the Japanese had captured in March, for a raid on Port Blair or an attack on Sabang.

Admiral Somerville's plan (Operation ' Stab ') was to suggest a landing in the Andamans by sailing three dummy convoys from Trincomalee, Madras and Vizagapatam respectively, covered by Force A to the eastward. W/T was to be used to ensure that the movement came to the knowledge of the Japanese, and subsequently to suggest postponement of the operation due to some accidental cause. Force A, comprising the *Warspite* (Flagship of Commander-in-Chief, Eastern Fleet), *Illustrious* (Rear-Admiral Aircraft Carriers, Eastern Fleet),[2] *Formidable*, *Birmingham* (Rear-Admiral Commanding 4th Cruiser Squadron),[3] *Mauritius* and the only four available destroyers, *Norman, Nizam, Inconstant* and *Van Galen*, sailed from Kilindini on 21st July for Colombo via the Seychelles. The *Napier* (Commodore (D))[4] joined at sea from escort duty two days later, and the *Heemskerck*, which had been delayed by defects, joined at Colombo on 28th July. Three dummy convoys with local escorts, termed forces V, M and T, were to sail from Vizagapatam, Madras and Trincomalee respectively in daylight on 1st August with orders to reverse course during the

---

[1] ' The fundamental nature of the mission of our submarines is as auxiliary to our fleet.' Interrogation of Vice-Admiral S. Miwa, I.J.N., successively Director Naval Submarine Department and Commander-in-Chief, Sixth (Submarine) Fleet.

[2] Rear-Admiral W. G. Tennant.   [3] Rear-Admiral D. W. Boyd.

[4] Captain S. H. T. Arliss.

night and return to their ports.[1] However, the sighting at 2325 on 28th July by the Dutch submarine *O–23* whilst on patrol in the Malacca Strait of an enemy force which she reported as two heavy cruisers and four destroyers in 5° 32′ N., 98° 50′ E. proceeding up the west coast of Siam caused the sailing of Force V, which was not provided with air cover as were Forces T and M, to be cancelled. The Commander-in-Chief considered this movement portended an enemy raid on shipping in the northern part of the Bay of Bengal rather than a move in reaction to the rumours ' planted ' in India of preparations by the British for a seaborne attack on the Andamans.

18

It is improbable, however, that the movement of enemy cruisers and destroyers had any special significance. The area in which they were sighted formed part of the South-West Area Command which had been constituted on 10th April 1942 and placed under Vice-Admiral I. Takahashi with headquarters at Surabaya.[2] It comprised the region of the Philippines, Sumatra, Malaya and Burma, and lay to the westward of the South-East Area Command which was formed in the summer of 1942 (*see* Section 25). The work of the force comprised principally local defence of ports, escort and anti-submarine operations, for which purpose Admiral Takahashi had under him three forces of minor vessels assigned to the following areas :—

1st Force—Malaya, Burma, Sumatra.

2nd Force—N.E.I., except Sumatra and Philippines.

3rd Force—Philippines.

A striking force, termed the 2nd Southern Expeditionary Fleet, was assigned to the Command. It was never more than a small cruiser force and consisted at this date of the 8-inch cruiser *Ashigara* and the 16th Cruiser Squadron (light cruisers *Natori, Kinu, Isudzu*). For the special duty of protection of shipping on the important lines of communication between the Southern Area and Japan, the ' oil route ' as it came to be known from the most vital commodity that passed along it, Admiral Takahashi's forces included A/S vessels comprised in the 1st Escort Squadron. For reconnaissance he had flying boats based on Port Blair, where a seaplane tender was sent at the beginning of August, the Japanese practice being to operate these aircraft from a tender ; and on 14th July the 30th Submarine Group (*I–165, I–166* and *I–162*) and its parent ship *Rio de Janeiro Maru* were detached from the Combined Fleet and placed under him. The 21st (Army) Air Regiment was incorporated in the South-West Area Command on 1st May 1942 and the 23rd Air Regiment on 14th July in that year.

In view of the report on 28th May by the Netherlands submarine *O–23* of Japanese cruisers off the coast of Siam, Admiral Somerville sailed from Colombo with Force A on the afternoon of the 30th July. Air searches were sent out, but

---

[1] Force V : Escort : H.M.I.S. *Jumna* (S.O. Force V), *Scout*.
             Convoy : H.T. *Blackheath*, s.s. *Trader Cranfield, Mahout*.
  Force M : Escort : *Manxman* (S.O. Force M), *Aster*, H.M.I.S. *Sonavati*.
             Convoy : s.s. *Tasmania, Hoperange, Clan McIver, Yvensang, Custodian*.
    Force T : Convoy : R.F.A.s *Appleleaf, Broomdale, Shenking, Maritmaersk*.

[2] *See Plan 22.* The word ' Fleet ' which the Japanese (or the American translators) apply to the South-East, South-West, North-East and Inner South Seas Area Commands is really a misnomer. They were in the nature of shore-based administrative commands supervising certain base forces and responsible for A/S and escort work, and thus corresponded fairly closely to Commands such as the British Western Approaches, Portsmouth and similar Commands, rather than to the Foreign Stations.

the enemy was not sighted. Force A was sighted by an enemy reconnaissance flying boat, however, at 1040 on 1st August and a broadcast of its presence went out from Tokyo. The following forenoon a Japanese flying boat was shot down in 9° 26′ N., 83° 16′ E. by a Martlet aircraft from the *Formidable*. The fleet returned to Trincomalee on the evening of the 2nd August for several of the ships were required to be at Kilindini on the 11th to prepare for an operation extending British control over the whole of Madagascar. A wireless diversion was arranged, to give the impression that Force A was still operating in the Bay of Bengal until 18th August.

The Commander-in-Chief, Eastern Fleet, thought the diversion succeeded in its object. At most, however, it may have caused the Japanese to send an additional bomber squadron to Sabang for they were sensitive on the subject of the valuable Sumatran oil refineries. The information available to the Admiralty was that the raid had no effect on the distribution of enemy surface ships or aircraft in the Solomons and New Guinea area.[1]

19

While planning the above diversion operation Admiral Somerville, though aware that for reasons of policy we must not fail our American allies, had expressed doubts whether it would have the desired effect of pinning down Japanese air forces in the Malay Barrier and had pointed out that it would be to the advantage of our common cause if he were to concentrate all his forces to meet the submarine menace to our Middle East and Indian communications. As the best method of putting an end to the depredation of these craft he advised that the whole of Madagascar should be occupied for the duration of the war. When Diego Suarez was occupied in May 1942, certain Allied leaders favoured the immediate extension of our hold on the island and operation orders for the capture of Majunga and Tamatave had been drawn up, but the operations were cancelled on 10th May. Complete occupation was deferred for various reasons chief among them being the hope that after the fall of Diego Suarez the French authorities in the rest of the island might adhere voluntarily to the Allies. This hope proved vain, and H.M. Government on 11th August gave authority to proceed with the occupation.[2]

The practice of employing joint naval and military commanders of equal rank, as at the capture of Diego Suarez in May 1942, which the naval commander of that operation had subsequently deprecated despite its success, was again successfully employed in ' Stream-Line-Jane ' as the series of operations of occupying Madagascar was named. On 18th August the Commander-in-Chief, Eastern Fleet, and the General Officer Commanding-in-Chief, East Africa, Lt.-General Sir William Platt, issued a joint directive to the Joint Commanders Rear-Admiral W. G. Tennant and Major-General R. G. Sturges, R.M. for three operations, namely

(*a*) the capture of Majunga (Operation ' Stream '),

(*b*) advance from Majunga and capture of Antananarivo (Operation ' Line '),

(*c*) capture of Tamatave (Operation ' Jane ').

In the event, however, no less than six naval and two military operations were found to be necessary in order to complete the occupation of the island.

---

[1] Tel. Adty. 1734A/23/10/42 to B.A.D., Washington.

[2] Tel. O.Z.969 11.8.42 (Air Min. 1925Z/11).

The forces engaged were known as Force M (*see* Appendix A). The naval forces in Operation ' Stream ' consisted of the cruisers *Birmingham, Dauntless, Gambia,* and *Caradoc,* aircraft carrier *Illustrious* (the other carrier, the *Formidable,* had been withdrawn to Home Waters on 24th August), the monitor *Erebus,* H.Q. ship *Albatross,* fast minelayer *Manxman,* twelve destroyers, three minesweepers, three A/S whalers and a netlayer. The Army carried out Operation ' Line.' The *Warspite* and an additional destroyer and minesweeper were available for Operation ' Jane.' The troops consisted of the 29th Independent Brigade and the 22nd East African Brigade with one squadron of South African Armoured cars. Fifty-three ship-borne and 46 land based aircraft were used. The operation was preceded by a practice (exercise ' Touchstone ') which was found of the greatest value.

Planning and execution of the operation were governed by the desire not to shed blood or antagonise more than necessary the authorities and a population whom we should subsequently have to rule with very slender forces and very few Political Officers. Secrecy of planning and the assembling of the naval forces and the 22 merchant ships engaged, without making it obvious to the world that an operation of some magnitude was about to take place, presented some difficulty but was successfully overcome. The French fortunately had no modern reconnaissance aircraft in Madagascar, and despite an approach to the island by the convoy at $8\frac{1}{2}$ knots, the speed of the slowest merchant ship, surprise was achieved ; this, coupled with timing which placed all landing and covering forces at the appointed places at the appointed time was largely responsible for success.

Little opposition was encountered by the Navy, there were neither mines, submarines nor hostile aircraft to contend with ; and, in the words of the Naval Commander the proceedings might be looked on as a ' super ' peace-time operation. Of the operation orders, Admiral Somerville wrote : ' It should be the aim to compile orders so they can be readily understood and appreciated without the necessity for personal contact with those to whom they are issued.'

20

The naval forces sailed, ostensibly for exercises, separately from the convoys carrying the assault forces. Three convoys sailed individually from Kilindini and one from Diego Suarez, making rendezvous with the Joint Naval and Military Commanders in the *Birmingham* with the *Illustrious, Heemskerck* and destroyer escort at noon on 9th September, about 90 miles south of Mayotta Island.

The main objective was Majunga (Operation ' Stream ') (Figure 1), which was required to be captured and held in order to establish a bridgehead for the military Operation ' Line ' and a combined service base for the control of the Mozambique Channel. The landings were carried out as scheduled. In the first, at 0100 on 10th September about 8 miles north-west of Majunga, the assault craft reached the beach almost exactly in the position planned and complete surprise was achieved. A second landing took place at 0520 just after first light, in Majunga harbour, where the French were found largely unprepared although the Commandant had received word of the first landing at about 0300. There were two subsidiary assaults. No bombardment from the sea was necessary in support of any of the landings. By about 0600 the airfield was captured and by 0900 the inner harbour had been swept and destroyers were ordered in to oil.

FULMAR FIGHTER LANDING ON DURING OPERATIONS AT MADAGASCAR

LANDING CRAFT AT THE CAPTURE OF MAJUNGA

Operation 'Line' was less successful. The order to cease disembarking the 29th Brigade (assault troops) and begin landing the 22nd Brigade was given at 0635 on D 1. Nevertheless, the first armoured cars of the forward body of the latter brigade did not leave the beach until 1100, nearly four and a half hours later. The subsequent unloading of the motor transport of this brigade was so slow that the first six ships were not released until D 19. The organisation for dealing with the unloading of M/T and stores seems to have left much to be desired and there was delay in bringing into use a number of lighters and tugs that were captured.

Arrangements had been made for the *Napier*, Captain S. H. T. Arliss (Captain (D)), to go alongside the s.s. *Empire Pride* at sea on D minus 2, to embark one troop of No. 5 Commando. The *Napier* then proceeded independently to Morondava 380 miles south of Majunga where, after some difficulty caused by the heavy surf the Commandos were landed in ships' boats and penetrated a considerable distance inland while bogus messages of a major British invasion were being telephoned to the capital. The desired effect of the operation ('Tamper') was completely achieved.

Nosi Bé, an island off the north-west coast of Madagascar, was captured on the same day (Operation 'Esmé (B)'). At 0300 on 10th September, the *Manxman*, Captain R. K. Dickson, with naval boarding parties under Sub-Lieutenant D. H. Hallifax, Marines from the *Caradoc*, under Captain R. E. Burton, R.M., and two platoons of Pretoria Highlanders (Captain A. B. Inglis) entered the harbour at Hellville on the island. Mooring head and stern the *Manxman* bombarded areas known or believed to contain machine guns commanding the pier head, afterwards sweeping the pier head with all short range weapons and military mortars. Some French casualties were caused. During these bombardments, boarding parties captured tugs and power boats. Under cover of fire the Pretoria Highlanders were then landed on the pier head in cutters pulled by Marines, and captured Hellville with only one casualty, the crews of the machine guns on the pier having been dazed or driven from their guns by the bombardment. Meanwhile, the 7th South African Brigade had been advancing southward from the Diego Suarez bridgehead (Operation 'Esmé (A)'). They were held up considerably by the retreating French troops burning the bridges behind them, and at the request of the local military authorities the *Manxman* escorted a party of Marines and South African Brigade troops and naval details, 85 officers and men in all, termed Force 'Backside,' to Sahamalaza Bay (14° 0' S., 47° 56' E. *See Figure 1*) and sent them up the river in small craft, where they landed. About dawn on 15th September they reached Maromandia. The French were faced with the alternatives of surrender or standing to fight one of the two forces, and they surrendered after a short engagement with the northern force.

The 29th Brigade at Majunga had begun re-embarking on D 2, and the ships left port on D 4 for the assault on Tamatave (Operation 'Jane') scheduled for D 9. In view of the slight opposition offered at Majunga the G.O.C.-in-C., East Africa, and the military commanders agreed to a proposal made by Admiral Tennant, to modify the plan of assault on Tamatave. The bombardment of an hour's duration from the sea, originally called for, was now abandoned in favour of an air demonstration and a display of force by all ships taking part, which included the *Warspite*. The honour of the Chef de Région having been satisfied with the exchange of a few shots, he surrendered : rather fortunately, because six of the nine landing craft which carried out the assault on the northernmost of the three beaches broached to, though there was little wind and swell, and had there been opposition the second wave would not have got ashore.

27

At the request of the military, on 29th September a force consisting of two companies of the Pretoria Regiment and a detachment of Marines from the *Birmingham*, supported by the Senior Officer Force M in the *Birmingham* with the destroyers *Napier, Inconstant* and *van Galen* landed at Tuléar (Operation ' Rose '). A policy similar to that at Tamatave was carried out. In this case, however, bombardment proved unnecessary. The white flag was hoisted and the landing was carried out without opposition. It was then learnt that the garrison had been withdrawn on the 20th, leaving but a few Malagache reservists in the place.

This completed the part of the Navy in the operations for the occupation of Madagascar. These operations had repercussions in another theatre of war, for preparations by the Commander-in-Chief, India, Field-Marshal Wavell, in the autumn of 1942 for a seaborne expedition to recapture Akyab had to be abandoned since the necessary shipping, troops and air forces were engaged in Madagascar.

21

The occupation of Madagascar saved the Eastern Fleet much trouble by putting an end to the sailing of Vichy French merchant ships. On 26th August, just before Operation Stream-Line-Jane began, the *Mauritius* sailed from Kilindini to intercept the s.s. *Amiral Pierre* which was suspected of having Japanese agents on board and was expected to sail from Manakara, on the east coast of Madagascar (22° 09′ S., 48° 11′ E.), for Réunion. The *Mauritius* arrived on patrol on the 29th, and apart from fuelling at Mauritius on 2nd September, remained on patrol until the 4th when she had to break off to meet and escort Convoy U.S.16 which was coming from Australia. The *Amiral Pierre* reached Réunion without being intercepted, and on 21st September, in consequence of intelligence that she was expected to try to escape to Lourenço Marques, the *Illustrious* carried out air searches to the southward of Madagascar, whilst the *Ranchi* was detached from Convoy C.M.31 (Capetown to Red Sea ports) and spent the next day in patrolling the area calculated to be the furthest-on position which the *Amiral Pierre* could reach. The Commander-in-Chief South Atlantic, Vice-Admiral W. E. C. Tait, also instituted air patrols covering the approaches to Lourenço Marques and sent the *Nizam* and *Hotspur* out on patrol, the *Norman* joining them on the 26th. On the 23rd the *Nizam*, acting on reports by the South African Air Force, intercepted and boarded the s.s. *Maréchal Gallieni* (1,559 tons) and sent her to Capetown with the S.A.A.F. whaler *Cedarberg*. On the 29th aircraft of the South African Air Force sighted and reported the s.s. *Amiral Pierre* but before the *Nizam* could reach her that afternoon she abandoned ship and scuttled herself in position 25° 45′ S., 21° E. Efforts to save her proved unavailing, and the *Nizam* eventually had to sink her in 26° 04′ S., 34° 54′ E.

22

On 30th November the Free French destroyer *Léopard*, independently and without support, by means of bold and ingenious action effected the release from Vichy control of the island of Réunion, 400 miles east of Madagascar.

The *Léopard* sailed from Port Louis, Mauritius at 1800 on 27th November with the Free French Governor-designate, Monsieur Choparry and the local representative of General de Gaulle, Captain Patureau, on board ; and arrived before midnight at a point 1,500 yards north of St. Denis, Réunion where an advance landing party put off. The moon had risen, but was obscured by clouds.

Captain Patureau, with a Sub-Lieutenant and seven ratings, all in plain clothes but with their uniforms ready to hand, paddled for the shore in two native boats brought from Mauritius, taking with them a portable wireless transmitter, an Aldis lamp and a pair of hand-flags. They took an hour to reach land, where they installed the transmitter in a cemetery unobserved, and the officer, with one rating, set off to find a landing place for the main party and make contact with likely partisans among the population.

No signals were received from the advance party until 0340 and assuming that it had been captured the main landing party put off for the shore in the *Léopard's* boats, and guided later by the advance party's signals, landed in bright moonlight at the jetty. Within half an hour the wireless station, barracks and Government House were seized, but the Governor himself was at his private house at Hellbourg, a hill station defended by 420 regular troops.

Meanwhile, St. Denis was full of crowds cheering for the British, who, the population assumed, had arrived. The First Lieutenant was busy telephoning to proclaim martial law to the mayors of all villages in the colony ; the illusion of the presence of an overwhelming force was created, the *Léopard* assisting by appearing off various points of the island in turn. At Pointe de Galets a coastal battery opened fire on the local de Gaullists, but surrendered after the *Léopard* had fired 200 rounds at it.

There still remained the considerable task of storming Hellbourg, and on the evening of the 28th the Commander-in-Chief, Eastern Fleet was asked for assistance. Early on the 30th, however, a threat to shell the sugar refineries of the island so shocked the sugar-kings that they forced the Governor to surrender. With the occupation of the island, the last potential base for enemy blockade-runners, submarines, raiders and aircraft in the western Indian Ocean passed under Allied control.

CHAPTER IV

Strategical Situation in the Pacific, July 1942

(*See* Plans 5, 6, 22, 24)

23

IT was at Guadalcanal, an island 75 miles long and 25 miles wide, in the Southern Solomons at the extreme periphery of Japan's defensive system, 3,000 miles from Tokyo, that the Allies in August 1942 began the offensive which in three years was to carry them to the shores of Japan. By the time Madagascar was taken under British control the Americans had landed on Guadalcanal Island and were fighting hard to maintain their foothold.

The Solomon Islands were of great strategical importance to the Japanese as stepping stones for attack on the line of communications from the United States and Hawaii to Australia. In 1942 little was known to us about these islands. They were thinly populated and undeveloped. Situated some 800 miles east of New Guinea, they form a double chain of tropical mountainous islands 600 miles long, stretching north-west to south-east between the parallels 5° S. and 12½° S. and the meridians 155° E. and 170° E. Several hundred islands with a total land area of 18,670 square miles compose the group. The largest in the north-eastern chain are Buka, Bougainville, Choiseul, Santa Isabel, and Malaita. The south-western chain consists of the Shortland, Treasury and New Georgia groups, the Russells, Guadalcanal, Florida, San Cristobal and Rennell. The chain was divided politically, the northernmost islands Bougainville and Buka, being part of the Australian Mandated territory of New Guinea, and the remainder forming the British Solomon Islands Protectorate. Situated in one of the world's wettest areas the humid climate is very enervating. There are few good harbours, but the narrow channels between the islands are usually calm. Guadalcanal was chosen as the first objective because it had a large grassy plain on which the Japanese were discovered to be constructing an airfield which threatened the route linking the U.S.A. with Australia and New Zealand, the bases of supply from which the process of defeating Japan was to be undertaken. In every operation in the Pacific to date the enemy had shown that he was aware of the importance of airfields. The Japanese used carrier based air power extravagantly when occasion demanded, but never for longer than necessary : at the earliest possible moment land-based air forces took over and the airfield replaced the carrier's flight deck. Carrier based air power was expensive and in short supply : shorter than ever since Midway had left the Japanese Navy with greatly reduced carrier strength, for although Japan still disposed of three fleet carriers and a similar number of light carriers she was at this time far from being able to man all of them with efficient air groups.[1] Tulagi Island, adjacent to Florida Island, where the Japanese had landed on 2nd May 1942, afforded no suitable land for an airstrip ; and on 4th July five transports escorted by cruisers and destroyers landed troops and labourers on the neighbouring island, Guadalcanal, and Allied reconnaissance aircraft soon saw a great airfield, later to become famous as Henderson Field, under construction on the north coast near Lunga Point (see Plan 12).

It was not, of course, known to the Allies, whose knowledge of the Japanese strategic as opposed to operational planning was based to a considerable extent on inferences, that the enemy were about to abandon their intention to invade New Caledonia, Fiji and Samoa. The Japanese landing at Tulagi in May, and the presumption that the establishment of an airfield was intended, was sufficient to threaten the still tenuous line of communication from the United States to Australia and New Zealand : in particular, it brought both the New Hebrides, where the Americans had landed at Efate and set up a minor base at the beginning of April, and even Kumac, the northern airfield in New Caledonia, within range of enemy land based aircraft.

24

The U.S. Joint Chiefs of Staff on 2nd July ordered Allied forces in the Pacific to mount a limited offensive (Operation ' Watchtower ') to halt the Japanese southward advance. It was a limited offensive because there were then available so few warships, transports and cargo ships, so few trained troops, so few weapons and supplies, that any offensive in the Pacific, for which the United States would have to produce the lion's share of the resources, would necessarily be on a restricted scale. The decision to mount such an offensive in the Pacific was a logical corollary to the strategic decisions taken at the ' Arcadia ' Conference at Washington in December 1941–January 1942 under which the strategy of the Allies was for the time being to be directed towards containing the Japanese with the limited forces then committed or allotted, whilst the main weight of their effort was brought to bear continuously against Germany until she was defeated. It was recognised, however, that the security of Australia and New Zealand as sources of supply, essential political and economic units of the British Commonwealth of Nations, and future bases for the defeat of Japan, must be ensured ; and this entailed, amongst other things, holding the air–sea island route from the U.S.A. to these territories.[2] As eventually established, there were two convergent routes.[3] One ran via Hawaii through Fiji and Numea in New Caledonia, which like nearly all French islands in the Pacific had declared for General de Gaulle, with minor bases at Palmyra, Christmas Island, Canton, Samoa, together with Efate and Espiritu Santo in the New Hebrides. The other route was from the west coast of U.S.A. and Panama via Bora Bora in the Society Islands and Tongatabu. Each route ran both to the main South-West Pacific Area bases Brisbane and Sydney, and the main South Pacific Area base Auckland.

---

[1] Fleet carriers *Junyo* (*Hayataka*) (commissioned May 1942), *Zuikaku*, *Shokaku* (under battle damage repair), light fleet carriers *Ryujo*, *Zuiho*, *Hosho*. Another fleet carrier, the *Hiyo* (*Hitaka*) was commissioned in July 1942.

[2] 'Arcadia' Conference Report, C.R. (JP) W.W. (WWJPC) Serial W.W.1 (Final). Though the security of New Zealand as well as Australia was premised the General Strategic Policy as laid down did not specifically mention holding the latter Dominion. The Joint Chiefs of Staff included New Zealand, however, with Australia (J.S.C.48 quoted in *United States Army in World War II—Guadalcanal, The First Offensive*).

[3] See Plan 5.

Reference has already been made to the difference of opinion between the U.S. Navy and Army Air Forces as to the most efficient means of defending the South Pacific islands.[1] The Joint Staff Planners made a thorough examination of the subject, and after studying their report the American Chiefs of Staff Committee decided that effective defence of the route must depend upon mutual support, neither forces nor equipment being available to develop the individual bases into impregnable fortresses. These must, however, be prepared to carry out direct ground and air defence. Shipping *en route* must be given direct naval and air escort, and important convoys must be covered by forces ready to accept battle with enemy striking forces. The enemy must be denied positions which would enable him to disrupt Allied sea and air communications, a task involving the employment not only of sea and air forces to prevent the enemy establishing himself in such positions but also of amphibious forces to dislodge him if established. It was concluded that seizure of positions which would in turn threaten Japanese control of vital sea and air communications offered the greatest promise of success in containing enemy forces in the Pacific.[2]

25

By July 1942 the Japanese strong defensive outpost system for Rabaul which was being developed as their main naval, air and military base in the south-west Pacific, was becoming consolidated. In New Guinea the enemy had for four months contented themselves with the beachheads at Lae and Salamoa which they captured in March ; but on 22nd July they landed 5,000 veterans of the Malayan campaign and moved into Buna and Gona, further down the coast, in preparation for a thrust southward across the Owen Stanley Mountains to Port Moresby, the Allied base, which they had failed in May to capture by sea. They certainly did not foresee that the Allied counter-attack to their offensive campaign in New Guinea would eventually develop into an advance that was to carry the Australian and American forces under General MacArthur triumphantly to the Philippines. The moving in of the Japanese Seventeenth Army and the construction of bases at Gasmata in southern New Britain, Kavieng at the north end of New Ireland, and at several places in Bougainville and the adjacent islands such as Buka, Kieta, Kahili, Buin and the Shortland Islands, bore witness to the intention of the enemy not only to provide for the defence of Rabaul, but to advance and sever the all important Pacific line of communications of the Allies.

Rabaul was destined within the month to become the headquarters of the new Japanese South-east Area Command consisting of some dozen destroyers and four minesweepers based at Truk and ten auxiliary vessels known as the 8th, 14th, 1st and 7th Base Forces, for local defence at Rabaul, Kavieng, Buin and Lae respectively and for escort and anti-submarine operations in the area of the Bismarcks, Papua, the Solomons and the Coral Sea eastward of a line running south-east from a point just west of the Admiralty Islands (2° 30′ S., 146° E.) through the Tobriand Islands.[3] The Commander-in-Chief, Vice-Admiral G. Mikawa, also controlled the Eighth Fleet, which was constituted in July 1942 and normally consisted of a small cruiser force. Under him, too, was the 25th Flotilla (Rear-Admiral S. Yamada) of Vice-Admiral N. Tsukahara's Eleventh Air Fleet. This was reinforced by a second flotilla, the 26th, after the Allied landing on Guadalcanal.

---

[1] *See* Vol. II of this history.

[2] *The Army Air Forces in World War II*, Vol. IV, pp. 14–15.   [3] *See Plan 22.*

The Allies had not been able to offer effective opposition to the Japanese incursions into New Guinea and the Bismarck Archipelago. The few Australian troops had been killed or driven out of the Bismarcks, whilst in the Australian Mandated area of North-east New Guinea and the British Dependency of Papua the meagre Allied strength was mainly concentrated in the south at Port Moresby, the only harbour in South-eastern New Guinea large enough to shelter a fleet. Reinforcements had been sent there after the outbreak of war, bringing the force there to the strength of two partly trained and inadequately equipped brigades.

The nuns and missionaries remained when the Japanese occupied the various islands, and under surveillance and in face of great difficulties for the most part continued to carry on medical and educational work. Though some Government officers quitted the islands when driven from their posts many remained and others returned as opportunity offered. In July 1942 it became a settled policy that for purposes of maintaining morale, officers should remain in concealment behind the enemy lines. The Allies were thus able to staff an organisation which with the assistance of the native populations, who proved immensely loyal, kept a remarkable watch on the enemy's movements.

In 1942 Australian radar was in its infancy, but it was fortunate that shortly after the conclusion of the First World War the Australian Government had created the Australian Coast Watching Organisation in the islands north and north-east of Australia, known by the code name ' Ferdinand ' from the Bull which did not fight but sat under a tree and just smelled the flowers.[1] It was administered by the Royal Australian Navy through the Naval Intelligence Division at Melbourne of which the organisation became an integral part in 1942.[2] This important reporting and communication service was composed for the most part of planters and civil servants who had lived in the islands for years. They remained in concealment behind the Japanese lines after invasions, near or on the coast, and by means of portable wireless sets informed the Allied fighting forces of the enemy's aircraft, ship and troop movements and other matters of defence interest.[3] They made a contribution to the Allied arms in the South and South-west Pacific out of all proportion to their numbers. Whilst Royal Australian Air Force radar equipment had a range of no more than 50 to 75 miles, the Coast Watchers' stations extended to hundreds of miles' distance from the areas held by the Allies. The Coast Watchers were at their posts on Guadalcanal and Tulagi when the Allies attacked in August 1942, and their stations covered the entire north and south shores of Papua and the islands of the Torres Strait (see Plan 6).

---

[1] See Ferdinand the Bull, by Munro Leaf.

[2] In March 1942, when General D. MacArthur arrived in Australia from the Philippines and was made Supreme Commander of all forces in the South-West Pacific Area the Coast Watching Organisation in that area became part of the Allied Intelligence Bureau which was formed as a unit from all Services, acting directly under General Headquarters for carrying out activities behind the enemy lines. The Coast Watchers in S.W. Pacific, like those in the South Pacific continued to be administered by the S.I.O. (D.N.I. Melbourne) (Comdr. E. Feldt, O.B.E., R.A.N.) who was responsible to ComSoPac for those in the South Pacific Area and to the A.I.B. for those in the South-West Pacific Area.

[3] Alternative channels were arranged, the final one being via Port Moresby, Townsville (Queensland) and Canberra to Pearl Harbour whose powerful transmitter broadcast the reports to the Pacific. It is said that when the Allies attacked Guadalcanal the report that a Japanese air counter-attack was on the way was received by the Allies by this route 25 minutes after the strike left Rabaul.

There was a conflict of views in the United States regarding the strategy of the forthcoming Allied offensive in the Pacific.[1] The War Department and General MacArthur wished to make New Britain and New Ireland the immediate objectives of attack in order to recapture Rabaul. Admiral King, in view of the precarious balance of naval power at the time, saw the danger of direct attack on a position so exposed to enemy counter attack as Rabaul and preferred a gradual advance through the Solomons from the south.

The problem of command, too, took some weeks to solve. General Marshall, Chief of Staff of the Army, argued that since the operation would take place in the South-west Pacific, which was General MacArthur's area, the latter should conduct it. General MacArthur had, however, neither troops nor aircraft for such an operation. Under his command in Australia he had, it is true, the 32nd and 41st U.S. Infantry Divisions and the 7th Australian Division ; but none of these was equipped or trained for combined operations, and whilst they could support an assault from the sea by moving ashore once a beachhead was taken, they could not take a beachhead themselves. The objectives of the offensive lay beyond the range of U.S. fighter aircraft even from Espiritu Santo in the New Hebrides, 560 nautical miles distant to the south-eastward, which the Americans had occupied at the end of May 1942, there to begin building a base and airfield which eventually became the principal advanced base for the Guadalcanal operation. Close support would consequently have to be provided by aircraft carriers, of which MacArthur had none, his naval force consisting only of two cruisers and six destroyers. As a corollary, unity of command was essential.

On the other hand, the Navy in the adjacent South Pacific Area, which was part of Admiral C. W. Nimitz's Pacific Ocean Areas Command, disposed of the necessary landing force in the shape of the 1st Marine Division, 9,000 highly trained professional fighting men, whilst there were now three American carriers in the South Pacific, the *Saratoga*, *Enterprise* and *Hornet* which with screens consisting of three or four of the ten cruisers in the area and some of the 28 destroyers constituted Task Forces 15, 16 and 17 respectively. At least two of these carriers would be available to take part in the assault on Guadalcanal. But like the British Admiralty a few weeks earlier, the U.S. Navy feared that if their carriers were placed under General MacArthur's control he might dangerously expose them in the waters of the Solomon Sea within range of Japanese shore-based aircraft. Though General MacArthur asseverated that his plan for assault on Rabaul envisaged a progressive advance against the Solomons and the north coast of New Guinea, in order to obtain airfields which would give him command of the air and thus remove the grounds of the Navy's objection, whilst General Marshall sought to allay the Navy's fears for the safety of the aircraft carriers by suggesting that the Joint Chiefs of Staff should approve any arrangements made for the employment of the naval forces, Admiral King whilst offering the workable compromise that the Commander-in-Chief Pacific should conduct the assault and MacArthur the subsequent consolidation foresaw the dangers of delay and directed Admiral Nimitz to proceed with the preparations for the occupation of the Santa Cruz Islands and an offensive in the Solomons. Eventually, on 2nd July, the matter was settled as proposed by Admiral King, on the basis that Vice-Admiral R. L. Ghormley, Commander under Nimitz of the South Pacific Area and South Pacific Force, should direct

---

[1] This section is based mainly on the official publication *United States Army in World War II*, Vol. I, since the Historical Section has not access to the U.S. Joint Chiefs of Staff papers.

the offensive until the Tulagi operation was at an end, and that thereafter General MacArthur should control the advance towards Rabaul. The boundary between the South-west and South Pacific Areas was moved westward on 1st August to longitude 159° E., thus placing Tulagi, Guadalcanal, the Russell Islands, Malaita and San Cristobal in Admiral Ghormley's area whilst leaving the remainder of the Solomons in the South-west Pacific Area under MacArthur.

28

Admiral Ghormley's directive, dated 2nd July 1942, specified that he was to hold island positions necessary for security of the line of communications between the United States and the South-west Pacific Area and for supporting naval, air and amphibious operations against the Japanese ; protect essential sea and air communications ; support the operations of forces in South-west and Central Pacific Areas ; and prepare to launch a major amphibious offensive against positions held by Japan.[1] The three tasks by which in their directive the Joint Chiefs of Staff envisaged that General MacArthur would expel the Japanese from the territories they had conquered in the Southern Pacific were never carried out in their entirety—indeed, the principal object itself of the offensive, namely the capture of Rabaul, was never carried out, for it was found eventually to be more economical and equally effective to isolate it and so render it both harmless to the Allies and useless to the enemy. The first task was the seizure and occupation of the Santa Cruz Islands, Tulagi and adjacent positions. No mention was made of Guadalcanal, the importance of which had not at that time become evident. The operation, as already stated, was to be under the command of an officer detailed by Admiral Nimitz. General MacArthur was to attach the necessary naval reinforcements and land-based aircraft to the South Pacific forces, and to interdict enemy air and naval activity west of the target area. Actually, the Santa Cruz Islands were found to provide no suitable site for an airfield, and the mortality rate from malaria was prohibitively high ; and they were never effectively occupied. The target date of Task One was 1st August. Task Two, the seizure and occupation of the remainder of the Solomons, Lae, Salamoa and the north-west coast of New Guinea, and Task Three, the seizure and occupation of Rabaul and adjacent positions in the New Britain–New Ireland area were to be carried out under General MacArthur's command.

The South Pacific Amphibious Force, which included the 1st Marine Division, transports and cargo ships was to carry out all three tasks supported by at least two aircraft carriers with their screens and aided by the Marine air squadrons and land-based aircraft in the South Pacific and the ground, air and naval forces then under General MacArthur. Troops from the latter's command would provide garrisons other than those for Tulagi and the adjacent positions which would be furnished by Army forces from the South Pacific. Naval task force commanders would exercise direct command of the amphibious forces throughout the conduct of all three tasks. The Joint Chiefs of Staff reserved the power to withdraw U.S. fleet units on completion of any phase of the operation if the aircraft carriers were jeopardised or if an emergency should arise elsewhere in the Pacific.

Meanwhile, Admiral Nimitz's plans were approaching completion. They recognised the importance of Guadalcanal as an objective to form a future advanced base for offensive operations against Rabaul. General MacArthur no

---

[1] Instructions issued by Cominch to Admiral Ghormley, prospective Commander South Pacific Force. M.051232/42.

less than Admiral Ghormley who was to exercise strategic control over the forces in the first task came to the conclusion that Tasks 2 and 3 would necessarily have to follow quickly on the heels of Task 1 and that for this purpose the forces available were insufficient. Though there was considerable Army troop strength in the South Pacific, these troops were engaged in holding bases on the line of communication and could not be withdrawn without relief.[1] Moreover, the shortage of shipping space precluded free movement of large numbers of men. Both MacArthur and Ghormley consequently recommended that the operation should be postponed. The Joint Chiefs of Staff rejected the recommendation. The southward advance of the Japanese must be halted immediately. They promised to provide such further forces as could be found to reduce the risks of this perilous adventure, and though urgency prevented thoroughgoing planning[2] orders were given to invade Guadalcanal and Tulagi at once. Thus was initiated six months of fighting as bitter as any that took place during the war.

---

[1] Morrison, *History of United States Naval Operations in World War II*, Vol. IV, quoting an official U.S. report, gives the following approximate numbers of army troops in May–June 1943 : Samoa 15,500, Tongatabu 7,800, Fiji one division, Numea 22,200.

[2] Admiral King, *Report to Secretary of U.S. Navy*, covering operations to 1st March 1944.

CHAPTER V

Invasion of Guadalcanal[1]

(*See* Plans 8, 9, 24)

29

THE directive of the Joint Chiefs of Staff for Operation ' Watchtower,' the invasion of the Southern Solomons with the ultimate object of capturing the Japanese main South Seas base of Rabaul, had barely been issued when a discovery was made which not only lent urgency to the undertaking, but rendered Guadalcanal the principal first objective. Air reconnaissance revealed that the Japanese had begun work on an airfield on Guadalcanal Island, and in consequence on 10th July the Joint Chiefs of Staff directed that Guadalcanal and Tulagi were to be invaded at once. The target date, 1st August, was three weeks distant. It was impossible to keep it, for the forces had to be gathered from far and wide, and the Atlantic as well as the Pacific was being drawn upon for ships. The landing was accordingly postponed for six days. It was made not a day too soon, for the airfield, when captured, was ready for almost immediate use by fighters and dive bombers.[2] Even when working to the postponed date of 7th August the military commander, Major-General A. A. Vandegrift, had to evolve his plan before leaving the United States, without knowledge of the plans of the Commander, South Pacific Area, Admiral Ghormley, whose headquarters were at Auckland, New Zealand, the main South Pacific Area base.

Shortage of time affected not only planning. When the ships bringing the 1st Marine Division to New Zealand left the United States there had been no reason to suppose the force would be employed immediately on active operations, and the ships of the First Echelon had been unloaded and released for landings in North Africa (Operation ' Torch '). Those of the Second Echelon were not combat loaded, and had now to be entirely restowed. At Wellington, almost the entire operation had to be carried out under press of time by the troops, many of whom were in bad physical condition after a long voyage in crowded transports.

---

[1] Tactical details of the operation and of all the naval engagements described in Chapter V to VIII will be found in Naval Staff History, Battle Summary No. 21 *Naval Operations in the Campaign for Guadalcanal, August 1942–February 1945*.

[2] It is stated in *The Army Air Forces in World War II*, Vol. II, p. 35, that Japanese aircraft were scheduled to move in on 7th August.

Work was carried out night and day, in three watches. Dockside equipment was meagre and there was no shelter from the wintry weather, so that supplies deteriorated no less than the men's morale in the persistent cold wind and rain. More than half the motor transport had to be left behind in New Zealand for lack of time to load it.

Both the naval and military commanders had to draw up their orders with very incomplete information of the geography and physical conditions of the Solomon Islands. Charts and surveys were imperfect and out of date. Former residents were hunted up and drawn upon for such information as they could supply, eight of them being given commissions or warrants by the Australian forces and attached to the 1st Marine Division as guides, advisers and pilots. For the rest, reliance was placed on aerial photography. As regards intelligence of the enemy the Coast Watchers on Guadalcanal sent regular telegrams via the Resident Commissioner, Mr. W. S. Marchant, on Malaita Island. These kept the Allies informed of the doings of the Japanese on Guadalcanal, the strength of the garrison and progress of the airfield.[1]

Admiral Ghormley issued his plan on 16th July, only eight days after receiving from the Commander-in-Chief, Pacific, his final orders, to capture the Santa Cruz Islands and the Tulagi–Guadalcanal area. A seaplane base was to be formed at Tulagi and air bases for four squadrons each at Guadalcanal and at Ndeni in the Santa Cruz Islands. The latter task was postponed until Tulagi and Guadalcanal should have been captured. In the event, the troops allotted to it had to be used to overcome unexpectedly stiff resistance in Florida Island, and this phase of the operation had in consequence to be cancelled. As already related, the Santa Cruz Islands were never effectively occupied.

30

Three ships of the Australian Squadron, which was detached from General MacArthur's South-west Pacific Force and placed under Admiral Ghormley, were to participate in Operation ' Watchtower.' This squadron, consisting of the cruisers *Australia*, *Canberra*, *Hobart* and *Adelaide*, had remained under its British Flag Officer when the Anzac organisation was abolished on 22nd April 1942 and Vice-Admiral H. F. Leary became commander of General MacArthur's naval forces. The remaining Australian ships comprised the armed merchant cruisers *Kanimbla*, *Manoora* and *Westralia*, the sloop *Moresby*, and the destroyers *Arunta*, *Stuart*, *Voyager* and *Vendetta*, one of which, the *Voyager*, was destroyed a few weeks later, as we have seen, whilst landing reinforcements for the Australian Imperial Force in Timor. None of the New Zealand ships in the South Pacific Force were to be employed in Operation ' Watchtower ' : all were engaged in convoy escort or local defence under Admiral Ghormley's orders. The two cruisers, *Achilles*, and *Leander*, had been transferred from the operational control of the Commander-in-Chief, Pacific, to that of Admiral Ghormley on 13th July. New Zealand retained control of the armed merchant cruiser *Monowai*,[2] the French light cruisers *Le Triomphant* and *Léopard*, the sloop *Chevreuil*, and the Fijian ship *Viti*.

Escort of shipping was the principal duty of the Australian and New Zealand ships, other than the cruisers of the Australian Squadron which were employed in furnishing support for carrier strikes and other operations. At that date, the

---

[1] The Coast Watching Officer-in-Charge on Guadalcanal was Captain M. Clemens.

[2] The other A.M.C., the *Ascania* was disarmed in June/July 1942. *See New Zealand, Extract from 33rd Monthly Report on war effort, Period ended 30th June 1942*, M.09616/42.

regular ocean convoys comprised the troop convoys from Australia to the Middle East, termed U.S. and the Trans-Tasman (VK, ZT) convoys between Sydney and Wellington, which sailed every ten days. Australian ships escorted the former as far as Colombo where the Eastern Fleet took over. The trainees under the Empire Air Training Scheme sailed to and from Australia in the regular American BT, TB military convoys[1] which ran every twenty-eight days ; and from New Zealand a convoy ran to Panama every ten days. Australian and New Zealand vessels assisted in the escort of ships effecting the movements of Allied troops and supplies between the Dominions and South Pacific bases on the lines of communication with the United States. Some of these troop movements were of considerable importance. For example, a large force of New Zealand troops had been sent to garrison Fiji after the outbreak of war, a movement which was covered by the *Achilles, Leander* and *Monowai*. During June 1942 the 38th (American) Infantry Division was moved to Fiji in readiness to replace the New Zealanders when the military command was transferred from New Zealand to the U.S. on 18th July.[2] Simultaneously, an extra-routine convoy termed 'Schooner' sailed from Colombo on 13th July for Australia, bringing back two brigades of Australian troops which had been diverted from the Malay Barrier to Ceylon at the beginning of March when the fall of Java was seen to be inevitable.

Besides the ocean convoys there were numerous Australian coastal convoys requiring anti-submarine escorts,[3] for enemy submarines were still working in Australian waters. Attacks continued until 7th August after which the submarines were withdrawn to operate in the Solomon Islands. But when Operation 'Watchtower' began the escort of Allied coastal shipping was still continuing.

31

The following diagram shows the chain of command for Operation 'Watchtower.'

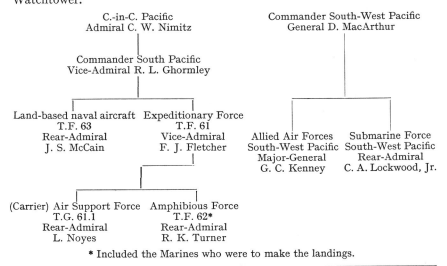

* Included the Marines who were to make the landings.

[1] Sydney, N.S.W. to U.S.A. and vice versa.

[2] The terms of transfer are given in C.O.S. (W) 210 and Tel. J.S.M. 298, 11th July 1942.

[3] The convoys are listed in Tel. A.C.N.B. 0557Z, 13th January 1942 to Admiralty.

Admiral Ghormley organised his ships, aircraft and troops in two forces : the Expeditionary Force (Task Force 61) (*see* Appendix B) and the land-based naval aircraft (Task Force 63).

The Expeditionary Force, which was under the command of Vice-Admiral F. J. Fletcher, Officer in Tactical Command of all naval forces afloat, was organised as the Air Support Force (Task Group 61.1) and the Amphibious Force (Task Force 62). The Air Support Force, under Rear-Admiral L. Noyes, had the duty of providing air support for the attack. The Americans had not yet gone the whole way in acceptance of the doctrine of concentration of carriers, for though the three available carriers, the *Saratoga* (Vice-Admiral Fletcher's flagship), *Enterprise* (flagship of Rear-Admiral T. C. Kinkaid) and *Wasp* (flagship of Rear-Admiral Noyes, Officer in Tactical Command of the Group) were organised in a single group, each carrier with its supporting ships and screen was organised as a separate unit. Support consisted of cruisers and the battleship *North Carolina*, the first of the great new capital ships laid down before the war as replacements for the limited number of battleships permitted under the terms of the Washington Treaty of 1922. The remaining battleships of the Pacific Fleet, seven in all, were covering Pearl Harbour, where the forth carrier, the *Hornet* (flagship of Rear-Admiral A. W. Fitch) lay at short notice for steam. On the security of Pearl Harbour rested the ability of the Americans to operate in the Pacific ; for it was to Pearl Harbour that, in the absence of a secure base in the South Pacific, all ships needing major repairs had to be sent. In the entire Pacific Ocean there was no other base capable of sustaining a fleet. Other than these seven battleships, the aircraft carrier *Hornet*, and the ships detailed for Operation ' Watchtower' every ship in the Pacific, with the exception of one light cruiser, on a special mission, was engaged on convoy duty.[1]

The Amphibious Force, Task Force 62, which was to transport, land and support the assault forces and protect the convoys against surface attack, was commanded by Rear-Admiral R. K. Turner, who flew his flag in the transport *McCawley*. Though he was part of Admiral Fletcher's Expeditionary Force he had in effect a free hand from the time of sailing of the expedition.[2] His force comprised two groups of transports and storeships, ' X ' for landing on Guadalcanal and ' Y ' for the Tulagi landings ; two fire support groups of cruisers and destroyers, and a screening group under the British Rear-Admiral V. A. C. Crutchley, V.C., who had succeeded Rear-Admiral J. G. Crace in command of the Australian Squadron on 13th June 1942, on expiration of the period on loan of the latter to the Royal Australian Navy. The Screening Group consisted of two 8-inch cruisers of the Australian Squadron, the *Australia* (flagship) and *Canberra*, and the 6-inch cruiser *Hobart*, reinforced by the U.S. heavy cruiser *Chicago*, with nine American destroyers. Admiral Crutchley was also second in command of the Amphibious Force.

It was estimated that the enemy garrison in the Guadalcanal area had a rifle strength of about 2,120 besides special weapons, with ancilliary troops and construction and labour units, a total of 5,000. In the Tulagi area the total was believed to be about a quarter of the above. The greater part of three regiments of the 1st Marines, with a Tank Division and a Special Weapons Battalion, engineers and pioneers, total 11,400, were assigned to the Guadalcanal landings, and rather less than a quarter of this number, including a Parachute Battalion 500 strong, to the landings in the Tulagi area which was separated

---

[1] Morison, *History of United States Operations in World War II*, Vol. IV, p. 276.

[2] The same, p. 269.

from Guadalcanal by the Sealark Channel, 20 miles wide. The 2nd Marines, 5,000 strong formed a reserve. Surface minelayers laid a minefield of 84 mines off Maramasike Island, Malaita Island, during the invasion, on 8th August, to prevent the use of the anchorage by the Japanese.

32

The Japanese were known to have seaplane bases in the Solomons, at Gavutu Island (near Tulagi, *see Plan 12*), Gizo Island in the New Georgia group (*see Plan 16*), Rekata Bay (Santa Isabel Island), Faisi Island in the Shortlands, and Buka Island off the north end of Bougainville (*see Plan 8*). The aircraft operating from these bases were largely engaged in reconnaissance, however, and the major threat came from Rabaul, 675 miles from Guadalcanal, base of the 25th (Naval) Air Flotilla, and from the base under construction at Kieta on Bougainville Island, only 300 miles from Guadalcanal, and from the Guadalcanal airfield itself. The Japanese air strength in the Bismarcks–Solomons area amounted at this time to some 150 first line aircraft, and a special staff officer had been sent from Tokyo to ensure their efficient employment. These machines belonged to battle-tried air units which had operated with great success in the advance to the south. The average pilot had at least 600 flying hours and considerable experience with tropical weather and the operational difficulties encountered in the Bismarcks area. The Americans attempted to neutralise this force on the day of the Guadalcanal landing by an attack on the Rabaul airfields, but at that date United States air power in Australia was so slender that only thirteen heavy bombers actually made the attack, and very little damage was done.[1]

To counter the serious Japanese air threat to Operation ' Watchtower ' strong air support was essential. Two forces of land based aircraft, one naval and one army, were detailed for this support. The naval force, Task Force 63, (land based naval aircraft), which was under Admiral Ghormley's orders, was commanded by Rear-Admiral J. S. McCain whose headquarters were located on board the U.S.S. *Tangier* at Numea, New Caledonia. Five Marine air squadrons were shipped to the South Pacific and the 11th Heavy Bombardment Group (army aircraft) was moved here from Hawaii. The total strength of Task Force 63 was 291 aircraft. One-third of these were U.S. army machines, and 30 R.N.Z.A.F. aircraft were included. Nearly half of the force operated from Numea, and the remainder from Efate, Tongatabu in the Friendly Islands, Fiji and Samoa. Admiral McCain's force had a threefold duty of conducting normal reconnaissance, covering the approach of the expedition to the objective, and covering and supporting the landings.[2] Throughout June and July men and aircraft poured into the new airfields in the New Hebrides, New Caledonia and Fiji, in preparation for the move to the Solomons. Jungles were flattened by bulldozers, and where time did not allow the ground to be hardened for the landing of heavy bombers, flexible steel grids termed Marston mats were laid down. A system of disseminating intelligence was rapidly organised.

Two forces standing outside Admiral Nimitz's command were ordered to cooperate in the operation. These were the Submarine Force, South-west Pacific, under Rear-Admiral C. J. Lockwood, Jr., and the Allied Air Forces South-west Pacific (Major-General G. C. Kenney), both of which were part of General MacArthur's command, which was now reinforced by the creation of a new Mobile Bombardment Group. There was no unity of command of the

---

[1] Japanese report.

[2] U.S. Battle Experience, *Solomon Islands Actions*, S.I.B. No. 3.

shore-based air forces employed in the operation. General MacArthur agreed that his air forces operating from Milne Bay in New Guinea and bases in Australia would patrol the northern and western approaches to the Solomons during the operations for its capture. Prior to D minus 5 they were to reconnoitre over eastern New Guinea, Lorungau (Admiralty Is.), Kavieng, Buka, Ontong Java ($5\frac{1}{2}$° S., $159\frac{1}{2}$° E.) and Tulagi. Thereafter, no South-west Pacific aircraft were to fly east of the meridian 158° 15′ E., close to the line of division between the South-west and South Pacific areas, which ran between Santa Isabel and Choiseul Islands, and north of 15° South, unless requested by Admiral Ghormley. From D minus 5 to D plus 4, South-west Pacific aircraft were to conduct daily reconnaissance flights over eastern New Guinea, Kavieng, and the easternmost point of New Georgia, and combat aircraft were to be ready to strike any Japanese naval vessels within a 500 mile radius of Port Moresby. From D–day to D plus 4, when the transports and cargo ships of the Amphibious Force would be unloading at Guadalcanal and Tulagi, Allied aircraft would thus be interdicting Japanese air operations in the Rabaul–Kavieng area. At the same time, Buka was to be attacked to prevent the Japanese from fuelling there, and Lae and Salamoa to prevent these bases from sending aircraft to reinforce Rabaul.[1]

Some of the 20 years' old ' S ' class submarines of Admiral Lockwood's Task Force 42, working from Brisbane, had been covering the Bismarck Archipelago–New Guinea area since May, performing special missions such as the landing of agents, and carrying out patrols of up to 45 days' duration in tropical waters, without air conditioning, under conditions of difficulty and extreme discomfort. Up to the time of the Guadalcanal operation they had sunk four ships, in an area where shipping was by no means plentiful. They were now to form a patrol line off Rabaul, to intercept any enemy forces attempting to interfere with the landings in the Solomon Islands, whilst one or two from the Pacific Fleet watched Truk. This resulted in dislocation of patrols, with consequent immunity of enemy shipping from attack for prolonged periods.[2]

The lack of unified command of the two land based air forces, Admiral McCain's and General MacArthur's, and the fact that the latter was not under naval command, were unsatisfactory features. South-west Pacific air support during the assault was negligible, and no ground troop support was ever forthcoming from that area.[3] Perhaps the explanation lies in MacArthur's shortage of aircraft and the distance from Tulagi of his bomber bases in Queensland, 975 miles,[4] and the fact that before the Guadalcanal operation began he was fighting hard to defend his base at Port Moresby against the Japanese overland attack.[5] Port Moresby was at that time defended by no more than two brigades of partly trained and inadequately equipped Australian troops hurriedly despatched there after the outbreak of war, much of whose time was necessarily devoted to road making and the unloading of ships. The result was that most of the work of delaying the enemy's advance fell on the air forces which were in consequence fully extended and thus unable to undertake many sorties outside the boundaries of their own area.[6]

---

[1] *U.S. Army in World War II, Guadalcanal, the First Offensive*, p. 34, quoting Telegram Commander-in-Chief S.W.P.A. to Comsopac, 1034/19/7/42.

[2] Report by Commander Miers, U.S./P/S.M.2 (Adm. (S) No. S.M.04094/844).

[3] Zimmerman, *The Guadalcanal Campaign*, p. 7 (Historical Division U.S. Marine Corps).

[4] The normal range of the B–17 was approximately 2,000 miles and of the B–24 2,100 miles without allowing for warm-up, take off, climb to altitude or reserve.

[5] The strength of MacArthur's air forces at this date is given in Section 83.

[6] *See* Chapter X.

Times, Z — 11

For a week previous to the landings in the Solomons, Admiral McCain's bombers softened up Guadalcanal and Tulagi, operating from primitive airstrips at Efate and Espiritu Santo in the New Hebrides. The runways were soft and frequently covered by water from the rains. For night flying they were marked by makeshift arrangements of truck headlights and petrol-soaked rags. At Espiritu Santo the tank wagons which then serviced the aircraft, had to be filled from drums. Heavy bombardment aircraft each required fifty drums for a single mission. The early operations taxed all hands to the utmost.

Meanwhile, the Amphibious Force, after carrying out in Fiji rehearsals, which owing to the shortage of landing craft were unrealistic, sailed on the evening of 31st July for the objective, 1,200 miles away, passing between New Caledonia and the New Hebrides in order to approach from the south. The carriers of the Air Support Force made rendezvous on 1st August and assumed their function of air support, reconnaissance and patrols. During the later stages of the passage there was fortunately much cumulus cloud and surface haze which grounded the Japanese aircraft at Rabaul ; and on 6th August, the critical last day, whilst the expedition was rounding the west end of Guadalcanal, conditions for reconnaissance were, to use Admiral Crutchley's description, ' hopeless ' for the enemy, and there were no hostile contacts. That night, the weather cleared, and at 0200 the Amphibious Force, still undetected, made their landfall and stole into the narrow waters of the Sound between Savo, Guadalcanal and Florida (*Plan 12*). The islands showed up clearly, lying peaceful under the rising moon.

Dawn galvanised the scene into sudden activity. Minesweepers began sweeping the shallow waters. The cruisers' aircraft flew off to their stations as anti-submarine and anti-M.T.B. patrols. The *Wasp's* aircraft appeared suddenly, launched by Admiral Noyes' carrier force from a position to the south-westward of Guadalcanal, and attacked enemy aircraft on the water.[1] The two convoys ' X ' and ' Y ' separated and passed, the one north and the other south of Savo Island, and as they neared the disembarkation area the guns of their escorts opened up at shore targets. At 0650 and 0720 respectively, the convoys reached their lowering positions some 4 miles from shore, lay to and lowered their assault craft, whilst Admiral Crutchley's screening force fanned out to provide each convoy group with an arc of destroyers to seaward, the cruisers lying between this screen and the transports.

The landing on Tulagi was timed to take place at 0800. Covered by bombardment by a cruiser and destroyers, a small force first seized the promontories covering the approaches to Gavutu and the main landing beach (' Blue ') in the northern part of Tulagi. Landing on the latter was made without opposition, the Americans rightly estimating that the enemy would not expect a landing to take place at a spot where the terrain was so unsuitable. But the stiff resistance met subsequently in the attack on the town and the southern half of the island was not overcome until next day. The landing on the small island of Gavutu took place at noon on the 7th, after a dive bombing attack by carrier aircraft and bombardment by the ships. It was strongly opposed. The parachute troops making the landing suffered from a wet boat

---

[1] It is reported that there were present at the Florida Island air base at Gavutu eight float fighters and the Yokohama Air Group of 18 four-engine flying boats from Rabaul, and that all eight of the former and 10 to 12 of the latter were destroyed on 7th August.

passage of several miles in a rough sea. The preliminary bombing and bombardment had not destroyed the enemy's caves and dugouts, the last of which were not secured until the following afternoon. Meanwhile, the tiny island of Tanambogo, which was connected to Gavutu by a causeway, was full of Japanese who put up a bitter resistance ; and it was not until nightfall on the 8th, after more than 6,000 troops, including the battalion of the 2nd Marines earmarked for the occupation of Santa Cruz had been thrown in, that the island was secured. Refusing quarter, the garrisons of the three islands, about 750 in all, were destroyed almost to a man. Some forty escaped to Florida by swimming. Only three surrendered. The Marines lost 144 killed and 194 wounded.[1]

The landing on Guadalcanal, to which forces four times as large as those for the Tulagi area had been allotted, was scheduled to take place at 0910 on the 7th. Lowering and loading of the assault boats began at 0650. The landing beach (' Red ') was just east of the Tenaru River, 5 miles east of the airfield (*see Plan 12*). The landing was preceded by a ten-minutes' bombardment, and was unopposed. The ship-to-shore movement of troops was well organised, and by nightfall, nearly 11,000 Marines were ashore.

Meanwhile, the Japanese at Rabaul had not been idle. At 1120 the Allies received warning from a coast watcher on Bougainville Island 350 miles to the west-north-westward, of a strong force of enemy bombers flying south-eastward.[2] These were from the 25th (Naval) Air Flotilla at Rabaul. Two hours later, fighters from the U.S. carriers, directed from the *Chicago*, attacked the enemy bomber formation 15 miles west of Savo Island. About 18 heavy bombers, supported by nine Zero fighters, penetrated to the transport assembly area, however, and carried out a pattern bombing attack. The transports remained at anchor. All bombs fell wide and no damage was done. An hour and a half later some ten bombers attacked the screening destroyers, and the *Mugford* was hit and damaged. The American fighters, to whom the problem of protecting a large force of transports was new, did well.[3] There were inevitably some losses. The Japanese also did not escape unscathed. The *Wasp*, *Saratoga* and *Enterprise* launched in all 700 aircraft on that day, of which 16 were lost.

On shore on Guadalcanal the troops encountered no opposition during their advance from the beach, but progress was very slow. The enemy had taken up a position covering Lunga, in the north-east part of the island, leaving the jungle to do the work of impeding the troops. The Marines were out of condition after being some weeks aboard the transports. So meagre and unsuitable had been the food that aboard one ship, the *Ericsson*, the one solid daily meal which was all the men had for the most part of the time, gave them but 1,500 calories, and men lost up to a stone and half in weight. Short of water and loaded with ammunition, mortars and heavy machine guns, they struggled through the thick and fetid jungle, crossing and recrossing the winding, unfordable Tenaru River. By dusk, they had advanced one mile.

The unloading of stores and equipment was also going badly. During the forenoon, when the report of the minesweepers was negative, the transports

---

[1] Historical Division, Department of the (U.S.) Army figures.

[2] The names of the Coast Watchers on Bougainville at this date are given as Lieutenant P. E. Mason, R.A.N. and Lieutenant W. J. Read, R.A.N.

[3] It appears that plans had not provided for fighter protection during enemy air raids. *U.S. Battle Experience*, Secret Intelligence Bulletin No. 2.

had moved closer in to shorten the trips to the beach. The loading of the landing boats from the supply ships proceeded precisely to schedule, it was at the beach that the bottleneck occurred. Many of the landing boats lacked bow ramps which could be let down, and the loads had consequently to be lifted up over the gunwales, an exhausting and almost impossible feat. In the expectation that the landing would be opposed an insufficient number of troops had been detailed to unload boats and move material off the beach. Though the shore party was empowered to call upon unit commanders for additional labour no units were thus detailed ; for a battle was momentarily expected against an enemy force with which, however, the scouts were unable to gain any touch whatsoever, though General Vandegrift felt that every movement of his own forces was under observation. Supplies became stacked ever higher on the beach, whilst by nightfall a hundred landing craft were beached, waiting to be unloaded, and another fifty lay off. Work continued under lights until nearly midnight, when the congestion compelled a halt until 1000 next day. At Tulagi, owing to enemy opposition, unloading of supplies had not even begun. On the whole, however, Admiral Turner had little reason for dissatisfaction, considering that this was the first American amphibious operation of the war. But it was fortunate that the Japanese had not seen fit to oppose the landing on Guadalcanal Island as at Tulagi. A bright feature of the operation was the revelation of the all-round usefulness of the unarmoured amphibian tractors. These could move directly from the ship's side to the dumps inland, crossing sea, reefs, beach and swamps without a halt. Later, they were to play a very important tactical role in the Pacific. But at Guadalcanal their numbers were all too few.

34

At 1027 on 8th August a message came in from one of the Coast Watchers on Bougainville that forty heavy bombers were flying south-eastward. The carriers had still no experienced fighter direction in the area, but three of the *Enterprise's* fighters which were in the air patrolling over the transports, shot down four or five of the Japanese, and one of the *Wasp's* bombing squadron meeting the enemy unexpectedly, shot down one more. The *Saratoga's* fighters failed to make contact. The warning from Bougainville enabled the transports to get under way and assume cruising formation at full speed before noon, when the survivors of the enemy, twenty-three or more torpedo bombers, appeared from behind the clouds over Florida Island coming in very low to attack Squadron 'X.' The ships put up a heavy barrage. The attack was determined rather than skilful for all aircraft attacked from the same direction, simplifying for the ships avoiding action and concentration of fire. In five minutes, the *Chicago* expended 142 rounds of 5-inch, besides over 2,000 rounds of 1·1-inch and smaller calibres. Most of the enemy aircraft dropped their torpedoes at long range, though many continued to close and attacked the ships' crews with machine guns. The destroyer *Jarvis* (Lieut.-Commander W. W. Graham) was hit by a torpedo but was able to reach shallow water. The transport *George F. Elliott* was set on fire by an aircraft which flew, apparently deliberately, into her superstructure; the fire could not be got under control, and the ship became a total loss. As the attackers withdrew, they passed close to the Tulagi squadron, which raked them. Altogether the ships gave a remarkable account of themselves and it is reported that no more than three of the two dozen Japanese torpedo aircraft returned safely to Rabaul. They consoled themselves, however, by making extravagant claims of the losses they had inflicted on the Americans.

At 1400, another air raid warning, which proved to be false, caused the transports to get under way again, and delayed unloading until 1630. The situation on the beach at Guadalcanal had not improved, despite the expedient of doubling the length of Red Beach by extending the boundary westward. Inland, however, matters were proceeding satisfactorily. The airfield was captured intact, as well as the enemy's Lunga Point positions, with the wharves, radio stations, electric plants and other installations on which the Japanese had done remarkable development work since their landing, little more than a month previously.

At 1807 Admiral Fletcher made a signal to Admiral Ghormley at Numea which caused Admiral Turner and General Vandegrift considerable anxiety. The original plan of operations envisaged that the majority of the transports and supply ships would have been unloaded and sailed from the objective area that night. Instead, none had sailed. The O.T.C. now reported that his fighter aircraft were reduced from ninety-nine to seventy-eight, fuel for the carriers was running low, and in view of the large number of enemy torpedo and bombing aircraft in the neighbourhood, he recommended immediate withdrawal of the Air Support Group. Senior officers in his force greeted the request with dismay.[1]

In proposing to withdraw the whole force simultaneously before the supply ships were unloaded, instead of sending the carriers south to fuel one at a time, there seems no doubt that Admiral Fletcher was influenced less by fuel shortage than by the possibility of air attack on his ships[2] and in this connection due weight must be given to the great value of aircraft carriers in the Pacific war and the need for safeguarding them.

Nevertheless it would seem that the proposal to retire from the battlefield at a critical stage of the operation was an error. That the proposal could ever have been made was no doubt due to a lack of precision in the operation orders. These failed to set a term to the carriers' responsibilities. That the request could ever have been approved was due to the location of the officer in supreme command, 700 miles away. With Admiral Ghormley the reported fuel shortage seems to have weighed more heavily than the likelihood of air attack.[3] From his headquarters in the south at Numea he was in no position to exercise more than a general direction over the forces at Guadalcanal ; and concluding that the man on the spot must know his own situation best, he approved the O.T.C.s recommendation at 0330 on the 9th.[4]

35

During the day, there had been a report that a Japanese force of three cruisers, three destroyers and two seaplane tenders or gunboats had been sighted at 1127, by an Australian Hudson aircraft, off the east coast of Bougainville in 5° 49′ S., 156° 7′ E., steering a course 120°, speed 15 knots. The report was much delayed and did not reach Admiral Turner until the

---

[1] S. E. Morison, *History of U.S. Naval Operations in World War II*, Vol. V, p. 28.

[2] The above history and other authorities quote figures from the ships' logs, to show that no fuel shortage actually existed.

[3] *The Guadalcanal Campaign*, Historical Division, U.S. Marine Corps, quoting from Admiral Ghormley's M.S. account.

[4] Morison, *op. cit*, pp. 27, 58.

evening.[1] He discussed it with Admiral Crutchley, and misled no doubt by the reported inferiority of the enemy force to his own, and the inclusion of two seaplane carriers, he sent shortly before midnight a message to Rear-Admiral McCain, suggesting the enemy force might be intending to operate torpedo aircraft from Rekata Bay, on the north-east coast of Santa Isabel Island, and recommending that a heavy air strike should be made on the seaplane station there next morning.

Unknown to the Allies, the reported composition of the enemy force was badly at fault, it actually comprised five 8-inch cruisers, two light cruisers and one destroyer. A few days earlier, the Japanese 8th Fleet consisting of the 8-inch cruiser *Chokai* and two light cruisers, which had been formed in July 1942, and constituted the striking force of the South-east Area Command, had been reinforced by the four heavy cruisers of the 6th Cruiser Squadron, the *Aoba* (flagship of Rear-Admiral A. Goto), *Kako*, *Kinugasa* and *Furutaka*. These were sighted on 2nd August at Balgai Bay near Kavieng, in New Ireland and reported by General MacArthur's headquarters as destroyers. On the 5th this was corrected, and they were stated to be probably cruisers.[2]

The first reaction of the Commander-in-Chief, 8th Fleet, Admiral Mikawa to the news of the invasion of Guadalcanal had been to despatch immediately the 500 troops available at Rabaul to reinforce the garrison. The transports carrying the troops and their escorts were sighted in the Buka–Bougainville area on the 8th, but the torpedoing that day of one of the transports, the *Meiyo Maru*, by *S–38* (Lieut.-Commander H. G. Munson), one of the twelve submarines of Task Force 42 which had been transferred temporarily from Fremantle to Brisbane, caused the reinforcement operation to be abandoned in favour of surface attack on the transport area. The 6th Cruiser Squadron was apparently on its way to the Admiralty Islands from Kavieng when news of the American invasion of Guadalcanal was received. Ordering Rear-Admiral Goto to make rendezvous with him, Vice-Admiral Mikawa sailed from Rabaul in his flagship, the *Chokai* with the light cruisers *Tenryu* (18th C.S.)[3] and *Yubari* (4th Fleet) and the only available destroyer, the *Yunagi*, and proceeded on a south-easterly course towards the Solomon Islands. Submarine *S–38* sighted the force as it debouched from St. George's Channel but could not attack. In the early hours of the 8th, the Commander-in-Chief made rendezvous with Admiral Goto's four heavy cruisers in the area between New Ireland and Buka, and proceeded north about the latter island for Guadalcanal. When sighted by a Hudson aircraft east of Bougainville at 1127 that day, he was

---

[1] No official explanation of the delay is forthcoming. The report of the Commander-in-Chief, U.S. Fleet, refers to it as ' an unexplained mystery ' and continues ' If the delay in getting the report through from the Army reconnaissance planes was the result of their being under a different supreme command, it certainly is an additional argument for unity of command certainly within the same operating area.' (*Battle Experience*, Secret Information Bulletin No. 2.) Morison, *History of U.S. Naval Operations in World War II*, Vol. V says the Australian pilot who made the sighting completed his patrol, landed and had his tea before reporting. The following general statement which may have some bearing on the subject, occurs in *Air Campaigns of the Pacific War*, U.S. Strategic Bombing Survey, p. 62 : ' An artificial barrier existed between the intelligence services of the Army and Navy. Throughout the war, lacking unified command in the Pacific, we operated without an intelligence system capable of meeting the requirements of co-ordinated land, sea and air warfare . . . a system was not established during the war which insured the timely production of balanced, objective intelligence and the timely dissemination of that intelligence for all those who needed it in the performance of their tasks.'

[2] Tels. G.H.Q.S.W.P.A. 1015Z/3/8 and 0631Z/5/8.

[3] The *Tatsuta* which also belonged to this squadron was engaged with two destroyers in escorting troops to Buna in Papua.

heading south-easterly, recovering his reconnaissance aircraft. This concluded, he took the precaution of steering towards Rabaul until the reconnoitring aircraft left him. As the aircraft passed out of sight Mikawa resumed his south-easterly course, making for Manning Strait (between Choiseul and Santa Isabel Islands) and the lower part of the Slot, as the Allies termed the passage between the eastern and western chains of the Solomon Islands. The *Aoba's* reconnaissance aircraft had been flown off and reported to him at noon the location and composition of the Allied forces off Guadalcanal and Tulagi, so he knew precisely what opposition to expect. His intention was to attack at 0200 on the 9th. The Japanese also called up five submarines of the 7th Flotilla, *I–121, I–122, I–123, RO–33* and *RO–34* and ordered them to sail early on the 9th to attack the American transports.

36

At 1830 on the 8th Rear-Admiral Crutchley ordered the Screening Group to take up night dispositions. Though these were the same as had been adopted on the previous night, there is no evidence that local enemy forces discovered and reported the positions of the ships. It was from his reconnaissance aircraft that Admiral Mikawa obtained the information. The destroyers *Blue* and *Ralph Talbot* were placed to the westward and north-westward of Savo Island on radar and anti-submarine patrol. When at the extreme ends of their patrols, the two vessels were 20 miles apart. Events were to prove the unwisdom of relying on two destroyers, so placed in relation to the land and each other that their radar was not to be depended upon to detect any approaching force. General Headquarters South-west Pacific Area (General MacArthur's) reported the sighting, in the course of reconnaissance that day over the Bismarck Archipelago, of various enemy forces, and it was considered there were in the Bougainville area five cruisers, including three heavy cruisers, with five destroyers and other warships. Two heavy cruisers, two light cruisers and one small unidentified vessel were sighted by an Australian Hudson at 1101 in 5° 42′ S., 156° 5′ E., approximately the position of the 1127 sighting by another Australian Hudson as already related. None of these sighting reports reached Admiral Turner or Admiral Crutchley. The latter, relying apparently on the superior numbers of his screening force over those of the Japanese in the area, considered it safe to divide the 8-inch cruisers into two sub-groups which were to operate independently but to afford each other mutual support. He did so partly because he considered this the most effective method of covering the approaches to north and south of Savo Island, and partly because two of the cruisers, the *Vincennes* and the *Quincy*, had not long arrived from the Atlantic ; these two cruisers and the *Astoria* had never worked under him, and for this reason both he and Rear-Admiral Turner considered it better that they should operate under the tactical command of their Senior Officer, Captain F. L. Riefkohl of the *Vincennes*, within the framework of Admiral Crutchley's plan. He stationed them to north of a line drawn 125° from Savo Island, screened by the *Helm* and *Wilson*, whilst to the south of this line were the *Australia*, *Canberra* and *Chicago*, screened by the *Patterson* and *Bagley*. The light cruisers *San Juan* and *Hobart*, screened by the destroyers *Monssen* and *Buchanan*, patrolled between the transport anchorages as cover against enemy light forces entering the area from the eastward. The speed of the cruiser patrols was 10 to 12½ knots.[1] The night was oppressive. The ships assumed the second

---

[1] *Battle Experience* Secret Intelligence Bulletin No. 20. The Commander-in-Chief, U.S. Fleet, criticised it as being too low, saying ' speed is the best protection for cruisers and destroyers.'

degree of readiness, with half the crews on watch. Captain F. L. Riefkohl made a note in his order book that the approaching enemy force could arrive and attack during the middle watch. Two of the captains turned in. They were to have a rude awakening.

Some two hours after taking up night dispositions, Rear-Admiral Crutchley received a message from Rear-Admiral Turner, requesting him to attend a conference on board the *McCawley* in Lunga Road. As the Amphibious Force flagship was several miles away, Admiral Crutchley, instead of proceeding in his barge, turned over the command of the southern patrol to Captain H. D. Bode of the *Chicago*, and sailed in his flagship, the *Australia*. At the conference, Admiral Turner announced that on account of the withdrawal of the Air Support Force at a time when heavy and more frequent air attacks on the ships were to be expected from Rabaul, which was receiving air reinforcements, he must withdraw his surface forces at 0730 on the 9th. Both General Vandegrift and Admiral Crutchley agreed with the decision, and orders were issued for the speedy disembarkation during the night of the more urgently needed items of equipment and supplies for the troops.

37

In the early afternoon of the 8th Admiral Mikawa's force passed out of the area of General MacArthur's air reconnaissance into that of Rear-Admiral McCain (*see* Section 32). McCain was responsible, within his area, for covering the approach of enemy ships to the Tulagi–Guadalcanal area, but he was not under Admiral Fletcher's orders and operated entirely independently of Admiral Turner, whose force he was covering, just as General MacArthur did. The schedule for 8th August comprised 650 and 800 mile searches to the north-west from Plaine des Gaiacs, in central New Caldonia : Espiritu Santo ; Malaita ; and if possible Ndeni in the Santa Cruz Islands. Owing to bad weather, however, the two sectors covering the lines of approach to Guadalcanal from Buka and Bougainville via New Georgia and Santa Isabel Island were incompletely covered that day. This was not reported to Admiral Turner until after midnight. During the evening, the enemy force passed through Manning Strait into the Slot (*Plan 8*) making for the transport area. Though two large Allied shore-based air forces were responsible for giving warning of the approach of such a force it had remained unreported since 1127.

Admiral Mikawa's aircraft reconnoitred the Sound between Guadalcanal and Tulagi as the Striking Force slipped into the Slot, repeating the reconnaissance shortly before midnight. A flaring beacon was provided for them by the transport *George F. Elliott* which had been hit during the day's air attack. She was still afloat and on fire though seven torpedoes had been fired at her in an attempt to sink her. Five of the nineteen transports were in the Tulagi area and the remainder off Guadalcanal, with all available destroyers, minesweepers and transport destroyers acting as anti-submarine screen. Between 2345 on the 8th and 0130 on the 9th several vessels, including the screening destroyers *Blue* and *Ralph Talbot*, heard or saw aircraft in the neighbourhood of Savo Island. The *Ralph Talbot* was the only ship to take any action. On sighting the first unidentified aircraft at 2345 her captain, Lieut.-Commander J. W. Callahan, called both the Task Force Commander and his Flotilla Leader on two transmitters for several minutes. Neither of them responded to the calls. Admiral Turner never received the warning, and Admiral Crutchley heard of it too late to take any action. Such vessels as intercepted the reports do not appear to have paid particular attention to them for it does not seem to have been the special responsibility of anyone to do so. The implications of the presence of these aircraft consequently went unrecognised.

On returning to the *Australia* after the conference, which did not break up until 0108, Rear-Admiral Crutchley decided not to rejoin his patrol group for the remaining hours of the night, but patrolled near the transports for the Guadalcanal Island landing within the anti-submarine screen. The *Chicago* and *Canberra* with the *Patterson* and *Bagley* about a mile on either bow were patrolling in line ahead on courses 310° and 130° at 12½ knots. Course was reversed every hour, the north-westerly turning point being about 5 miles south-east of Savo Island. The *Chicago* had been rear ship in the original formation ; Captain Bode had not altered this order when he became senior officer, but directed the *Canberra* to remain ahead of him and conduct the patrol. To the north, the *Vincennes* group was carrying out a box patrol, steaming at 10 knots clockwise round a square whose sides ran 045° and 135°, course being altered 90° every half hour. The cruisers were in line ahead in the order *Vincennes* (Senior Officer), *Quincy*, *Astoria*, with the destroyers *Helm* to port and *Wilson* to starboard, 1,500 yards on the bows of the *Vincennes*. At about 0145 on 9th August, flares of the type used by aircraft for illuminating areas were seen over Transport Area X and almost simultaneously the *Bagley* and *Patterson* sighted ships slightly on the port bow of the formation, steering approximately 125°. The Japanese force had already passed the radar screen undetected. As the ships came in south of Savo Island the eyesight of these supposedly myopic sailors proved more efficient than American radar, and they sighted the *Blue* on the starboard bow and also the *Ralph Talbot* to port.[1] Admiral Mikawa at once reduced speed to 12 knots to render his ships' wakes less conspicuous, and his eight ships passed unseen by the destroyers' lookouts and undetected by their radar. As the force entered the Sound, Mikawa ordered the destroyer *Yunagi* to reverse course and remain outside as a picket and to deal with any American destroyer that should attempt to follow him. On her way out, the *Yunagi* engaged a destroyer, which she believed she damaged heavily. This was probably the *Jarvis* which had been hit by an aircraft torpedo on the previous day and was now returning to Sydney for repairs, having sailed without her escort. She was sunk later in the day by enemy air attack.

Admiral Mikawa's ships had not previously operated together and he consequently disposed them in a single column in open formation, to avoid confusion, in the order the *Chokai* (fleet flagship), *Aoba* (flagship of 6th Cruiser Squadron), *Kinugasa*, *Kako*, *Furutaka*, *Tenryu*, *Yubari*, *Yunagi*. Though his ships were without radar they enjoyed the advantage of knowing that every vessel they might encounter would be hostile, and they were ready to open fire instantly. As they came in west of Savo Island they sighted the silhouettes of the *Canberra* and *Chicago* and kept these ships under observation for some minutes before the Commander-in-Chief, shortly before 0145, ordered torpedoes to be fired and began his attack on the southern patrol of Admiral Crutchley's force.

On sighting the enemy, the *Bagley* and *Patterson* turned to port to fire torpedoes to starboard. The *Patterson* broadcast a warning by short wave voice signal, repeating it by light signal, but neither destroyer fired a gun or

---

[1] The *Ralph Talbot* would seem to have been very near the limit of visibility which that night was about 12,000 yards (*see Plan 9*). No doubt the *Blue's* look-outs were not keeping a look-out astern—a common failing.

rocket or turned a searchlight on the enemy. The *Bagley* swung past the safe torpedo firing bearing before the primers could be inserted ; the ship continued her swing and fired four torpedoes from the port side some three or four minutes later ; by that time the enemy had passed and could be but dimly seen. On board the *Patterson* the order to fire torpedoes was drowned by the roar of her guns as she opened fire on one of the enemy light cruisers ; she was hit but not seriously damaged, and no further opportunity of firing torpedoes occurred before the last enemy light cruiser disappeared in the darkness. Neither the *Canberra* nor the *Chicago* received the *Patterson*'s signal. The *Canberra*'s first warning of the enemy came from sighting torpedo tracks passing down either side of the ship from ahead. The rudder was put hard to starboard to open the ' A ' arcs, but before the turrets could be trained the ship was raked at almost point blank range by 5·5-inch shells and within an incredibly short space of time, perhaps no more than one minute, was reduced to a blazing defenceless wreck : her Commanding Officer, Captain F. E. Getting, R.A.N. was mortally wounded and most of the officers and men on the bridge were disabled or killed.[1] It is believed that two torpedoes and a few shells were fired before steam failed and the ship came to a standstill. Ten officers and 74 ratings were lost. The *Chicago* sighted torpedo tracks on the starboard bow just as the *Canberra* started to swing to starboard. The rudder was put to starboard, but the helm was reversed a few seconds later as torpedo tracks were seen to port. It was in vain, for a minute later a torpedo struck the ship in the port bow. The resultant structural damage did not for the moment affect the cruiser's fighting efficiency, and after shoring up bulkheads a speed of 25 knots was considered safe. As nothing could be seen of the enemy, Captain Bode ordered four salvoes of four star shells each to be fired ; all sixteen proved to be blind. Continuing on a westerly course the *Chicago* chased and engaged a ship which may have been the destroyer *Yunagi*. On returning soon after 0500 she had a short engagement with a vessel she took to be a destroyer, which was apparently the *Patterson* standing by the *Canberra* ; she returned the *Chicago*'s fire until her nationality was recognised. No damage was done on either side in this encounter.

After giving the *Canberra* and *Chicago* a burst of fire, Admiral Mikawa led his column round to port to attack the northern group of cruisers of which he had received a report from an aircraft launched by his flagship about an hour before reaching Savo Island. During the turn, the Japanese column divided. The *Furutaka*, fifth ship in the column, turned short. The two light cruisers did the same and soon found themselves ahead of the *Furutaka*. As they passed the *Canberra* they completed the wrecking of the ship. Having turned inside the four leading heavy cruisers, the *Furutaka* and the two light cruisers passed close up the east side of Savo Island, to westward of the American northern group, whilst the main body of the heavy cruisers proceeded on a nearly parallel course some 600 yards to the eastward. The *Chokai*, owing to the difference of turning circle, followed a track about a mile eastward of the *Aoba*, *Kako* and *Kinugasa* and finished up in the rear. The Americans were caught between cross fire.

Captain Riefkohl's group was in the southern part of its patrol area, on the north-westerly leg of its patrol, when at 0145 flares appeared to the south-westward, followed by gunfire to the west and south-west. The ships increased to 15 knots and sounded the alarm. In the darkness, the second ship, the *Quincy*,

---

[1] The Japanese state that the 8-inch cruisers also engaged the *Chicago*'s group with their main armament. Captain Getting died of his wounds next day.

alone of Captain Riefkohl's three cruisers caught a glimpse of the enemy before the force was suddenly illuminated by searchlights and a devastating fire was opened on them at close range from the port quarter. The ships' companies were still closing up at action stations. The *Vincennes* altered course to port and got off a few salvoes in local control, some of which are reported to have hit and damaged the *Chokai*. But she was hit ' innumerable times '[1] by cross fire, and two or more torpedoes striking her on the port side completed the ruin. The ship floated for half an hour longer, then sank, a blazing and abandoned wreck. The *Quincy* had sunk a few minutes earlier. She got off one nine-gun salvo at 6,000 yards range as she received her first hit. After following the *Vincennes* round to port she turned out of line to starboard, apparently to avoid collision with the *Vincennes*, but within a very few minutes all her guns were disabled, her commanding officer, Captain S. N. Moore, killed, her decks a shambles and below decks an inferno. With her gun-deck and forecastle awash, the senior surviving officer present ordered her to be abandoned, and she sank between 0235 and 0240. The *Astoria* (Captain W. G. Greenman) opened fire at a radar range of 5,640 yards as the *Vincennes* and *Quincy* came under fire, and saw one enemy vessel hit. She followed the two leading ships round to port. As the bearing of the four Japanese heavy cruisers to starboard drew aft, she fouled the *Quincy*'s range. She, therefore, altered hard under the latter's stern, and steered to the northward ' under the heaviest concentration of enemy fire,' still engaging the enemy to starboard whilst the Japanese light cruisers and the *Furutaka* engaged her from the port quarter. After firing some ten salvoes, her main armament was put out of action by the heavy cross fire, but the secondary batteries continued in action until their crews were killed or driven off by the fires raging throughout the ship. Then, just as power failed, the enemy ceased fire and disappeared. The destroyer *Wilson* (Lieut.-Commander W. H. Price) on the starboard bow of the *Vincennes* opened fire at once at the leading enemy searchlight, at an estimated range of 12,000 yards, firing over the American cruisers. She continued in action with the *Aoba*, *Kako* and *Kinugasa* until the searchlights were switched off. The *Helm* (Lieut.-Commander C. E. Carroll) received orders from the *Vincennes*, just after firing began, for the screening destroyers to attack, but smoke from the guns and fires prevented her from finding any opponent, though for a time she chased a ship which turned out to be friendly, probably the *Bagley*. The *Ralph Talbot* on seeing the attack on the *Vincennes* group, left her patrol and stood towards Savo Island. About 0217, however, before she had got far, she was illuminated, fired on and hit by a ship, perhaps one of the *Furutaka* group, which her captain, Lieut.-Commander J. W. Callahan, felt certain was friendly. He switched on his identification lights and the firing ceased, but just then the dim shape of an enemy cruiser, probably the *Yubari* or *Tenryu*, was sighted 3,300 yards off. A short engagement ensued, in the course of which the destroyer fired four torpedoes at her antagonist and was herself hit and damaged, before the enemy vessel switched off her searchlight. The *Ralph Talbot* entered a rain squall, and the engagement ended, leaving the destroyer listing heavily, with a large fire in her chart house.

38

The enemy ships ceased fire at 0215 and all soon disappeared up the Slot to the north-westward by much the same route as they came. Apart from the flagship, the *Chokai*, which had been hit four times, they were little damaged. Admiral Mikawa's original intention had been to attack the American transports,

---

[1] Signalled report of Captain Riefkohl.

but he abandoned his object when his objective lay all but defenceless within his reach. Knowing nothing, of course, of Admiral Fletcher's intention to withdraw his carriers, which the Japanese air reconnaissance had not succeeded in locating, Mikawa was unaware that local command of the air had passed to his own 25th Air Flotilla at Rabaul, and he feared attack by carrier aircraft after sunrise. He had lost touch with the *Furutaka* and the two light cruisers, and the day might almost be at the dawn before he could assemble his entire force once more. An additional deterrent was that he disliked the idea of entering the unfamiliar pilotage waters of the Sound at night.[1]

The Americans made no attempt to dispute the withdrawal of the Japanese force. It had been arranged that if Admiral Crutchley so ordered, Captain C. W. Flynn, Commander Destroyer Squadron 4, should form a striking force of seven destroyers drawn from the transport screen and the other two units, to attack any enemy surface force.[2] Not all the destroyers detailed seem to have received or understood the signal, but certain of them proceeded to a concentration area north-west of Savo Island, where they began to arrive independently about 0400. After remaining on patrol till shortly before daylight, they returned to the transport area. At the time of the battle Admiral Fletcher had not yet received permission to withdraw his carriers and they were still in the area steering north-westward off San Cristobal Island. The *Wasp* whose air group was trained in night operations and was intact, was only 150 miles distant from the scene of the encounter. But neither Noyes, Fletcher nor Ghormley ordered an attack[3] (*see* page 39 for the chain of command).

The Japanese were not, however, to escape entirely without loss. Whilst the 8th Fleet ships, the *Chokai*, the two light cruisers, and the *Yunagi* went in to Rabaul, the 6th Squadron continued on to Kavieng. In the approaches to the port the four heavy cruisers were sighted on the morning of the 10th by the U.S. submarine *S–44* (Lieut.-Commander J. R. Moore). The submarine fired four torpedoes at the last heavy cruiser, the *Kako*, from a range of 700 yards, and sank her immediately. This was a poor return, however, for the loss of the four 8-inch cruisers H.M.A.S. *Canberra*, which had to be sunk as she could not be made to steam in time to join the withdrawal ; U.S.S. *Astoria*, which despite all attempts to save her, sank at 1215 on the 9th ; the *Vincennes* and the *Quincy* ; serious damage to the destroyer *Ralph Talbot* ; and the loss of 1,023 officers and men. The main consolation which the Allies had was that at least Admiral Mikawa had failed in his attempt to attack the transports. But he drove these out of the area before they had discharged their function of supplying the troops, thereby placing the success of the operation in serious doubt.

The engagement necessitated a reconsideration of the opinion, promulgated earlier by the Admiralty on evidence furnished by Admiral Layton when Commander-in-Chief, Eastern Fleet, that the Japanese were not good night fighters. It demonstrated also the necessity for providing proper facilities for ships to carry out regular practices if efficiency was to be maintained, a course

---

[1] One of the reasons usually ascribed to the Japanese Commander-in-Chief for the decision to withdraw, was that the flagship's charts had been destroyed by shell fire. Unless we are to believe the force had no other charts of the Sound this scarcely appears a valid reason.

[2] *Selfridge, Patterson, Mugford, Helm, Henley, Bagley, Wilson.* The authority for this rests on Morison, *op. cit.*

[3] Morison, *op. cit.*, p. 58 says that Captain Sherman of the *Wasp* three times asked Admiral Noyes to launch an attack, but Noyes declined to forward his request to Fletcher.

which Admiral Nimitz had already enjoined on his task force commanders as the result of experience at the Battle of the Coral Sea in May. No ship in Rear-Admiral Crutchley's group that got into action on the night 8th–9th August had done target firing more recently than May or a night target firing within eight months. The *Chicago* had not carried out a surface firing since October in the previous year. But the fundamental lesson was the importance of a bold offensive spirit.

39

The engagement off Savo Island had still further delayed the unloading programme, for when flares appeared over the transport anchorage and it became apparent that a battle was in progress, all the transports got under way independently and stood out clear of the anchorage. They did not return until dawn. The survivors of Rear-Admiral Crutchley's force then took up day screening positions and the transports resumed unloading. Admiral Turner had intended to begin the withdrawal of the Amphibious Force at 0630, but in order that more stores might be landed for the Army he postponed its departure until the afternoon. The risk of remaining without air protection, which he took, was justified, for the enemy made no further attempt to attack him. It is believed that a force of sixteen torpedo aircraft accompanied by fifteen fighters of the 25th Air Flotilla, which sank the damaged *Jarvis* that day, were after bigger game, probably Admiral Noyes' carriers. These they failed to find, for they were on the way to Numea, and they did not molest the Amphibious Force. The latter withdrew in two groups, the first at 1530 and the remainder at 1830. Numea was reached on 13th August.

The Marines were left ashore with less than half their ammunition and food for only thirty days, including Japanese rations for ten days.[1] None of the 3rd Defence Battalion's 5-inch coast defence guns, nor any long range warning or fire control radar sets had been landed. Very little barbed wire had been brought ashore, and there was a shortage of entrenching tools and sandbags. Heavy construction equipment was still in the ships' holds. Since the liaison aircraft detailed for the Division had been destroyed on board the cruisers in the battle, no air reconnaissance of Guadalcanal was possible. The Marines were exposed to Japanese air raids and naval bombardment without air cover or naval surface support. They were virtually a besieged garrison.

---

[1] These are the figures given in *U.S. Army in World War II—Guadalcanal the First Offensive.*

CHAPTER VI

Japanese First and Second Attempts to Retake Guadalcanal

(See Plans 8, 11, 24)

40

IN landing on Guadalcanal, the Americans had obtained a foothold on a strategic position from which future operations in the Bismarcks, notably against the ultimate objective Rabaul, could be strongly supported. But both Admiral Ghormley and Major-General M. F. Harmon, Commanding General South Pacific, felt considerable uneasiness concerning the situation. Admiral Ghormley's position was that unless he used his carriers to support the garrison on Guadalcanal this and other South Pacific positions might fall. But the Japanese using aircraft carriers for ferrying purposes, were building up their shore-based air strength in the South Pacific. Consequently, the use of the American carrier-based aircraft in supporting the garrison and providing air cover for ships engaged in supplying Guadalcanal would jeopardise an arm which was the principal defence of the line of communications between the United States and the bases in Australia and New Zealand. It was even desirable that the American carriers should be kept out of range of Japanese air reconnaissance except in special circumstances. Reliance had therefore to be placed on Admiral McCain's shore-based air force operating from bases in the deep south.

Japanese destroyers carrying reinforcements and supplies came down the ' Slot ' with such regularity that they earned the name of the ' Tokyo Express.' They bombarded Guadalcanal with impunity by day and night before Henderson Field was in operation. Submarines also carried out nightly nuisance bombardments and the greater part of two flotillas is reported to have been concentrated on the Guadalcanal supply routes at the time. One of these, *I–123* was sunk on 28th August by the converted minesweeper *Gamble* in Indispensable Strait, between Guadalcanal and Malaita.[1] The few Allied transports and cargo ships in the South Pacific were too valuable to be risked

---

[1] The Japanese report (War Diary of Sixth Fleet, 1942) that *I–123* signalled at 2325 on 28th August (0125 Z–11 on 29th) that she was being attacked by an enemy *aircraft*, and was not heard of again. Their War Diary is, however, frequently at fault.

in the supply of Guadalcanal in these conditions, until aircraft were based ashore on the island. Recourse was had to old converted destroyers of high speed, though their carrying capacity was so limited that one brought little more than a day's rations for the 17,000 troops ashore on Guadalcanal. After 17th August Admiral Ghormley made these operations the responsibility of Admiral Turner's Task Force 62.[1] They uncomfortably resembled blockade running. Admiral McCain's shore-based naval air force also undertook the movement of airborne supplies and reinforcements to the island, as well as furnishing support and serving Admiral Ghormley as a scouting and attack force.

Immediately after the first fighter aircraft flew in on 20th August, the naval cargo ships *Formalhaut* and *Alhena* were sent up, escorted by the destroyers *Blue, Henley* and *Helm*. During the dark hours of the morning of 21st August, the *Blue* (Commander H. N. Williams) was torpedoed and sunk by the destroyer *Kawakaze*, Japanese eyesight again proving keener than U.S. radar. The enemy strong land-based air forces at Rabaul and his superiority in surface ships caused the Americans some losses and seriously reduced the flow of supplies to Guadalcanal. On 30th August, the Japanese bombed and sank the fast transport (converted destroyer) *Colhoun* (Lieut.-Commander G. B. Madden) whilst engaged in covering the landing of stores at Guadalcanal. Redesigned specifically as troop carriers, the *Colhoun* and her sister ships had had their armament drastically reduced to permit the stowage of landing boats. This reduction left them with meagre protection against surface and air attacks. They were equipped with listening gear and depth charges, however, and thus could be used as escort vessels in case of need. It was whilst acting as escort vessel and anti-submarine screen that the *Colhoun* was attacked during the afternoon, by 18 bombers, and by unusually bad luck, for the bombing was horizontal, was sunk with the loss of 51 of her crew. During the night of 4th/5th September, her sister ships, the *Gregory* and *Little* were sunk off Lunga Point by Japanese destroyers sent into the Sound to provide diversionary bombardment to cover the landing of reinforcements. In this case, too, the luck was with the enemy. The two American ships were on a routine patrol. The night was exceptionally dark. At 0100 on the 5th flashes of gunfire were seen and were thought to be from a Japanese submarine engaged on the customary shelling of the beach. A few moments later a Catalina, mistaking one of the two destroyer transports for a submarine, dropped a string of flares, the effect of which was to silhouette them both within view of a group of enemy ships, the destroyers *Yudachi, Hatsuyuki* and *Murakumo*, on the starboard quarter. The Japanese opened fire, to which the *Gregory* and *Little* replied. But the issue was never in doubt. Overborne by superior fire power the two ships were sunk with considerable loss of life, including both Captains[2] and the Divisional Commander, Commander H. W. Hadley, who was on board the *Little*.

The Japanese no less than the Americans found difficulty in maintaining the reinforcement and supply of their troops on the island, though their problem was simplified through the fact that they held all the islands to the north and west and could land cargoes and troops for Cape Espérance, their main base, on the west side of Guadalcanal, without running through Savo Strait. On 28th August, in an attempt to throw reinforcements into the place, the destroyer *Asagiri* was sunk and the *Shirakumo* and *Yugiri* seriously damaged by Marine aircraft, after which the Japanese virtually limited themselves to running in troops and supplies by night in fast ships.

---

[1] *U.S. Army in World War II, Guadalcanal, the First Offensive*, p. 104.

[2] Lieutenant-Commander H. F. Bauer, *Gregory*, Lieutenant-Commander G. B. Lofberg, Jr., *Little*.

Left to his own resources on Guadalcanal, General Vandegrift centred his defence around the vital airfield. This had to be lengthened by 1,000 feet. Without adequate equipment the work was difficult. No power shovels or dump trucks had been landed, and the single bulldozer was not at first available. But by using antiquated equipment captured from the Japanese the airfield was made fit, on 20th August, to receive 19 Marine fighters and 12 dive bombers flown off from the escort carrier *Long Island*. Thereafter enemy surface craft confined their bombardments of Guadalcanal to the dark hours. Fortunately, the Japanese had at that time insufficient troops in the area to mount a serious attempt to drive out the Americans, and they made the mistake of trying to do so with the inadequate force available. On 17th August elements of the 5th Yokosuka Special Naval Landing Force were put ashore near Tassafaronga, wide of the west flank of the Allied bridgehead, and on the night 18th–19th the first echelon, about 1,000 men, of a special force known from the name of its commanding officer as the Ichiki[1] Force, conveyed in six destroyers, landed to the east.[2] These were part of Lieut.-General H. Hyakutaka's 17th Army. Fortunately, discovery of the landing before the second echelon was ashore enabled the Americans to exterminate the intruders ; whilst the Japanese destroyers, which stayed to bombard the U.S. positions, were caught in daylight by Army bombers from Espiritu Santo which hit and seriously damaged the *Hagikaze*.

In the first attempt to reinforce Guadalcanal the Japanese, who had been unable to discover the strength of the Americans on the island, greatly underestimated their opponents. Japanese Intelligence reported that less than 1,000 U.S. troops were involved.[3] In the second attempt, made a few days later, the force of troops employed was but little stronger, for the operations in the Solomons were at the time considered less important than those in New Guinea, a state of affairs which was soon to be reversed. Powerful naval co-operation was, however, provided. The second echelon of the Ichiki Force, 700 strong, with 800 of the Yokosuka 5th Special Naval Landing Force were used. They sailed from Rabaul in four old destroyer transports and the auxiliary cruiser *Kinryu Maru*, escorted by the light cruiser *Jintsu*, flagship of Rear-Admiral R. Tanaka, Commander of the Occupation Force, with three destroyers. Vice-Admiral Mikawa in the *Chokai*, with the three remaining cruisers of the 6th Squadron and three submarines gave close cover.[4] The organisation of the support and distant convering groups was as complicated as usual.[5] The light carrier *Ryujo*, supported by the 8-inch cruiser *Tone* and screened by two destroyers, formed a Detached Force under Rear-Admiral T. Hara whose function seems to have been to draw the teeth of the American carriers, as the *Shoho* had done at the Battle of the Coral Sea. The Carrier Group, consisting of the *Shokaku*, Vice-Admiral Nagumo's flagship, and *Zuikaku*, screened by six destroyers, and supported by a Vanguard Group of two battleships, a cruiser squadron and a destroyer flotilla, under Rear-Admiral H. Abe, completed the

---

[1] Colonel Ichiki's name is sometimes, but it is said erroneously, rendered Ikki.

[2] *The Guadalcanal Campaign*, by Major J. L. Zimmerman, gives the names of the destroyers as *Arashi, Hagikaze, Hamakaze, Tanikaze, Urazaze, Kagero*.

[3] *U.S. Army in World War II, Guadalcanal, the First Offensive*, quoting Major-General S. Miyazaki, later Chief of Staff, 17th Army, and *Japanese Military and Naval Intelligence Division* (U.S. Strategic Bombing Survey), p. 52.

[4] One of these was *I-123* which the *Gamble* sank on 28th August.

[5] The organisation of the Japanese forces is given in Appendix C.

Striking Force. The seaplane carrier *Chitose*, escorted by a battleship and four destroyers, the whole being termed the Support Group, operated seaplanes in the general neighbourhood of the Occupation Force. A group of two cruiser squadrons and a destroyer flotilla, termed the Main Body, under Vice-Admiral N. Kondo, Commander-in-Chief, Second Fleet, who was in command of all support and distant covering groups, had some part in the complicated plan of operations, but what this was is not apparent. Submarines of the Sixth Fleet formed a screen termed the Advance Expeditionary Force ; and the 11th Air Fleet at Rabaul co-operated. The Commander-in-Chief, Combined Fleet, Admiral I. Yamamoto, remained at or near Truk in the new battleship *Yamato*.

42

The concentration of these powerful forces at Truk and Rabaul was duly reported by Coast Watchers and the Allied aircraft in the South Pacific Area based on Espiritu Santo, Efate and New Caledonia and those of the South-west Pacific Area based in Australia and New Guinea which maintained constant reconnaissance. There was no information about the Japanese aircraft carriers, but it was suspected that two or even three would be used as a striking force, as well as shore-based aircraft. Accordingly, the *Hornet* was ordered to leave Pearl Harbour to reinforce Admiral Ghormley. She sailed on 17th August and joined Task Force 61 on the 29th, after the battle which was about to take place.

At this date there were in the South Pacific Area the three carriers *Saratoga*, *Enterprise* and *Wasp*. The latter had come from service in the Atlantic via the Mediterranean, the Americans having generously lent her to ferry aircraft to Malta. These three carriers were organised as Task Force 11, 16 and 18 respectively, under Vice-Admiral Fletcher in the *Saratoga*, the whole command being known as Task Force 61.[1] The total number of aircraft borne was 253, of which 100 were fighters. The Japanese air force was 168 strong, including 69 fighters ; whilst 22 reconnaissance aircraft were based on the *Chitose*. In addition, about 100 naval aircraft were operational in the 11th Air Fleet at Rabaul.

As reports began to be received indicating that the Japanese preparations were nearing completion, Admiral Fletcher moved up his carriers. Rear-Admiral Crutchley, with the *Australia*, *Hobart* and three U.S. destroyers joined on 21st August. During the next two days Task Force 61 operated to the south and east of Guadalcanal, within a hundred miles of the island.

43

On 23rd August aircraft of the dawn reconnaissance flown by the *Enterprise* to a distance of 180 miles between the bearings of 345° and 045° located and attacked two enemy submarines proceeding to the southward at high speed on the surface. They were suspected of being part of a screen ahead of surface forces, and indeed two or three hours later one of Admiral McCain's shore-based reconnaissance aircraft reported an enemy force—Admiral Tanaka's Occupation Force—of two cruisers, four destroyers and four transports at 1030 near Ontong Java (5° 30′ S., 159° 30′ E.), steering a southerly course at 17 knots. During the afternoon, when the enemy were estimated to be 320° 260 miles from Task Force 61, the *Saratoga* despatched a striking force of six torpedo and 31 dive bombers, armed with 1,000 lb. bombs, to attack. The Marine aircraft at

---

[1] *See* Appendix D.

Guadalcanal also sent an attack group. Both aircraft forces searched until dusk without result, for Tanaka, on sighting Admiral McCain's aircraft, had reversed course, the covering forces following suit, but the Allied aircraft did not report the alteration. The *Saratoga's* aircraft landed on Henderson Field and rejoined their carrier next morning, and thus missed participating in repulsing an attack made that afternoon on Henderson Field by a combined force of aircraft from Rabaul and the *Ryujo* in which the enemy lost 21 aircraft and the Americans but three. Whilst the *Saratoga's* aircraft were landing on the carrier, an incident, the first of its kind, occurred, which trivial though it was in itself, yet foreshadowed what was to become commonplace in the future, namely, the shooting down of an enemy reconnaissance flying boat located 20 miles from the carrier, by fighters vectored out to attack it.

During the night the Japanese forces once more reversed course and steered towards the Allies, and their Diversionary Group was advanced. At daybreak on the 24th Admiral Fletcher was some 50 miles to the eastward of Maramasike, Malaita Island. Only two carriers were with him, for on the previous evening he had detached Rear-Admiral Noyes' group, with the cruisers *San Juan, Salt Lake City, San Francisco* and destroyers to refuel at sea in 13° S., 164° E., some 250 miles to the southward ; the group had just begun fuelling (*see Plan* 11). At 1005, a shore-based aircraft reported a carrier, two heavy cruisers and a destroyer in position some 300 miles north of Fletcher's force at 0905 steering south, and the Admiral manoeuvred to close the enemy. The carrier was the *Ryujo*, but there were no reports of any other Japanese carriers, and the information the American Admiral was receiving was so curt, confusing and delayed that at 1300 he ordered the *Enterprise* to send out a search group. This search group was made up of 29 bombers and torpedo-bombers. It proceeded to the northward and half an hour later the *Saratoga* launched similar force to attack the enemy carrier. The *Enterprise's* search group sighted the *Ryujo* and her escorts at 1410. Twenty minutes later they sighted the *Shokaku* and *Zuikaku*, screened, as they thought, by four heavy cruisers, six light cruisers and eight destroyers. Several of the group attacked the carriers inflicting slight damage on the *Shokaku*. Actually, the identification was somewhat at fault, for the escort of the two large carriers consisted of the battleships, cruisers and destroyers of Admiral Abe's Vanguard Group. They bore 340° distant 198 miles. This important sighting report never reached the flagship, though the report, half an hour later, of a group of four heavy cruisers and destroyers (presumably the Covering Group and Bombardment Force) got through without delay, apparently even before that of the sighting of the *Ryujo*. Other ships in Task Force 61 intercepted the report of the two large carriers, however, and Admiral Fletcher attempted to direct the *Saratoga's* attack group on to them, but without success. He was in the galling situation of having committed most of his attack aircraft, and though the *Enterprise* prepared to launch a further 25 the hour was too late to send them off at such long range ; with the south-easterly wind that was blowing the carriers when launching had to head away from the enemy who were to the north-westward of them, and the Admiral could not close.

Unaware of the two great carriers then but 75 miles distant the *Saratoga's* strike group made a co-ordinated attack on the *Ryujo* at 1550, coming in on both bows to counter any shift of helm either way. This was followed by a small strike by heavy bombers from Espiritu Santo. The carrier sank in a smother of bombs, but like the *Shoho* a few weeks earlier, she had played her part and diverted attack from the more important target, the large carriers. No single aircraft was lost by the Americans in the attack[1] despite heavy anti-aircraft fire and the efforts of the fighters in the *Ryujo* which still survived the attack made that forenoon as related above on Henderson Field. The seaplane carrier *Chitose* also received damage and withdrew to Truk with a flooded engine-room.[2]

44

Admiral Fletcher's task force had been under observation by Japanese aircraft since 1100 or earlier. The 25th Air Flotilla at Rabaul had two air groups searching. Four of the observation aircraft were shot down by the protective air patrol over the U.S. carriers before reporting, but at about 1400 one of these aircraft succeeded in making a report of the American carriers.[3] If Admiral Nagumo timed the despatch of his strike in the hope of attacking the Americans whilst their air groups were committed to the attack on the *Ryujo*, he was destined to suffer disappointment, for no less than 53 American fighters were in the air over Task Force 61 when the attack came in. The first warning was given at 1602, when the *Enterprise* picked up a large flight bearing 302°, 88 miles distant. Both carriers flew off their remaining striking forces in order to clear their decks : the *Saratoga* launched two dive bombers and five torpedo bombers with orders to attack the Japanese battleship group, and the *Enterprise* eleven dive bombers, seven torpedo bombers, and seven fighters to finish off the *Ryujo*. Two of the dive bombers of the *Saratoga*'s small group near-missed and put out of action the seaplane carrier *Chitose*, but the torpedo bombers had no success ; all of them launched their torpedoes, but the Japanese battleships avoided every one by the use of helm. The *Enterprise*'s group failed to find the *Ryujo*, which by then had sunk. Her returning search group was told to keep clear of their ship, but not all the aircraft received the message, and it is thought the Japanese may have followed them in.

When the attack came, Task Force 61 was in two groups, steaming at 27 knots, with frequent alterations of course, the *Enterprise* being some 10 miles to the north-west of the *Saratoga*, the fighters of each carrier group operating independently of the other. The battleship *North Carolina*, 180° 2,500 yards from the *Enterprise* of whose screen she formed part, was able to keep station even at this high speed ; the remainder of the *Enterprise*'s screen, namely the cruisers *Portland* and *Atlanta* and six destroyers, was disposed on a 1,800 to 2,000 yards circle. With the *Saratoga* were the *Minneapolis*, *New Orleans*, H.M.A.S. *Australia* and *Hobart*, and five destroyers, disposed on a similar tight circle. The weather was fine and visibility excellent. A moderate south-easterly wind was blowing. The bearing of the sun was about 325°.

The first visual contact occurred at 1625, when one section of the fighter patrols sighted 36 bombers and many Zero fighters, 33 miles from the *Enterprise* ; they attacked and shot down several of the enemy. At about 25 miles from the carriers the Japanese strike split into numerous sections and veered to the northward. The Americans' radar screens then became confused with the great number of aircraft in the air : the enemy groups ; U.S. returning search aircraft ; the *Enterprise*'s group returning from the attempt to attack the *Ryujo*, the *Saratoga*'s second attack group also returning ; and the

---

[1] One B–17 crashed when landing at Espiritu Santo, however.

[2] Four B–17's from Espiritu Santo claimed to have done the damage, but the Japanese attributed it to two dive bombers.

[3] Interrogation No. 97. But Morison, *History of U.S. Naval Operations in World War II*, Volume V, says it was an aircraft from the *Chikuma* that sent the report.

numerous American protective fighters. Communication by voice radio became impossible with so many aircraft on one narrow frequency. Many pilots failed to observe radio discipline. The Commander-in-Chief, Pacific Fleet, subsequently found excuse for them owing to the number of machines in the air and the lack of recent opportunity for drill ; but it is significant that this was no isolated instance of radio indiscipline. The loquacity of the American airmen continued to frustrate fighter direction officers until a late stage in the war, when the authorities at length succeeded in enforcing obedience.[1] At 14 miles distance a fighter reported that the Japanese were at 18,000 feet. Previous estimates had placed them at 12,000 feet, and the U.S. fighters had to climb to the attack through a cloud of Zeros. This, combined with the difficulty of the fighter director officer in the duty carrier (*Enterprise*) in making himself heard, resulted in the majority of the enemy remaining unmolested till they were in their dives.

The first attack was concentrated on the *Enterprise*. A 20-mm. battery officer caught a momentary sight of one of the enemy aircraft in its dive, at 12,000 feet, and promptly turned his tracers on it to indicate the target. Simultaneously the *North Carolina*, which had sighted the enemy at 15,000 feet, and the other screening ships, opened fire with 5-inch guns. For the next four minutes, except for two short breathing spaces, there was continuous gunfire and the roar of aircraft diving on the target. The dives were made in sections of five aircraft at short intervals, evidently in order to saturate the defence. But the A.A. fire of the Americans was excellent, and no more than half of the attackers, the number of which was variously estimated at between 15 and 30, succeeded in pushing home their dives to point of release at 1,500 feet or lower. For three minutes the *Enterprise* remained unscathed, but she then received in quick succession a damaging near-miss and three direct hits. At least ten Japanese aircraft crashed into the sea near-by, and others flew away smoking heavily. In order to divert the fire of the *North Carolina* from their aircraft attacking the *Enterprise* the Japanese made on the battleship two dive-bombing attacks, one supported by a real or simulated torpedo attack, together with a high level bombing attack which, incidentally, passed unnoticed by the *North Carolina*, since she was not keeping a lookout overhead. But war experience had gone to the designing of the *North Carolina*'s A.A. armament,[2] and whilst refusing to be distracted from the defence of the *Enterprise* she could still spare guns to shoot down several of her attackers. To onlookers she appeared to be ablaze throughout. Out of 80 Japanese aircraft which attacked Task Force 61, not less than 70 were shot down, about 23 of them by ships' gunfire and the remainder by the carrier air groups. No torpedoes were sighted nor was any torpedo attack apparent, and it seems likely that the whole of the 12 or so Japanese torpedo aircraft which were included in the strike became operational or combat casualties before launching their torpedoes.

The *Enterprise*'s damage control was very efficient. She had filled her fuel lines with inert gas and blanketed her tanks, and she had no inflammable aircraft on board ; within the hour the ship was able to steam at 24 knots. At 1821 however her steering gear broke down and for 38 minutes she was immobilised. There was still an enemy attack group in the air, evidently searching for Task Force 61. The *Saratoga*'s aircraft returning from attacking the *Ryujo*, sighted them at 1700 in 7° 45′ S., 162° 10′ E., about 180 miles distant, flying on a course 140° which, had they maintained it, would have

---

[1] Morison, *op. cit.*, p. 94, says the American authorities never throughout the war succeeded in entirely stopping the ' aimless chatter ' of the pilots.

[2] 20×5-in./38, 4×1·1-in. mounts (16 barrels), 40×20-mm., 26–50 calibres.

brought them to the temporarily immobilised *Enterprise*. But they altered course several times, apparently flying a box, and did not come within visual range. As soon as the *Enterprise* regained steering control, Admiral Fletcher withdrew to the southward, meeting the *Wasp* at 0300 on the 25th.

The Japanese Occupation Force, *raison d'être* of these great carrier air battles, continued to close Guadalcanal during the forenoon of the 25th. It was attacked by Marine aircraft from Henderson Field which had taken off soon after daylight with the intention of attacking the enemy carriers. They failed to find these but found instead and sank the transport (converted light cruiser) *Kinryu Maru*, and damaged the flagship, the light cruiser *Jintsu*, whilst eight army heavy bombers from Espiritu Santo, which also had as their objective the Japanese carriers, sank the destroyer *Mutsuki* whilst she was alongside the *Kinryu Maru* taking off troops and crew. The destruction and disorganisation of the greater part of three Japanese air groups on the previous day rendered it impossible for the enemy to force a daylight landing ; the expedition turned back and by the afternoon of the 25th all surface forces had reversed course and were retiring northward. But Admiral Fletcher had missed an opportunity of converting a Japanese reverse into a Japanese defeat.[1] On 25th August the Americans had destroyed 90 Japanese aircraft and definitely won control of the air. With two undamaged carriers and practically two full air groups immediately available and a third carrier, the *Hornet*, closing him at high speed Fletcher disposed his forces with the idea of repelling further Japanese attacks instead of following up the destruction of the Japanese air power with the destruction of their fleet.

45

When the Americans first appeared off Guadalcanal the Japanese had called up the 3rd Submarine Flotilla from Australian waters and the 7th Flotilla from the Mandates, and also despatched the 1st Flotilla from Japan to co-operate with the fleet and operate on the Allied lines of communication with the Solomons. On 30th August they ordered the submarines in the Guadalcanal area to concentrate and attack the ships in the anchorage. In this they had no success, but the I–class quickly achieved some disconcerting results against Admiral Fletcher's carriers at sea. These, after the Battle of the Eastern Solomons were reorganised as three groups of Task Force 61.[2] Two of the groups, the *Saratoga*'s and *Hornet*'s, were patrolling east of San Cristobal on 31st August, the *Wasp*'s having been detached to Numea for fuel, provisions and stores. There had been a number of recent reports of enemy submarines in the area, and at 0330 on the 31st several ships had radar contacts of an

---

[1] Battle Experience *Solomon Islands Actions, August and September 1942*, S.I.B. No. 2, U.S. Fleet, H.Q. of Commander-in-Chief, p. 12/17.

[2] TASK FORCE 61
Vice-Admiral F. J. Fletcher

Task Group 61.1	Task Group 61.2	Task Group 61.3
(Task Force 11)	(Task Force 17)	(Task Force 18)
Vice-Admiral Fletcher	Rear-Admiral G. D. Murray	Rear-Admiral L. Noyes
Saratoga (flag)	*Hornet* (flag)	*Wasp* (flag)
North Carolina	*Northampton*	*San Francisco*
Minneapolis	*Pensacola*	*Salt Lake City*
New Orleans	*Phoenix*	*Australia*
Atlanta	*San Diego*	*Hobart*
7 destroyers	7 destroyers	7 destroyers

SINKING OF THE U.S.S. *Wasp*, 15TH SEPTEMBER 1942

TWO JAPANESE TORPEDO-BOMBERS ATTACKING U.S.S. *South Dakota* DURING
BATTLE OF SANTA CRUZ, 26TH OCTOBER 1942

unidentified object which, owing to a communication failure, was not investigated. At 0746, whilst the fleet, though zigzagging, was steaming only 13 knots, the destroyer *Macdonough*, 3,500 yards on the starboard bow of the *Saratoga*, made sound contact close at hand and a moment later sighted a periscope 10 yards off. She dropped two depth charges, unfortunately without depth setting, and broadcast a warning that a torpedo was approaching the *Saratoga*. The latter took avoiding action, but she was moving at slow speed and paid off sluggishly. Two minutes later the torpedo struck her. In five minutes power failed and the ship, which had electric propulsion, came to a standstill. During this time four other torpedoes, none of which hit, were seen. *I–26* had fired them from outside the destroyer screen, which was stationed approximately on the 4,000 yard circle. A depth charge attack on the submarine was immediately organised, but although the Americans believed they sank her, *I–26* in fact escaped. The cruiser *Minneapolis* took the *Saratoga* in tow ; and the latter using both engines and tow flew off her aircraft in the 12 to 16 knot wind. These were eventually sent to Henderson Field to operate from there. The ship was later able to proceed under her own power and sailed to Pearl Harbour for repairs.

With the dispersal of the *Saratoga*'s task group, the *North Carolina* was attached to the *Hornet*'s group commanded by Rear-Admiral G. D. Murray. The group patrolled south of latitude 12° S., in an area centred about longitude 164° E., just south of the cruising area of the previous week. At 1240 on 6th September, when in 13° 20′ S., 162° 40′ E., steering south-west, the force changed course into the wind to 135° to permit the *Hornet* to launch a patrol of torpedo bombers. At 1251 one of these aircraft sighted a torpedo approaching the *Hornet* and dropped a depth charge near it. The torpedo broke surface and exploded, though it is not certain that this resulted from the explosion of the depth charge. A few seconds later a second torpedo exploded about a hundred yards from the first. A third missed the *Hornet* and passed to port of the *North Carolina*. All three had been fired by *I–11*, which believed she had made two hits on a carrier. Destroyers of Task Force 17 attacked and damaged her, so that she could not submerge. Later that afternoon two aircraft returning from an extended search sighted and bombed a submarine on the surface in a position reported as 13° 29′ S., 163° 25′ E. This may have been *I–11*. She reached Japan safely via Truk, and was there repaired. After the attack, Task Force 17 cleared the suspected area and spent the following day cruising at a distance of 120–180 miles to the south-eastward.

On 15th September the *Wasp* and *Hornet* groups were cruising between San Cristobal and Espiritu Santo engaged in covering an important convoy carrying reinforcements of Marines and supplies of aviation fuel to Guadalcanal.[1] The two task groups maintained their own independent dispositions about 7 miles apart, with their inner screens at 2,500 yards and destroyers on the 4,000 yard circle. At 1420 the *Wasp*, which was duty carrier, turned into the wind to a course about 120°, and reduced speed to 13 knots for flying operations. At 1444 she turned back to the westerly course of the fleet and increased speed to 16 knots. With the destroyers racing to regain their stations, their sound gear was temporarily ineffective, and the first hint that a submarine was about came when three torpedoes were sighted close aboard, three points before the starboard beam of the *Wasp*. They had been fired by *I–19*. Before the rudder could take effect all three hit the ship, whilst a fourth passed ahead. The shock

---

[1] The convoy consisted of the *McCawley* (flagship of Admiral Turner), and five transports escorted by the *Minneapolis, Boise*, H.M.N.Z.S. *Leander* and destroyers.

of the three almost simultaneous explosions was tremendous. The fuel lines were ruptured and soon great fires were raging throughout the ship. She had to be abandoned and sunk, Captain F. C. Sherman leaving at 1600. Some 26 officers and 167 ratings of her crew were lost out of a total of 201 and 2,046 respectively. The *Hornet* safely took aboard all but one of her 25 aircraft that were in the air when the *Wasp* was torpedoed. *I–19* escaped to report her success.

Meanwhile, the *Hornet*'s task group had also been attacked. When the *Wasp* was hit this group was just beginning to conform to a change to course west. As the ships turned the *Wasp* was seen to be on fire. The *North Carolina* (Captain G. H. Fort) had just steadied on the new course of 280° at 1450 when she intercepted a broadcast warning from one of the *Wasp*'s screen that a torpedo was heading for her, course 80°. Full starboard helm and full speed were ordered, but at 1452, when the ship had turned 15° she was hit on the port side by a torpedo which was not seen until just before it struck. Despite a rent in the hull below water 32 feet long by 18 feet high, and severe structural damage, the ship built up speed to 25 knots and remained in the formation. About 2 minutes later, the destroyer *O'Brien* (Lieut.-Commander T. Burrowes) on the *North Carolina*'s port quarter was hit. None of the crew was killed, or even seriously wounded, and the ship was able to proceed under her own power to Espiritu Santo, where she was temporarily repaired ; but she broke in two and sank later whilst on passage for permanent repairs. The *North Carolina* was repaired at Pearl Harbour. It is not known what submarine was responsible for torpedoing the *North Carolina* and the *O'Brien*. *I–15* confirmed the sinking of the *Wasp* by *I–19* but made no claim to have herself torpedoed any ship about that time. It consequently seems possible that the salvo which sank the *Wasp* was responsible also for torpedoing the *North Carolina* and *O'Brien*.[1]

In his report, Admiral Nimitz stated :—

> The torpedoing by submarines of four warships, with the loss of two of them was a serious blow that might possibly have been avoided. Carrier task forces are not to remain in submarine waters for long periods, should shift operating areas frequently and radically, must maintain higher speed, and must in other ways improve their tactics against submarine attack.[2]

During this offensive *I–9*, *I–17*, *I–121*, *I–174*, and *I–5*, in addition to *I–11* as already described, all received damage but all reached port safely.

Times, Z — 11

The Japanese had a submarine base in Guadalcanal, near Cape Espérance, and early in October the Japanese Submarine Force A proceeded to the Solomons together with four submarines which on 19th October were

---

[1] The *Wasp* was torpedoed at 1444, the *North Carolina* eight minutes later, at 1452, and the *O'Brien* soon after 1454. The two task groups were 5–6 miles apart, *i.e.*, 6–7 minutes running time for a 49-knot torpedo, a speed which the Japanese claimed for their Type 93 Model 1 (U.S. Naval Technical Mission to Japan report). Thus it would have been possible for a torpedo fired by *I–19* as part of the same salvo that hit the *Wasp* to have hit the *North Carolina* and *O'Brien*, and there was the circumstance that though *I–19* got clear away she only claimed one carrier and was presumably, therefore, unconscious of having torpedoed the *North Carolina* and *O'Brien*. Morison, *op. cit.*, Vol. V, thinks that *I–15* was probably responsible for torpedoing the *North Carolina* and *O'Brien*.

[2] A 16–3/F.F. 12 Serial 034372, *Reprint of Commander-in-Chief, Pacific, Reports of Actions and Campaigns, February 1942 to February 1943.*

incorporated in a force of six known as Force B.[1] Early in the month the Americans had formed a small cruiser and destroyer force, part of Rear-Admiral W. A. Lee, Jr.'s Task Force 64, termed Task Group 64.2, to counter the Japanese night reinforcement and supply and bombardment activities. Late on 20th October the force was cruising just east of San Cristobal. At 2120 the ships were on the port leg of a zig-zag, the destroyers screening up to 75° from ahead on either bow. It was a bright moonlight night, in calm weather, with visibility 4 miles. Without warning the cruiser *Chester* was suddenly struck by a torpedo. This had been fired by *I-176*, one of the submarines of Force A. The torpedo was not seen, but the wake bore 140°. A second torpedo passed about 20 yards ahead of the ship from the same direction and broke surface apparently at the end of its run, 700 yards on the port bow. From the fact that the wake was clearly visible after the torpedo struck the ship it was concluded that the training of the *Chester*'s lookouts was incomplete and they were not keeping a proper lookout on bearings abaft the beam. *I-176*, for her part, believed she had made two hits on a *Texas* class battleship. The *Chester* had to be sent to Norfolk, Virginia, for repairs, and was out of service for many months.

The only other ship torpedoed during this offensive was the unescorted s.s. *Edgar Allen Poe*, by *I-21* on 9th November, 56 miles south-east of Numea. The ship reached port safely. Both submarine forces were diverted on 26th October to co-operate in a fresh reinforcement operation which the Japanese were carrying out at Guadalcanal,[2] but between 11th November and 24th December 1942 a total of ten boats of Forces A and B again operated in the Solomons, being joined by a fresh force D.[3] Meanwhile, *I-31*, *I-21* and *I-9* carried out aerial reconnaissance and offensive patrols in the Suva, Numea and San Cristobal areas, and *I-7* reconnaissance and offensive patrol in the Santa Cruz Islands. Each of the three submarines of Force A launched two or more midgets, but none of them had any success, and all were lost, though some of the crews made good their escape.[4] *I-172* was sunk on 10th November on the way to patrol off San Cristobal, by the minesweeper *Southard* whilst on passage to Aola Bay, San Cristobal (9° 40' S., 160° 25' E.) with troops. On 17th December certain Japanese submarines, including some of those in Forces A, B and D, were diverted to the supply of Guadalcanal, where stores were running low (*see* Section 66). The only success of the ten submarines during the six weeks of their offensive in the Solomons was the sinking of the A.A. cruiser *Juneau* during the Battle of Guadalcanal (*see* Section 59). The Japanese attributed their lack of success to the increasing strength of the American land-based aircraft forces and the development of American radar.

46

The reinforcement convoy for Guadalcanal which the *Hornet* and *Wasp* were covering when the latter was torpedoed was shadowed for an hour at 1100 on 15th September by a 4-engined bomber. Since the troops embarked were the

---

[1] Force A—*I-4, I-5, I-7, I-8, I-22, I-176.*
   Force B—*I-9, I-15, I-21, I-24, I-174, I-175.*

[2] Their activities are described in Sections 54–56.

[3] Force A : *I-16, I-20, I-24.*   Force B : *I-15, I-17, I-26.*   Force D : *I 122, I-172, I-175, R.O. 34.*

[4] Launchings : By *I-16*, Midgets *30* (11th November), *10* (27th November), *22* (14th December). By *I-20*, Midgets *37* (19th November), *8* (2nd December). By *I-24*, Midgets *12* (22nd November), *38* (7th December). After the capture of Guadalcanal a midget submarine was discovered aground off the north-west coast of the island, but this is the only trace of their presence known to the Historical Section.

only reinforcements in the South Pacific which could be made available for some weeks, Admiral Turner did not feel justified in risking attack by strong surface forces during disembarkation, an attack which he expected would follow the air shadowing. He therefore altered course to the south-eastward after dark to await a more favourable opportunity of landing. At 1500 next day, as the enemy were quiescent, the Admiral turned the convoy towards the eastern end of San Cristobal Island, a position from which it could reach Guadalcanal on the morning of the 18th if the situation warranted the attempt to land the troops. Early on the 17th conditions appeared to be shaping fair. It was known that Japanese cruisers and destroyers had landed troops at Guadalcanal during the night 15th/16th, and withdrawn northwards, and it was thought they would be unable to return in time to interfere with an American disembarkation on the 18th. Admiral Ghormley sent a message from Numea saying that, in his opinion, the enemy had temporarily withdrawn from the area. An enemy expedition escorted by four cruisers and destroyers was sighted at 0900 on the 17th at Gizo, 200 miles from Guadalcanal, but Admiral Turner appreciated that the enemy, no less than himself, had difficulties to contend against, and having their own transports to protect, were unlikely to attack him. Accordingly, he ran his transports in to Lunga and at 0550 on 18th September began disembarking, under the guns of his destroyers. By the close of day, the 7th Marines, nearly 4,000 men, with all weapons, essential equipment, most of their motor vehicles, three units of fire[1] and 40 days' rations had been landed, in addition to much needed petrol, oil and stores from three auxiliaries which arrived during the day. At 2030 all ships withdrew. The landing had been reported by the enemy 45 minutes after it began, but at 0015 on the 19th, when as expected by the Americans, a force of Japanese cruisers and destroyers arrived, they were too late and had to be content with shelling the U.S. positions ashore.

47

After the failure of the second attempt to recapture Guadalcanal, the Japanese flew in air reinforcements, this time from south-east Asia. They continued to land small reinforcements and bombard the American positions on the island at night, whilst 300 miles to the north-westward they were preparing an expeditionary force at their advanced base in the Buin–Faisi (Shortland Islands) area. Admiral Ghormley planned to break up the concentration. The only land-based bombers capable of a strike at such a range were B–17's which were not suitable for attacking ships, and it was therefore decided to employ a carrier. Accordingly, on 2nd October, Rear-Admiral G. D. Murray sailed from Numea with Task Force 17, consisting of the *Hornet* (flag), 8-inch cruisers *Northampton* and *Pensacola*, A.A. cruisers *San Diego* and *Juneau*, and six destroyers, intending to launch an attack on the concentration of enemy shipping on the 5th, his subsequent retirement being covered by shore-based air attacks on Rabaul and the Buka–Kieta area of northern Bougainville in order to contain the enemy air forces.

To reduce the chances of detection, the run in to the launching position at 1000 on the 4th was made at 28 knots, the destroyers, whose fuel endurance was insufficient for such high speed, following at 19 knots, a speed calculated to enable them to rejoin on completion of the raid and resume their screening duties. The bombers, in two groups of 18 and 15 respectively, each group

---

[1] ' A unit of fire is a quantity of ammunition for any given weapon, based on the average daily consumption for that weapon in combat.' S. E. Morison, *History of U.S. Naval Operations in World War II*, Vol. V, p. 59.

escorted by eight fighters, were flown off from a position about 120 miles south of Buin at daylight on the 5th in unsettled weather, though the indications were that improved conditions would be encountered in the target area. But the weather deteriorated further whilst the groups were on passage and few of the bombers found the target. The ceiling was so low as to prohibit dive bombing, and though the aircraft reported several hits the Japanese aver that no ship was damaged. The raid illustrated the dependence of the carrier aircraft of 1942 on the weather, for it was on the promise of clear weather at the target that the torpedo bombers had been armed with bombs rather than with torpedoes. All aircraft returned safely to the *Hornet*, and the force retired up wind unmolested.

48

By the beginning of October the strength of the Americans in surface ships in the South Pacific had increased sufficiently to enable them to form a striking force to counter the enemy's activities in reinforcing and supplying Guadalcanal. The Japanese practice was to run reinforcements down the ' Slot ' and land them at the north-west end of the island during the night, or to bombard Henderson Field and the American positions, and retire before daybreak. Enemy destroyers landed up to 900 troops on some nights until the Japanese strength on Guadalcanal reached a peak of 26,000 army troops and 3,000 special naval attack troops.[1] On 7th October, Rear-Admiral N. Scott took out from Espiritu Santo Task Group 64.2, comprising the 8-inch cruisers *San Francisco* (flag) and *Salt Lake City*, 6-inch cruiser *Boise*, A.A. cruiser *Helena* and destroyers *Farenholt, Laffey, Duncan, Buchanan* and *McCalla*. He arrived in his cruising area two days later. His orders were to search for and destroy enemy ships and landing craft. He intended to remain well to the southward of Guadalcanal beyond the range of enemy bombers by day and to close the western approaches by night, in order to intercept enemy reinforcements. A large convoy with 6,000 U.S. Army reinforcements was leaving Numea about that date, and cover had been arranged by the *Hornet's* task group to the westward and the fast battleship and cruiser force under Rear-Admiral W. A. Lee in the *Washington* to the eastward. Admiral Scott's force had no operational connection with the convoy, though its covering forces would also afford him cover to the westward.

The formation of Task Group 64.2 coincided in point of time with a decision on the part of the enemy to alter their method of reinforcement of the island. Infiltration was proving inadequate : the small fast craft employed could carry few troops and no heavy material, guns or tanks. The Japanese decided instead to bring in transports at night, run them aground if necessary, on the unloading beaches, and trust to getting the personnel and as much material as possible ashore before the ships were destroyed by air attack in daylight, as seemed inevitable. The first operation of this nature was planned for the night of 11th/12th October, when the seaplane carriers *Chitose* and *Nisshin* escorted by six destroyers[2] were to land reinforcements, heavy artillery, and supplies at Tassafaronga (*see Plan 12*). Rear-Admiral Goto with a bombardment group, consisting of the heavy cruisers *Aoba* (flag), *Furutaka* and *Kinugasa*, and the destroyers *Fubuki* and *Hatsuyuki*, provided cover. The landing operations were to be completed by about midnight 11th/12th, after which Admiral Goto's force was to bombard Henderson Field, whilst the transports and escort withdrew.

---

[1] Figures based on the *U.S. Army in South Pacific Report* quoted in *The Guadalcanal Campaign* (Historical Division U.S., Marine Corps).

[2] *Akizuki, Asagumo, Natsugumo, Yamagumo, Murakumo, Shirayuki.*

On the 10th air search by the aircraft of Admiral Scott's cruisers drew blank; but early next afternoon an American shore-based reconnaissance aircraft reported Admiral Goto's force of cruisers and destroyers 210 miles north-westward of Guadalcanal approaching the island at high speed.   An attack on Guadalcanal by some 75 enemy aircraft was made that afternoon and successfully prevented the American air groups from attacking the approaching Japanese. At 1810 the enemy were reported to be 100 miles nearer, and Admiral Scott estimated they would reach the landing area about 2300.   Each of his cruisers had retained one aircraft, the others having been flown to Tulagi.   At 2200 these remaining aircraft were catapulted to search for the enemy.   The *Salt Lake City's* machine crashed and burst into flames, but the Japanese, then some 50 miles off, mistook this for a signal from the shore and were not alarmed.

At 2325 the *Helena* obtained contact on S.G. radar[1] of ships bearing 315°, 27,700 yards off, and tracking began ; the flagship, *San Francisco*, was not fitted with this type of radar, and was handicapped by having to wait for reports

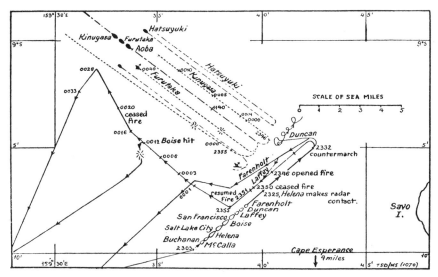

FIG. 2. BATTLE OF CAPE ESPERANCE 11th–12th OCTOBER 1942

from other ships.   At 2333, eight minutes after the *Helena's* contact, the squadron being then about 4 miles due west of the northern point of Savo Island, course was altered sixteen points, from 050° to 230°.   Ships were in column in the order *San Francisco, Boise, Salt Lake City, Helena*, with the destroyers *Farenholt, Duncan* and *Laffey*, trying to regain their positions ahead which they lost on the turn, and the *Buchanan* and *McCalla* astern of the cruisers.   Some confusion was caused by a report from the *Boise* at 2344 of five ' bogies ' bearing 065° ; it was uncertain whether ships or aircraft were meant.   This was intended as the relative bearing, but it was interpreted as the true bearing except by the flagship.   The uncertainty was increased by the fact that at the moment of contact the *Farenholt, Duncan* and *Laffey* were still trying to regain station at the head of the column after the sixteen-point turn.   Having received no radar contacts they were unwittingly passing to

---

[1] Designed for installation in large vessels and used primarily for detection of surface craft.

starboard between the U.S. cruisers and the enemy. Admiral Scott knew only that from three to five of his destroyers were somewhere to the rear and to starboard.

The enemy were sighted to starboard at 2345, and a minute later the *Helena*, owing to a signal-book uncertainty, opened fire at a range of 4,000–5,000 yards, followed by the other cruisers. Admiral Scott, believing the ships were firing at their own destroyers, tried to make them cease fire, without entirely succeeding. By 2351 the matter was cleared up and the O.T.C. ordered ' commence firing.' The Japanese had been taken by surprise and at first thought their own supply group was firing at them. Their cruisers were in column, in the order *Aoba*, *Furutaka*, *Kinugasa*, with the destroyer *Hatsuyuki* on the left and the *Fubuki* on the right flank, course 125°. The two leading cruisers and the *Fubuki* at once altered course sixteen points to starboard, the *Hatsuyuki* and the *Kinugasa*, owing to the heavy shell fire and bunching, turned to port, a manoeuvre which stood them in good stead, for both escaped serious damage and the *Kinugasa* was able later to inflict considerable injuries on the Americans. But the latter were in the classic position across the enemy's T, and the remaining Japanese ships, as they turned, received the fire of the entire American squadron. The *Fubuki* sank almost immediately, the *Furutaka* a few minutes later, whilst the *Aoba* was hit about forty times and suffered very severe damage and casualties, including Rear-Admiral Goto, who was mortally wounded early in the action.

The American ships remained unhit for eight minutes, when the *Boise* was hit. A quarter of an hour later she came under heavy fire from the *Kinugasa* and the *Hatsuyuki*, received seven hits in three minutes, lost a hundred and seven of her crew, and was forced to break off the engagement. Despite an explosion in her handing room, the ship was saved by good damage control, and when the Task Group 64.2 retired, her commanding officer, Captain E. J. Moran, brought her out in the formation in a spectacular manner steaming at 20 knots with flames streaming from her damaged bow. The *Salt Lake City* was hit, and the destroyer *Duncan* whilst making an independent torpedo attack, was caught between two fires and sunk, though her commanding officer, Lieut.-Commander E. B. Taylor and most of her crew were saved. No other torpedo attacks appear to have been made by the U.S. destroyers whose disposition in a single long column with the cruisers was not favourable for such action. The enemy also did not fire torpedoes. At 0025 (12th) Admiral Scott ceased fire. None other than burning enemy ships were then on the radar screens. His formation was disorganised, and there was danger of his ships engaging each other. At 0027 he withdrew to the south-westward. The *Boise*, *Salt Lake City* and *Farenholt* were damaged and the *Duncan* lost, but the enemy had lost the 8-inch cruiser *Furutaka* and the destroyer *Fubuki*, whilst the *Aoba* was severely, and the *Kinugasa* slightly damaged. Aircraft followed up the victory after daylight, and sank the destroyers *Murakumo* and *Natsugamo*, two of the seaplane carriers' escort, which had returned to the scene to rescue survivors.[1] More than one hundred of the latter were picked up by another American task group, though with some difficulty, for they refused to take heaving lines. Though he lost his life, the Japanese Admiral had effected his object, for whilst he was fighting it out with Scott, the *Chitose* and *Nisshin* landed their guns and the destroyers their troops. The U.S. Army reinforcements also landed in Guadalcanal, on 13th October, without interference on the part of the enemy.

---

[1] *The Imperial Japanese Navy in World War II*. G.H.Q., F.E.C. The Assessment Committee found that the *Natsugumo* was sunk on the 11th by surface craft.

In the effort to reduce the enemy's reinforcement and supply of Guadalcanal the submarines of the South-West Pacific naval forces were called upon. On 20th October the joint Chiefs of Staff transferred the depot ship *Holland* and eight submarines of Task Force 42 from Fremantle to Brisbane until the completion of the Guadalcanal campaign.[1] An attempt by the Japanese, at the end of August, to capture Milne Bay, in south-east New Guinea, had failed (*see* Section 84) their overland advance from Buna was also held up, and the enemy had consequently relegated the campaign in Papua to second place and given preference to the recapture of Guadalcanal.[2] Japanese troops and aircraft were being steadily moved from regions as distant as the Philippines and Netherlands East Indies towards the Solomons, and the concentrations in the Rabaul and Shortland Islands areas were increasing daily. To stop this traffic the Americans sent six of the Fremantle submarines to reinforce those already operating south-east of the Solomon Islands, and six to Indispensable Strait, between Guadalcanal and Malaita ; and submarines were also sent to patrol in the Bismarck Archipelago. But although the *Grayback* (Lieut.-Commander E. C. Stephan) on 2nd January sank *I-18* off the coast of New Georgia submarine operations in the Solomons were disappointing. The enemy traffic, though heavy, proceeded at high speed and at night, and only a few of the Brisbane boats were fitted with surface radar. In the Bismarcks, however, conditions were less difficult and results were better. Between December 1942 and February 1943 thirteen merchant ships were sunk. The *Seadragon* (Lieut.-Commander W. E. Ferrall) on the 20th sank *I-4* off St. George's Channel (between New Ireland and New Britain) whilst engaged on transport service to Buna in New Guinea[3] ; and the *Guardfish* (Lieut.-Commander T. B. Klakring) on the 23rd sank the destroyer *Hakaze* near New Hanover. Two old destroyers used as patrol boats were sunk in December and January. The submarines from Brisbane also carried out a number of special missions in connection with the Solomons strategy. They scouted and reconnoitred in support of fleet operations, escorted convoys and landed coast watchers at strategic points. The shortage of aviation fuel at Guadalcanal was so acute that, on returning from a successful patrol in the Bismarcks–Carolines area, the *Amberjack* was placed under the orders of Rear-Admiral McCain, Commander Air South Pacific, and on 22nd October took out from Espiritu Santo a load of aviation fuel and bombs for Tulagi, the only occasion on which an American submarine was employed as a tanker during the war.

---

[1] This is the number of submarines which Admiral Lockwood states that he sent.

[2] A.T.I.S. translation of *South East Area Operations, Part I* (*Navy*).

[3] The Japanese were unaware of her loss and reported her as missing, cause of loss—air attack.

CHAPTER VII

Japanese Third and Fourth Attempts to Retake Guadalcanal

(Plans 8, 12, 24, 25, 26)

50

THE Japanese were ready to begin their third major attempt to retake Guadalcanal by the middle of October. On the night of the 13th–14th the battleships *Haruna* and *Kongo*, screened by a light cruiser and eight destroyers bombarded Henderson Field for over an hour. The airfield had been bombed all the previous afternoon by Japanese bombers circling at 30,000 feet, out of reach of the available American fighters, and had barely been held in operation. The battleships' bombardment wrecked it so thoroughly that it was useless for heavy and medium bombers for more than a month. Large numbers of American aircraft were destroyed. Cruisers and destroyers repeated the bombardment on the two succeeding nights, though with less effect. On 15th October before dawn, the Japanese succeeded in landing the greater part of the 2nd Division and its equipment from six large transports near Kukum to the west of the American lines (*see Plan 12*), though scout bombers from Henderson Field and heavy bombers from Espiritu Santo after daylight sank three of the transports, the *Kyushu Maru*, the *Sasako Maru*, and the *Azumasan Maru*, and damaged an escorting 8-inch cruiser. All available fighter aircraft were flown into Henderson Field after the bombardments, but their numbers were small. On 16th October there were only thirty-four aircraft operational on Guadalcanal, but they were reinforced by twenty on that date. By the 29th only twenty-nine of the fifty-four were fit to fly. They were handicapped by shortage of fuel. For over a week, during a period of increasing Japanese air attacks, their only fuel was that which could be flown in by Marine transport aircraft, assisted by such aircraft as were available from the 23rd Troop Carrier Squadron of the Army Air Force. The Americans made an attempt to pass aircraft fuel and bombs into Guadalcanal in six barges towed by two cargo vessels, an M.T.B., a fleet tug, and the two destroyers *Vireo* and *Meredith*. The attempt was unsuccessful, and the *Meredith* was sunk on 15th October by air attack from the carriers *Junyo* and *Hiyo* which operated against the U.S. supply line as far south as 13° S. The *Meredith's* captain, Commander H. E. Hubbard, and 184 officers and men were lost. A further supply train casualty occurred next day, when the destroyer-seaplane tender *McFarland*, which had gone up from Espiritu Santo, was bombed and damaged whilst discharging aircraft fuel and torpedoes in Lunga Road. The ship subsequently carried out a remarkable emergency self-repair whilst lying camouflaged in the shelter of mangroves in the Maliali River, about 2 miles north-west of Tulagi.

51

On 16th October Admiral Ghormley reported to the Commander-in-Chief, Pacific, that the enemy appeared to be preparing to make a supreme effort. He represented that the South Pacific forces, which were being held in readiness to intercept the expected expedition, were ' totally inadequate ' and he needed air reinforcements.[1]   Battle damage had played havoc with his capital units and the *Enterprise, Saratoga* and *North Carolina* were all away, undergoing repairs at Pearl Harbour. Admiral Nimitz had already recognised that the situation was critical,[2] whilst the authorities even appeared to be preparing the public in the United States for the possibility of being unable to hold on to Guadalcanal.[3]   He ordered work on the *Enterprise* to be rushed, and on 16th October she sailed for the South Pacific in company with the new fast battleship *South Dakota* and nine destroyers. On the 22nd on the way south two of the latter, the *Lamson* and *Mahan* under the command of Commander L. A. Abercrombie in the *Lamson*, were detached to raid the Japanese patrol line on longitude 175° E. between the Gilbert Islands and Ellice Islands. They sank the converted gunboat *Hakkaisan Maru* 630 miles south-south-east of Mili.

On 17th October Admiral Ghormley sent an urgent telegram pointing out the need for reinforcements.[4]   Next day Vice-Admiral W. F. Halsey, Jr., was appointed to succeed him as Commander South Pacific Area. Halsey was destined to reap the benefits of Admiral Ghormley's representations, for within a week President Roosevelt intervened to secure the despatch of reinforcements ; and arrangements were made to divert to the South Pacific a fast new battleship, six cruisers, two destroyers and a Task Force (T.F.42) of 24 submarines, including those already temporarily transferred from the South-west Pacific Area. Seventy-five fighter aircraft, 41 dive and 15 torpedo bombers were also sent, in addition to the number already detailed by Admiral Nimitz to bring Admiral Fitch's force at Espiritu Santo up to a strength of 85 patrol aircraft and bombers. One of the difficulties of the South Pacific Commander was to find sufficient transports for the reinforcement of Guadalcanal with troops. Accordingly, 30 vessels were allocated to Halsey for November, and 20 additional 7,000 ton ships were to follow later.[5]

In the adjacent South-west Pacific Area, in addition to lending twelve submarines General MacArthur did everything possible to relieve the pressure on the Solomons. In New Guinea an advance was made, in part, as a diversion.

[1] *U.S. Army in World War II—Guadalcanal*, quoting Tel. Comsopac to Cincpac, 0440, 16th October 1942.

[2] Morison, *History of U.S. Naval Operations in World War II*, Vol. V, p. 183.

[3] Idem, p. 178, quoting the *New York Times*.

[4] *U.S. Army in World War II—Guadalcanal : the first offensive*, quoting Tel. Comsopac to Cincpac, 1230, 17th October 1942.

[5] *Ibid.*, quoting memo. Cominch for President F. D. Roosevelt, 26th October 1942.

The South-west Pacific Air Force employed its entire long-range bomber strength to maximum capacity in strikes on hostile shipping and air and supply installations in the Bismarcks and northern Solomons, using in support of the New Guinea operations only short-range aircraft. Immediate priority was given to requests from the South Pacific Area for reconnaissance or attack.[1]

52

East longitude dates

About 20th October the indications of the massing of Japanese forces for a further major attempt to retake Guadalcanal prompted the Americans to renew their request for action by the British Eastern Fleet in the Bay of Bengal or along the Malay Barrier, which Admiral Nimitz believed would result in lessening the pressure on Halsey's forces in the Solomons.[2] The Australians, too, had been asking Admiral Somerville for action. The Admiralty re-examined the matter but still could not discover anything effective which they could do, for as they pointed out, the diversion operation undertaken in August had had no effect.

At the time when the request for British action was received, detachments from the Eastern Fleet had been made to assist in providing the necessary forces for the Allied landings in North Africa (Operation ' Torch '), and the force under Admiral Somerville's command was temporarily reduced to the battleships *Valiant* and *Warspite* and the carrier *Illustrious*. Even this reduced fleet was for the moment immobilised by the loan of six destroyers and three corvettes which had been temporarily detached to the South Atlantic Station to help to check a heavy German submarine offensive which developed on 7th October in the Cape of Good Hope area. The Admiralty offered to consider the immediate withdrawal of the loaned destroyers from the Cape, accepting the consequent losses to merchant shipping, if they could find anything practicable which the Eastern Fleet could do. A week later, on 27th October, Admiral Halsey made a request which was backed by Admiral Nimitz, for reinforcement of his force by one or more of the Eastern Fleet carriers. The Americans were in a desperate situation at the time, as the result of the losses they had suffered in repulsing on the previous day, at the Battle of Santa Cruz (*see* Section 55), the third Japanese major attempt to retake Guadalcanal, in which the *Hornet* had been sunk and the *Enterprise* reduced to 50 per cent. operating efficiency through battle damage. The only other carrier, the *Saratoga*, was not expected to complete her repairs until the latter half of November.

Both the Admiralty and the Commander-in-Chief, Eastern Fleet, laboured under the difficulty of having no clear picture of the situation in the Pacific. They knew almost nothing of the American plans and the dispositions, present and proposed, of their forces.[3] No British carrier could arrive in the South Pacific in time to affect the immediate issue, and a decision to send one could not be made until it was seen how the type fared in the North African operations. The one carrier which it might be possible to send to the South Pacific could,

---

[1] *Employment of Forces under the South-West Pacific Command*, U.S. Strategic Bombing Survey, p. 15.

[2] The message, which was received through Admiral Stark, Commander of the U.S. Naval Forces in Europe, was apparently a personal one from Admiral King. Neither the Navy Department nor the British Admiralty Delegation, Washington, knew anything of it.

[3] *See* Appendix E.

according to Admiralty estimate, be countered by three or even four Japanese which could reach the area first. ' If the south-west Pacific area is fed with weak reinforcements at intervals, the United Nations capital ship and carrier strength will be liable to suffer further attrition and we may have the command of the sea wrested from us.'[1] To assist, however, in ferrying aircraft to the South Pacific Area on 24th November 1942, the seaplane carriers *Engadine* and *Athene* were ordered to proceed to Numea via Australia, to come under the operational control of the Commander-in-Chief, Pacific Fleet, on their arrival in the South Pacific. The *Engadine* reached Brisbane on 30th December 1942, and the *Athene* Numea on 20th February 1943. The carrier *Victorious* was withdrawn from the Home Fleet and left for Norfolk, Virginia, in December 1942, and after refitting there, joined the U.S. Pacific Fleet at Pearl Harbour on 11th March 1943, by which time the Japanese had been driven out of Guadalcanal. At Pearl Harbour the *Victorious* received accidental damage from her own aircraft, and she remained there until May.

53

The Japanese troops on Guadalcanal had by now been built up to their peak strength (*see* Section 48). The enemy planned to carry out a series of shore-based fighter sweeps followed by bomber attacks in order to neutralise the American air power on Guadalcanal and support an advance by the troops, whilst the carrier force contained the American naval forces in the area. Beginning about 20th October a series of heavy air attacks on Guadalcanal took place. On the evening of the 23rd, the enemy land forces on the island attacked along the Matanikau River (*see Plan 12*) with Henderson Field as their objective. Hard fighting took place throughout the next two days, the Japanese being supported on the 25th by the gunfire of cruisers and destroyers as well as by aerial bombing. Henderson Field was out of action during the opening stages as the result of damage and heavy rains. But the American lines held, and Admiral Nagumo, who was in command of the naval forces covering the main Occupation Force, the landing of which, originally planned for the 21st, had been three times postponed, informed the Japanese Island Commander on the 25th that he would be forced to retire through lack of fuel if the attack was not carried out immediately.

On the morning of the 25th a Japanese bombardment unit consisting of the light cruiser *Yura* and destroyers approached Guadalcanal to support the attack. They encountered and engaged in the Sound various American vessels occupied in the supply and reinforcement of General Vandegrift's forces, had an inclusive engagement with the destroyer-minesweepers *Trever* and *Zane*, and stayed to sink the tug *Seminole* and the patrol vessel *YP–284*. The delay cost them the *Yura*, for American aircraft were able to take off about noon from the rapidly drying Henderson Field, and they caught and sank the light cruiser east of Indispensable Strait, besides breaking up a number of bombing attacks made in support of the Japanese attack on the Matanikau River. That night, the enemy succeeded in breaking through the American lines on shore, but after desperate fighting were driven back with heavy losses. On this, the main Japanese occupation force, which had remained in an area 200 to 400 miles north-east of Malaita during the night of the 24th-25th finally turned back.

---

[1] Tel. Personal from 1st Sea Lord to B.A.D. Washington, 0010A/28/10/42.

In the Solomons at the time the Japanese had a powerful naval force which had acted as distant cover for the transports making the large troop landing near Kukum on the 15th (*see* Section 50) ; it subsequently performed the same service for the light forces engaged in supporting the land attacks by their gunfire. The force was organised in three groups under the supreme command of Vice-Admiral Nagumo. The organisation, although it had served the Japanese none too well since they first encountered effective resistance in the Coral Sea in May, resembled the familiar pattern, and was as follows :—

The Advance Force under Vice-Admiral N. Kondo, Commander-in-Chief, Second Fleet, consisted of the battleships *Kongo* (flag of Vice-Admiral T. Kurita) and *Haruna*, the light carrier *Junyo*, the four heavy cruisers *Atago* (flag of Admiral Kondo), *Takao*, *Myoko* and *Maya*, the light cruiser *Isudzu* and 13 destroyers.[1]

The Carrier Striking Force, under Admiral Nagumo's own command, consisted of the fleet carriers *Shokaku* (flagship) and *Zuikaku*, the light carrier *Zuiho*, heavy cruiser *Kumano*, and a screen of seven destroyers.[2] The aircraft pilots in this force were the best men then remaining in the Japanese Naval Air Force and included many of the few remaining veterans of Pearl Harbour, Ceylon and Midway.

The Battleship Striking Force, under Rear-Admiral H. Abe, was formed by two battleships, the *Hiyei* (flag) and *Kirishima*, the heavy cruisers *Tone*, *Chikuma* and *Suzuya*, screened by the light cruiser *Nagara* and seven destroyers.[3]

The Supply Group consisted of four oilers and three cargo vessels, escorted by a destroyer. Submarine Forces A and B co-operated, as did also the Eleventh Air Fleet at Rabaul, in command of which Vice-Admiral J.Kusaka had in the early autumn succeeded Admiral Tsukahara.

As the Japanese preparations advanced, the Americans assumed the following dispositions. The fast battleship *Washington*, with the three cruisers *San Francisco*, *Helena* and *Atlanta* and ten destroyers, under Rear-Admiral W. A. Lee, Jr., cruised to the westward of Guadalcanal, ready to attack any enemy forces supporting landings. Beyond the New Hebrides, some 800 miles to the eastward, Task Force 17, consisting of the carrier *Hornet* (flag) with the remaining four cruisers[4] and six destroyers[5] of the South Pacific Area Force, under Rear-Admiral G. D. Murray, awaited news of the departure of enemy occupation forces from the Shortlands area. Task Force 16, consisting of the *Enterprise* (flagship of Rear-Admiral T. C. Kinkaid) with the *South Dakota*, the cruisers *Portland* (flag of Rear-Admiral M. S. Tisdale), *San Juan* (A.A.) and eight destroyers[6] was on the way from Pearl Harbour, and was able to join the *Hornet* on 24th October in 13° 45′ S., 171° 30′ E., between Fiji and Santa Cruz Islands. Rear-Admiral T. C. Kinkaid assumed command of the whole force

---

[1] Morison *op. cit.* lists 13 destroyers, the *Naganami, Makinami, Takanami, Umikaze, Kawakaze, Suzukaze* (screen of cruisers), *Kuroshio, Hayashio* (screen of *Junyo*), *Oyashio, Kagero, Murasame, Samidare, Yudachi.*

[2] Morison lists the following eight destroyers: *Amatsukaze, Hatsukaze, Tokitsukaze, Yukikaze, Arashi, Maikaze, Terutsuki, Hamakaze.*

[3] *Kazagumo, Makigumo, Yugumo, Akigumo, Tanikaze, Urakaze, Isokaze.*

[4] *Northampton* (Rear-Admiral H. Good), *Pensacola, San Diego* (A.A.), *Juneau* (A.A.).

[5] *Morris, Anderson, Hughes, Mustin, Russell, Barton.*

[6] *Porter, Mahan, Cushing, Preston, Smith, Maury, Conyngham, Shaw.*

which was termed Task Force 61. In this task force each of the two carriers operated as a separate group with her own screen, in contradistinction to the Japanese practice of operating two or more carriers with a single screen. The advantages of operating two or more carriers in a single group for strike as opposed to search were at that date clearly recognised by the British, and there was not lacking support for the practice in the United States fleet, though there was still some diversity of opinion on the subject of the defensive advantage, the Admiralty inclining to the view that it came from the greater concentration of fighter aircraft, and the Americans from the resultant superior fire power against the most dangerous of all forms of air attack, that from close range. The unsoundness of the practice of operating each carrier with a separate screen was to be disastrously demonstrated within forty-eight hours when a battle over his carriers was forced upon Admiral Kinkaid.

55

The directive under which Admiral Kinkaid was operating was as follows :—

Proceed around the Santa Cruz Islands to the north, thence proceed south-westerly and east of San Cristobal to the area in Coral Sea and be in position to intercept enemy forces approaching the Guadalcanal–Tulagi area. There are many enemy submarines concentrated south of San Cristobal.[1]

On learning that the Japanese offensive had begun, Task Force 61 shaped course to the north-westward as directed. During 25th October air reports were received of strong enemy forces, including battleships and carriers, some 360 miles to the north-westward. The Admiral steered for the contact at 27 knots, launched a search group and flew off an attack group of 18 scout and torpedo bombers and 11 fighters. Neither the search nor attack group made contact, for the enemy had not been shadowed and had altered course to the northward unnoticed.

Admiral Kinkaid continued to steer towards the reported position of the enemy during the night. At 0612 on the 26th, whilst the *Enterprise* was flying off fighter patrols and a search group of 16 aircraft, a report came in from a shore-based aircraft of a large carrier and six other vessels about 200 miles distant from Task Force 61 (*Plan 25*). At 0730 the first report of the search group was received : two battleships, one heavy cruiser and six destroyers, steering north, 275° 170 miles from the *Enterprise* at 0717. Half an hour later a report from the group timed 0750 placed two carriers and their escort steering 330°, 75 miles north of the squadron first sighted ; four aircraft of the American search group had attacked the *Zuiho* and made two hits which put her flight deck out of action. Between 0830 and 0910 the *Enterprise* and the *Hornet* launched striking forces of a total strength of 36 bombers and torpedo bombers armed with bombs, 14 torpedo bombers with torpedoes and 23 fighters. Owing to the distance to the target, estimated to be 200 miles, the strike took departure in three groups without waiting to form up as a single force.

Meanwhile the Japanese had sighted the *Hornet* and Admiral Nagumo had launched an air striking force to attack her. It subsequently transpired that the enemy aircraft which made the sighting was encountered by two aircraft of the search group launched by the *Enterprise*, flying in the opposite direction,

---

[1] For a detailed description of the battle, *see* Battle Summary No. 21. *Naval Operations in the Campaign for Guadalcanal, August 1942–February 1943.*

but they did not attack it. Fighters of the Japanese strike group attacked the *Enterprise*'s air group as they passed, shot down five aircraft and so severely damaged three more that they returned to the carrier and landed in the water. The remainder of the *Enterprise*'s group went on, and failing to find the enemy carriers, attacked Admiral Kondo's Advance Force but caused no damage. The *Hornet* groups found and attacked Admiral Nagumo's carriers. The dive bombers made four 1,000 lb. bomb hits on the *Shokaku* and damaged her so badly that in the evening the Commander-in-Chief shifted his flag to a destroyer. They seriously damaged and set on fire the *Chikuma* and damaged two destroyers, the *Terutsuki* and *Akikaze*. All this was done with bombs : no hits were made by torpedoes.

Meanwhile the enemy striking force had attacked the *Hornet*. The American ships had already received warning both by radar and from reports by their attack groups as they passed the Japanese while on the way to the *Shokaku* and *Zuikaku*. The *Hornet*, with her screen at 2,000 yards and fuel lines blanketed ready for the attack was in 8° 38′ S., 166° 43′ E., the *Enterprise* group being eight or ten miles to the north-east of her. The latter carrier's fighter director was charged with control of the fighters protecting both carrier groups, an arrangement subsequently criticised by the Commander-in-Chief, Pacific. Fifteen fighters were over the *Hornet*, whilst eleven more launched by the *Enterprise* made for the enemy groups attacking her. The *Hornet* was fitted with an old type radar set removed from the battleship *California* after the Pearl Harbour disaster, and she was late in identifying the approaching enemy aircraft. The *Enterprise* found difficulty in vectoring out the fighters to meet the many groups in which the enemy made their approach, and it was not until shortly before 1000, when they were but 15 miles distant that the first defensive fighters, those of the *Hornet*'s combat air patrol, encountered them.[1] The fighters shot down several of the enemy, but about 15 dive bombers and 12 or more torpedo aircraft got through and made a well coordinated attack on the *Hornet*. The torpedo planes attacked low and from various directions ; like the bombers they suffered heavily from the ship's fire, eight or more torpedo aircraft and some 12 of the 15 bombers being shot down ; but two torpedoes and three 500 lb. bombs hit the *Hornet*, and two bombers crashed into her. The torpedoes did great damage. Two boiler rooms and the forward engine room were flooded ; all propulsion, power and communications failed ; large fires broke out, and the ship took a list of 7° or 8°. Within an hour, however, with the assistance of destroyers which went alongside despite her heavy rolling all fires were under control and the *Northampton* began taking the ship in tow.

The *Enterprise* which was landing-on and servicing returning aircraft low on fuel, was now coming under attack from a second enemy striking force. About 1027 the Japanese had intercepted a radio voice transmission which revealed to them that a second American carrier was present. Admiral Nagumo reacted immediately, and during the next two hours launched three heavy strikes at the *Enterprise*. The first attack was made between 1115 and 1119 by about 24 dive bombers which were not seen until well in their dives, owing to broken clouds and radar screens cluttered with friendly and hostile aircraft. About ten of them were shot down, but the *Enterprise* received heavy damage from two hits and a near miss. Half an hour later, at 1145, 15 torpedo aircraft

---

[1] ' Unfortunately the *Enterprise* fighter-director officer was new to the job. Admiral Halsey had taken the veteran of Midway for service on his staff.' (Morison, *History of U.S. Naval Operations in World War II*, Vol. V, p. 210.)

accompanied by fighters began a protracted attack, being immediately followed by 12 dive bombers, most of which attacked the screening ships : none of these attacks caused any damage, though a torpedo aircraft crashed into and damaged the destroyer *Smith*, and some minutes later a solitary bomber made a direct hit on the *South Dakota* which put out of action two guns of her main armament. About 12 torpedo aircraft and five or more dive bombers were shot down by the ships' fire.

As already noticed, the Japanese had called up submarines. The destroyer *Porter* (Lieut.-Commander D. G. Roberts), whilst rescuing survivors of a friendly aircraft which had crashed, was torpedoed about five minutes before the air attacks on the *Enterprise* began, and so severely damaged that she had subsequently to be abandoned and sunk, two torpedoes and 14 four-gun salvos being required to sink her. At 1155 a submarine fired four torpedoes at the *Portland*, of which three probably hit but were either blind or else had not run far enough to arm as the submarine (believed to be *I–21*) appeared within 300 yards but escaped. Ten minutes later the *San Juan* was attacked by a submarine whose periscope she sighted ; but she succeeded in combing all torpedo tracks.

At 1221 a second series of air attacks began on the *Enterprise*, 25 dive-bombers attacking in shallow dives. About half of them were shot down, but damage was caused by a near miss. They were followed by 15 dive-bombers accompanied by nine fighters, which damaged the *San Juan* severely with five near misses and a direct hit : ten were shot down. This ended the air attacks on Task Force 16, in which over 80 aircraft had taken part. At least 60 of these had been destroyed, more than two-thirds of them by the ships ; for the *Enterprise* and *South Dakota* had been rearmed with an American version of the Bofors gun, which did tremendous execution, the latter ship alone shooting down 26 of the enemy.

Whilst these air attacks were taking place the *Hornet* remained unmolested, and by the early afternoon was in tow of the *Northampton*, with good hopes of saving the ship. At 1620, however, her group was attacked by nine torpedo aircraft and six dive-bombers. The two American forces were out of visual touch with one another. The *Hornet* asked for air cover, but the *Enterprise* could not help. Her flight and hangar decks were crowded with her own and the *Hornet*'s aircraft : fighters, bombers and torpedo aircraft were mingled together just as they landed and one lift was jammed. Nothing could be done until the excess aircraft were refuelled and flown off the ship. Unfortunately, too, the A.A. cruiser *Juneau* misunderstood a signal addressed to the *Hornet*'s returning aircraft, and joined the *Enterprise*'s group ; and the *Hornet* was thus deprived of the protection of her sixteen 5-inch guns in the hour of need. The *Northampton* cast off the tow and manœuvred successfully, but the *Hornet* was hit by a torpedo, the third she had received, which flooded the remaining engine room, and by a bomb dropped in a high level attack. An hour later another bomb struck her. By then, Admiral Murray had transferred to the *Pensacola* and the ship was in process of being abandoned. After her commanding officer, Captain C. P. Mason, left her at 1727 an attempt was made to sink the ship, but she was still afloat, though sinking, after the destroyers *Mustin* and *Anderson* had fired at her 15 torpedoes and 430 rounds of 5-inch ; and it was left to the Japanese to give her the *coup de grace*.

Whilst the two destroyers were thus engaged the enemy fleet was approaching under Admiral Kondo, who was temporarily in command whilst the Commander-in-Chief was shifting his flag from the damaged *Shokaku*. Japanese air reconnaissance had sighted Admiral Lee's Task Force 64 to the southward of Guadalcanal : judging that it would move east to cover the damaged carrier Admiral Nagumo had ordered a night attack by cruisers and destroyers supported by the battleships. Submarine Forces A and B were also ordered to proceed to the north of the Santa Cruz Islands to intercept damaged ships. The American task forces had however already retired independently to a position about 185 miles south-east of Espiritu Santo, where they fuelled next day. They encountered two submarines, one of which, *I–21* (Force B), too optimistically reported damaging a battleship of the *Colorado* class on the 27th. Damage was, however, caused to the *South Dakota* which collided with the *Mahan* during avoidance of a submarine attack.

56

The Battle of Santa Cruz was unsatisfactory to both antagonists. The Americans lost a carrier they could ill spare. The Japanese had a carrier badly damaged and emerged from the battle with a considerably weakened air arm. Neither side was in a position to exploit the weakness of the other. Nevertheless, given the war aims of the Americans and Japanese respectively, the encounter was inevitable. The aim of the Americans was the reduction of the Japanese fleet by attrition : destruction of enemy ships wherever and whenever found. The Japanese were under the paramount necessity of destroying the American South Pacific force in order to clear the way for a bold reinforcement of Guadalcanal in place of passing in small detachments by evasion. Nagumo reversed course and retired during the night 26th–27th October : he might well have done so early on the 26th when he learnt that the land attack on Henderson Field had failed ; but he would thereby have missed what, on the intelligence available to him, appeared an excellent opportunity of destroying American carriers in detail.

The Americans gained from the encounter the valuable conclusion that their standard method, or rather lack of standardised method, of operating carriers must be remedied. ' Until that is done,' wrote the Commander-in-Chief, Pacific, ' we will continue to suffer losses.'[1] Nevertheless the Americans were still far from abandoning the practice of operating their carriers separately, each with its own screen.[2] In their discontent with their shore-based search, shadowing and reporting, the inexperience of their radar operators consequent on continual drafting away of skilled men to man new construction, and the disconcerting liability of their ships to steering breakdowns during high speed manoeuvring the only bright gleam was afforded by the excellence of their anti-aircraft gunnery, though even this was clouded by the criticism that too many of the enemy aircraft were shot down only after they had released their bombs or torpedoes. The Americans were harsh self critics ; but it paid them to be so.

57

In the third major attempt to retake Guadalcanal the enemy had come perilously close to destroying American air strength on the island. This recovered during November with the lessening of the Japanese attacks, though until the 10th of the month shortage of fuel prevented heavy bombers from using

---

[1] *Battle Experience, October 1942.* S.I.B. No. 3.

[2] Morison, *op. cit.,* Vol. V, p. 223 says the older practice was abandoned during sorties of the carrier task forces early in 1943. The Historical Section has been unable to discover any instance of a change of technique in actual strikes until the air attacks on Rabaul in November 1943.

Henderson Field. A supporting airfield was projected close by on the coastal plain, and to cover its construction the Americans during the first week of November landed at Guadalcanal a force of Army troops and naval construction troops escorted by a task force commanded by Rear-Admiral D. J. Callaghan. The landing was unopposed, but on the 7th the naval cargo ship *Majaba* was torpedoed by *I–20* and had to be beached. The Japanese continued their reinforcement of the island almost nightly by destroyers. On the 7th U.S. aircraft from Henderson Field damaged the *Takanami* and the *Naganami* whilst thus engaged, and the Tulagi M.T.B. flotilla torpedoed the *Mochizuki* next day. The *Mochizuki* however did not sink. The U.S. submarines in Indispensable Strait effected no sinkings.

The enemy during the last half of October succeeded in causing serious interruption of the logistic supply to the U.S. forces in Guadalcanal and Tulagi. The Americans consequently drew up a comprehensive plan for expediting the movement of supplies and reinforcements as well as disorganising enemy operations. This involved the movement to the island of 6,000 officers and men of the 182nd Infantry in two groups of transports supported by strong combatant forces. The first group was scheduled to arrive on 11th November, and the second on the following day. Both contingents were under the operational control of the Commander Amphibious Force, South Pacific, Rear-Admiral R. K. Turner. The first of the convoys, termed Task Group 62.4, consisted of the attack cargo ships *Zeilin*, *Libra* and *Betelgeuse* escorted by Read-Admiral Scott in the A.A. cruiser *Atlanta* with the destroyers *Aaron Ward*, *Fletcher*, *Lardner* and *McCalla*. The force sailed from Espiritu Santo on 9th November and was scheduled to land at Lunga Point on the 11th. The second contingent of four transports (the *McCawley*, flagship of Rear-Admiral Turner, *President Jackson*, *President Adams* and *Crescent City*) termed Task Group 67.1, sailed from Numea on 8th November escorted by the heavy cruiser *Portland*, A.A. cruiser *Juneau*, and destroyers *Barton*, *Monssen*, *O'Bannon* and *Shaw*. Task Group 67.4 sailed from Espiritu Santo on 10th November. It consisted of the heavy cruisers *San Francisco* (flagship of Rear-Admiral D. J. Callaghan) and *Pensacola*, light cruiser *Helena* and destroyers *Buchanan*, *Cushing*, *Gwin*, *Laffey*, *Preston* and *Sterett*. The convoy, escort and covering force were collectively known as Temporary Task Force 67. On arrival of this force at Guadalcanal on 12th November it was intended to amalgamate Task Group 62.4 with it.

The unloading of Admiral Scott's three ships on 11th November was twice interrupted, once by a bombing attack from the carrier *Hiyo* and once by land based aircraft attack from Rabaul. During the *Hiyo's* attack the *Zeilin* was damaged by a near miss, but about thirteen of the attacking aircraft were shot down by fighters from Henderson Field, and several more by A.A. fire. Though it was clear that the Japanese had begun another large scale attack on Guadalcanal, Rear-Admiral Turner determined not only to land the remainder of the reinforcements due to arrive next day, but also to protect the vital Henderson Field by engaging with his escort forces the enemy bombarding forces which were known to be on the way, a bold decision to accept heavy risks for an adequate object. At dawn on 12th November the cargo ships of the first contingent resumed unloading and the four transports of the second contingent began to disembark their troops. They were interrupted at 1405 by an attack by 21 torpedo bombers escorted by 12 fighters ; able manœuvring, good gunfire, and fighter protection from Guadalcanal enabled the store ships to escape, though the cruiser *San Francisco* was crashed by a torpedo aircraft on fire. Several of the enemy fighters and, it is believed, all the torpedo aircraft except one were destroyed.

Japanese transports preceded by a bombardment group containing two battleships had been located by air reconnaissance early that morning approaching Guadalcanal from the north.[1] Air search during the past few days had revealed the number and characteristics of the enemy forces, and reports during the 12th left little doubt that they intended either to attack the transports or bombard Henderson Field during the night, with a force likely to consist of two battleships, four to six cruisers, and ten or more destroyers. Consequently at 1815 Admiral Turner withdrew from Guadalcanal with the transports and three escorting destroyers and sailed for Espiritu Santo. Recognising that only by preventing bombardment could Henderson Field be preserved and the enemy offensive stopped he directed Rear-Admirals Callaghan and Scott with five cruisers and eight destroyers (Task Group 67.4) to deal with the greatly superior Japanese force which was approaching. The *Enterprise* and the two new battleships *Washington* and *South Dakota* (Task Force 16) were coming up from Numea, the former with orders to be in a flying off position south of Guadalcanal on the morning of the 13th ; but neither force was near enough to render assistance before daylight.

From these dispositions there developed the decisive battle known as the Battle of Guadalcanal (*see Plans 12, 26*) which consisted of separate night actions on the nights of the 12th–13th and 14th–15th November, with air operations spread over the whole period.[2]

58

The enemy expedition and its powerful bombardment unit, the approach of which caused Admiral Turner to withdraw his transports on the evening of 12th November whilst 10 per cent of the troops and much of their supplies were still on board the ships, was the outcome of determination by the Japanese to put ashore on Guadalcanal the tanks and heavy artillery which destroyers could not carry and for lack of which the troops ashore were unable to make progress against the Americans. The Japanese plan was to neutralize Henderson Field by air attack and bombardment by battleships and then to run in a large troop convoy under powerful escort. The nine submarines of Force B were ordered to cooperate.[3] Eleven or twelve large transports were assembled in the Buin–Faisi area during the first part of November and loaded with 10,000 army troops, 3,500 special naval attack troops, heavy field artillery, equipment and supplies. Owing to the losses and damage caused to their carriers and, in particular, the decimation of their air groups in the recent Battle of Santa Cruz, little fleet air support was available and the Japanese relied chiefly upon the protection of shore-based fighters in the Bismarcks and northern Solomons whose effort naturally decreased with the increase of the distance of the force from its base. This was not known to the Americans, however, who estimated that two enemy carriers were available and indeed they were correct, as will soon appear, though neither of the two enemy carriers intervened in the surface ship actions of the forthcoming battle.[4] Since they themselves had only the *Enterprise* operating at reduced efficiency, the situation appeared critical. The

---

[1] The composition of the Japanese force is given in Appendix H.

[2] Details of the battle will be found in Naval Staff History Battle Summary No. 21 ; a summary only is given here.

[3] *I–9, I–11, I–15, I–17, I–19, I–26, I–31, I–174, I–175.*

[4] Several sighting reports of enemy carriers were received. Enemy transports and cargo ships, in consequence of camouflage, looked like converted carriers at a distance.

assembly of the expedition was noted by Coast Watchers, who on 10th November reported it to consist of at least 60 ships, including four battleships. The U.S. army aircraft attacked the concentration of shipping early on the 11th and again on the morning of the 12th, but no significant damage resulted.

59

After escorting the transports to the south-eastward, Rear-Admiral Callaghan first swept through Indispensable Strait and encountering no enemy re-entered Lengo Channel at midnight 12th–13th November. The night was dark, with a heavy overcast. The ships were in line ahead in the order *Cushing* (Commander Destroyer Division Ten), *Laffey, Sterett, O'Bannon*, the A.A. light cruiser *Atlanta* (flagship of Rear-Admiral Scott), heavy cruisers *San Francisco* (flagship of Rear-Admiral Callaghan), *Portland*, light cruisers *Helena, Juneau* (A.A.), destroyers *Aaron Ward* (Commander Destroyer Squadron Twelve), *Barton, Monssen* and *Fletcher*. This formation was subsequently criticised both by the Commander-in-Chief, U.S. Fleet and the Commander-in-Chief, Pacific. The flagship, *San Francisco*, was not equipped with SG radar, consequently much of the advantage to be expected from the superiority of the American radar equipment over the Japanese was wasted : the ship equipped with the best radar should have been chosen as flagship. The four destroyers in the rear could have been more effectively employed in the van, concentrated with the other destroyers, since destroyer gunfire at night was secondary to torpedoes, but the destroyers in rear were not in a position to attack unless the enemy placed himself in a position to be attacked. The employment of A.A. light cruisers in the battle line did not appear sound to Admiral King. There is no record of any operation order or tactical plan issued by Admiral Callaghan, who lost his life in the engagement.

At 0124 on the 13th the *Helena*'s SG radar picked up ships bearing 310°–312°, range 27,000–32,000 yards, closing rapidly on a south-easterly course (*see Plan 12*). The Japanese force consisted of the battleships *Hiyei* (flagship of Vice-Admiral H. Abe) and *Kirishima*, in single line ahead, about 8 cables apart, screened by the light cruiser *Nagara* about a mile and a half ahead, and three destroyers in line ahead, about 7½ cables apart, on each flank, the rear destroyer being about a mile abeam of the battleships.[1] Two destroyers of the Sweeping Unit were stationed 3 miles on the port bow of the flagship and three others about the same distance on the port quarter. Three destroyers[2] patrolled between Russell Islands and Guadalcanal, as a protection against M.T.B. attack.

At the moment of contact the American force was near Lunga Point steering 280°. Admiral Callaghan altered course to 310° and shortly afterwards to north. The two forces were closing very rapidly, and before the Admiral could get a clear picture of the situation the head of his column became mixed with the enemy and confusion arose even before firing began, some of the American ships having to haul round to port to avoid collision while others maintained the northerly course. The advantage of surprise afforded by radar was lost. At that juncture, at 0148, enemy ships close aboard switched on searchlights, and a fierce action began. The American fire seemed to them very effective. Within five minutes one ship in the enemy northern column appeared to blow up and others were believed damaged before they could retire on the main body. Most of the American ships were hit, but the enemy were firing bombardment ammunition from their main armament, and the only ship

---

[1] *See* Appendix H.   [2] *Shigure, Shiratsuyu, Yugure.*

seriously damaged during this phase of the action was the *Atlanta* ; Admiral Scott was killed and the ship was hit by one or two torpedoes fired by the Japanese destroyers. But the American formation was in confusion, and at 0155 Rear-Admiral Callaghan ordered ' cease fire,' in the belief that some of his own ships were firing on the *Atlanta*. A minute later the enemy battleships arrived. The *Hiyei* was repeatedly hit by gunfire, probably by the *San Francisco* and *Portland*. Three destroyers also claimed to have torpedoed her, but the ranges were very short and perhaps the torpedoes failed to arm, for the Japanese reported that she received no damage from torpedo hits during the night action, all hurt being caused by some 85 shell hits. She withdrew to the westward with the *San Francisco* engaging her. The *San Francisco* herself came under a cross fire and was severely damaged. Rear-Admiral Callaghan, her commanding officer Captain C. Young, and about 85 officers and men, including most of the Admiral's staff were killed. Her situation was somewhat relieved by the *Helena*, which engaged with her main battery one of the larger ships firing at her.

The Americans had suffered severly in the melee. The *Laffey* had been torpedoed, the *Barton* sunk by two torpedoes, the *Cushing* heavily hit by gunfire and brought to a standstill, the *Juneau* put out of action by a torpedo in her forward engine room, and the *Portland* hit by a torpedo aft which damaged her steering gear so that she could only steam in circles. About 0230 the *Sterett* torpedoed a destroyer, probably the *Akatsuki*, which blew up ; the explosion illuminated the *Sterett*, which was thereupon fired at, hit and damaged. Ten minutes earlier, the *Monssen* on flashing her recognition lights had at once come under fire and had been wrecked and abandoned ; her commanding officer, Lieut.-Commander C. E. McCombs, and bridge personnel were trapped, and all suffered more or less serious injury in getting clear. The immobilised *Cushing* came under heavy fire ; having fired her torpedoes she was abandoned. The *Aaron Ward*, hit by three 14-inch, two 8-inch and smaller shells engaged a cruiser until she too lost power and stopped. Only a single American ship, the destroyer *Fletcher*, remained undamaged.

About 0230 firing ceased and the enemy withdrew, ordering his transports back to Buin. The *Akatsuki* had been sunk and four destroyers damaged ; one of these, the immobilised *Yudachi*, was sunk at 12,500 yards range after daylight, by the damaged *Portland* which was still capable only of turning in circles when under way. The damaged battleship *Hiyei* was scuttled during the day after being further injured by numerous air attacks. Her toughness was probably less a tribute to her British designer, Sir George Thurston, than to the American torpedoes of that date, only three of which exploded. All that struck her probably did so on her armoured belt, for the ship was low in the water and the depth setting of the torpedoes was 10 feet. At least two were seen to bounce off her side.

In addition to the *Barton*, the Americans lost the *Cushing* and the *Laffey*. The *Monssen* burned all night and blew up about noon. The *Atlanta*, which had lost 40 per cent. of her crew and was shockingly damaged, could not be kept afloat and was scuttled off Lunga Point in the evening, her commanding officer, Captain S. P. Jenkins, who was amongst the wounded, being saved. The *Aaron Ward* and *Portland* reached Tulagi with the help of tugs. The six American ships still capable of steaming and steering limped away from the grisly scene. These were the badly damaged *San Francisco*, *Juneau*, and *Sterett*, the less seriously damaged *Helena* and *O'Bannon*, and the *Fletcher*. They had not proceeded far towards Espiritu Santo when the *Sterett* made a submarine contact. She dropped several depth charges, but without result. At 1101 three torpedoes were seen, one of which struck the *Juneau* at the spot on the port side where she had been hit during the night. The ship broke in two and disappeared in a matter of seconds, Captain L. K. Swenson and all except ten of the crew being lost. The submarine which sank her was *I–26,* one of the nine detailed to cooperate in the reinforcement operation.

60

Meanwhile, Task Force 16 coming up from Numea reached the position to which it had been ordered, some 300 miles south of Guadalcanal, that morning. Admiral Kinkaid was flying his flag in the *Enterprise.* As she steamed north, artizans strove to free her jammed forward lift. With her were the battleships *Washington* (flagship of Rear-Admiral W. A. Lee) and *South Dakota*, the heavy cruiser *Northampton*, the light cruiser *San Diego*, and eight destroyers.[1] Dawn search by aircraft from the *Enterprise* showed that the enemy survivors of the night's engagement had retired out of range. As the carrier's forward lift was still out of action the number of aircraft on board was reduced by flying off to Guadalcanal nine torpedo-bombers escorted by six fighters. On the way, they fell in with the *Hiyei* lying north of Savo Island, and added to the damage caused in the night action followed by an attack by Marine aircraft from Guadalcanal that morning. The *Enterprise's* aircraft formed a valuable reinforcement to Henderson Field, and continued to work from there. Accompanied by the heavy cruiser *Pensacola* (flagship of Rear-Admiral M. S. Tisdale), which joined the force early in the afternoon, Admiral Kinkaid increased speed to 23 knots and steered northward under orders received from Admiral Halsey, to support the ships damaged in the night's action, keeping south of the parallel 11° 40′ S. until conditions required otherwise.

The Japanese had not abandoned their plan to bombard Henderson Field and land reinforcements. The Transport Unit of 12 ships escorted by 13 destroyers under Rear-Admiral Tanaka sailed again from Buin that night (13th–14th November), whilst a fast cruiser force under Vice-Admiral Mikawa, consisting of the *Chokai, Kinugasa* and *Maya*, with the light cruisers *Tenryu* and *Izudzu* and six destroyers was approaching Guadalcanal to bombard the airfield.[2]

During the late afternoon of the 13th, by Admiral Halsey's directions Admiral Kinkaid organised a striking force (Task Force 64) consisting of the two battleships with the destroyers *Preston, Gwin, Benham*, and *Walke*, in readiness to intercept the enemy bombarding force. The orders to proceed, though timed 1652, were not received by the Commander of the force, Admiral Lee, until 1929 ; he was unable to arrive in time and the naval defence of Guadalcanal devolved upon the six M.T.B.s at Tulagi. From 0120 to 0240 on the 14th the enemy bombarded the airfield, whilst the M.T.B.s discouraged them to the best of their power, bringing off three attacks. The Japanese then retired, having, fortunately, done little damage to the airfield, though they destroyed three U.S. aircraft and damaged 17, most of them slightly. As the enemy retired, they were sighted south of New Georgia Island by a reconnaissance flown from the *Enterprise* to test the accuracy of a report of two Japanese

---

[1] *Clark, Hughes, Benham, Anderson, Morris, Mustin, Russell* and *Walke.*

[2] For composition of the forces *see* Appendix H. Interrogation No. 109 says Mikawa's force was termed Outer South Seas Supporting Unit (South).

carriers 265 miles to the westward of Guadalcanal on the 12th.[1] The *Enterprise* had been closing Guadalcanal during the night and at dawn on the 14th was about 200 miles south of the island. She already had in the air 17 bombers and ten fighters which had been launched both in order to clear the flight deck in case of attack and to be ready for an early strike on targets which it was felt sure would be found in the area. These 27 aircraft were sent to attack the Japanese bombarding force, which they reached soon after 0800, just as an attack group from Henderson Field consisting of three naval torpedo bombers and three Marine torpedo bombers, seven scout bombers and seven fighters was completing a strike on the same targets. The combined attacks resulted in the sinking of the heavy cruiser *Kinugasa* which went down under less punishment than Japanese armoured ships usually withstood, and severe damage to the *Chokai, Isudzu*, and the destroyer *Michisio*.

Half an hour later, shore-based aircraft reported a convoy of 12 ships escorted by light cruisers and destroyers steaming down New Georgia Sound towards Guadalcanal. This was Rear-Admiral Tanaka's Transport Unit, and as soon as possible aircraft from Guadalcanal went out to attack it.[2] They were augmented by heavy bombers from Espiritu Santo and a striking group of eight bombers escorted by 12 fighters from the *Enterprise* which after flying them off withdrew to the southward and took no further part in the operations being too valuable to risk unnecessarily. She retained on board for her protection 18 fighters, whilst her striking group continued to work from Henderson Field as far as lack of servicing equipment and crews rendered this possible.

The Japanese had provided a carrier group under Vice-Admiral Kurita, consisting of the *Junyo* and *Hiyo*, the battleships *Kongo* and *Haruna*, the heavy cruiser *Tone* and destroyers, to support the Bombardment and Transport Units. But the force was some distance away to the northward, and the aircraft complement of the carriers, less than fifty apiece, was insufficient to carry out all they had to do. For Kurita's effort had been reduced by a large strike which he sent off against the *Enterprise*. This strike failed to find the *Enterprise*, due it is said to the squally weather conditions.

Attacks by Allied aircraft on Tanaka's meagrely covered transports went on all day and continued after dark. Aircraft landed on Henderson Field, hastily bombed up and refuelled and took off again. The lesson that it was tantamount to suicide for a surface force lacking control of the air or at least adequate fighter cover, and with no better screen than lightly gunned destroyers, to remain within range of an airfield in active operation, was demonstrated that day by the slaughter. As the Japanese steered south-eastward between New Georgia and Santa Isabel seven transports were hit and set on fire.[3] Destroyers went alongside and took off such of their troops as they could and continued with the surviving transports to steer for Guadalcanal with crowded decks. For Admiral Tanaka possessed the indispensable military virtue of resolution : his losses did not shake his determination to effect his object, though he chose a desperate method. Daylight on the 15th found four of his transports beached or beaching themselves on the Japanese-held coast between Tassafaronga and

---

[1] The report was in error. These were not the two carriers *Junyo* and *Hiyo* referred to later on, which were away to the northward at the time, though no details of their movements are known.

[2] *See* Appendix H for the actual composition of the force.

[3] *Shinanogawa M., Nako M., Nagara M., Sado M., Canberra M., Brisbane M., Arizona M.*

Aruligo.[1] Though they never landed the tons of supplies which were badly needed by the Japanese garrison some of their troops swarmed ashore as the Allied dawn air strikes began. Throughout the day the *Enterprise*'s air group and Marine and Army aircraft bombed, machine-gunned and dropped incendiaries on the doomed transports. A Marine heavy battery on Guadalcanal bombarded them, and the destroyer *Meade*, which had arrived at Tulagi on the previous afternoon escorting a fleet auxiliary, encompassed with her guns their final destrouction. The carnage was so great that the waters along the ten-mile stretch of coast are said to have been strewn with human remains and stained with blood. The Americans lost but five aircraft in destroying those eleven Japanese transports.

61

A few miles away to the northward, between Cape Espérance and Savo Island, the first battleship action of the war had just been fought. Admiral Lee's battleship force had arrived at a position some 50 miles to the south of Guadalcanal towards the close of the forenoon of the 14th.[2] An enemy force, somewhat diversely reported but apparently containing one or more battleships, had been sighted early that morning in 8° 9′ S., 157° 55′ E., preceding the transport unit ; whilst at 1700 four heavy cruisers, one light cruiser and a destroyer flotilla were reported about 130 miles north of Florida Island, steering 165°, closing Indispensable Strait. Commander South Pacific Area considered that the enemy would renew the bombardment of the airfield that night, probably using capital ships. In the hope of surprising them Admiral Lee, unaware that he himself had been sighted and his force reported as a possible battleship, a light cruiser and four destroyers, stood off to the south-westward of Guadalcanal. At about 2035 he passed between Russell Islands and Savo Island, and from a point 10 miles north of the latter, ran down on a south-south-easterly course into the Sound, passing east of Savo Island. From 2030 onwards the *South Dakota* heard Japanese radio voice transmissions intermittently, but she had no interpreter on board. South Pacific Headquarters learned about 2230 that an enemy convoy was coming through the passage off Savo Island, and at once presumed that the battleships sighted earlier in the day formed its covering force. Lee knew, however, only that the Japanese were coming down in strength.[3]

The Japanese force was an Emergency Bombardment Group which had been formed from ships of the various forces engaged in the operations of the previous three days and had no connection with any convoy. It consisted of the battleship *Kirishima*, the heavy cruisers *Atago* (flagship of Vice-Admiral

---

[1] *Kinugawa M., Yamaura M., Yamatsuki M., Hikokawa M.* It is not known what happened to the twelfth ship the oiler *Kumagawa M.*, or whether she in fact accompanied the expedition. She was sunk on 12th January 1945 off Cape St. Jacques.

[2] For composition of the force *see* Appendix H. For a plan of the battle *see* Plan 26.

[3] Between 0455 on 14th and 0106 on 15th 25 enemy reports were received by the *Washington*, but the latter evidently did not receive the 2230 report. The *Washington's* Action Report (M.053022/42 in R.O. Case 8644) lists no enemy report between 2000 (Z–11) and 2306 (Z–11) on the 14th. Morison, *History of U.S. Naval Operations in World War II*, Vol. V, p. 272 says : 'As he had been assigned no call sign in the hurry of departure, he tried to contact radio Guadalcanal, asking for any late information and signing with his last name. To this he received the snub, ' We do not recognise you.'

N. Kondo) and *Takao*, screened by the light cruiser *Nagara* (flagship of Rear-Admiral S. Kimura) and six destroyers,[1] with the light cruiser *Sendai* (flagship of Rear-Admiral S. Hashimoto) and three destroyers[2] as a scouting group or advanced screen.[3]

An hour before midnight Task Force 64, 20 miles south-east of Savo Island, was in column formation. Lee had just altered course to the west, to pass south of Savo, speed 19 knots. The four destroyers led by the *Walke* were 2 miles ahead of the *Washington*. The distance between the battleships was 1,700 yards. The moon was in the first quarter and visibility was good. At 2307 the *South Dakota* sighted three ships bearing 330°, dimly illuminated by the setting moon. It was considered that the leading ship was a battleship or heavy cruiser and the other two light cruisers. Actually there were only two ships, the light cruiser *Sendai* and the destroyer *Shikinami*, part of Admiral Hashimoto's scouting group. They had sighted the American force at 2210 whilst the latter was running down into the Sound, but mistook the battleships for cruisers. Admiral Kondo had ordered Hashimoto to keep the *Shikinami* with him and follow the enemy, whilst his other two destroyers, the *Uranami* and *Ayanami*, were to pass west and south of Savo Island, followed by Rear-Admiral Kimura in the *Nagara* with four destroyers. Admiral Kondo himself, with the Emergency Bombardment Group and Kimura's two remaining destroyers, the *Asagumo* and *Terutsuki*, would pass north and east of Savo. There was yet a fourth force approaching the area, namely the four transports, with a destroyer escort, which as already stated, were about to beach themselves on the north-east shore of Guadalcanal (*see* Section 60). Thus, although his ships were incompletely equipped with radar and were operating in restricted waters Kondo was practising nevertheless the complicated dispersal of forces customary among the Japanese.[4]

The *Washington* opened fire on the leading enemy ship at 2316, radar range 18,000 yards, whilst the *South Dakota* engaged the next astern. Faced with such heavy metal, both Hashimoto's ships made smoke and withdrew at high speed to the northward, undamaged, but so promptly that the Americans thought they had sunk them out of hand. Five minutes later the rear ship, or another, appeared on the *South Dakota's* starboard quarter and was engaged. By now, the American column was steering 300°, heading between Cape Espérance and Savo Island. At 2322 the leading American destroyers sighted a group of enemy destroyers fine on her starboard bow and opened fire. These were the *Uranami* and *Ayanami*, followed by Admiral Kimura in the *Nagara* with four destroyers. The enemy replied and also fired their torpedoes prematurely at the U.S. destroyers instead of the still unseen battleships. They did great execution. The *Walke* and the *Benham* were both hit; the former sank in a few minutes, with heavy loss of life, the latter was able to retire but had to be sunk later. The Japanese also used their guns to good effect. The *Preston* came under cross fire, and with her vitals torn out sank after being abandoned; and the *Gwin* suffered severe damage. The American battleships joined with their secondary armament in the firing at the enemy ships in the shadow of Savo Island, severely damaging the *Ayanami*, so that she subsequently sank. At 2348 when Admiral Lee ordered the destroyers to retire only the *Benham* and *Gwin* were able to comply.

---

[1] *Terutsuki, Shirayuki, Hatsuzuki, Asagumo, Samidare, Ikazuchi.*

[2] *Uranami, Shikinami, Ayanami.*   [3] *See* Appendix H.

[4] The fitting of radar in Japanese warships did not begin until after the Battle of Midway in June 1942.

The *South Dakota* in consequence of electrical trouble at 2333 had been for three minutes without power or propulsion, with her SG radar out of action. Of this Admiral Lee knew nothing at the time. The *South Dakota* lost touch with the flagship, and coming within the glare of the burning destroyers was sighted by Admiral Kimura's force (the *Nagara* and four destroyers). These fired at her no less than 34 torpedoes. Every one missed. The loss for three minutes of a radar picture already highly confused left the *South Dakota* in uncertainty of the position. Altering course to starboard to avoid the burning *Preston*, she inadvertently steered towards the enemy. At 2400 she was illuminated with searchlight, and came under heavy fire from three or four ships—Kondo's Emergency Bombardment Group—at about 6,000 yards range. The *Washington* came to her help. The flagship had been tracking by radar a group which appeared to her as eight enemy ships closing on her starboard bow. These were the *Dakota's* present opponents, the *Kirishima* and heavy cruisers, which had been manœuvring to the north-westward of Savo Island and were coming down on a south-easterly course on receipt of Kimura's report, to attack the American battleships. The *Washington* immediately opened fire on the leading enemy ship, the *Kirishima*, the *South Dakota* joining in shortly after at a ship illuminating her. The duel lasted but 10 minutes. The *Dakota* had taken enough punishment and retired to the south-westward. No more than a few minutes' intense gunfire at short ranges had sufficed to render this modern battleship impotent for the time being through the destruction of radar, radio and fire control circuits.[1] The *Kirishima* was in far worse shape, however. The *Washington* had so pounded her that the Japanese scuttled her about three hours later. The *Atago* and *Takao* escaped with slight damage.

At 0033 (15th) Admiral Lee, appreciating that by now the transports had been sufficiently delayed to prevent them from reaching Guadalcanal before daylight, decided that the time had come to retire. He withdrew to the south-westward. For more than an hour the Japanese destroyers pursued him with torpedoes, all of which were avoided by manœuvring. The *South Dakota* was met at 0900.

The enemy, apart from the destroyers pursuing the *Washington*, had already retired before Lee quitted the scene. They had made their effort with a force not far short of the strongest they could muster. It had failed, with the loss of the battleships *Hiyei* and *Kirishima*, the heavy cruiser *Kinugasa*, the destroyers *Akatsuki*, *Yudachi* and *Ayanami*, and seven transports or cargo ships whilst a further four transports were about to undergo destruction on the shores of Cape Espérance. The American losses though numerically severe had all been in light units, the A.A. light cruisers *Atlanta* and *Juneau* and the destroyers *Barton*, *Cushing*, *Laffey*, *Monssen*, *Benham*, *Preston* and *Walke*. But a further eight ships had been damaged, including the heavy cruisers *Portland* and *San Francisco* ; whilst the *South Dakota* was so badly damaged that she had to be despatched to the United States for repairs. The fate of Guadalcanal had been decided in favour of the Allies.[2]

---

[1] The *South Dakota* was commissioned on 20th March 1942.

[2] Reprint of Cincpac Reports of Actions and Campaigns, February 1942/February 1943 O (145).

CHAPTER VIII

Conquest of Guadalcanal

(*See* Plans 8, 13, 24)

62

AFTER the repulse of their fourth and greatest attempt to retake Guadalcanal the Japanese fell back to Rabaul, and the amount of shipping in the Buin–Faisi area, an unfailing indication of their intentions, diminished rapidly and remained low for a week or ten days. The Americans were in no shape to follow up their victory. They withdrew their naval forces to Espiritu Santo and Numea to reorganise and make good damage. With the exception of destroyers, the only ships remaining to Admiral Halsey were the *Enterprise*, the *Washington* and the light cruiser *San Diego* at Numea, and the heavy cruisers *Northampton* and *Pensacola* at Espiritu Santo. Reinforcements were, however, on the way. At Nandi in the Fijis lay the carrier *Saratoga*, the battleships *North Carolina, Colorado* and *Maryland* and the light cruiser *San Juan*. The heavy cruisers at Espiritu Santo were reinforced by the *New Orleans* and *Minneapolis* and the light cruiser *Honolulu*. Light craft were sent to reinforce the Tulagi base known as ' Ringbolt.'

The Battle of Guadalcanal almost sealed off the Japanese on Guadalcanal from their rear bases and made the task of the Americans in reinforcing the island much less dangerous. The landing of the 182nd Infantry on 11th and 12th November was the last movement of reinforcements which had to be effected in the face of the enemy fleet. Thereafter American troops were to be landed on Guadalcanal fairly regularly, and although Japanese air attacks continued, the danger of attack by warships diminished. On shore, the U.S. Marines passed to the offensive and by the end of November had driven the main Japanese forces well to the westward of Point Cruz and dispersed the enemy detachments to the east of the Tenaru River (see *Plan 12*). For these operations they had the support of naval bombardment. By the end of November General Vandegrift's force numbered 39,416 men, and the Lunga area was securely held.

Enemy submarines were still operating off Guadalcanal, though certain of them were withdrawn from their usual advanced positions south of the island, towards the Shortlands, probably to protect Rabaul. Early on the morning of 28th November the 6,200 ton cargo auxiliary *Alchiba* which had come up from Numea with a cargo of aviation fuel, bombs, ammunition and provisions, whilst unloading at Guadalcanal screened by five destroyers, was torpedoed by a Japanese midget submarine launched by *I–16* (Force A). Though badly damaged the ship was saved.

89

By 24th November Japanese shipping concentrations in the Shortlands began to grow. Coast Watchers and aircraft reported the number of vessels in Buin and Shortland Harbours three days later to have mounted from the previous week's dozen to two or three times that number, in addition to small craft. An enemy move in strength to supply and reinforce his southern Solomons positions appeared imminent. The American appreciation was correct. Rear Admiral Tanaka with the 2nd Destroyer Flotilla[1] had been detailed for the duty of dropping supplies in watertight drums off the Japanese-held beaches of Guadalcanal : these drums would be towed ashore later by small craft. In order to intercept the attempt, Rear-Admiral Kinkaid on 27th November was given a striking force (Task Force 67) consisting of the five cruisers *Minneapolis* (flagship), *New Orleans*, *Northampton*, *Pensacola* and *Honolulu* (flagship of Rear-Admiral M. S. Tisdale), with the destroyers *Drayton*, *Fletcher*, *Maury* and *Perkins*. Admiral Kinkaid was ordered to other duty next day, and was succeeded in command of the force by Rear-Admiral C. H. Wright who had just arrived at Espiritu Santo in the *Minneapolis*.[2] The destroyers *Lamson* and *Lardner* joined the force on the evening of 30th November. Admiral Kinkaid had divided Task Force 67 into one destroyer and two cruiser units, and this organisation stood. Each unit included at least one ship equipped with SG radar for detection of surface craft and CXAM or SC–1 radar for detecting both surface craft and aircraft at medium range. The *Minneapolis*, *New Orleans* and *Pensacola* formed one unit under Admiral Wright. Admiral Tisdale led the second unit composed of the *Honolulu* and *Northampton*. The destroyer unit was under the command of Commander W. M. Cole in the *Fletcher*. Before handing over command of the force Admiral Kinkaid had prepared a set of operation orders based on the experience of previous surface engagements in the Solomons. These Admiral Wright adopted. The plan aimed at obtaining surprise in a night action.[3] The destroyers were to be stationed 4,000 yards 30° on the engaged bow of the cruiser line with one or more pickets advanced a distance of 10,000 yards in the direction of the enemy. The engagement was to open with a torpedo attack, the range, until this was completed, being kept above 12,000 yards if possible. The destroyers, after launching their torpedoes, were to clear the range quickly, and engage with gunfire when the cruisers opened fire. Ships unable to maintain fire by radar control were authorised to illuminate by star shells. Searchlights were not to be used.

On the evening of 29th November, Rear-Admiral Wright received orders to proceed to sea with all despatch, in order to intercept an enemy force of eight destroyers and six transports expected off Tassafaronga, to the westward of the American perimeter on Guadalcanal, at 2300 next night. By steaming at full speed (28 knots) he reached and cleared Lengo Channel at the moment when the Japanese destroyers, making their final approach from the northward, were to the westward of Savo Island, just turning to a south-easterly course for Tassafaronga. It was a dark night, glassily calm, with an overcast sky and surface visibility of about 2 miles. The Japanese formation was divisions in line ahead disposed astern, Rear-Admiral Tanaka in the *Naganami* leading, with the *Takanami* stationed on his port bow as a lookout. Rabaul had informed

---

[1] 30th Division, *Naganami* (Flag), *Makinami*, *Takanami* ; 15th Division, *Oyashio*, *Kurashio*, *Kagero* ; 24th Division, *Kawakaze*, *Suzukaze*.

[2] Admiral Kinkaid assumed command of the North Pacific Force on 3rd January 1943.

[3] The tactical plan is reproduced in the Report of the Commander-in-Chief, Pacific Fleet, T.S.D. 6684/43.

him that American cruisers were in the Guadalcanal area, but he knew no details ; whilst the only intelligence Admiral Wright had received since the original signal ordering the operation was a coast watcher's report of the sailing of 12 destroyers from Buin on the night of the 29th/30th, and a signal from the Commander, South Pacific, which however gave him no definite enemy intelligence. Despite special aircraft searches from Guadalcanal on the 30th giving 100 per cent coverage in the good weather which prevailed the approaching enemy force was not detected ; a tribute, perhaps, to Admiral Tanaka's skill in choosing evasive courses.

At 2238 the American cruisers formed on a line of bearing 140° on course 280°. (See *Plan 13.*) They were in the order *Minneapolis* (flag), *New Orleans, Pensacola, Honolulu* (flagship of Rear-Admiral Tisdale), *Northampton*, the destroyers *Fletcher, Perkins, Maury* and *Drayton* being stationed 300° 2 miles from the flagship. These four destroyers had never operated together as a unit and no divisional commander was present. No destroyer picket was stationed ahead, as provided for in Admiral Kinkaid's plan. The *Lamson* and *Lardner*, which were taken from escort to join the force, were too late to receive the plan of attack ; they were astern of the *Northampton*. At 2306 the *Minneapolis* obtained a SG radar contact of ships off Cape Espérance bearing 284°, 23,000 yards, and three minutes later the squadron turned together to 320°, bringing the cruisers into line ahead. There seemed to be seven or eight ships in the enemy group. At the same time, another group of six vessels, about 4 miles to the south-eastward of the first, was reported by aircraft to be approaching Tassafaronga close inshore. This report did not reach Rear-Admiral Wright.

At 2319, when Task Force 67 was on course 300° the destroyers having radar contact launched torpedoes but by firing star shells at the moment of launching, they destroyed any chance of surprise. The bearings, too, were drawing aft and the range was excessive, in view of the fact that the enemy ships were already abaft the beam. The *Fletcher* fired ten torpedoes at 7,300 yards and the *Perkins* eight at 5,000 yards. The *Drayton*, owing to an erratic radar plot fired only two torpedoes, whilst the *Maury*, which was without SG radar, could not identify any targets, and fired none. There were apparently no hits. Almost simultaneously the *Minneapolis* opened fire and the action became general.

The Japanese, whose ships were without radar, had no indication of the approach of the enemy. Though taken by surprise, their reaction was rapid and effective. Increasing speed to 24 knots they carried out a manœuvre which they had practised frequently, reversed course by divisions (leaders together, the remainder in succession) and all ships fired torpedoes as fast as they were able. In accordance with previous orders, gunfire in general seems to have been withheld. The *Takanami*, however, the nearest ship to the enemy opened fire : she was overwhelmed by American gunfire and quickly sunk. Apart from shell splinters through the funnel of a second destroyer, not another Japanese ship was touched. The enemy torpedoes played havoc with the American heavy cruisers. The *Minneapolis* was hit by two, one of which blew off her bow. She got off a few more salvoes with her 8-inch guns, however, before power failed. With his ship immobilised and communications failing Rear-Admiral Wright at 2333 directed Rear-Admiral Tisdale in the *Honolulu* to take over the conduct of the battle ; the message took 28 minutes to reach him. The *New Orleans* was struck a minute after the flagship, the torpedo detonated her fore magazines and tore off her bow as far as her fore turret.

Deprived thus suddenly of its two leading ships, the American formation was thrown into some confusion. The *Pensacola* hauled out to port to clear the *New Orleans*, and continued to the westward roughly parallel to the coast, firing at two enemy targets until a torpedo struck her on the port side at 2339. She developed a 13° list and fires broke out which were not fully under control 12 hours later. The *Honolulu* followed by the *Northampton* altered course sharply to starboard. The two ships gradually hauled round to the westward, firing at the enemy, until the *Northampton* was hit by two torpedoes at 2348 which brought her to a standstill and the action to an end. The enemy, except for the *Takanami*, got clear away to the westward, though once again their attempt to land reinforcements and supplies had been frustrated. Admiral Tisdale in the *Honolulu* searched the area, without finding any Japanese ships, made contact with his four van destroyers north of Savo Island, and then returned to direct salvage and rescue operations. The *Northampton* had a heavy list which increased until she was ordered to be abandoned at 0245, 1st December. Twenty minutes later, just after her Commanding Officer, Captain W. A. Kitts, III, left her, she turned over on her beam ends and sank. She was the thirteenth ship to be sunk in the South Pacific Area by Japanese torpedoes. Good seamanship together with damage control of a very high standard enabled the three other cruisers to reach Tulagi, where temporary repairs were effected at the M.T.B. base, with minimum resources.

Tassafaronga witnessed the defeat of a fully alerted, superior American force in an encounter battle in which the Japanese were taken by surprise. The torpedo attack of the enemy after they came upon the Americans unexpectedly, was masterly and the result of long training. This was precisely what the Americans lacked, for they had during the war consistently been under the necessity of organising task forces quickly without opportunity for the Commander to indoctrinate his units with his views. The American gunfire was described by Admiral Tanaka as inaccurate. Arrangements had been made for aircraft from Guadalcanal to illuminate the enemy who were distinguishable with difficulty against the dark shore, after action was joined. The aircraft however did not arrive in time, and the flares which they eventually dropped, after most of the fighting had ceased, actually illuminated damaged American ships rather than the enemy. M.T.B.s might have operated effectively. Eight additional boats had been sent to Tulagi during the last week in November, to counter such a Japanese attempt as had just taken place, bringing the number there to sixteen. They were ordered to remain in port, however, to avoid possible errors in identification. This latter difficulty was one which had dogged the Americans in night actions throughout the war and at that date was far from being overcome.

64

The intentions of the Japanese after the Battle of Tassafaronga were not clear to the Americans. Early in December the enemy showed increased interest in strengthening New Guinea and the Dutch East Indies. Convoys to the region increased; and on 18th December an occupation force of Army troops landed at Wewak, Madang and Finschafen in north eastern New Guinea and began the construction and expansion of air bases. On the other hand, the strengthening of the Japanese positions and developments in the central Solomons seemed to the Americans to point to the probability of an offensive to recapture Guadalcanal. The Japanese had occupied most of the small islands immediately north of Guadalcanal such as the Russells and also Rendova and Kolombangara near Munda in New Georgia. From these bases they appeared to be infiltrating troops into Guadalcanal. Air strength in the Solomons was being built up, and the construction of a new airfield was begun at Munda, only 150 miles from Guadalcanal. This, though suspected, was so cleverly concealed by natural camouflage of palm fronds that its existence was not definitely established till December. Rekata Bay, on Ysabel Island, was developed as a seaplane base. Further north, a large air base at Buin, in the Bougainville Strait, was in full operation and had a garrison of an entire division. Buka in the extreme north of the Solomons, was also fully developed.

By this date the Japanese forces ashore on Guadalcanal had been greatly reduced in numbers and condition, and there was no danger of the enemy recapturing the island if he could be prevented from landing heavy reinforcements. The policy of the Americans at the moment was to let them wear themselves out in attacks on their strong positions. Admiral Nimitz was sending every ship he could spare to the South Pacific Area, and by the end of the third week in December, the whole effective Pacific Fleet was concentrated there. Two more 14-inch battleships were sent from Pearl Harbour, leaving there only three cruisers, whilst one heavy and one light cruiser and two auxiliary carriers were on their way from the Atlantic.

Actually the enemy had not yet abandoned their intention of retaking Guadalcanal. Practically the entire Combined Fleet, except half the battleships, was concentrated in the Truk–Bismarcks area ; this was insufficient to maintain the naval superiority in the South Pacific which the Japanese had previously enjoyed. On 2nd December, General H. Imamura arrived at Rabaul from Java, to assume control of operations in the Solomons and Eastern New Guinea, operating directly under the orders of Imperial General Headquarters. An attack aimed at driving the Americans out of Guadalcanal was planned to take place about 1st February 1943, but problems of transportation and supply caused it to be cancelled ; for after the disaster on 14th and 15th November 1942 the Japanese never again used transports to reinforce or supply Guadalcanal. Although Imamura had 50,000 men of the 8th Army at his disposal, which he had brought from Java to Rabaul, he could not deploy them.

On 31st December the Japanese abandoned the proposed attempt to reconquer Guadalcanal, and four days later the Imperial General Staff ordered General Imamura together with Admiral J. Kusaka who had recently assumed command of the South East Area Fleet to evacuate the troops : instead of Guadalcanal, defensive positions in New Georgia were to be held as outposts for Rabaul.[1] The decision came too late to save half the garrison. For during December reinforcements for the Americans consisting of the battleships *Indiana, New Mexico* and *Mississippi*, six cruisers, including H.M.N.Z.S. *Achilles*, and ten destroyers arrived in the South Pacific.[2] The Japanese were consequently in naval inferiority, and evacuation had to be effected by evasion.[3]

---

[1] *U.S. Army in World War II, Guadalcanal.* General Imamura and Admiral Kusaka worked in co-operation, as far as can be discovered, both being directly reponsible to Imperial H.Q. in Tokyo.

[2] The other cruisers were the *Columbia, Cleveland, Louisville, Nashville, Wichita.* The *Achilles*, with her sister ship, the *Leander*, had been continuously employed on convoy escort duty throughout the earlier stages of the Guadalcanal campaign. In November a serious defect which occurred in the *Leander* put the ship out of action until March, 1943.

[3] The composition of the Allied fleet in the South Pacific at this date is given in footnote 1 p. 100 and of the Japanese fleet in footnote 3, p. 102.

65

Meanwhile Japanese supply and certain troop replacement operations in preparation for the evacuation went on.   The traffic was constantly attacked by aircraft and by the motor torpedo boats, based on Tulagi.   Ten Japanese destroyers with air cover landed their stores safely on the night of the 3rd/4th December, incurring nothing worse than slight damage to the *Makinami* by air attacks from Guadalcanal.   For some reason the American motor torpedo boats were not ordered out, whilst Task Force 67 was not available, having not yet been reorganised after the Battle of Tassafaronga.   The enemy made another attempt, four nights later.   Eight American M.T.B.s were moved into position consequent on the sighting by air reconnaissance of nine or more Japanese destroyers approaching Guadalcanal.   Two of the M.T.B.s (*PT–109, PT–43*) established a patrol between Kokumbona (*see Plan 12*) and Cape Espérance and two (*PT–48, PT–40*) off the north-west coast of Guadalcanal, whilst a striking force of four boats (*PT–59, PT–44, PT–36, PT–37*) was stationed near Savo Island.   Aircraft from Guadalcanal attacked the enemy at nightfall and disabled the *Nowaki*.   Some seven of the remaining Japanese destroyers reached Cape Espérance at 2320, but the attack of *PT–48* and *PT–40* was spoilt by an engine failure in the former, and *PT–40* had to cover her withdrawal with smoke.   The M.T.B.s of the striking force got into action at 2335, and though they apparently caused no damage to the enemy their attacks caused the Japanese destroyers to withdraw without effecting their purpose of landing reinforcements.   A force of eleven destroyers came down on the night 11th/12th December, and M.T.B.s from Tulagi sank the *Terutsuki*.[1]   The Japanese made no further important effort at reinforcement until the night 2nd/3rd January 1943 when ten destroyers came down.   Off Rendova (*Plan 8*) they were attacked from the air, and the *Suzukaze* was damaged and her speed reduced.   Eight of the destroyers made Guadalcanal, where M.T.B.s attacked them.   The M.T.B.s were themselves .bombed by enemy aircraft but without damage.   The Japanese destroyers threw overboard their supplies, which were in watertight drums, and retired.   In the late afternoon of 10th January, a coast watcher sighted eight destroyers north of New Georgia, heading south-west.   It was not possible for aircraft to attack before dark.   Six M.T.B.s from Tulagi,[2] however, met the Japanese force off Cape Espérance soon after midnight, and directed by a Catalina which illuminated the enemy with flares the M.T.B.s attacked with torpedoes and damaged the *Hatsukaze* ; but *PT–43* (Lieutenant (jg) C. E. Tillen, U.S.N.R.) and *PT–112* (Lieutenant R. E. Westholm, Commander of the patrol) were sunk by gunfire.   One destroyer unloaded supplies, and more than 250 drums were sunk by the M.T.B.s after daylight on the 11th.[3]   On 14th January, enemy destroyers were seen *en route* to the island, though again too late for daylight air attack.   By that date Catalina aircraft were operating from Guadalcanal, equipped with landing wheels as well as pontoon hulls, so that, painted black, they could work at night from Henderson Field, having satisfactory radar installations for night operating ; the name ' Black Cats ' followed automatically.[4]   One of these night

---

[1] For some reason the Assessment Committee give the position of sinking of the *Terutsuki* as off North New Georgia.

[2] *P.T.s 112, 40, 43, 59, 46, 36.*

[3] A description of this engagement is given in U.S. *Battle Experience No. 5*, p. 34–1, where, however, no mention is made of illumination by Catalina.

[4] Another innovation of this date was the Catalina specially equipped for life-saving and known as ' Dumbo.'

search aircraft shadowed the force to Savo, where 13 M.T.B.'s[1] attacked it. The enemy retired, without landing supplies or dropping supply drums; they were attacked east of New Georgia next morning by dive bombers from Henderson Field, which damaged the *Arashi* and slightly damaged the *Urakaze*. Allied and Japanese light forces had plenty to do during the weeks preceding the Japanese evacuation of Guadalcanal. But to the Americans, the Japanese activity appeared as operations of reinforcement and supply, not evacuation preparations.

66

Now that the Japanese had decided not to attempt further the reconquest of Guadalcanal they diverted to other duties certain of the submarines of Forces A, B and D operating against the American supply line to the island. At least one flotilla of submarines was regularly employed to supplement the efforts of the 'Tokyo Express' in running supplies and reinforcements to Guadalcanal, and during the last ten or twelve weeks of the Japanese occupation of the island the garrison was forced to rely largely on supplies brought in by submarines. The Japanese report that some 300 tons of supplies and about 1,000 troops were transported in this manner. It was the first manifestation of a practice which at later stages of the war was to claim the services of a substantial proportion of the Japanese submarine force. The instructions for the operation are reported to have been issued by the Commander-in-Chief, Combined Fleet, on 16th November 1942. The submarines had one gun removed and were left with only two torpedo tubes. They embarked their supplies at Buin in south Bougainville, and landed them on the north-west coast of Guadalcanal. The round trip took four days and was made submerged apart from surfacing for four hours to charge batteries. After various methods of transporting the supplies had been tried, these were packed in drums which could if necessary be released off the landing point, whilst the submarine was submerged. Another method was to employ cargo tubes. These also could be released from a submerged submarine. They were piloted by one man, motive power being supplied by two torpedoes which gave them an endurance of about 4,000 yards. They could carry about 2 tons of supplies.

There was also a submarine supply line to Buna in New Guinea. About 11 submarines were engaged in the supply of Guadalcanal and, including the submarines running to New Guinea, it is said that at maximum, in January 1943, 20 submarines were engaged in the work of supply. One submarine could carry two days' supplies for 30,000 men.

The work was not carried on without loss. On the night 9th/10th December, *PT-59* sank *I-3* off Cape Espérance with 30 tons of supplies which she was hoping to land. A week later, land based Navy aircraft of Squadron 55 sank *I-15* in the same area, though according to the Japanese she was not being employed on supply duty. Both these were of the 2,000-ton cruiser type[2] but as the Allied advance in the Solomons and New Guinea progressed the Japanese were compelled to use for the supply of by-passed and isolated garrisons small submarines having a loading capacity of no more than 10 tons. Some of the enemy continued to patrol the supply route from Numea and Espiritu Santo to

---

[1] Outer Patrol *P.T. 59*, *P.R. 38*. Inner Patrol *P.T. 39*, *P.T. 115*. Striking Force *P.T.s 109, 37, 45, 40, 36, 48, 47, 46, 123*, operating in three groups.

[2] Standard displacements : *I-3* 1,995 tons, *I-15* 2,212 tons.

Guadalcanal. It was whilst engaged on this duty that *I–18* was sunk (*see* section 49) ; and on 11th February, an aircraft from the cruiser *Helena*, which was on A/S patrol, assisted by the destroyer *Fletcher*, sank *RO–102* in 14° 15′ S., 161° 59′ E.

A fourth blockade-running submarine, *I–1*, was sunk by the 25th Mine-sweeping Flotilla, composed of the New Zealand trawlers *Matai, Kiwi, Moa, Tui, Breeze* and *Gale* which had been placed under the orders of Commander, South Pacific Area, for service in the Solomons. On the night 29th/30th January the *Kiwi* (Lieut.-Commander G. Bridson, R.N.Z.V.R.) and *Moa* (Lieut.-Commander P. Phipps, R.N.Z.V.R.) were patrolling off the enemy held coast about Cape Espérance when the former detected a submarine. The latter had just raised her periscope at the entrance through the reef. The *Moa*, which was astern of the enemy, forced her to the surface with depth charges, about 2,000 yards away. This was *I–1*, and she made off at full speed against the dark background of the shore. Both the trawlers pursued her, firing first of all star shell, then following up with high explosive, to which the submarine replied with her 5·5 inch gun. The *Moa* scored one hit when the *Kiwi*, which was the nearer vessel and had decided to ram, firing every gun that could be brought to bear struck the submarine squarely on the port side abaft the conning tower putting the enemy's 5·5 inch gun out of action and damaging the landing craft which were stowed on deck. Troops, of which the submarine was said to be carrying 200, began jumping into the water. The *Kiwi* backed off and at a third attempt to ram, under rifle and machine gun fire from the submarine's deck, struck *I–1* on the starboard side just abaft the conning tower. A dull fire was seen to be raging inside the submarine and a horrible smell of roasting flesh came from the Japanese trapped below. By this time, the *Kiwi's* 4-inch gun had been firing for an hour and had become too hot to use ; accordingly Lieut.-Commander Bridson withdrew to enable the *Moa* to finish off the enemy, which had now got both her 6 pounder and her machine guns into action. Failing to escape by manœuvre, *I–1* headed for the beach, but ran ashore on a reef in a sinking condition. She was gutted by fire and 30 tons of supplies were lost with her. Only one prisoner (a Japanese officer) was picked up, but important confidential documents were recovered, for the Japanese failed to complete their destruction. One fatal casualty was sustained in H.M. ships. Damage to the *Kiwi* was merely superficial.[1] That night the *Moa* was again in action, and with the *Tui* engaged four Japanese landing barges with troops, sinking two and damaging a third. The *Moa* ended her service a few weeks later, on 7th April when she was sunk off Tulagi in a Japanese air attack.

The Japanese also sent submarines to operate once more on the lines of communication from the U.S.A. and Hawaii to Australia. On 18th January 1943, the tanker *Mobilube* was torpedoed off Sydney, but made port, and a few hours later the British s.s. *Kalingo* (2,051 tons) was sunk nearby, presumably by the same submarine. On the 22nd the s.s. *Peter H. Burnett* was torpedoed further east, in 32° 54′ S., 159° 32′ E. but was towed to port. The operations, however, were merely sporadic.

67

The use by the enemy of fast light craft and submarines to support Guadalcanal was foredoomed to failure. The use of light craft had been thoroughly tried out during October and November and found inadequate ; and the inability to transport heavy guns, tanks and large scale reinforcements by this

---

[1] The above account is based on W.I.R. 165/14.

THE BOW OF THE JAPANESE SUBMARINE *I–1* DESTROYED BY
H.M.N.Z.S. *Moa* AND *Kiwi*, 29TH JANUARY 1943

AMPHIBIOUS VEHICLES LANDING SUPPLIES AT RENDOVA, 30TH JUNE 1943

means had contributed to the Japanese decision to launch the expedition which resulted in the disastrous Battle of Guadalcanal. Now it proved more inadequate than ever, for American troop and air superiority on the island were developing at a rate which no stopgap system of supply could hope to counter.

During December, relief took place by the Army of the U.S. 1st Marine Division on Guadalcanal. These men were enervated with malaria and combat fatigue after double the tour of duty that medical officers considered possible under the conditions.[1] On the 9th Major General Vandegrift turned over his command to Major-General A. M. Patch who, like his predecessor, was responsible to Commander South Pacific Area for the Guadalcanal airfields, the seaplane base at Tulagi, and the naval bases, as well as the troops of all services. On the 10th Admiral Turner was relieved of responsibility for defending Guadalcanal, but retained the duty of transporting troops and supplies to the area, General Harmon being responsible for providing supplies. By the end of the month, out of approximately 58,000 American troops stationed in the Guadalcanal–Tulagi area, 31,600 were Army forces. The final stage of the relief of the Marines involved a particularly large troop movement early in January, 1943. Six transports and one cargo vessel carrying part of the 25th Division were to leave Numea on New Year's Day, arriving at Guadalcanal on 4th January. As soon as their troops were landed they were to embark the 7th Marine Regiment and leave next day for Melbourne. As a diversion, a bombardment was arranged of the newly discovered enemy airfield at Munda in New Georgia. The airfield constituted a serious threat to the American position in the Solomons, its importance lying in the fact that it was within easy fighter range of Guadalcanal. Regular air attacks had been made on Munda airfield throughout December, but none of these succeeded in putting it out of action for more than a day or so. By the end of December a fighter strip at Munda was in operation by Japanese bombers, increasing the threat to the American forces in Guadalcanal. It was therefore decided to try the effect of naval bombardment, the bombardment being synchronised with the landing of the 25th Division and acting as a diversion for this landing.

To cover the operation of landing the 25th Division and embarking the 7th Marine Regiment, Rear-Admiral Lee took out Task Force 64, consisting of three battleships and four destroyers, whilst Task Force 67,[2] comprising seven cruisers and five destroyers, commanded by Rear-Admiral W. L. Ainsworth, sailed from Espiritu Santo on 2nd January 1943, to escort and support the transports. The group detailed for the bombardment of Munda airfield, consisting of the three 6-inch cruisers Nashville (flag), St. Louis and Helena and the destroyers Fletcher and O'Bannon, was detached on the 4th. The submarine Grayback was stationed off Rendova to assist the navigation of the group ; this, in conjunction with the use of radar, enabled the operation to be carried out exactly as planned. A total of 4,149 rounds of 6-inch and 5-inch was fired. The enemy reply was weak and caused no damage. The bombardment group rejoined Task Force 67 to the westward of Guadalcanal on the morning of the 5th. Shortly afterwards, the force was surprised by four Japanese dive bombers. At the time, some of the ships were in a condition of complete readiness and some in one-third readiness. The cruiser Honolulu was exercising guns crews against friendly fighters ; radar failed to distinguish the approaching enemy from these, for the Japanese aircraft resembled the Grummans covering the task

---

[1] Morison, op. cit., Vol. V, p. 288.

[2] Nashville (Flag, Rear-Admiral Ainsworth), St. Louis, Helena, Honolulu (Flag, Rear-Admiral Tisdale), Columbia, Louisville, H.M.N.Z.S. Achilles ; destroyers Fletcher, O'Bannon, Nicholas, Lamson, Drayton.

force and none of the American aircraft were showing I.F.F. signals. However, with the exception of the *Achilles* which had barely time to man her A.A. guns and was damaged by a direct hit which wrecked No. 3 turret, the force escaped unhurt. ' The *Achilles*,' says the American report, ' took the damage in her stride, and never lost position.' Her A.A. fire continued throughout the brief engagement.' This was the first occasion of the use by A.A. guns of the new American Mark 32 proximity-influence fuze.[1] Though the bombardment served as a deterrent against air attack on Guadalcanal during troop replacement the damage to the airfield at Munda was so quickly repaired that enemy aircraft were operating from it in less than 18 hours. ' The damage to airfields or other land positions is so transient that ships should not ordinarily be risked to bombard airfields and other positions except in close support of ground operations,' Admiral Nimitz subsequently directed.[2] At the time, however, the Americans wished to divert enemy attention both from their extensive troop replacements and from the preparations for amphibious operations on the north-west coast of Guadalcanal, for which bombardments were considered to be of considerable value.

The discovery of an airfield under construction at the Vila and Stanmore Plantations, in the south part of Kolombangara Island, north of New Georgia (*see Plan 16*) initiated a bombardment on 24th January by the cruisers *Nashville* and *Helena* and the destroyers *Nicholas*, *De Haven*, *Radford* and *O'Bannon*, whilst the cruisers *Honolulu* and *St. Louis* with three destroyers operated to seaward. Task Force 11 (Rear-Admiral De W. C. Ramsey) consisting of the carrier *Saratoga*, the light cruiser *San Juan* and six destroyers, was south east of Rennell Island (*see Plan 8*), in support. The bombarding force was picked up south of Guadalcanal by enemy reconnaissance aircraft at 1030 on 23rd January, and was shadowed all day while making to the westward, but with the setting of the sun the whole sky became overcast, and at 2000 when course was altered to the northward, it was too dark for the turn to be detected. The bombardment was carried out at 0200, 24th January, as planned. During the withdrawal the force was again shadowed. Later, enemy aircraft made some attempts to attack, but were driven off by the gunfire of the ships or were avoided by making use of the intermittent heavy black squalls. The ships had scarcely completed the bombardment before the Japanese began to repair the airfield. Six hours later, 42 bombers and torpedo bombers armed with bombs, escorted by 24 fighters from the *Saratoga* attacked the same area flying from Henderson Field, to which they had been flown on the previous day. They encountered no air opposition and only sporadic A.A. fire which caused no damage, and they rejoined their carrier off Rennell Island that afternoon.

Construction of the air base continued at a rapid rate, seemingly little interrupted by the bombardment and bombing. The field was completed and aircraft were operating from it by early February 1943. It had perhaps taken the Japanese as many weeks to complete as the Americans would have required days. The ability of the Americans to build airfields, and indeed piers, buildings, oil tanks, roads and installations of all kinds needed to form bases, with astonishing speed, gave them a great advantage over the Japanese. It was brought about through the formation of Construction Regiments and Battalions. The officers belonged for the most part to the Civil Engineer Corps. The men had both the usual naval substantive rates and in addition non-substantive

---

[1] Morison, *op. cit.*, Vol. V, p. 329. One hit was claimed, but it is not stated whether it was allowed.

[2] *Commander-in-Chief, Pacific, Reports of Actions and Campaigns*, Serial 00617 18th March 1943.

rates such as Bulldozer Operator, Wharf Builder, Pipe Layer, Longshoreman, Truck Driver and Hatch Boss which sufficiently indicate their peace-time employments. The organisation was purely Naval, and the units were armed with mortars, machine guns and personal weapons. They were familiarly known as ' Seabees.'

68

To prevent absolutely and entirely the reinforcement and supply of Japanese forces in Guadalcanal by fast craft and submarines was a task which could not be accomplished by U.S.A. naval forces alone. What Admiral Halsey did was during December to order General Harmon to take the necessary action to eliminate all Japanese forces on the island.[1] This order gave the General, temporarily, direct authority over tactical operations which he had not previously possessed, his former authority having been limited to administrative matters ; and he immediately flew to Guadalcanal to concert the necessary measures. Preliminary operations to provide manœuvre room for an offensive in January 1943 were begun at once. General Patch launched his offensive to clear Guadalcanal of the enemy early in the New Year. It continued vigorously throughout January, constantly confining the Japanese to an ever dwindling portion of the island. Four U.S. destroyers based on Guadalcanal under the Commander Advanced Naval Base, termed Task Group 67.5, from 16th January onwards assisted the army by bombarding enemy positions as required.[2]

69

Late in January, the Americans had information of a forthcoming operation by a powerful Japanese fleet of battleships, carriers, and heavy cruisers ; knowing nothing of the enemy decision to evacuate Guadalcanal they believed that another major attempt was about to be made to regain possession of the island. It was thought that sufficient time had elapsed for the Japanese to repair their ships and replenish their air groups, and it was believed that they now had five carriers in the South-West Pacific. An increase of enemy shipping at Buin and Rabaul, intensification of air activity, and indications of the movement of strong forces towards the Southern Solomons pointed to prospective vigorous operations by the enemy. A force of 15 to 20 Japanese submarines, termed the Advanced Expeditionary Force, the usual name for a submarine force engaged in fleet operations, was already maintaining a line of patrols south and south east of Guadalcanal. A force of four battleships, two carriers, six heavy cruisers and 12 destroyers was sighted on 5th February, 400 miles south east of Truk steering south west, and the Commander, South Pacific ordered his main forces to assume dispositions suitable for interception. At the same time, Rear-Admiral R. C. Giffen, with a strong force of cruisers, destroyers and two auxiliary aircraft carriers, known as Task Force 18 was to cover an American troop convoy bound for Guadalcanal.[3]

In actual fact, the enemy were engaged in deception operations to cover the evacuation.[4] They were enabled to increase their air activity both because a carrier group was stationed at Buin during the evacuation of Guadalcanal and

---

[1] *U.S. Army in World War II—Guadalcanal*, p. 232.

[2] Task Group 67.5, *Nicholas, De Haven, O'Bannon, Radford*.

[3] Task Force 18 :   8-inch cruiser *Wichita* (Flag, Rear-Admiral Giffen), *Louisville, Chicago ;* 6-inch cruisers *Montpelier* (Flag, Rear-Admiral A. S. Merrill), *Columbia, Cleveland ;* auxiliary carriers *Suwannee, Chenango ;* eight destroyers.

[4] *U.S. Army in World War II, Guadalcanal.*

also because now for the first time Army air forces became involved in the Solomon Islands campaign. In the previous autumn the Japanese Navy, whose air arm alone had up till then sustained these operations, made an urgent request to Tokyo for air reinforcements, one reason given being the excessive demands of the Army forces in the area for ground support. In December, there were less than a hundred naval aircraft at Rabaul. The majority of the pilots were fresh from Japan with an average of less than 300 flying hours, only about half of which had been spent in a combat aircraft. Two of the best Army fighter units were consequently despatched from Surabaya to Truk by carrier, with a hundred aircraft. From Truk they were flown down to Rabaul, where elements from them intercepted an attack by heavy bombardment aircraft on 5th January 1943.

Halsey, who had been promoted Admiral on 26th November, now disposed of a large fleet which had been re-organised on 12th January in seven task forces, comprising in all two carriers, three auxiliary carriers, three modern and four old battleships, 11 cruisers and 37 destroyers.[1] Towards the end of January these forces, except the four old battleships and the three auxiliary carriers and their screen were ordered to concentrate in the area bounded by latitude 14° to 17° 20' S., longitude 157° to 162° E., where they were so placed as to be in a position to intercept the enemy in the event of another large-scale attempt on Guadalcanal developing, or to cover Rear-Admiral Giffen's convoy. The four old battleships under Vice-Admiral H. F. Leary, remained in reserve at Nandi, in the Fiji Islands.

Task Force 18 left Efate on 27th January under Rear-Admiral R. C. Giffen to rendezvous with the four destroyers of Task Group 67.5 based on Guadalcanal and sweep up the ' Slot.' It reached a position south of Guadalcanal on the evening of the 29th, when the escort carriers were detached as their slow speed was delaying the force. During the day there had been many aircraft contacts, but American air groups were in the area, their I.F.F. was erratic, and it was difficult to determine which were hostile. There seems little doubt that at least one group of enemy aircraft while remaining beyond gun range, spent the early evening in getting into position for attack from the eastward whilst the American ships were silhouetted against the western horizon. Task Force 18 was in special approach formation, cruisers in line of divisions, interval 2,500 yards, distance 700 yards, with destroyers disposed in anti-submarine screen ahead on the 4,000 yards circle, a formation adapted for meeting submarine but not air attack which was the immediate threat. The sea was smooth, wind from south-east, force 2, sky eight-tenths to nine-tenths overcast, ceiling about 2,000 feet. The first attack developed as it was growing dark, about 1923, and was preceded by an aircraft dropping dim white marker floats and red and green parachute lights. Admiral Giffen at once increased speed to 27 knots. The cruiser

---

[1] T.F. 16—*Saratoga* (Flag, Rear-Admiral De W. C. Ramsey), *San Juan* (A.A. cruiser), four destroyers.

T.F. 11—*Enterprise* (Flag, Rear-Admiral F. C. Sherman), *San Diego* (A.A. cruiser), five destroyers.

T.F. 64—Battleships *Washington* (Flag, Rear-Admiral W. A. Lee), *North Carolina*, *Indiana*, four destroyers.

T.F. 67—6-inch cruisers *Nashville* (Flag, Rear-Admiral W. L. Ainsworth), *Helena*, *Honolulu*, *St. Louis*, four destroyers.

T.F. 18—Heavy cruisers *Wichita, Louisville, Chicago*, light cruisers *Cleveland, Columbia, Montpelier, Chenango, Suwannee*, destroyers *La Vallette, Waller, Conway, Frazier, Chevalier, Edwards, Meade, Taylor*.

T.F. 65—Battleships *Maryland, Colorado*, three auxiliary carriers, six destroyers.

T.F. 69—Battleships *New Mexico, Mississippi* with destroyers as necessary.

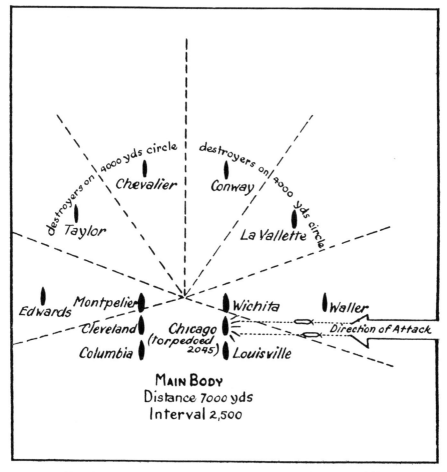

FIG. 3. AIR ATTACK ON TASK FORCE 18, 29th JANUARY 1943

Louisville sighted torpedoes and turned out of line and manoeuvred to avoid them, but apparently no other cruiser changed course after 1930, when zig-zagging was discontinued in order to reach the rendezvous in time. Twilight had given place to night when the air attack ended. Several waves of attack by small groups of aircraft followed, however, though no hits were made, and a number of the enemy were shot down. The aircraft employed artifices to induce the ships to open fire and disclose their positions in the dark, such as machine-gunning, the use of running lights and flares to resemble aircraft running lights, more powerful surface flares being used for illumination. At 1945 the cruiser *Chicago* whilst illuminated by an aircraft which she had just shot down in flames, was hit by two torpedoes. The ship lost all power, and after being towed by the *Louisville* during the night was subsequently taken in tow by the fleet tug *Navajo* which was diverted whilst on passage with the escort vessel *Sands* from Guadalcanal to Espiritu Santo. Task Force 18 remained with the *Chicago* until ordered by Commander South Pacific at 1500 on the 30th, to proceed to Efate. Five destroyers and the *Sands* were left to screen the damaged ship.

This was the first night torpedo attack made by Japanese aircraft during the war. Admiral Giffen had apparently not made adequate arrangements for air cover by his escort carriers in case of emergency.[1] Admiral Halsey consequently ordered the *Chenango* and *Suwannee* together with the *Enterprise* to provide this cover, and during the 30th the two former maintained a fighter patrol of aircraft over the damaged ship. Between 1527 and 1543 warning of impending air attack was received by the *Chicago* and her screen. The *Suwannee* and *Chenango* did not receive the message until late, but anticipating that the damaged cruiser might be attacked during the afternoon they launched a special flight of 19 fighters and four torpedo bombers at 1545. Owing to some mistake these arrived over the *Chicago* too late. The *Enterprise* which was about 40 miles from the *Chicago*, also intercepted the warning. At 1605 she launched an additional patrol of ten fighters, six of which were to reinforce the fighter patrol over the damaged ship, the enemy aircraft having been reported by radar, at 1554, 67 miles away making for the *Enterprise*. The Japanese, however, on sighting these fighters, turned and headed for the *Chicago*. At about 1615, the latter sighted 11 Japanese torpedo aircraft coming in to attack. Though there were sufficient fighter aircraft present there was no fighter direction and the combat patrol was unable to establish communication with the *Chicago* or the screening destroyers.[2] Some of the enemy were shot down by the combat patrol and the cruiser and her screen, though the latter were not very effective being on a 4,000 instead of a 2,000 yard circle. Being towed as the *Chicago* was, at three to four knots, she was unable to manoeuvre. She was hit by four torpedoes in rapid succession and the crew had barely time to abandon ship before she rolled over and sank in 2,000 fathoms, in 11° 25' S., 160° 56' E., 30 miles east of Rennell Island. In the screen, the destroyer *La Vallette* was hit by a torpedo but reached Espiritu Santo safely on 3rd February. The American transports unloaded their troops without molestation.

70

The Japanese effected the evacuation of Guadalcanal between 1st and 8th February, totally unsuspected by the Americans. Destroyers came down on three occasions and evacuated troops on the nights 1st/2nd, 4th/5th and 7th/8th, whilst the entire effective strength of the Japanese fleet in the South Pacific covered the operation from a position near Ontong Java, to the eastward of Bougainville Island (Plan 8)[3]. Increased landing barge traffic between Guadalcanal and the Russell Islands, which latter, it will be remembered, had been temporarily occupied by the Japanese in the middle of January, was interpreted by the Americans as a reinforcement operation instead of the reverse as it actually was.

---

[1] Admiral King in *Battle Experience No. 6*.

[2] *Ibid.*, also the Action Reports in M.053038/43.

[3] The organisation of the forces for the operation is reported to have been as follows :—
    STRIKING FORCE—Battleships *Yamato*, *Musashi*, one carrier (63 aircraft), one carrier (42 aircraft), two 8-inch cruisers, nine destroyers.
    ADVANCED FORCE—two 14-inch battleships (*Haruna*, *Kongo*), one carrier (54 aircraft), four 8-inch cruisers, nine destroyers.
    ADVANCED EXPEDITIONARY FORCE.—15–20 submarines (already on patrol south and south-east of Guadalcanal).
    REINFORCEMENT FORCE—two 8-inch cruisers, four seaplane carriers, 20–25 destroyers, transports.
    BASE AIR FORCE—two Air Wings   150 shore based aircraft.
    EASTERN DIVERSION FORCE—two 8-inch cruisers.

On 1st February the Americans landed a force at Nugu Point in six L.C.T.s from Lunga covered by Task Group 67.5. The group was attacked by Japanese dive bombers and the *De Haven* was sunk with the loss of her captain, Commander C. E. Tolman and 167 of her crew. On the same day 20 Japanese destroyers came down with fighter cover for the first of the three evacuation operations. They were attacked to the eastward of New Georgia by aircraft from Henderson Field, and the *Makinami* was immobilised. The 11 available boats of M.T.B. Flotilla One took up positions to intercept.[1] They were attacked by enemy aircraft at 2140 and scattered. An hour later, the M.T.B.s encountered the enemy destroyers and attacked. *PT–111* and *PT–37* were sunk by gunfire and *PT–123* by a bomb dropped by an aircraft during the engagement. But the *Makigumo* was sunk by a mine in Déma Cove between Tassafaronga and Cape Espérance, whilst avoiding the attacks of the American M.T.B.s. This minefield, the first offensive field to be laid by American surface craft in the Pacific, had been put down as recently as 2100 that evening by the destroyer minelayers *Tracy*, *Montgomery* and *Preble*, which laid 255 mines, as part of a campaign to mine the channels most likely to be used by the enemy in his attempts to reinforce his garrison; and its immediate success attracted the attention of the Americans to the tactical possibilities of this type of attack. Attempts to attack the enemy off Cape Espérance by the three remaining destroyers of Task Group 67.5 were frustrated by an air group working in co-operation with the Japanese; on each attempt enemy aircraft from 15 to 20 miles away closed the destroyers causing them to turn to unmask batteries and preventing them from making a surprise attack. Three days later, a Japanese cruiser and 22 destroyers came down from Buin-Faisi with strong fighter protection. Thirty-three American bombers and torpedo aircraft escorted by 31 fighters attacked them. Seventeen Japanese and 10 U.S. fighters were shot down. The *Maikaze* and *Shiranuhi* were damaged in the attack, but the remaining enemy vessels got through to Guadalcanal and 10 of them lay for three hours off the north-west coast of the island, evacuating troops unmolested, whilst the remainder apparently patrolled in support.[2] The force was sighted retiring on the morning of the 5th, but a striking force sent from Henderson Field at 0620 could not locate it, and it was later seen arriving at the Shortlands. The evacuation force 18 or 19 strong came down for the third and last time on the night 7th/8th February. Dive bombers from Henderson Field, attacked it at 1735 south of Rendova (New Georgia) and damaged the *Hamakaze*. Whilst some of the enemy embarked troops from the Russell Islands, to which they had been ferried, the remainder proceeded to Guadalcanal, where the *Isokaze* was slightly damaged by Allied air attack. ' For reasons not explained ' reported the Commander-in-Chief Pacific, no attack was made on them by the American destroyers, and all 19 of them returned to Faisi next day. The evacuation was complete; 13,000 troops had been embarked without the Americans having an inkling of what was toward.[3] In his report the Commander-in-Chief, Pacific Fleet wrote :—

> Until almost the last moment it appeared that the Japanese
> were attempting a major reinforcement effort. Only skill in
> keeping their plans disguised and bold celerity in carrying

---

[1] *P.T.s 47, 39, 111, 48, 59, 115, 37, 124, 123, 109, 36.*

[2] Task Group 67.5 had been withdrawn for rest, and the report of Commander-in-Chief Pacific Fleet says : ' Reports do not indicate why P.T. boats failed to make contact.'

[3] *The Guadalcanal Campaign* (Marine Corps History) states that the figure of 13,000 given by the Japanese after the conclusion of hostilities is perhaps too high, and estimates that 9,000 were evacuated, including 2,100 ' normally removed.'

them out enabled the Japanese to withdraw the remnants of the Guadalcanal garrison. Not until after all organised forces had been evacuated on 8th February did we realise the purpose of their air and naval dispositions ; otherwise, with the strong forces available to us ashore on Guadalcanal and our powerful fleet in the South Pacific, we might have converted the withdrawal into a disastrous rout.[1]

The powerful Japanese covering force retired to Truk, carrier air groups operating ashore in the Solomons returned to their ships, and most of the land-based aircraft brought to the Solomons for the evacuation operation returned to New Guinea. In the fighting for Guadalcanal the Allies had lost two aircraft carriers, eight cruisers and 14 destroyers and their losses in officers and men included 1,600 Marine and Army troops killed in action. The Japanese lost two battleships, an aircraft carrier, five cruisers and 13 destroyers. The Japanese losses of ships were of less importance than the damage caused to the land-based Naval Air Force. This was soon to be aggravated by the irreparable damage suffered by the carrier air groups in the fighting in New Guinea. The turning point of the war had come. From now onwards the Japanese were on the defensive in the Pacific.[2]

---

[1] Serial 00712, dated 17th April 1943.

[2] Statements by Fleet Admiral O. Nagano, I.J.N., Supreme Naval Adviser to the Emperor and (from April 1941 to February 1944), Chief of the Naval General Staff ; and Lieutenant-General Kawabe, former Chief of the Japanese Army General Staff.

CHAPTER IX

Submarines, Raiders and Blockade Runners in the Indian Ocean

(See Plans 1, 7)

71

DURING the two years which elapsed before the course of the war and the development of our resources permitted us to build up the Eastern Fleet naval operations in the Indian Ocean were sustained largely by coastal forces and submarines. When reconstituting the Eastern Fleet the Admiralty intended also to include a substantial reinforcement for the submarines in the Indian Ocean, where there were only one British and three Dutch boats, which was about the average number during the first eighteen months of the war. Of these, *O–21* was engaged on special operations from Australia until the end of September 1942 ; *O–23* was due to leave Ceylon early in that month for refit in the United Kingdom ; *O–24* was operational ; and the *Rover* was undergoing a prolonged refit at Bombay. Up to date, the submarines had sunk no more than seven ships though they damaged several others.[2] They had also been engaged on special operations. The Americans carried out one trial patrol in the Malacca Strait–Martaban area, but targets were found to be scarce and unsuitable ; and in view of the need for offensive patrol nearer Australia Admiral King, Commander-in-Chief U.S. Fleet, on 16th April 1943 decided that a second submarine would not be sent.

On 30th July Admiral Somerville reported that there were opportunities for the effective use of submarines in the Malacca-Andamans area, and asked for the projected reinforcement to be substantially advanced. The Admiralty had already (27th July) instructed the Commander-in-Chief, Mediterranean, to release eight long-endurance submarines to the Eastern Fleet. Admiral

---

[1] Details of the operations will be found in the Naval Staff History, *British Submarine Operations in the Second World War.*

[2] Sunk : *Yae M.* (6,781 tons) by *Truant*, April 1942 in 5° 42′ N., 98° 57′ E.
Shunsei M. (4,939 tons) by *Truant*, 1st April 1942 in 5° 42′ N., 98° 57′ E.
Toyohashi M. (7,031 tons) by *Trusty*, 4th June 1942 in 7° 30′ N., 98° 10′ E.
Zenyo M. (6,441 tons) by *O.23*, 2nd August 1942 in 5° 36′ N., 99° 53′ E.
Bandai M. (165 tons) on 21st February 1942 in 7° 50′ N., 98° 9′ E.
Kasuga M. No. 2 (3,967 tons) by *O.21*, 13th March 1943 in 11° 40′ N., 92° 50′ E.
Yamazato M. (6,925 tons) (escorted) by *O.21*, 22nd April 1943 in 3° 28′ N., 99° 47′ E.

Cunningham detailed the *Severn, Tally Ho, Templar, Tactician, Taurus, Trespasser, Surf* and *Simoon*. The first of them, the *Trident*, which took the place of the *Taurus*, left Aden on 4th August for Colombo. On her first patrol, on the 29th of the month, she fired eight torpedoes at the Japanese cruiser *Kashii* as the latter was entering Sabang (Sumatra), but the cruiser was not hit. The submarines had to wait until 12th November for their first success against a warship, when the *Taurus* attacked a submarine from submerged with six torpedoes, and sank her. The enemy was the Japanese submarine *I–34*. The submarines carried out ten more patrols before the end of the year, resulting in the sinking of but a single ship.

On 4th September the Admiralty decided that all new construction and refitted T and S class submarines and ultimately A class submarines, with the exception of a few earmarked for training and operations in Home Waters, should join the Eastern Fleet.

The first aerial mining of the Rangoon river was carried out by American naval aircraft on 23rd February 1943. By the end of the year minelaying and the operations of the submarines had denied the use of Rangoon to the Japanese.

72

In October 1942 there was a report that a Japanese raider or supply ship was in the Indian Ocean. On the 21st, in the area north-east of the Seychelles, the S.S. *Karagola* reported sighting a suspicious vessel of 20,000 tons, nine miles distant, which so far as she could be discerned between rain squalls, appeared to resemble one of the Nippon Yusen Kaisha Pacific passenger ships. Though the report was doubted Vice-Admiral Danckwerts, Second-in-Command, Eastern Fleet, the Commander-in-Chief in the *Warspite* being at the time at Durban for the docking of the flagship, decided to employ the *Devonshire, Enterprise* and *Mauritius* which were then at Kilindini with no immediate task, to search for the ship and any enemy supply ships or raiders which might use that area for refuelling submarines about to engage in operations which the enemy were suspected of preparing in the Gulf of Aden and the Gulf of Oman. R.A.F. flying boats co-operated. The search (Operation ' Demcat ') continued from 27th to 30th October, and was without result, other than the sighting on 30th October by one of the Catalinas of a submarine on the surface, which was believed to be one that had been bombed and damaged by aircraft off Ras-el-Hadd five days previously. In the hope of intercepting the enemy as she passed eastwards between the Maldive Islands and the Chagos Archipelago an organised hunt was carried out by the A.S.V. Catalinas then on passage from Ceylon to Mombasa together with all available A/S vessels in the Addu Atoll area. The *Fritillary, Lismore* and *Cairns* were quickly assembled and carried out a patrol to the south-westward of Addu Atoll whilst Catalinas carried out cross-over patrols further to the westward of them as far as the shortage of their numbers allowed, and the *Hoxa* patrolled the one-and-half Degree Channel. The search in this vast area[1] proved unsuccessful and was abandoned on 1st November.

German submarine activity in the Cape area which had necessitated the despatch thither of Eastern Fleet destroyers during October (*see* Section 52), diminished during November. Simultaneously, sinkings by Japanese submarines began within the East Indies Station limits, close to the boundary with

---

[1] The distance between Haddummatti Atoll (southern Maldives) and Speakers Bank (northernmost of the Chagos Archipelago) is 400 miles.

the South Atlantic Station, which had been moved on 15th September 1942, from longitude 36° E. to longitude 35° E. and now ran south from a point near Inhambane about 120 miles north-east of Lourenço Marques (*see Plan 1*). On 13th November the S.S. *Louise Moller* (3,764 tons) was sunk in 30° 50′ S., 35° 54′ E., and on the 20th the American *Pierce Butler* (7,191 tons) was torpedoed and sunk in 29° 40′ S., 36° 35′ E. By the end of the month the German submarines had moved northward to the southern approaches to the Mozambique Channel, where three sinkings occurred : the Greek S.S. *Cleanthis* (4,153 tons) on 30th November in 24° 29′ S., 35° 44′ E., the S.S. *Saronikos* (3,548 tons) on 7th December close by, and the S.S. *Empire Gull* (6,408 tons) on the 12th in approximately 26° S., 35° E. These sinkings were the work of Japanese submarines, for German submarines did not reach the boundary between the South Atlantic and East Indies Stations until the end of January 1943.[1] In view of the increased Japanese submarine activitity in the area of Eastern Fleet responsibility Admiral Somerville asked for the release of the destroyers and corvettes loaned to the South Atlantic Station, not only to strengthen his own anti-submarine forces, but to restore mobility to the fast detachment of the Eastern Fleet, and to enable training of the battleships and carriers to be resumed.

In the Arabian Sea at least four Japanese submarines had been working since the middle of September, but with little result. The threat to the Persian Gulf and sinking of the S.S. *Ocean Vintage* on 22nd October off Ras-el-Hadd has already been referred to (Section 16). Further east, the American S.S. *Paul Luckenbach* (6,606 tons) was sunk in 10° 03′ N., 63° 42′ E., on 22nd September, possibly by a submarine homeward bound from the Gulf of Aden, the S.S. *Losmer* (5,549 tons) two days later in 7° 40′ N., 74° 15′ E., and the Russian S.S. *Mikoyan* (2,332 tons) on 3rd October in 19° 24′ N., 85° 24′ E., 300 miles south-west of Calcutta. The S.S. *Cranfield* (5,332 tons) was sunk on 23rd November off Alleppey in 8° 26′ N., 76° 42′ E., and the S.S. *Tilawa*, a 10,000-ton British India liner, was torpedoed during the night 22nd/23rd in 7° 36′ N., 61° 8′ E. The latter had a large number of native passengers on board, including more than a hundred women and children. They panicked at once and rushed the boats. The Master endeavoured to recall the boats, as the vessel did not seem to be in danger of sinking, but without success. Some two hours later the vessel was struck by a second torpedo and sank in a few minutes. The *Birmingham* rescued approximately 675 persons out of a total of 950 and the A.M.C. *Carthage* searched the area and picked up four more ; but the loss of life was heavy.

Further north, there were suspicious activities near Jask, suggestive of the landing of arms and agents. On the east side of the Indian Ocean three ships were unsuccessfully attacked by submarines off Ceylon and Madras. On 16th November a patrol vessel sighted a submarine off the latter port but lost contact. These enemy submarine operations were conducted from Penang, with Port Blair as an advanced operating or fuelling base, and were independent of supply ships such as the raiders which during the offensive in the Mozambique Channel in June and July had acted in that capacity.

Analysis of 93 attacks by Japanese submarines in the Indian Ocean and Australian waters, about which sufficient details were known, confirmed conclusions already arrived at, as to the value of resolute defence by the merchantman when attacked. On 13 out of 15 occasions when merchant vessels engaged a submarine on the surface with gunfire the submarine broke off the

---

[1] *The U-Boat War in the Atlantic.* German Naval History Series, C.B. 4523 (2), p. 84.

engagement and the vessel escaped. On three occasions the ships did not use their gun although the submarine came within gun range on the surface : two of these vessels were sunk. Two ships, one of them unarmed, attempted to ram their opponents. Both escaped. The value of keeping a good lookout was shown by the escape of ten vessels which avoided torpedoes through sighting tracks in time for an alteration in course to be effective. Thirty-six vessels were lost through sighting torpedo tracks too late or not at all. Only on six occasions did a submarine press home an attack at risk to herself until her victim was sunk.

73

East Longitude Dates

Two German raiders operated in the Indian Ocean during 1942. In January 1943 the Japanese announced that the area south of 25° S. and west of 108° E. was reserved for German and Italian raiders.

The German *Raider 10 (Thor)* (Kapitän Zur Zee G. Gumprich) which left Germany at the end of November 1941 entered the Indian Ocean in the last half of April 1942 after laying mines off Cape Agulhas. She met the supply ship *Regensburg*, which was on passage to Japan, on 4th May, in about 23° S., 75° E. Six days later she captured the S.S. *Nankin* (7,131 tons) in 26° 43′ S., 89° 56′ E. The *Nankin* succeeded in sending a distress message, although attacked by the raider's aircraft. The raider put a prize crew on board and sent the ship to Yokohama, where she was renamed *Leuthen*. On 14th June about an hour after dark, the *Thor* sank the laden Dutch tanker *Olivia* (6,307 tons) from Abadan in approximately 26° S., 77° E., having located her, it is reported, by R.D.F. One D.E.M.S. gunner, who managed to escape from the blazing tanker, was taken aboard the raider, and three Europeans and one Chinese reached Madagascar on 14th July in one of the ship's boats. On 19th June *Raider 10* captured the laden Norwegian tanker *Herborg* in approximately 28° S., 90° E., and sent her to Japan with a prize crew ; her aircraft destroyed the tanker's W/T aerial by diving between the masts with a trailing hook and no distress message was made. The same method of preventing a distress message from being sent, was used on 4th July when another Norwegian tanker, the *Madrono*, was captured in about 29° S., 70° E. She was sent to Japan. On 20th July the raider sank the British merchant vessel *Indus* (5,187 tons) in 26° 44′ S., 82° 50′ E., taking prisoners about half the crew. The *Indus* replied to the raider's fire, which resulted in casualties on board both ships.

Raider 10 found no further victims and arrived at Yokohama on 9th October. On 30th November, whilst lying near the German fleet tanker *Uckermark* in Yokohama, explosions occurred on board the latter which started fires. The *Uckermark* was destroyed, as was also the *Leuthen (Nankin)* which was being used by the Germans in Yokohama as a depot and accommodation ship and was lying near them.[1] A Japanese ship, believed to have been the *Unkai Maru No. 3* also caught fire and was destroyed.[2] *Raider 10* was damaged beyond

---

[1] The *Nankin* was to have been handed over to the Japanese some two weeks later. Most of her stores and officers had already been transferred to the *Havelland* (6,334 tons), a ship which had for long been lying immobilised in Yokohama awaiting new engines. The *Havelland* was sunk by a submarine south of Japan in December 1943.

[2] The U.S. Army Joint Assessment Committee were unable definitely to establish the details of the loss of the *Unkai Maru No. 3*. The Japanese report that she was sunk by air attack at Rabaul on 5th November 1942.

108

repair and several of her ship's company lost their lives. British prisoners on board the *Speybank*, which had been captured on 31st January 1941 in the Indian Ocean and was in harbour at the time, watched the flames, fanned by a south-east wind, rapidly spreading to the warehouses surrounding the basin. They were in high hope that all Yokohama would be destroyed, but the Japanese managed to extinguish the fires.

The second raider *No. 28* (the S.S. *Bonn*, operating as the *Michel*—Kapitän zur See H. von Rückteschell), which carried two motor torpedo boats to assist her operations, entered the Indian Ocean from the South Atlantic, and on 18th November 1942 met the *Rhakotis* which had been working in Japanese controlled waters since she arrived at Yokohama from Chile, in the summer of 1941. The *Rhakotis* was homeward bound, having sailed from Yokohama in October 1942 as a blockade runner. The meeting probably took place in the area of 30° S., 80° E., and the raider transferred to the blockade runner some personnel and mails, together with some British official papers and documents discovered on board one of her victims. The *Rhakotis* never reached home : she was intercepted and sunk by the *Scylla* on 1st January 1943 in the Bay of Biscay. On 29th November *Raider 48* sank the m.v. *Sawolka* (5,882 tons) south-east of Madagascar, in 28° 52′ S., 52° 51′ E., and she was probably responsible for the sinking after dark on 7th December of the Greek S.S. *Eugenie Livanos* (4,816 tons) in 27° 21′ S., 53° 30′ E., whilst that ship was on passage from Capetown to Bombay. No distress message was received but the British S.S. *Matheran* reported rockets or flares followed by heavy gun-fire between 1645 and 1745, in 27° 48′ S., 53° 58′ E. On 15th February 1943 *Raider 28* was seen in Batavia. Her subsequent career is unknown, but she is said to have been sunk by an American submarine during the night 17th/18th October 1943, off the coast of Japan.

74

On 11th November, the *Hokoku Maru* which had returned to Japan in the late summer of 1942 after the raid in the Indian Ocean, returned to those waters with a confederate of the *Kiyosumi* or *Kunikawa* class. At 1145 that day, in 19° 45′ S., 92° 40′ E., H.M.I.S. *Bengal* (act. tempy. Lieut.-Commander W. J. Wilson, R.I.N.R.) a minesweeper armed with one 12-pounder and three smaller guns, which was escorting the Dutch tanker *Ondina* (one 4″ gun) (William Horsman, Master), from Fremantle to Diego Garcia, sighted a ship on the port bow proceeding at high speed and steered towards her. Ten minutes later a second ship was sighted and the *Bengal* ordered the *Ondina* to make off and save herself, an order which the latter courageously disregarded. The first vessel sighted was the *Hokoku*, and when the range was over 3,500 yards, she opened fire. The *Bengal*, with the *Ondina* supporting her, engaged the enemy, the other raider being still out of range. The *Bengal* was hit and had a fierce fire, but the two ships succeeded in hitting the *Hokoku* aft ; she caught fire and sank at 1215 after an explosion which blew off her stern. Before this happened, however, the second raider came within range and opened fire. The *Bengal* was hit again and set on fire, and with her ammunition supply almost exhausted, she disengaged under cover of smoke floats. The raider then turned her guns on to the *Ondina* and hit her repeatedly. The Dutch tanker's ammunition soon ran out, the Master and Chief Engineer had been killed, and the crew abandoned ship. After the survivors had taken to the boats the raider closed, machine gunned them and fired two torpedoes into the *Ondina*. She then proceeded to pick up the survivors of the *Hokoku*, returned to fire another torpedo at the *Ondina*, which missed, and finally made off to the north-eastward. The *Ondina*'s crew then reboarded their ship. They found the engines intact, corrected a very heavy list, put out a fire in the forecastle, and headed for Fremantle, which they reached a week later. The *Bengal* had reached Diego Garcia on the previous day.[1] She had no casualties.

Apart from a single sinking in July 1943[2] the Japanese undertook no further operations by merchant ship raiders in the Indian Ocean. They had paid little attention and made few preparations for such activities before war broke out ; and during the war so meagre was the economy of the country, that the effort necessary to equip ships for raiding could be put to better use. For a country as short of shipping as was Japan from the very outset of the war, this was probably a wise decision, as it was a fortunate one for us in view of the shortage of long-range escorts. The absolute answer to the merchant ship raider was convoy ; yet even in the Indian Ocean, where the shortage of escort vessels prejudiced the thorough-going adoption of convoy until the war was well advanced, raiders accomplished little in comparison with the effort entailed.

75

Though certain war material which the Germans could supply would have been welcome to the Japanese the latter had no surface ships to spare for blockade running to and from Europe, and they used submarines for this purpose only on a very limited scale. The Germans on the other hand during the war sent to the Far East various surface ships and submarines, to bring back cargoes of essential materials, such as rubber and tin. On the outward voyage the ships carried cargoes for Japan, principally prototypes or high grade machinery which the Japanese were unable to manufacture themselves in sufficient quantity. The casualties of this traffic were very heavy and could only have been justified by the Axis needs. But if the casualties were high, so were the rewards of success. For example, before sailing from the Far East for Europe, the crew of the *Ramses* were told that if the ship ran the blockade successfully it would be the equivalent of winning an important battle. This was scarcely an over-statement, for the 4,000 tons of rubber in the ship's holds would have equipped eight new armoured divisions or maintained half that number in the field for an entire year, whilst the 3,000 tons of whale oil carried by this one ship was more than sufficient to meet one week's consumption of fats in Germany.

Substantial quantities of valuable goods which Germany had purchased for transport by the Trans-Siberian route remained in warehouse in the Far East after she attacked Russia, and the Germans made plans for running them through the blockade in vessels with sufficient cruising range to enable them to reach Europe or Vichy-controlled African territory without refuelling *en route*. Five of the German ships which were in Japan on the outbreak of the war in Europe were sold to Japan.[3] Others were operated either by the Germans or by the Japanese on charter, in waters adjacent to territory controlled by

---

[1] For this gallant action Lieut.-Commander Wilson received the D.S.O., and eight of his crew (all Indians) received decorations. Captain Horsman was posthumously mentioned in despatches and a number of awards were made to his Dutch crew and to the D.E.M.S. gunners, all except one of whom were British (H. & A. 1044/42, 82/43).

[2] The American S.S. *Samuel Heintzelman* (7,176 tons) sunk on 3rd July 1943 off Abrolhos (Western Australia).

[3] *Augsburg, Fulda, Bremerhaven, Saarland, Scharnhorst.*

Japan.[1] Others acted as blockade runners between Japan and Europe. Such blockade runners were liable to be given the task of supplying German submarines or raiders whilst either outward or inward bound. The Axis requirements of Far East trade were said to be 250,000 tons (25 ships) during twelve months. Only 257,770 tons can be traced as having been shipped during the entire war, of which Germany received 111,490 tons, or less than half her needs for one year, the remainder failing to get through the blockade. Japan during the same period is known to have received 57,000 tons out of a total of 69,300 tons despatched. Both the route via Cape Horn and that round the Cape of Good Hope were employed, the latter becoming the principal one after the Japanese obtained control of the Sunda Strait early in 1942, being approximately 3,000 miles shorter than the route via Cape Horn.

The practical difficulties preventing the Allies from stopping this traffic were great. Intelligence regarding the arrival or departure of ships in the Far East was non-existent and though information about shipping at Bordeaux, which was the usual European terminus, was more satisfactory in that it could generally be ascertained by reconnaissance that some ship had arrived or that another was no longer in the port, yet reports of actual dates and times of departure of outward bound blockade runners were not obtainable. A system known as ' Checkmate ' was instituted on the East Indies and South Atlantic Stations for the purpose of enabling warships to obtain quick corroboration of the bona fides of suspicious merchant ships. Towards the end of May 1943 this was extended, and an organisation was set up at the Admiralty to deal with ' Checkmate ' signals from any part of the world.[2]

The only possible points of interception in the Pacific and Far East were the Sunda Strait and the Malacca Strait, the latter of which the Japanese opened to blockade runners in March 1942. Blockade runners in these areas could only be attacked by submarine. The Sunda Strait was in the American sphere of responsibility, and there on 12th October 1942 a U.S. submarine torpedoed the blockade runner *Regensburg*. She beached herself, however, on the coast of Sumatra and was repaired by the Japanese at Singapore. Despite the Japanese lack of vigilance, which shocked the master of more than one German ship on arrival at the Sunda Strait from Europe, no other sinkings occurred in the Strait. The density of traffic there was low and the Americans during the early part of the war employed their submarines in more important areas. Later, when more American submarines became available, blockade running in surface ships had greatly diminished and was coming to an end. Though the Allies sank at least 20 enemy ships in the Malacca Strait during the war, no blockade runner was amongst them.

Of the Axis ships in Japan on the outbreak of the war in Europe eight German and three Italians reached Europe safely between April 1941 and May 1942.[3] Two were sunk in the Atlantic, the *Elbe* by aircraft from the *Eagle* on 6th June

---

[1] According to a German report (N.I.D. 3879/46) the following ships were so engaged. Date when taken on charter by Japan is given in brackets, *Mosel* (November 1942), *Winnetou* (October 1942), *Havelland*, *Rhakotis* (*see* Section 73), *Bogota* (October 1942 to May 1943, then under German flag again), *Spreewald* (July–September 1941, then as blockade runner to Europe), *Kulmerland* (before being used as blockade runner to Europe), *Elsa Essberger* (same), *Havenstein* (July 1941), *R. C. Rickmers* (spring 1941), *Ursula Rickmers* (August 1941. Under German flag again February 1944), *Quito* (1942 for short period).

[2] Admiralty Tel. 241910B, May 1942, *see* Appendix S.

[3] German : *Ermland, Regensburg, Anneliese Essberger, Burgenland, Elsa Essberger, Osorno, Rio Grande, Portland ;* Italian : *Cortellazo, Pietro Orsoleo, Fusiyama.*

111

1941, and the *Spreewald* accidentally by *U.333* on 31st January 1942. The *Odenwald* was captured in the Atlantic, and the *Ramses* turned back to Japan. During the blockade runner season 1941–1942 five German ships left Europe and arrived safely in Japan. The first was the *Rio Grande*, which sailed from Europe on 17th September 1941. The *Dresden* arrived at Yokohama on 23rd June 1942 with guns for arming German merchantmen in Japan, and sailed again from Saigon on 8th September in that year. The *Tannenfels* sailed from Europe on 16th March 1942 and also arrived in Yokohama on 23rd June. The *Regensburg* returned from Europe, reaching Yokohama on 7th July 1942. The S.S. *Speybank*, renamed by the Germans *Doggerbank*, after laying mines off Capetown in March 1942 and Agulhas Bank in the following month, made her way into the Indian Ocean in the summer of 1942, and on 31st July passed through the Sunda Strait and anchored in Tandjong Priok next day. Her arrival was unexpected. No patrol boats of any kind were met on entering the Strait, and a lighthouse to which she flashed did not answer. On 19th August the *Doggerbank* arrived in Yokohama, where she handed over to the Japanese the remainder of the mines and torpedoes she carried after German specialists had shown the Japanese the working of them. These five ships brought 32,540 tons of cargo, principally engines and engine parts, commercial goods, chemical products and potash.

During the second blockade running period, from August 1942 to May 1943, a programme was arranged under which Germany was to receive from Japan 140,000 tons of dry goods and 70,000 tons of liquid edible fats. Allied counter-measures disrupted this programme, and only 29,600 tons reached Germany. Six ships out of 17 which sailed, got through successfully. These were, the *Tannenfels*, the *Kulmerland* (which had been in Far Eastern waters for over two years), the *Munsterland*, *Elsa Essberger*, *Dresden* and the Italian *Pietro Orsoleo*. Four ships were recalled to Japan.[1] Seven were sunk : the *Rhakotis* as already noticed (Section 73), the tanker *Hohenfriedberg*, the *Karin*, *Irene*,[2] the *Regensburg* and the *Doggerbank* were sunk in the Atlantic. The latter before sailing from Japan, had her original character as a merchant ship restored ; she left Batavia for Europe on 15th January 1943 after taking on board at Yokohama, Kobe and Singapore a cargo of 2,000 tons of crude rubber, 1,854 tons of coco-nut oil and 1,000 tons of sebacic acid for Germany. Entering the Indian Ocean through Sunda Strait she proceeded on a southerly course until meeting what the Master considered to be the Allied convoy track from Australia to the Cape. He followed this and passed close around the Cape, instead of taking the route prescribed by Berlin, which he considered dangerous. On the night 3rd/4th March 1943 the ship was sunk in error by the German submarine *U.43* (the second Axis ship to be sunk thus), 600 miles south-west of the Azores. Only one man was saved, after 26 days spent adrift in a boat, during which time he stated that he had nothing to eat except two flying fish. The former Dutch vessel *Kota Nopan*, renamed by the Germans *Karin* sailed from Singapore for Europe on 4th February with a cargo which, in addition to a large quantity of rubber, included also 2,000 tons of tin, loaded partly at Penang and partly at Singapore. The ship made her way into the Indian Ocean through the Malacca Strait, this route being chosen on account of the recent torpedoing of the *Regensburg* in Sunda Strait. When approaching the Cape of Good Hope the *Karin* received warning of a convoy to the southward of her course, bound from the Cape to Australia. She, therefore, steamed on an approximately opposite course and could not turn south as soon as intended,

---

[1] *Rossbach* (Tanker), *Weserland, Burgenland, Rio Grande.*
[2] Ex-Norwegian *Silvaplana.*

with the result that she came within 200 miles of Madagascar before clearing the convoy. She rounded the Cape successfully, but was sunk during March in the South Atlantic.

One of the ships which sailed from Japan during the 1942–1943 blockade runner season was sunk in the Indian Ocean. This was the *Ramses* which sailed for Europe from Kobe via Batavia. She was intercepted on 28th November 1942 in 23° 20′ S., 99° 13′ E. (about 700 miles south of the Cocos Islands), and scuttled herself, assisted by gun-fire from H.M.A.S. *Adelaide* and the Dutch anti-aircraft ship *Heemskerck* which were escorting Convoy O.W. 1. A dog, 78 Germans and a pig were taken on board, as well as ten Norwegian survivors of the S.S. *Aust* which had been sunk by *Raider 10* (*Thor*) on 20th May.

Amongst the 17 ships which left Europe for Japan during the 1942–1943 season the Italian *Cortelazzo*, believed to be carrying six months' supply of mercury for Japan, was intercepted and sunk 600 miles west of Cape Finisterre. The *Annelise Essberger* left Europe early in November 1922 for the Far East, but got no further than the Atlantic ' Narrows ' where she was intercepted on the 21st of the month and scuttled herself. The *Portland* which cleared the Bay of Biscay towards the end of March, was also sunk in the Narrows, on 13th April 1943. Since the width of the Atlantic at this point is only 100 miles less than the distance from Ireland to Newfoundland interception unless aided by sailing intelligence could but be considered highly fortuitous. Two ships, the *Elsa Essberger* and the *Himalaya*, turned back, but 15 reached the Far East successfully with 24,447 tons of cargo.[1] One of these, *Karin* which left La Pallice on 5th November, 1942, and proceeded via the Cape of Good Hope and Sunda Strait, dropped anchor at Tandjong Priok on 22nd December. She reported that the main entrance to the port was still blocked by sunken ships at that date and that vessels had to load from lighters outside the harbour. The *Karin* also stated that she passed through Sunda Strait unchallenged. Though about half her crew were German naval ratings she was a merchantman engaged in trade, unarmed and with none of the characteristics of a raider or regular supply ship. The *Karin* was, however, equipped to refuel submarines in emergency and to accommodate prisoners taken by raiders, secondary functions which she never exercised. One ship reached Japan from Las Palmas during the 1942–1943 season. This was the tanker *Charlotte Schliemann*, with a naval crew, which arrived at Yokohama in October 1942 and was employed as a submarine supply ship until sunk in the Indian Ocean on 12th February 1944 by the destroyer *Relentless* (Operation ' Canned ') in 23° 23′ S., 74° 37′ E. (about 960 miles east-south-east of Mauritius) after being sighted and reported by a Catalina on the previous day.[2]

The third blockade running period extended from July 1943 to February 1944. Only five ships were available in Japan, and the Germans sailed them from Batavia in two groups. Only one, the *Osorno*, carrying a cargo consisting of 3,944 tons of rubber and 1,288 tons of tin, arrived in the Gironde. The other four were all sunk or scuttled in the Atlantic.[3] No ships left Europe for the Far East, for the Germans considered the risk of breaking out to be too great.

---

[1] *Weserland, Uckermark* (tanker), *Brake* (tanker), *Burgenland, Rio Grande, Irene, Karin, Alsterufer, Pietro Orsoleo, Osorno, Charlotte Schliemann, Spicheren* (tanker), *Portland, Elsa Essberger, Himalaya.*

[2] The operation will be described in Volume IV of this history.

[3] *Alsterufer, Burgenland, Rio Grande, Weserland.*

On 12th January 1944 the Admiralty sent information that a possible blockade runner was proceeding from Japan to Europe via the Sunda Strait–Cape route[1] and Admiral Somerville organised a force to intercept the ship in an area to the south-east of Mauritius (Operation ' Thwart '). The *Newcastle* (flag of Rear-Admiral A. D. Read), *Kenya*, *Suffolk*, the escort carrier *Battler* (12 Swordfish and six Seafire aircraft), A.M.C. *Canton* (with Kingfisher aircraft), the destroyer *Nepal*, the frigate *Bann*, and three Catalinas from East Africa assembled at Mauritius and were organised in three forces, 62, 63 and 64, as follows :—

Force 62 (*Newcastle*, *Suffolk*, *Battler*, *Bann*) sailed from Mauritius between 19th and 21st January ; searched an area 900 miles south-east of the island from dawn on 22nd to dusk on 30th January.[2]

Force 62 (*Canton*) searched an area 750 miles to the south of Mauritius from 23rd to 30th January.

Force 64 (*Kenya*, *Nepal*) and Catalinas operating from Tombau Bay, Mauritius, searched an area to the south-eastward from 23rd to 30th January. No sign of the blockade runner was seen, and Admiral Somerville suspended the operation at dusk on 30th January as the weather had deteriorated and the *Battler's* air effort was by that time considerably extended, whilst the majority of the ships needed to refuel at Mauritius. They had steamed a distance of 15,000 miles, whilst the aircraft had flown 40,900 miles, and had searched an area equal to that of Germany (1939), France, Spain and Italy.

A further operation (' Sleuth ') to intercept a possible blockade runner from Japan to Europe was carried out during the following month in an area to the south-west of the Cocos Islands, merchant shipping on the Australian run being diverted to the westward clear of the area of operations. The *Illustrious* (flag of Rear-Admiral C. Moody, Rear-Admiral Eastern Fleet Aircraft Carriers) and *Gambia*, forming Force 66, with the *Rotherham* and *Tierk Hiddes* as A/S escort, sailed from Trincomalee on 22nd February to the southward. The A/S escort was detached on the 24th on reaching latitude 2° S. and returned to Trincomalee. The Cocos area was reached two days later and daily air searches began to the south-westward of the islands. On the 28th further information indicated that the enemy could not reach the area for some days, and as the *Gambia* needed fuel and the *Illustrious* would have to leave on 1st March, to refuel, the Commander-in-Chief, Eastern Fleet, ordered these ships to return to port, the former to Fremantle and the latter to Trincomalee. The *Sussex*, which had joined the force on 28th February remained in the area carrying out daily search, until 6th March, when shortage of fuel made it necessary for her to withdraw to Fremantle. The operation was without result, nothing being sighted.[3]

Germany abandoned blockade running by surface ships early in 1944. Between 1941 and 1944 some 21 ships sailed from Biscay, of which 15 reached the Far East ; whilst of 36 or 37 ships which sailed from the Far East, only 16 or 17 reached Europe. The losses were too high to be borne, and the report

---

[1] It is uncertain to which of the five blockade runners that sailed from Japan about this time, the Admiralty's information referred.

[2] The *Suffolk* and *Bann* did not join the search until the 24th.

[3] It was decided, at the time when Operation ' Sleuth ' was planned to carry out an operation (' Covered ') on similar lines to Operation ' Thwart ' to the south-east of Mauritius, in the event of Operation ' Sleuth ' being unsuccessful. This resulted in the sinking of the German tanker *Brake* whilst engaged in refuelling U-boats. The operation will be dealt with in Volume IV of this History.

of the German Special Staff for Economic and Commercial Warfare on blockade running in 1943 indicated that traffic by surface ships was to be discontinued in favour of submarines.

76

Most of the sinkings, as we have seen, took place outside the Indian Ocean, for during the greater part of 1943 the status of the Eastern Fleet was little more than a trade protection force. The heavy and widespread calls on our resources not only precluded building up the Fleet, but compelled the Admiralty to use the East Indies as a source of reinforcement for more hard-pressed areas. The containing effect on the Japanese fleet of the operations in the Solomons, where the Americans opened their offensive in August 1942, and the naval losses suffered by the enemy were considered to rule out for the time being any further raids by enemy carriers or modern cruisers in the Bay of Bengal.[1] Nevertheless, Admiral Somerville was taking no chances, and when the 9th Australian Division sailed from Suez on 1st February 1943, to return to Australia, in Convoy ' Pamphlet ' made up of five of the greatest liners afloat, the *Queen Mary, Aquitania, Ile de France, Nieuw Amsterdam* and the A.M.C. *Queen of Bermuda*, in addition to being given air cover during their approach to Addu Atoll for refuelling and after their departure, they were both escorted and were also given cover in the Indian Ocean by Force ' A ' of the Eastern Fleet consisting of the *Warspite, Resolution, Revenge, Mauritius* and six destroyers. The escort was joined by the *Gambia* en route, and when nearing Australia was reinforced by the Dutch cruiser *Tromp*, the anti-aircraft cruiser *Heemskerck* and the destroyers *Van Galen* and *Tierk Hiddes*. The three latter ships were amongst those that escaped to Britain when Germany attacked Holland and were sent out from British home waters to join the Eastern Fleet after the outbreak of war with Japan.[2]

The year 1943 witnessed a number of withdrawals of ships for operations in more active areas, which reduced the Eastern Fleet temporarily below the strength even of a trade protection force. The *Illustrious* was withdrawn to the United Kingdom in January 1943 to be brought up to date for prospective operations in northern waters. No carrier was available for relief, and the risk of having none with the Eastern Fleet until the arrival in the spring of the air supply and repair ship *Unicorn*, which was capable of rapid conversion to an operational carrier for 35 aircraft, was accepted. Meanwhile, the Eastern Fleet was confined to the west side of the Indian Ocean, as both the Commander-in-Chief and the Admiralty were of one mind that it was undesirable for it to operate in the Ceylon area without an aircraft carrier. However, the Fleet soon ceased to exist temporarily for all practical purposes. Admiral Somerville's flagship, the *Warspite*, and the 6-in. cruiser *Mauritius* were withdrawn to take part in the invasion of Sicily, three sloops and eight Royal Australian Navy *Bathurst* class minesweepers being also taken for the same operation. No less than 48 ships were detached from the Eastern Fleet for service in the Mediterranean between April and July, including, in addition to the *Mauritius* and eight Bathursts, the *Raider* and five sloops. At the end of 1942 the Commander-in-Chief, Mediterranean, had also asked for reliefs for his destroyers working from Aden, but these Admiral Somerville could not supply ; seven of his 14 destroyers were on the South Atlantic Station, three were refitting, and only four were under his own hand, two of which were needed to escort ships in and out of Kilindini.

---

[1] Tel. Admiralty 1758A/10/11/42 to F.O.C.R.I.N., Commander-in-Chief, E.F.

[2] Other Dutch ships which joined the Eastern Fleet were the destroyer *Isaac Sweers* (February 1942), *021, 025, 024* (1943).

Other calls were made on the Fleet for help to counter the submarine menace in the South Atlantic Station. The Commander-in-Chief, Eastern Fleet, considered that though single enemy submarines could, and undoubtedly would, continue to operate throughout the Indian Ocean the Japanese threat was unlikely to be as great a menace as the danger that had arisen with the appearance of German U-boats in South African waters and in the southern approaches to the Mozambique Channel. Recent events had shown that long-range German submarines, refuelled from supply vessels could operate in those waters and it was thought probable they would return. A redistribution of A/S forces was therefore undertaken during January 1943 to meet the threat. Two destroyers were detached from the Eastern Fleet to the South Atlantic in addition to four corvettes already lent, and a force of 13 Catalinas was moved south. Eight months earlier in June 1942 when the Japanese launched their submarine offensive in the Mozambique Channel the all too few aircraft which could be spared for transfer from Ceylon had been handicapped by lack of bases and could only give very limited cover. Now the bases of Madagascar were at our disposal and complete air cover of the whole of the Mozambique Channel was considered to be possible.

Within a few weeks Admiral Somerville's prediction of renewed submarine activity in South African waters came true. On the night 3rd/4th March 1943 an attack was made on Convoy DN 21 (Durban northward and westward) escorted by the corvette *Nigella*, the A/S whaler *Sondra* and A/S trawler *Viviana*, about a hundred miles south of Durban and six ships were torpedoed. The sloop *Falmouth*, the four remaining corvettes, and every available destroyer of the Eastern Fleet were lent to the South Atlantic Command to meet the menace. Convoy was withdrawn from ships in the northern Indian Ocean, A/S escort being confined to local areas such as the entrance to the Persian Gulf (from which now the 'Insect' class gunboats were withdrawn to the Eastern Mediterranean), off Bombay and Colombo.

At the beginning of the year, before these detachments were made to the South Atlantic, the anti-submarine measures in force in the Indian Ocean included the running of regular escorted convoys in and out of the Persian Gulf to and from Aden and Bombay; outbound shipping to Australia and South Africa was sailed in convoy and dispersed well to seaward of the Gulf of Kutch; Indian coastal traffic proceeded up and down the east coast in escorted convoys or small escorted groups; and local anti-submarine escorts were provided for important ships entering and leaving the Gulf of Aden direct from the south from certain larger ports such as Kilindini, Colombo, Bombay and Diego Suarez. By July, detachments to the Mediterranean, the South Atlantic and Western Australia had reduced convoy escorts to little more than nominal proportions, and the number of ships in each convoy had to be reduced to conform more nearly to the number of escort vessels available, with consequent increase of unescorted ships. Local anti-submarine escort, other than by air, could be provided only for troop transports and a few specially valuable ships. The Commander-in-Chief, pointed out that the re-opening of the Mediterranean, where the first convoys went through in May 1943, would increase the importance and volume of Aden, Bombay and Colombo traffic to an extent which would reduce escort throughout its passage, whilst he also wished to institute convoy in the Mozambique Channel, and was anxious about the heavy and valuable traffic from Australia to India and the Persian Gulf.[1] The elimination of the

---

[1] Commander-in-Chief E.F.211033Z, July 1943 to Admiralty.

enemy submarine threat on the South Atlantic Station made more escort vessels available in the Indian Ocean in September; whilst the conclusion of the campaign in Sicily in August, followed by the signing of an Armistice with Italy on 3rd September enabled the Admiralty to take steps to reinforce the escort vessels of the Eastern Fleet. Arrangements were made to return the 12 escort vessels lent to the Mediterranean; five coastguard cutters were ordered out from home; and the first seven corvettes of new construction were ordered to be sailed for the fleet as soon as they were ready for service.

78

These measures, though holding hope for the future, were no help in the emergency which arose in May 1943, when an offensive by five German submarines developed in the Mozambique Channel and south and east of Madagascar. Only two of the 19 Eastern Fleet destroyers were at Admiral Somerville's disposal. In an area 1,000 miles square there were no more than 10 anti-submarine vessels and 22 flying boats. The 19 A/S vessels in the northern Indian Ocean were pooled (Arabian Bengal Ceylon Escort Force) to facilitate operation and administration, and divided into a Bombay group and a Colombo group. The 24 vessels of the Coastal Anti-Submarine Force were organised in three groups, East and West Coasts of India and Hormuz respectively.

Japanese submarines were also showing renewed activity. The Japanese in May had informed the Germans that they intended to intensify operations against Allied communications. Within a month they were active in the Gulf of Oman and off the shores of Arabia in the neighbourhood of Masirah Island (off the coast, about 140 miles south-west of Ras-el-Hadd), where three vessels were sunk. They also operated to the south-east of Ceylon and to the west of Addu Atoll and Diego Garcia, where one ship was sunk in May, two in June, and one in July. In the case of the first the Dutch freighter *Berakit* (6,608 tons), the master was taken prisoner, this being the first recorded occasion of a Japanese submarine taking prisoner a member of the crew of one of her victims, though German and Italian U-boats often did so. A submarine entered the Gulf of Oman about the 22nd or 23rd June, and after sinking the tanker *British Venture* (4,696 tons) sank the S.S. *Dah Pu* (1,974 tons) in Muscat harbour on the 24th. For some time it was considered, from the position of the ship, that she was sunk by internal explosion or sabotage, but the finding of remnants of a Japanese torpedo near the wreck was considered to prove that a submarine was responsible.

During May and June German U-boats operating in South African waters continued, from time to time, to enter the East Indies Station. One merchant vessel was sunk in the southern approaches to the Mozambique Channel in May. In June 1943 Italian submarines (blockade runners) entered the Indian Ocean. The German submarines *U.177*, *U.178*, *U.179*, *U.181*, *U.198*, which were operating off the South African coast, moved eastward after sinking the S.S. *Hopetarn* (5,231 tons) on 29th May in 30° 50′ S., 39° 32′ E. On 19th June a U-boat (probably *U.178* which was carrying a cargo to Japan) was plotted by D.F. as having moved to a position south of Madagascar. As there was no D.F. or other indication that the other U-boats known to be in the area were proceeding homeward this gave some reason to suppose that the whole force might have moved to the relatively calm weather area to the south-east of Madagascar to refuel and replenish from a supply ship or supply U-boat before recommencing operations. On 24th June the Admiralty had information that the German tanker *Charlotte Schliemann*, which arrived at Surabaya from the Atlantic on 7th June, was due to refuel Axis submarines in the Indian Ocean towards the end of June in one of three alternative positions 360 or 800 miles to the southward of Madagascar or 500 miles east of the first position. Acting on Admiralty instructions, Admiral Somerville organised a sweep of the area (Operation ' Player ') from the 24th to 30th June, using the *Suffolk, Newcastle*, and the destroyers *Relentless, Nizam* and *Racehorse* with an oiler, whilst Catalinas from the South Atlantic Station made an extensive search. The only result was an A.S.V. contact of a possible U-boat in 32° 54' S., 50° 06' E. on the 29th, and though we now know that *U.178* (Commander W. Dommes) refuelled from the *Charlotte Schliemann* in approximately 34° 30' S., 46° 30' E. he was not seen. On the 29th, too, a German U-boat was plotted by D.F. to be within 50 miles of position 29° 00' S., 50° 00' E. No actual contact was made, however, with any supply vessel or U-boat, and the search was abandoned on 30th June. The total tonnage lost in the Indian Ocean in that month was 67,000.

On 1st July, a U-boat was plotted by D.F. to be within a hundred miles of 21° 00' S., 60° 00' E. This tended to confirm the supposition that the German submarines after replenishment might operate to the eastward of Madagascar in order to avoid the increased air cover given to shipping inshore, and the increasingly bad weather off shore, along the South African coast. This surmise was borne out in part, for three vessels were sunk and one attacked unsuccessfully south of Madagascar and four were sunk east of the Island, between 27th June and 29th July. Eight vessels were sunk in the Mozambique Channel during July, five of them by *U.178*.[1] Total sinkings during the month rose to 89,000 tons and the Commander-in-Chief Eastern Fleet asked for the return of twelve escort vessels in the Mediterranean for use in the Arabian Sea. He also requested ten additional corvettes for escort duties in the Mozambique Channel and twelve more frigates or corvettes to be used on the Aden–Colombo route. After refuelling and revictualling south of the Cape of Good Hope from an Italian blockade running submarine, later named *U.It.23, U.178* proceeded in company with the Italian to Sabang, and after repairs at Penang and Singapore sailed in December 1943 for Bordeaux. The remaining German U-boats continued active operations in the Mozambique Channel and the waters south and east of Madagascar during August, gradually withdrawing to Penang as the month progressed. During the month they sank six vessels totalling 37,954 tons, one vessel being sunk in convoy.[2] One of their number *U.197* was destroyed by Catalinas N/265 and C/259 in the southern part of the Mozambique Channel on 20th August, in 28° 40' S., 42° 36' E.

U.178 which committed such depredations in the Mozambique Channel was not the first German submarine to reach the Far East, for *U.511* had arrived at Penang a month earlier, in July 1943. These arrivals were the result of a somewhat sudden offer which Japan had made about December 1942 to Germany and Italy. She was willing to place at their disposal a submarine base, either at Penang, Sabang or a port in the Andaman Islands, together with the fuel supplies necessary for a campaign. Early in 1943 the Germans, finding

---

[1] Greek S.S. *Michael Livanos* (4,774 tons) and Norwegian S.S. *Breiviken* (2,669 tons) a straggler from Convoy D.N.50, sunk in the south part of the Channel on 4th July ; Greek S.S. *Mary Livanos* (4,771 tons) in the Narrows 11th July ; American S.S. *Robert Bacon* (7,191 tons) south-east of Point Mozambique on 14th July and the S.S. *City of Canton* (6,692 tons) in the north part of the Channel on the 16th.

[2] The S.S. *City of Oran* (7,232 tons) sunk 2nd August in 13° 45' S., 41° 16' E. by *U.752*, from Convoy C.B.1, escorted by the *Falmouth*.

that the Japanese submarine campaign in the Indian Ocean was not having the effect they hoped for, decided to enter the area themselves, and accepted the offer of a base. Sabang had no dock facilities or workshops, but at Penang the Japanese workshops carried out all normal repair work for the Germans, though docking had to be done at Singapore. The Germans report that repairs were slow but well done. Delays were caused by the necessity of obtaining all materials from Japan. The dockyard could just maintain five German and two or three Japanese submarines. Surabaya and Tanjong Priok (called by the Germans Jakarta or Djarkarta) were also used by the Germans. Co-operation with the Japanese was not entirely satisfactory. The Japanese Navy was helpful but the Army was not co-operative. The Japanese authorities would not until late 1943 agree to the setting up of a German wireless station, and the method of communication used was through the German embassy at Tokyo, orders for the Germans coming from Admiral Wenniker, the Chief German Liaison Officer. The Germans at Penang were obliged to rely for intelligence on a few personal contacts : they had no intelligence service of their own. There was no form of harbour defence against submarines and surface craft, and no anti-submarine organisation or vessels. Torpedo stocks were derived from German armed merchant cruisers and blockade runners. Some of the torpedoes had deteriorated due to the climate, causing frequent failures ; and at the beginning of 1944 two torpedo transport U-boats, *U.1562* and *U.1059* sailed from Europe for the Far East with replenishments. German U-boats operated in the same areas as Japanese, and to avoid clashes each were forbidden to attack submarines and the Japanese also undertook that the aircraft they carried would not attack submarines.

79

Times, Z — 4

At the end of June 1943, 11 German U-boats, known as Group ' Monsun ' sailed from Europe for the Indian Ocean. Six of them were sunk on the way out, amongst them being two tankers *U.462* and *U.487*.[1] The survivors fuelled from *U.155* and *U.156*, 600 miles west-north-west of Cape Verde between 21st and 27th July.

On 11th September, the five surviving German submarines of the ' Monsun ' group met together 450 miles south of Mauritius where they refuelled from the *Brake* which had been sent from Penang. They then proceeded to operate against shipping in the Indian Ocean, Gulf of Aden and the Arabian Sea. Despite the increased number of A/S vessels becoming available the wide dispersal of the patrol areas of the enemy submarines presented a problem. The focal points of Allied shipping, such as the mouth of the Red Sea, the Mozambique Channel and the One and a Half Degree Channel, might be as much as 1,500 miles apart ; and there were few land bases in the centre of the Indian Ocean at which flying boats or ships could refuel. Moreover, Pacific weather normally favours the submarine as against the aircraft. Generally speaking, either the visibility is so good that the submarine can sight the aircraft first, or visibility is very poor.

To meet the threat, the Commander-in-Chief decided to put as many ships as possible into convoy, and to cover such shipping as still had to proceed independently by the establishment of approach positions outside focal areas,

---

[1] The six U-boats sunk were *U.514* (by R.A.F. 8th July 1943), *U.506* (by U.S. Liberator 12th July 1943), *U.487* (by aircraft from U.S.S. *Core* 13th July 1943), *U.160* and *U.509* (by aircraft from U.S.S. *Santee* 14th July 1943 and 15th July 1943), *U.462* (by R.A.F. 30th July 1943).

air patrols being provided to cover the route between the approach position and the port. This policy necessitated the institution of regular convoys for ships of 9–13 knots speed between Aden and Bombay direct (B.A., A.B.) (1st October) and Colombo and Bombay (B.M., M.B.) (9th October) and the provision of A/S units for these convoys. The reduction of the U-boat threat in the Mozambique Channel made A/S vessels available during September for escort of convoys further north, from Durban to Aden (D.K.A., A.K.D.). Increased escorts had also to be provided for the convoys in and out of the Persian Gulf (P.A., A.P. ; P.B., B.P.). Owing to increased U-boat activity on the west coast of India vessels had to be withdrawn from the east coast to increase the number of escorts for the B.M. and M.B. convoys. More than half the 98 Catalina flying boats on the East Indies Station worked in the Western and Southern areas.[1] A detachment of eight from the former area operated in South Africa, and aircraft were detached to advanced bases and operated to meet the U-boat threat in the Mozambique Channel and south and east of Madagascar. In the southern area, aircraft, including a detachment of Catalinas from Mombasa and Catalina amphibians from Ceylon operated mainly to the eastward of Durban ; they were aided by aircraft of the S.A.A.F.

It quickly became apparent that the German submarines were penetrating much more deeply into the East Indies Station than before, whilst the Japanese entered the Mozambique Channel once more after a long absence. The Germans soon moved north and by October were operating in the Gulf of Oman, off the east coast of Africa and the west coast of India, and in the Maldives and Ceylon area. Four of them moved at the end of October to Penang. They had done less damage than usual and lost one of their number, *U.533*, sunk 16th October in the Gulf of Oman in 25° 28′ N., 56° 50′ E. by Bisley aircraft E/244 and H/244 whilst on patrol. This submarine had left Lorient on 6th July and proceeded into the Indian Ocean passing well south of the Cape of Good Hope. After fuelling from the German tanker *Brake* she was ordered to the Persian Gulf in the hope of intercepting tankers coming down from Abadan. Reaching the Gulf of Oman on 6th October, she spent ten fruitless days. She failed until too late to sight the aircraft which attacked her. In her crash-dive she had reached a depth of 100 feet when the first of four depth charges dropped at her, exploded. The only survivor was a torpedo rating who was blown to the surface and swam for 28 hours before reaching land on the Arabian coast at Khor Fakkan, whence he was rescued by H.M.I.S. *Hiravati*.

East Longitude Dates

Twenty-one ships of 125,625 tons were sunk during the period September to December 1943, a great reduction on the figures for the Spring (when the offensive began) and Summer. Four convoys were attacked. At 0537 Z–3 on 5th October Convoy A.P.47, consisting of nine ships escorted by the minesweepers *Bengal* and *Burnie*,[2] off the Arabian coast in position 14° 20′ N., 50° 47′ E., saw the tracks of four torpedoes apparently fired from long range from the starboard quarter of the convoy. The Norwegian tanker *Anna Knudsen* (9,095 tons) was hit forward by one torpedo but remained afloat and reached Aden on the 7th. The *Burnie* carried out an attack, which was unsuccessful and search of the area failed to establish asdic contact.

---

[1] The Southern Area included the Cape and Mozambique Channel as far north as 25° S. The Western Area included the remainder of the east coast of Africa, Madagascar, Seychelles and Mauritius. The Northern Area included approaches to Aden and Persian Gulf and Arabian Sea north of 10° N. The Eastern Area included Ceylon and the Indian coast except that part in the Northern Area (M.053076/43).

[2] Manned by R.A.N.

Convoy M.B.50, the first Bombay to Colombo convoy, consisting of nine ships escorted by the Indian minesweeper *Carnatic*, was attacked on the night 11th/12th October off Cochin the SS. *Jalabala* (3,610 tons), the leading ship of the port column, being torpedoed on the port side at 0223 Z–5. H.M.I.S. *Carnatic*, whose Asdic transmitting set was giving trouble, was before the attack zigzagging 40° each side of the mean course and 3,000 yards ahead of the convoy. She closed the convoy and dropped depth-charges. A quick search of the area was made, but no contact was obtained. The *Jalabala* sank in 11° 40′ N., 75° 19′ E.

At 2230 Z–5 on 20th October the tanker *British Purpose* (5,845 tons), one of the 14 ships in Convoy B.M.71 from Colombo to Bombay escorted by the *Carnatic*, the A/S–M/S Trawler *Baroda* and the sloop *Shoreham*, was struck by a torpedo in the bows and badly damaged in the Calicut area, in 11° 49′ N., 74° 54′ E. The ship managed, however, to make Cochin under her own power where the cargo was discharged and temporary repairs carried out. Contact was not made with the enemy submarine.

In November, air escorts were given to convoys. There were no attacks on convoys in that month, though in the previous month three out of the nine ships sunk or damaged were attacked in convoy.[1] For more than two months there were no further attacks on convoys. On the afternoon of 23rd December Convoy J.C.30 which left Colombo on the 19th for Vizagapatam escorted by the minesweepers *Ipswich* and *Orissa*, was attacked to the southward of Madras and the British SS. *Peshawur* (7,934 tons) was torpedoed, and sank later in 11° 11′ N., 80° 11′ E. Aircraft had reported a submarine near this position at 1000 that day, and the destroyers *Quality* and *Quiberon* sailed from Trincomalee to hunt, with air cooperation, but no result was reported.

80

The efficiency of enemy submarine attacks increased in 1943 over the previous year.

Percentage of ships sunk, damaged or escaped of total number attacked
(attacks reported to British naval authorities)

	1942	1943
Sunk	54 = 59·5 per cent.	50 = 65·8 per cent.
Damaged	4 = 4·5 per cent.	8 = 10·5 per cent.
Escaped	33 = 36·0 per cent.	18 = 23·7 per cent.

Total number of ships attacked in 1942, 91 ; in 1943, 76.

Though fewer ships were attacked, fewer escaped undamaged. The increase in efficiency was attributed by the Commander-in-Chief to the arrival of German submarines in the Indian Ocean. There was a great increase in the percentage of ships attacked by night or in twilight with corresponding decrease in the number attacked by day.[2] The torpedo gained in popularity at the expense of

---

[1] The total number of ships involved, namely nine, is too small to form a firm indication of German U-boat doctrine, but it is significant that experience in the Atlantic was similar, *i.e.* that U-boats disliked attacking convoys with air cover. A Catalina escorting convoy M.B.53 on 3rd November attacked a submarine on the surface but there is no record that the submarine attacked the convoy.

[2] This may have resulted in unsuccessful attacks not being reported.

121

the gun.[1] The Commander-in-Chief attributed this almost entirely to the increase in the number of ships adequately armed, practically every ship operating in the theatre being so armed by the end of 1943. Attacks recorded in 1942 numbered 91. Only one ship was attacked in convoy. During 1943 out of 76 vessels attacked six, that is 7·9 per cent., were in convoy. In no case was more than one vessel lost out of a convoy attacked. The Commander-in-Chief reported that the institution of the convoy system undoubtedly contributed greatly to reducing the total number of attacks during 1943.

Instances of atrocity by Japanese submarine commanders began to come to light. The Norwegian m.s. *Scotia* (9,972 tons) on passage from Bahrein to Melbourne with a full cargo of 13,800 tons of Navy diesel oil was torpedoed by a Japanese submarine at 1725 ship's time on 27th November, 300 miles south-west of Addu Atoll in 03° 00′ S., 69° 03′ E. and began to sink. After the crew were in the boats, the submarine surfaced took the Captain prisoner and machine-gunned the men in the lifeboat and the chief engineer who was alone on a raft near by and disclosed his position by flashing a torch. One able seaman dived into the sea and survived ; the remaining boats and rafts were sighted by searching Catalinas and the survivors picked up by the *Okapi* on 29th and 30th November. The s.s. *Daisy Moller* (4,087 tons), on passage from Colombo to Chittagong, was torpedoed at 0920 Z–5 on 14th December in 16° 21′ N., 82° 13′ E. and sank rapidly. All boats got away from the ship before she sank. The submarine surfaced, rammed the boats and machine-gunned the water over a wide area. Only 16 survivors succeeded in making land five days later out of a total complement of 69 crew and two passengers. Atrocities were to become commonplace during 1944 and created a serious problem.[2]

81

On 30th November the Admiralty asked the Commander-in-Chief, Eastern Fleet to make such relaxations in the convoy system as the submarine situation permitted from time to time, with the dual object of expediting the turn round of shipping generally, and releasing faster ships from convoys in which, owing to the slow convoy speed, they were difficult to handle. Admiral Somerville had just decided (27th November) to institute convoy between Calcutta and Colombo, as the enemy submarine threat in the Bay of Bengal appeared to be increasing ; the first convoy, J.C.8 left Colombo on 3rd December and C.J.8 Calcutta on the 8th.[3] He felt unable to release any ships from standard orders for convoys either in the Gulf of Aden or on the east coast of India, though he proposed to release ships of higher speeds when enemy submarine activity permitted. Meanwhile he was releasing ships of 13 knots and above from the Persian Gulf–Bombay (P.B./B.P.), Colombo–Bombay (M.B./B.M.) and the Durban–Kilindini (D.K./K.D.) portions of the Durban–Kilindini–Aden (D.K.A./A.K.D.) convoys ; they would be routed from port to port on straggler's routes. These measures did not satisfy the Admiralty, who were of the opinion that the existing shipping situation justified the acceptance of some risks to expedite turn round. In each month, under the existing system, some 1,800 ship-days were being lost in insuring against ' relatively modest and local threats.' In general, they considered the system should now be made more elastic : convoys should be operated only on routes actually or potentially threatened, escorts

---

[1] Perhaps in consequence of the increased number of ships sailing in convoy, *i.e.* protected by A/S vessels.

[2] *See* Volume IV of this History.   [3] Convoy numbers 1–7 were not used.

thus released from other routes operating wherever as practicable as hunting groups in areas of known probability.[1] In response, Admiral Somerville decided to discontinue convoys from 13th December, with the exception of those between Bombay–Colombo and Colombo–Calcutta, though on the latter run ships of 13 knots speed and over would proceed independently. Personnel and combined operations ships would continue to be sailed in convoy and where possible, shipping from Aden was to be escorted clear of the Gulf.

---

[1] In the light of experience in the Atlantic the view expressed that ship days were being lost in insuring against ' relatively modest and local threats ' may be questioned. Such threats had caused many losses when ships were sailed independently. This in turn resulted in a higher loss rate and a greater adverse effect upon shipping delivery rates than if the ships had been in convoy.

Experience had also shown that ' hunting groups in areas of known probability ' achieved little success. The subject is fully discussed in Volume I of the Naval Staff History *The Defeat of the Enemy Attack on Shipping*.

CHAPTER X

Campaign in New Guinea :

Reconquest of Papua

(*See* Plan 14)

82

WHILST in the Indian Ocean we were engaged at that date (1943) almost exclusively in protecting our shipping, in the adjacent South-West Pacific Ocean the Allies were still engaged in a series of amphibious operations which began in August 1942. The conquest of Guadalcanal had completed the first of the three tasks comprising the offensive plan for the reduction of Rabaul. Plans for the continuation of the advance under General MacArthur in the South-West Pacific Area (Tasks 2 and 3) were based upon the progressive forward movement of air echelons culminating in the isolation of Rabaul prior to assault. Two drives were to be made. One task force was to advance along the north coast of New Guinea securing in succession Salamoa–Lae–Madang–Wewak together with Gasmata, Cape Gloucester and Talasea in New Britain and Lorungau (Manus) in the Admiralty Islands ; whilst the other worked through the Solomon Islands and New Ireland to seize Faisi–Kieta–Buka and Kavieng. Both task forces were to cooperate in the capture of Rabaul. The speed of advance and timing of the various operations were governed by the availability of shipping and the speed of development of bases and airfields necessary to ensure air superiority. General MacArthur transferred his headquarters from Melbourne to Brisbane, to be near the headquarters of the Allied Air Forces and Allied Naval Forces and Advanced Land Headquarters which dealt with operational matters.

New Guinea was divided politically into three parts. The western half was a Dutch possession ; the south-eastern portion, known as Papua, was a dependency of the Commonwealth ; whilst North-East New Guinea and the Bismarck Archipelago had been taken from Germany during the First World War and in 1921 were made an Australian Mandate. The island of New Guinea, one of the largest in the world, is mountainuous on its northern coast, and the south-eastern end is formed by the slopes of the Owen Stanley range terminating at East Cape. The southern part of this peninsula is completely encircled by mountain ranges, attaining a high altitude. The country on the northern side of the island is rich and has an abundant supply of water ; the rivers, though generally small, pass through wide plains extending for many miles, and covered with tall grass. To the southward, in the direction of Torres Strait, there is a vast alluvial plain, traversed by large rivers, and the coast hereabouts consists of low muddy shores covered with mangroves and dense forests of large trees. The tropical climate is bad. The shape of the island resembles some huge and horrid lizard-like denizen of the primeval slime ; and it was in primeval slime, amid clouds of malaria-bearing mosquitos that the troops fought, lived and slept, tortured by sores and ulcers, fed perforce on tinned food and often too little of that. The sickness rate was very high, and there were times when a brigade could not muster a battalion.

Land routes of communication at the beginning of the war were almost non-existent and because of the difficult country and heavy jungle were never developed to the point where they became of military importance. Consequently, the movements of both contestants were confined largely to amphibious advances along the north coast, and the various Japanese and later the Allied bases may be considered for all practical purposes as islands dependent for reinforcement and supply upon sea or air transport. Papua was only partially occupied by the enemy. In the south-west where the Allies had a base at Merauke (8° 22' S., 140° 13' E.),[1] the Japanese showed no activity until a late stage in the campaign, and Australian and Dutch troops maintained their positions. On the north coast, movement by sea was restricted by the navigational difficulties of the reef-strewn waters, which were very imperfectly surveyed, particularly in that part between Milne Bay and Dampier Strait, where the early fighting took place. Consequently, a survey was undertaken by the Royal Australian Navy, whilst the operations proceeded, under frequent attack. The difficulties of movement were enhanced by the shortage of the only craft suitable for working in those uncharted waters, such as landing craft and motor torpedo boats, almost the entire American output of landing craft in 1942 being required for the landings planned to take place in North Africa. Troops, equipment and stores carried by sea had usually to be transferred for landing into native canoes outside the extensive shore reefs.

The plan for the capture of the central and northern Solomons, New Guinea and the Bismarck Archipelago was not made until after Guadalcanal had been captured and the Japanese driven out of Papua. When in February 1942 General MacArthur, by President Roosevelt's orders, handed over the command in the Philippines to become Supreme Commander South-West Pacific Area, his directive from the Combined Chiefs of Staff included holding Australia, checking the enemy's advance along the Melanesian Barrier, protecting land, sea and air communications with the South-West Pacific, as well as maintaining the U.S. position in the Philippines.[2]

The Joint Chiefs of Staff in their directive issued on 28th March 1943 outlined a campaign in two phases. The first phase was divided into two parts. Initially, the north coast of New Guinea was to be occupied as far west as Cape d'Urville (approximately 1½° S., 138° E.). Secondly, an air base was to be established on the south-west coast of New Guinea, as a preliminary to seizure of the Aru Islands and possible occupation of the Tanimbar Islands ; these latter operations, however, were not proceeded with, for though the Japanese during 1943 reinforced south-west New Guinea and extended their establishments the Australian Air Force kept the region sufficiently in subjection to obviate the necessity of land operations. The second phase of the campaign comprised the capture of the Vogelkop area of New Guinea, including Waigeo Island, and was to be accomplished by seizing the Schouten Islands and Japen Islands on the north coast. Positions were to be established in McCluer Gulf and in Ambon before the seizure of the south and west part of Vogelkop. These operations

---

[1] *See* Section 94.   [2] General Marshall's First War Report.

too were not proceeded with. Indeed, the time table was only adhered to by making full use of the technique, which was later successfully employed by Admiral Nimitz in the Central Pacific, of by-passing enemy occupied positions not required by the Allies as bases for further advance.

Though the campaign in New Guinea, as fought, divided itself into two phases, this was not in the manner directed by the Joint Chiefs of Staff. There was first a period of slow and costly fighting against the main Japanese concentrations in the south-east of the island between Bogadjim and Buna. Since Allied naval power was lacking, land fighting and an expensive air effort had to take its place. Of the two years of the Allied offensive, eighteen months were spent in fighting to break the Japanese power in this relatively small area. The enemy were defeated in a series of three enveloping movements. The first of these ended in January 1943 when Buna fell to a combined Australian and American assault. There was then a long pause until mid-1943 when the advance was resumed in an enveloping movement around the next Japanese concentration at Lae and Salamoa. These two strongholds fell in September. In January–February 1944 the third and last envelopment began. The Americans landed at Saidor and the Australians pushed on from Finschafen, trapping all the Japanese forces between them. Rabaul was already threatened, for in December of the previous year, the Americans had crossed the straits and landed in New Britain. These movements closed the first phase of the New Guinea fighting. The second phase was more rapid. Ships and landing craft had become available and a series of sea-borne landings by the Allies eliminated Japanese bases or outflanked enemy concentrations, and by September 1944 carried General MacArthur's forces to Morotai in the Moluccas, where an air base was formed for the attack on the Philippines.

No major Allied naval forces were engaged in the New Guinea campaign subsequently to the Battle of the Coral Sea until a late stage when aircraft carrier forces from the adjacent South Pacific Area co-operated temporarily. In the absence of adequate charts of the north coast of the island and on account of its exposure to Japanese air attacks from their airfields in New Britain it was dangerous even for destroyers to operate there. By the time the Allies gathered sufficient strength to begin the second phase of the campaign the Japanese Fleet based at Rabaul and Truk had been so reduced by continual losses in the Solomons and by carrier-based aircraft attacks by the Pacific Ocean Area forces that it did not move to oppose the amphibious operations of General MacArthur's naval forces. The latter, which were later known as the Seventh Fleet, were the descendants of Admiral Leary's Anzac Force. They consisted at first of only two cruisers and six destroyers, in addition to local defence forces; for the Australian squadron of four cruisers, though detached for service in the South-West Pacific Area, operated under the Commander, South Pacific Area in the Solomons, until after the Battle of the Eastern Solomons at the end of August 1942.

In contrast to the Allied organisation which provided separate commands for the South Pacific and the South-West Pacific until 29th March 1943 when General MacArthur was given strategical control of further operations in both areas, the Japanese South-East Area Command and the Eighth Army, established at Rabaul, directed all operations in the South-East Area, namely east of the 140th meridian. Since it involved a direct threat to their bases at Rabaul and Truk, the Japanese soon came to consider the campaign in the Solomons more important than that in New Guinea, and consequently the greater proportion of their naval, air and surface strength was brought to bear in the Solomons.

In view of the Allied lack of amphibious force to support the army, the poor land communications, and the unsuitability of the area for naval surface activity, air power and air transport acquired a special importance in the campaign in New Guinea. Where in other countries a railway station would be found, in New Guinea there would be an airstrip.

Command of the Allied Air Forces South-West Pacific was taken over at the beginning of August 1942 from Lieutenant-General G. H. Brett who had been Deputy-Abdacom, by Major-General G. C. Kenney, Commander of the U.S. Fifth Air Force. Regarding the strength of the air forces of which he took command General Kenney wrote :

> ' On the books I had, in the United States part of the show, 245 fighters, 53 light bombers, 70 medium bombers, 62 heavy bombers, 36 transports, and 51 miscellaneous aircraft, or a total of 517.
>
> This didn't look too bad, until I found what the real story was. Of the 245 fighters, 170 were awaiting salvage or being overhauled at Eagle Farms. None of the light bombers were ready for combat, and only 37 mediums were in shape or had guns and bomb racks to go to war with. Of the 62 heavy bombers, 19 were being overhauled and rebuilt. There were 19 different types among the 36 transports and less than half of them were in commission. The 51 miscellaneous turned out to be light commercial or training types which could not be used in combat.
>
> The Australian Royal Air Force listed 22 squadrons, but most of these were equipped with training planes doing anti-submarine patrol off the coasts of Australia itself. Two fighter squadrons in New Guinea had a total of 40 planes, and four reconnaissance squadrons had a total of 30 aircraft.
>
> There was also a Dutch squadron of B–25s (medium bombers), supposed to be training at Canberra, but they were a long way from being ready for combat.
>
> All told I had about 150 American and 70 Australian aircraft, scattered from Darwin to Port Moresby and back to Mareeba (approximately 17° S., 145½° E.) and Townsville, with which to dispute the air with the Japanese. He probably had at least five times that number facing me and could get plenty more in a matter of a few days by flying them in from the homeland.'[1]

Allocations were small and replacements over a line 7,000 miles long uncertain. The Japanese however were only two days from factory to combat zone. This made it difficult for the Allies to reduce the hostile airfield complexes at Rabaul and later Wewak. Fortunately, the Japanese could not easily replace their skilled pilots.

Under General Kenny Air Vice-Marshal W. D. Bostock, R.A.A.F., commanded the Royal Australian Air Force. The Allied Air Forces had many duties. They had to operate against the enemy air force, his airfields, his installations and his shipping ; provide close support to local ground force operations ; and carry out reconnaissance both over land and sea. To carry out these tasks,

---

[1] *General Kenney Reports*, pp. 61–62.

air force units were moved into Cape York Peninsula (Australia) and New Guinea as rapidly as the completion of airfields and limited shipping resources permitted. Prior to August 1942, the scale of Allied air effort was restricted by the availability of operational airstrips within range of enemy bases. Strips had been constructed on the mainland of Australia in anticipation of a Japanese drive south of Rabaul. But these strips were not within fighter range of the fighting in New Guinea, and bombers starting from Australia to attack Japanese airfields in the Lae–Salamoa area in support of South Pacific operations on Guadalcanal consequently found it necessary to refuel at Port Moresby on each run. To add to the operational difficulties of those early sorties, the navigational hazard of crossing the Owen Stanley mountains was interposed between the staging airfield at Port Moresby and the objective areas.

Though the Japanese Army Air Force was responsible for operations in New Guinea it was not established in the island until July or August 1943. Air operations in New Guinea and cover for the Japanese convoys were the responsibility of the Fourth Air Army which was based at Ambon with advance forces at Rabaul. The Japanese moved the carrier *Junyo* to the Bismarcks and her fighter aircraft gave cover to at least one attempt to land reinforcements in New Guinea in December 1942; but except in the U.S. strikes on Hollandia carrier-based aircraft were little used in New Guinea by either contestant after the Battle of the Coral Sea, until a later stage when Admiral Nimitz's forces made carrier-based air attacks on the northern Solomons and the Bismarck Archipelago in connection with General MacArthur's operations in New Guinea.

84

The first phase of the projected Allied advance involved an amphibious attack on Lae and Salamoa. In order to provide fighter cover for the movement of the convoy and the actual assault, the construction of an airfield at Buna was projected. In the absence of sufficient air lift a light force of four infantry companies was to move overland from Port Moresby via Kokoda to occupy the place prior to the arrival of troops by sea, including anti-aircraft, engineer and air force ground units. The operation was timed to take place under cover of the landings in the Solomons, but the Japanese forestalled it. After the repulse of their seaborne expedition aimed at Port Moresby in the Battle of the Coral Sea in May 1942 the enemy decided to take the base by a land advance from Buna over the Owen Stanley Mountains. Its possession, whilst depriving us of our base for reconquest of Papua, would have enabled the Japanese to control the sea routes between the waters south of Papua and those to the north. On 21st July they brought from Rabaul three transports escorted by the light cruisers *Tenryu* and *Tatsuta* and three destroyers, and that night landed troops at Gona, north-west of Buna. The ships were attacked by American and Australian aircraft, and the large transport *Ayatosan Maru* was sunk. These Japanese troops were advance elements, 4,400 strong, of a force of veterans of the Malaya campaign under Major-General T. Horii. They were opposed by the Papuan Infantry Battalion and an Australian company. The Allies planned reinforcement by air, but only 30 men had been flown in when the Japanese in three days' fighting on 26th–28th July secured Kokoda and its landing ground. In the next three and a half months the enemy landed re-inforcements numbering several thousand, and moved slowly across the mountains towards Port Moresby. Since the Japanese Army Air Force had not yet been brought into New Guinea and the campaign was under the same control as that in the Solomons, the Japanese Seventeenth Army which was carrying out the operations in New Guinea under Lieutenant-General H. Hyakutake, had to look for air support to forces under the command of Army and Navy Air Headquarters, South-East Area Command, at Rabaul. The planning was poor. It reflected a lack of co-operation between the Army and Navy and a failure to appreciate the value of air power. The Japanese showed however great skill in jungle and mountain fighting.

Times, Z — 10

The Japanese plan was to make a simultaneous advance from the south-east with Special Naval Landing Force troops from Rabaul, carried in a small convoy consisting of the transports *Kinai Maru* and *Nankai Maru* with two tankers, escorted by the light cruisers *Tenryu* and *Tatsuta*, destroyers *Tanikaze*, *Urakaze* and *Hamakaze*, and two gunboats. The troops began landing at 0140 on 26th August near the head of Milne Bay, at the south-east tip of New Guinea, where the Allies were constructing an air base. The ships disembarked, it is believed, nearly 1,200 men and sailed again at 0730. They were without air support. Bad weather prevented Allied aircraft from attacking the expedition before its arrival in Milne Bay; but, later, Australian and American medium bombardment aircraft inflicted severe damage on the troops and stores ashore. The Japanese effected further landings at night but lacking air/sea command they could not bring in enough reinforcements. Australian troops which had been sent to garrison the area about a month earlier, counter-attacked them. They killed about half the total number of invaders landed, and by the end of the month the enemy forces had been destroyed.[1] Some were evacuated under cover of heavy weather to Goodenough Island, off which on 11th September American and Australian aircraft sank the destroyer *Yayoi* whilst she was trying to rescue them. The rest were dispersed by the Australians with the loss of all their supplies and heavy equipment, including tanks. Japanese ships subsequently carried out some bombardments of Allied shipping and positions at Milne Bay; and on the night 6th/7th September two cruisers sank the supply ship *Anshun* at the wharf in this manner. To put a stop to these attacks Rear-Admiral Crutchley took up a task force composed of the R.A.N.S. cruisers *Australia* (flagship) and *Hobart*, and the U.S.S. *Phoenix*, and the destroyers *Selfridge*, *Bagley*, *Henley* and *Herm*, which patrolled outside air range, south of Milne Bay; after which no further attacks took place. The submarine *RO–33* patrolling in the Milne Bay area, was sunk by H.M.A.S. *Arunta* on 29th August in 9° 36′ S., 147° 6′ E.

Milne Bay became a base for Allied naval operations in the area, and in January 1943 was established as a defended port.

85

Despite poor planning and inadequate support by the Japanese naval air forces at Rabaul, by 12th September the enemy forced the Allies back to within 30 miles of Port Moresby. However, reinforcement of the Australian troops coupled with well co-ordinated air support finally enabled the 25th Australian Brigade to halt the Japanese at Eoribawa Ridge on 17th September; and the Allies were able at the end of the month to break out of their narrow coastal strip at Port Moresby and counter-attack with Buna and Gona as their ultimate

---

[1] The Australians ' were fighting mad, for they had found some of their captured fellows tied to trees and bayoneted to death, surmounted by the placard, ' It took them a long time to die,'.' Morison, *History of U.S. Naval Operations in World War II*, Vol. VI, p. 38.

objective. General Sir Thomas Blamey, Commander of the Allied Land Forces in the South-West Pacific Area proceeded to Port Moresby to direct the operations. A considerable force was soon concentrated in New Guinea, taxing the shipping resources and supply services to the utmost.[1] Shipping was in short supply : it consisted chiefly of some 2,500 to 4,500 ton steamships of the K.P.M. (Koninklijke Portetvaart-Maatschappij) and other lines which plied in Indonesia before the war, together with a few Australian and American ships. Consequently, many of the troops were flown up from Queensland in one of the biggest air lifts of the war. Base installations were almost wholly deficient at Port Moresby, practically non-existent at Milne Bay, and entirely lacking in forward areas. Heavy equipment could not be taken over the Owen Stanley mountains, and the problem of supply was responsible for the development of an axis of advance by infiltration northward from Milne Bay. General MacArthur had sought to obtain trained Marine amphibious troops and suitable landing craft for operations northward along the coast from Milne Bay, but in the allocation of troops priority had to be given to Guadalcanal, where the Americans were in danger of being driven into the sea, and no landing craft were available in the Pacific, for the first shipment from the United States would not be ready for despatch until October. He consequently decided to take the north-east coast of New Guinea by an airborne, air-supplied movement of the 32nd (U.S.) Division from Port Moresby, co-ordinated with a drive by the Australians over the Kokoda Trail. After an Australian battalion had been flown in covered by air attacks on Buna and Rabaul, American troops were flown to Wanigela, south of Cape Nelson, where there was an airstrip, and moved forward by means of a coastwise ferry service using local craft, including even canoes manned by primitive natives. Stores for the army were carried from Milne Bay through the shoal infested passage between the d'Entrecasteaux Islands and the mainland, of which little more information was available than was given by Admiral John Moresby's running survey of 1874. A survey was accordingly undertaken and a channel from East Cape to Cape Nelson was buoyed by Commander K. E. Oom, R.A.N., with the Australian ships *Polaris* and *Stella*, covered by Australian corvettes. The ships worked in the intervals of hiding amongst the mangroves from enemy air attacks, but they did not escape without casualties. Despite many air attacks, the extension of sea control resulting from the bitterly contested encounters in the adjacent South Pacific area, made it possible for the Navy to keep pace with the Army's supply requirements. From Milne Bay, Government vessels and coasters of 50 to 500 tons carried the army's stores to Oro (Oifabama) Bay, 30 miles south-east of Gona. It was dangerous for ships to remain at Oro Bay in daylight so loads were transferred to smaller craft which made nightly runs to advanced supply bases. Beach-heads were established under Australian naval beachmasters. All along the coast corvettes, H.D.M.L.s, barges and lighters and native-manned auxiliary fishing vessels slipped in and out of creeks and bays with stores and men, and gathered intelligence, in which they were greatly aided by the Coast Watchers. The seaborne supply line remained always under threat of interruption. Enemy air attacks on 16th/17th November put it out of action for three weeks, and on 23rd December it was attacked by M.T.B. type vessels and a ship was sunk.

Concurrently with the advance from Wanigela a reconnaissance in force was made of Goodenough Island, which lay off the north-eastern coast of New Guinea, to clear it of the enemy and to determine its suitability for an airfield.

---

[1] The organisation of the Allied forces is given in Appendix K.

On the night 22nd/23rd October Australian troops carried from Milne Bay in H.M.A.S. *Stuart* and *Arunta* landed at Mud and Taleba Bays. On the island were approximately 300 Japanese troops, including some who had been stranded there in August when Allied aircraft destroyed the barges in which they were moving from Buna for the assault on Milne Bay. The Australians attacked, and after indecisive fighting on 23rd/24th October the Japanese escaped from the island by sea, and the Allied task force remained in occupation. Shortage of garrison troops necessitated postponement for several months of the project to construct an air base on the island.

86

The Australians recaptured Kokoda on 2nd November, and by the end of the month converging attacks by Australian and American troops had driven the enemy right back to the area he originally occupied along the north-east coast with strong bridgeheads at Buna and Gona. The Australian corvettes *Katoomba* and *Ballarat* were sent up to Buna on 27th November, to discover how the enemy were receiving supplies. They were dive-bombed, but escaped undamaged. It was found that the Japanese were bringing in supplies both in cargo ships and by barges from Lae and Salamoa, ports to which they were carried from Rabaul by destroyers. Attempts were made to reduce the traffic by air attacks on the barges in harbour, and on 2nd November U.S. army aircraft attacked two ships escorted by two destroyers off Buna, and sank one of the ships, the 6,710-ton *Yasukawa Maru*.

The Japanese also used warships for landing troops. Two light cruisers and eight destroyers were attacked by Fortresses whilst thus engaged, on the 17th and again on 21st November. On the latter day a number of enemy aircraft were destroyed whilst covering the landing of troops. The Japanese then gave up sending their destroyers across the open sea between Rabaul and Buna, in favour of following the north coast of New Britain and running down through Dampier Strait, a route which afforded some protection from air observation and was convenient if stores were to be dropped at Lae and Salamoa. On the 24th a force of destroyers and torpedo boats bringing reinforcements from Rabaul was caught and attacked by aircraft in Dampier Strait, but got through with the loss of the destroyer *Hayashio* and damage to the torpedo boats *Hiyodori* and *Otori*. On 2nd December another force of destroyers succeeded in reaching Buna, but had to retire after landing a few troops, after 23 of its escorting aircraft had been shot down and the destroyer *Isonami* hit by a bomb in an attack by five heavy and six medium army bombers. The destroyers changed their course after dark and landed their troops on the beach 40 miles north-west of Buna, where however they were detected and heavily attacked from the air, suffering many casualties. A reinforcing attempt by six destroyers was frustrated on 8th December by American heavy bombardment aircraft which intercepted the enemy off Cape Orford, on the south side of New Britain, bombed and damaged the *Asashic* and *Isonami* and turned back the enemy before reaching the coast of Papua, Seven of the Japanese fighter aircraft escort were shot down by the Fortresses without loss to themselves. The Americans had intelligence that another attempt to land reinforcements near the Kumusi River, 20 miles west of Buna, was expected to take place on 14th December. It duly did so. A Japanese force of two light cruisers and three destroyers left Lorungau in the Admiralty Islands on the 13th, carrying reinforcements for Southern New Guinea. It was sighted off Madang and attacked by aircraft when passing through Vitiaz

Strait. Ten of the fifteen Zero fighters protecting the convoy were shot down. The ships reached the Mambare River however, 42 miles north-west of Buna, on the 14th, where about 250 troops probably succeeded in getting ashore before the force retired in the direction of New Britain after Allied air attacks had caused considerable casualties to troops and damage to landing craft and stores.

The Japanese at this date were also reinforcing northern New Guinea. Hollandia was occupied on 25th December by two companies of troops brought in the light cruiser *Natori* and the minelayer *Itsukushima*. This led to a surmise that they might have decided to abandon southern New Guinea and the Lae airfields. There were indications that the enemy were preparing to land in strength at Wewak about the 18th. A naval force consisting of three 8-inch cruisers and at least one carrier, the *Junyo* (54 aircraft), flying the flag of the Vice-Admiral Commanding Carrier Force, was in the Admiralty Islands (between New Ireland and New Guinea), and there were 24 transports and one more 8-inch cruiser at Rabaul. The operation took place on the 18th as expected. Three separate forces, all starting from Lorungau, landed troops at Wewak, Madang and Finschafen. The landings at Wewak and Finschafen were on a small scale and were made by destroyers. The main convoy of two transports was escorted by four destroyers and a light cruiser which subsequent events showed to be the *Tenryu*, one of the 18th Cruiser Squadron in Admiral Mikawa's force based on Rabaul. The convoy was sighted between the Admiralty Islands and the Hermit Islands and was unsuccessfully attacked by Allied aircraft when it had reached the coast of New Guinea near the entrance to the Sepik River. Zero fighter aircraft, believed to have flown from the *Junyo*, intercepted the Allied aircraft and spoilt their attack. The convoy moved south down the coast and was again attacked off Karkar Island (40 miles north of Madang), where the light cruiser was apparently hit and damaged. The two transports and the remainder of the escort were seen later in the day anchored off Madang. After dark the *Albacore* (Lieut.-Commander R. C. Lake), one of the submarines which had been sent up in September from Brisbane to defend the New Guinea coast during the threat to Port Moresby, after unsuccessfully attacking one of the destroyers, fired two torpedoes at the light cruiser *Tenryu*, and sank her. The two transports escorted by the destroyers left for Rabaul next day. The *Albacore* was also successful on 20th February in sinking the destroyer *Oshio*, off the Admiralty Islands.[1]

In December a force of M.T.B.s, beginning with six boats, was moved into New Guinea to cut off supplies for the enemy's advanced forces passed down the coast in power barges. A base was formed at Porlock Harbour, Cape Nelson, with the converted yacht *Hilo* as parent ship. The Allied air offensive and the activities of the M.T.B.s, ultimately forced the Japanese to supplement their destroyer and barge landings by using aircraft and submarines to supply their ground forces opposing the Australian and American advance. On 28th November three groups of enemy submarines were seen coming down the coast of New Guinea from the direction of Dampier Strait, believed to be bringing supplies. On 25th December, the motor torpedo boat *PT–122* sank *I–22* off Gona, though the Japanese report that the submarine was not engaged on transport duty at the time. Japanese naval medium bombardment aircraft, on which the Army Air Force called for help in November, also dropped supplies for the troops, but much is reported to have been lost in the jungle.

---

[1] A frigate, which has never been identified, is also reported in the list prepared by the Joint Army–Navy Assessment Committee, to have been sunk, but the ship is not shown in the list given in *The Imperial Japanese Navy in World War II*, Japanese Monograph No. 116.

In the final stages of the Allied drive the American Army Air Forces without interrupting their offensive campaign against the shipping employed by the enemy in his attempts to supply his troops, flew 15,000 American troops, with equipment and food, over the Owen Stanley range from Port Moresby to the Buna district, using bombers as well as transport aircraft. The Australians, however, fought their way across every foot of the steep, bloody, fever-haunted Kokoda trail, driving the Japanese northwards and downwards until they were pressed against the sea at Buna and Gona. On 16th November, American troops were ferried around East Cape and landed 7 miles south of Buna, the capture of which, with the neighbouring villages Gona and Sanananda, was required in order to secure the Dobodura plain for the construction of airfields. Speed in construction was vital, for as already related (Section 85) the enemy cut the coastal boat supply line on 16th/17th November. Essential materials for the final assault on Buna and Gona were sent in to Oro Bay in Dutch merchant ships escorted by Australian corvettes. The Australians, on whom fell the brunt of the fighting in the campaign, captured Gona on 9th December ; and on the 13th H.M.A.S. *Colac, Broom, Whyalla* and *Ballarat* embarked Australian troops at Milne Bay, and making a swift passage through the night, landed them at Oro Bay next day. On the 17th the Australians ferried eight tanks up the coast from Milne Bay on rafts and landed them near Cape Endaiadere, just north of Oro Bay. Buna fell on 2nd January 1943 after a month of fighting, and the Australians captured Sanananda on the 18th. By the 22nd when organised resistance ceased Papua had been cleared of the enemy by Allied troops as far north as Buna–Gona–Sanananda, though only after the Japanese had been systematically routed out of their foxholes along the beaches. Losses were heavy on both sides, mainly from disease. The food situation on shore for the Allies was meagre since there was insufficient shipping to bring up supplies. For the Japanese, however, it was much worse, and many died from starvation. The 7th Australian and 32nd United States Divisions had to be withdrawn to Australia for reconstitution after the protracted campaign in which the Australians lost 2,037 officers and men killed, the Americans 671. Many of the casualties and months of time would have been saved if the Allies had possessed the necessary beaching craft for coastal landings and carrier-based aircraft to protect them : in other words the campaign was one more instance of the mobility conferred by sea power.

87

Before the campaign in Papua was completed the Japanese began their second overland offensive against Port Moresby. They could no longer move by sea from their advance bases at Lae and Salamoa so they planned an attack by another overland route through the mountains and jungles of the interior of New Guinea. Wau, a gold mining centre on the Bulolo River, near where the Australians operated a primitive airfield, was the key to the control of the inland routes from Lae and Salamoa to Port Moresby. There, a band of miners and prospectors, reinforced by a small Australian commando-type unit and known as the Kanga Force, had throughout the war held out against superior Japanese forces. As a first step the Japanese sent reinforcements to Lae, their main base in south-east New Guinea, where there was an airfield which they used for refuelling, withdrawing troops from Manchuria and North China for the purpose. On 4th January 1943 a total of 87 ships of all types were seen in the Rabaul area. Allied bombers made a daylight attack on them next day and sank one ship.[1] On the same day, the Japanese sailed a convoy of five high speed transports from Rabaul for Lae carrying the 102nd Regiment of the 51st Division escorted by a light cruiser and four destroyers, with strong fighter air protection. It was not sighted until late on the 5th when off Gasmata on the south coast of New Britain. Allied aircraft attacked it next day, but without success. On the 7th they made 16 attacks. Every attack was intercepted by the Japanese protective fighter aircraft, but one transport, the *Nichiryu Maru*, was sunk. The remainder of the convoy reached Lae that evening, being joined just before arrival by two more ships. They were attacked whilst unloading on the 8th and the cargo vessel *Myoko Maru* was set on fire and destroyed. The remaining vessels sailed from Lae next day. Allied aircraft attacked them on the way back to Rabaul, but without success. Though the Japanese succeeded in landing between 5,000 and 6,000 troops, they paid a high price, for in all the Allied aircraft shot down between 85 and 90 of the enemy fighters covering the convoy. On 19th January however the Japanese landed a large force at Wewak, 380 miles up the coast from Lae, unmolested.

The shipping concentration at Rabaul continued high. Intelligence estimated that it sufficed to lift two divisions. Allied Army aircraft and submarines kept it under attack, the claims of the former being remarkable for optimism.[2] Results might have been better if Rabaul had been within range of torpedo bombers operating from the existing Allied airfields. Moreover, a proportion of the Allied air effort had to be directed, not against shipping, but against the three airfields at Rabaul in order to interfere with Japanese air reinforcements for the Solomons.

88

The Japanese attacked Wau on 30th January 1943. They were repulsed with heavy loss and counter-attack pushed them back. They sent a call to Rabaul for reinforcements, and the Japanese decided to bring in a division of troops. So considerable a force necessitated the employment of large transport ships, and before long, Allied reconnaissance began to report a build-up of shipping in the harbour at Rabaul and preparations at Gasmata airfield to receive fighters for the protection of a convoy. On 25th February the Allies got information that a large Japanese convoy was scheduled to arrive at Madang or Lae early in the following month. If the Allied troops, debilitated by malaria and poor food and decimated by losses, had had to cope with a fresh Japanese division there would have been no certainty as to the outcome ; and arrangements were made to attack and destroy the convoy from the air before the troops could land. Three days later, the 115th Regiment of the Japanese 51st Division, a total of 6,912 officers and men, commanded by Lt.-General Alachi, embarked at Rabaul and Kokopo (in the St. George's Channel), and sailed to reinforce the garrison at Lae and under the terms of the Japanese operation order establish a strong strategic position along the Lae, Salamoa and

---

[1] The cargo vessel *Keifuku Maru* (5,833 tons). The bombers claimed to have sunk or set on fire nine ships in all.

[2]

Date	Ships claimed sunk.	Ships actually sunk (Joint Army and Navy Assessment Committee Report)	(Japanese Official list)
7th January	2	1	1
8th January	2	1	0
18th January	5	1	0
21st January	3	1	1
Total ..	12	4	2

Markham Valley areas. There were at that time 2,500 Japanese Naval and 1,000 Army troops at Lae, and 1,500 Naval and Army troops at Salamoa. The Japanese underestimated the strength of the Allied air forces in New Guinea, and believed they could fight a convoy through as they had done early in January : they were prepared to lose half the ships. This explains the ill-advised plan to despatch a convoy with the slow speed of 7 knots, along a route where for two days it would be within effective range of Allied air attack. The operation was in charge of Rear-Admiral M. Kimura. The convoy consisted of seven transports and a collier, escorted by the eight destroyers *Shirayuki* (flagship), *Yukikaze* (with the G.O.C. embarked), *Shikinami*, *Asagumo*, *Uranami*, *Asashio*, *Arashio* and *Tokitsukaze*.[1] All destroyers except the flagship and the *Asagumo* which was detailed as rescue ship for aircraft and damaged vessels, carried 150 troops as well as one or two small M.L.C.s and six to nine collapsible boats. One small vessel, the 953-ton *Kembu Maru*, a new type known as a sea truck, was loaded with aircraft fuel and spare parts for the airfield at Lae. The transports were tactically loaded, to allow for losses. Strong air protection for the convoy was arranged, and its departure was prefaced by an air attack on the Buna area, but this failed.

The expedition took a course north about New Britain as the Allied Command had appreciated it would do, to take advantage of the bad weather which was forecast. When first sighted on the afternoon of 1st March off Talasea, on the north coast of New Britain, the weather was such as to give the convoy a certain amount of protection. It passed through Vitiaz Strait during the night, and at dawn next day the Allies began to attack it. During the morning 27 heavy bombardment aircraft escorted by 16 fighters sank the *Kyokusei Maru* and damaged two more ships which, however, continued to stay with the convoy.[2] Two enemy destroyers picked up the survivors of the sunken ship's troops and landed them at Lae under cover of darkness. Several of the enemy fighters protecting the convoy were shot down. In the afternoon the weather deteriorated and a subsequent attack force of heavy bombers was unable to find the convoy. Naval seaplanes found and kept in touch with the enemy during the night and dropped bombs intermittently without result. General Kenney had just introduced in the Fifth Air Force a new technique of ' skip bombing ' by B–25 (medium bombardment) aircraft fitted with a large armament as commerce destroyers, which enabled the aircraft to attack at low level without being blown up by the explosion of its own bomb. It was employed on 3rd March in a series of co-ordinated and rehearsed attacks. On that morning a total of 17 heavy, 32 medium and 12 light bombers covered by 29 fighters, shuttled from the Moresby and Milne Bay airfields, attacked the convoy in the Huon Gulf area. During the afternoon a further 13 heavy bombardment aircraft attacked it and several reconnaissance aircraft also bombed the convoy. Numerous hits were made from an altitude so low that it is reported the Japanese believed the aircraft to be attacking with torpedoes, and consequently the ships waited to sight non-existent torpedo tracks before taking evasive action. At dusk the only ships left afloat were four destroyers and two cargo vessels. Both the latter were on fire, and one sank after dark. American motor torpedo boats came out and sank the remaining cargo vessel, the *Oigawa Maru*, during the night. The four destroyers sunk that day were the *Arashio*, *Asashio*, *Tokitsukaze* and *Shirayuki*. Air attacks on the four surviving destroyers were resumed next morning, but all escaped. At least a third of the Japanese troops were lost ;

---

[1] The organisation of the convoy is given in Appendix F.

[2] The *Teiyo Maru* and the *Oshima*.

a few, in addition to a thousand saved from the *Kyokusei Maru*, reached the shore: the remaining survivors were rescued by Japanese destroyers and submarines. Losses of Japanese protective fighter aircraft were so heavy that they brought about the decision to disembark carrier air forces and base them ashore, a decision which was destined to have a far-reaching effect on the Naval Air Force (*see* Section 91). In defence of the convoy, the Japanese employed some sixty naval and a similar number of army aircraft, the latter experienced fighter units brought in from the Netherlands East Indies. Two-thirds of both the naval and army aircraft were shot down. The Allied air losses were no more than five aircraft.

The failure of the Lae convoy to arrive resulted in a shortage on shore of food and ammunition. Attempts were made to send in supplies by submarines from Rabaul, the practice being for the submarines to arrive off the coast at dusk and unload their cargoes into barges during the night. Allied M.T.B.s caused considerable havoc amongst these barges, and towards the middle of March the Japanese attempted to run to Wewak a convoy of four or five merchant ships escorted by three destroyers. Allied aircraft attacked the convoy after dark on the 13th and sank the cargo vessel *Momoyama Maru*. The remaining ships reached Wewak which the enemy was now making his main base and port of entry into New Guinea.

By the end of March the Japanese had begun to use the same method of reinforcing central New Guinea as they formerly used for Guadalcanal. Troops and stores were brought to Kavieng and carried from there in destroyers to Finschafen, where they were unloaded into barges and taken down the coast to Lae and Salamoa. The destroyers' round trip Kavieng–Finschafen–Kavieng took 24 hours. They left Kavieng in the evening, completed unloading at Finschafen early the following morning and returned to Kavieng by that evening. The first of these destroyer movements took place on 29th/30th March. Allied aircraft attacked the four destroyers whilst stationary off Finschafen, but results were indefinite. On 12th April the enemy successfully ran a convoy of four medium cargo vessels and two small vessels with two destroyers to Hansa Bay, between Madang and Wewak. Four further transports escorted by destroyers reached there on the 13th. The ships were attacked by heavy bombers on the 12th and again on the 14th in Hansa Bay and the *Sydney Maru* (4,105 tons) was sunk. On the 14th the Japanese also ran into Wewak a convoy of six merchant vessels, escorted by a light cruiser, a destroyer and a gunboat. Three squadrons of army heavy bombers attacked the enemy from low level at dusk in the approaches to the harbour and continued the attack during the night and early morning, sinking the cargo vessel *India Maru* (5,872 tons). The growing Allied air power in the South-West Pacific was intensifying the Japanese logistic problems in supplying his New Guinea garrisons. With the isolation of Rabaul before the end of the year, it was to reach a climax.

CHAPTER XI

Japan Adopts Defensive Strategy

(*See* Plans 1, 8, 14, 24)

89

AFTER the destruction of the Bismarck Sea convoy the Japanese Army, for lack of reinforcements, virtually abandoned offensive operations in eastern New Guinea and concentrated its efforts on strengthening defences. The loss of the convoy necessitated hurried despatch of troop reinforcements from the Solomons to Hansa Bay and Wewak in New Guinea, thus depleting the strength of the ground forces in the former area. These reinforcements were unable, however, to prevent the build-up of Allied air strength in the Markham Valley. The Japanese considered flying in reinforcements to the valley, but air support in the Solomons claimed so many aircraft that the idea was discarded. The Allies were consequently able to construct in the valley a series of airfields from which subsequent advances along the New Guinea coast were launched. The advance did not begin, however, until June 1943. The American Chiefs of Staff on 9th January had asked General MacArthur to submit plans for the capture of Rabaul. The place could only be captured by amphibious assault, for advance from the west along the 250 mile roadless length of New Britain was not a feasible operation. General MacArthur informed the Joint Chiefs of Staff that he could not undertake further offensive operations without a relatively long period of preparation. The rapid conquest contemplated in the early plans had been shown to be impossible. The Japanese had proved to be desperate and capable fighters, and their strength was sufficient to make the planned campaign a long one. They were estimated to have between 79,000 and 94,000 troops in New Guinea, New Britain and the Solomons. In opposition to these forces the Allies had in the South-West and South Pacific areas $15\frac{2}{3}$ divisions and two more divisions were scheduled to arrive during 1943. Seven additional Australian divisions which were neither completely trained nor equipped, were retained for the defence of Australia and as garrison and service troops in rear areas. The ground force superiority of the Allies was somewhat discounted, however, since the Japanese had the advantage of position. The heavy jungle forests limited the effect of bombing and artillery bombardment, and each isolated enemy garrison had to be exterminated by Allied infantry, entailing much hand-to-hand fighting, a costly process for the attackers. The Japanese had been trained and equipped for precisely this type of fighting, whereas General MacArthur's troops needed additional training in landing operations to fit them for offensive operations in the South-West Pacific. On the other hand, the Japanese forces were scattered as garrisons of ports and airfields throughout an archipelago extending over 900 miles from Manus in the Admiralty Islands to New Georgia in the Solomons, and 400 miles from Kavieng to Lae. The Allies were able to isolate each enemy strong point and crush or neutralise it through the concentration of superior forces. Neutralisation through the domination which air power was able to achieve, was to be clearly exemplified in the coming campaign.

The shortage of landing craft and other special equipment, which had impeded training in the South-West Pacific in the Summer of 1942, was alleviated by detailing the VII Amphibious Force and an Engineer Special Army Brigade to join the forces in that area. Whereas the Amphibious Force was designed for major amphibious movements, the Engineers had small boats with a radius of action of 60 miles designed for shore-to-shore operations. The VII Amphibious Force had been formed, under the title Amphibious Force South-West Pacific in the latter part of 1942 and placed under Rear-Admiral D. E. Barbey towards the end of December in that year. Its beginning was slender, for it consisted at first of no more than the liner *President Jefferson* renamed the *Henry T. Allen* and converted into an attack transport, and the three Australian armed merchant cruisers *Westralia, Manoora*, and *Kanimbla* converted to infantry landing ships. The force was gradually built up, partly by borrowing from Admiral Halsey's Third Fleet ; but it was not until June 1943 when the advance against Lae began, that it could be considered in any respect an adequate organisation.[1] The Royal Australian Navy offered Admiral Barbey the facilities of their amphibious training base, H.M.A.S. *Assault*, at Port Stephens, north of Sydney. Here the Admiral, who on 8th February 1943 was made responsible for amphibious training, set up an Amphibious Training Command, similar organisations being subsequently established at Toorbul and Cairns in Queensland. In 1943 one U.S. Marine, four U.S. Army and two Australian divisions were trained by the Command. Each task force detailed to carry out a particular operation was given a complete rehearsal, including the unloading of supplies and equipment, immediately before the operation was undertaken.

90

On 15th March 1943 Admiral King introduced a new numbered-fleet system under which all fleets in the Pacific were odd-numbered, all in the Atlantic even-numbered. Each fleet was further divided into task forces, as requisite for each operation with emphasis on the particular type of ship needed for the task. In the numbering of such forces the first digit was the number of the fleet. Task forces were divided into task groups, with numbers following a decimal point, and the groups into task units, with numbers following a second decimal point. The South Pacific Force under Admiral Halsey became the Third Fleet. It consisted of six battleships, two carriers, three escort carriers, thirteen cruisers, some fifty destroyers and twelve submarines. Attached to it was the III Amphibious Force under Rear-Admiral Turner (relieved on 15th July by Rear-Admiral T. S. Wilkinson). The former Central Pacific Force, Vice-Admiral R. A. Spruance's Command, became the Fifth Fleet, and in August 1943 the V Amphibious Force was set up under Rear-Admiral Turner. Command of

---

[1] Repair ship *Rigel* (Flagship of Admiral Barbey), four high speed transports, 17 L.S.T.s, 20 L.C.I.s, 20 L.C.T.s, 10 destroyers, 10 submarine chasers, four motor minesweepers, one civilian-manned salvage tug. Like the flagship of the Fleet Train, British Pacific Fleet, at a later date, acommodation on board the *Rigel* was so limited that the wardroom was used also as office and sleeping quarters.

General MacArthur's naval forces was taken over on 11th September 1942 from Vice-Admiral Leary by Vice-Admiral A. S. Carpender (relieved 26th November 1943 by Vice-Admiral T. Kinkaid), and renamed by Admiral King the Seventh Fleet on 19th February 1943. The Fleet comprised five cruisers, 15 destroyers and 23 submarines. Its primary function was the support of landing operations by the VII Amphibious Force under Rear-Admiral D. E. Barbey.

The task organisation of the Seventh Fleet finally resolved itself into the following :—

Task Force 70	Administrative designation for Commander Seventh Fleet under which the only operational units were M.T.B.s as Task Group 70.1 and the Guerilla Supply Group as Task Group 70.4.
Task Force 71	Submarines (Fremantle).
Task Force 72	Submarines (Brisbane) under operational control of Commander South Pacific Area.
Task Force 73	Service Force, Seventh Fleet.
Task Force 74	Australian cruisers (Rear-Admiral V. A. C. Crutchley).
Task Force 75	Cruisers (Rear-Admiral R. S. Berkey).
Task Force 76	Amphibious Force (later termed VII Amphibious Force).
Task Force 77	Operational name for Admiral Kinkaid at Leyte and Lingayen and on several occasions operational designation for Amphibious Forces.
Task Force 78	At first escort and mine craft, but when these were absorbed by the Service Force, used for operational purposes as Amphibious Force designation.

91

In April 1943 the Japanese opened an air offensive in the Papua–Guadalcanal–northern Australia triangle, in an attempt to obtain control of the air. It was largely sustained by carrier air groups based ashore at airfields in the Bismarck Archipelago, and it resulted in such heavy losses that the enemy were never thereafter able to reconstitute the groups. The numerical air superiority of the Allies was overwhelming, but they still lacked bases within easy reach of Rabaul. Serviceability was very low. Admiral Halsey had 350 carrier-based and 500 land-based aircraft, and there were 1,000 American and Australian aircraft in General MacArthur's area. The Japanese had some 650 naval and 200 Army aircraft.[1]

The decision of the Japanese to disembark and shore base their carrier air groups was surely a desperate one. Opinion within the Naval Air Service was divided on the question. As already noticed, in the autumn of 1942, soon after the struggle for possession of Guadalcanal began, the Navy made an urgent call for reinforcements for the 25th and 26th Air Flotillas at Truk and Rabaul, giving as one reason the excessive demands of Japanese Army forces in the area for ground support. In December 1942 Army fighter units with experience in the Malayan campaign were moved from Surabaya to Truk by carrier, with a

---

[1] It seems probable, however, that the Japanese figures included only combat types whereas the figures for Allied aircraft included transports and other non-combatant types in forward areas, A/S patrols and aircraft undergoing overhaul or modification. *The Army Air Forces in World War II*, Vol. IV, p. 87 footnote.

hundred aircraft. From Truk they were flown down to Rabaul where some of them arrived in time to intercept an attack by heavy bombardment aircraft on 5th January 1943. In defending the Bismarck Sea convoy in March they lost two-thirds of their operational aircraft, and most of the remainder were seriously damaged. They were returned to Japan to refit, having lost 98 aircraft and 38 pilots since their arrival in Rabaul, little more than a month previously. Meanwhile the Japanese Navy was urging on the High Command that the Army should commit its strategic reserve of units based in Manchuria. This the Army refused to do, though ultimately they compromised by sending in four bomber and fighter units. The former were for the most part incompletely trained and the latter poorly equipped. Since the crews lacked training in oversea navigation losses in ferrying were particularly heavy in groups which were not piloted by a naval aircraft. One unit alone is said to have lost half its strength en route from Truk to Rabaul.

After the loss of Guadalcanal in February 1943, the Japanese decided that the central Solomons and Rabaul should be held at all costs, to protect the main fleet base at Truk, a decision which, however, had soon to be reversed. The naval command at Rabaul, who were charged with the defence of the base, maintained that the air groups of the carrier force were the only remaining units in the Japanese Naval Air Force with sufficient experience to offer effective opposition to the Allied advance, and urged that they should be employed from land bases. The carrier force strongly opposed the suggestion and argued that the force should be kept intact ; and for a time their views prevailed with the High Command. In March, after the Bismarck Sea disaster, the decision was reversed, and all fully trained carrier groups were ordered to airfields in the Bismarcks. They arrived about 1st April, with approximately 350 aircraft flown by the best remaining naval pilots. At the time, there were some 200 aircraft in the Eleventh Air Fleet at Rabaul, where the 25th Air Flotilla, after being withdrawn to prepare for rehabilitation during the winter, had rejoined the 26th in March 1943. In addition, the 22nd Air Flotilla had been brought into the area from the Marianas towards the end of the previous year.

92

With these reinforcements the Japanese stepped up the determined attempt which they had already begun to secure domination of the air over New Guinea and the Solomons. On 9th March they unleashed at widely separated points a series of heavy air attacks. The most destructive was made on the 28th at Oro Bay, New Guinea, where the U.S. auxiliary *Masaya* was sunk and the Dutch freighter *Bantam* (3,322 tons) was set on fire and beached, subsequently becoming a total loss. This little port, situated about 15 miles south-east of Buna, had become the main supply port for the area. So far as the enemy's resources permitted, strikes continued, though somewhat sporadically, all over eastern New Guinea, the Solomon Islands and northern Australia, which at that time comprised a single Japanese air command, that of the Eleventh Air Fleet in the South-East area.

On 1st April Operation P.A. was begun with Naval air forces and the Solomons were attacked. The first heavy raid, on 7th April, coincided with an unusually large concentration of Allied ships in the Guadalcanal area in preparation for a bombardment of Munda and Vila–Stanmore which had been arranged for that night. Rear-Admiral Ainsworth's Task Force 68 had for some time past been based at Tulagi in order to be in a position to attack enemy shipping running under cover of darkness from Buin to Vila–Stanmore, night air cover being given him. The strength of his force varied from three cruisers and six destroyers to two cruisers and four destroyers. Including these ships, there were approximately 40 vessels of corvette size or larger in the Guadalcanal area when shortly after noon on 7th April, coast watchers sent warning of an impending raid by an enemy force estimated to number 160 aircraft. On receiving the warning the ships began to get under way from their various berths to clear restricted waters and obtain sea room ; and when the attack came in at 1500 they were in six main groups. Task Force 68 was in Indispensable Strait ; one small group lay east of Koli Point ; three groups were proceeding east of Sealark Channel towards Espiritu Santo ; and one large group, composed for the most part of small vessels, was still in Tulagi harbour. The first attacks were directed against the latter ships. The oil hulk *Erskine Phelps* was damaged ; the New Zealand A.S./M.S. trawler *Moa* was sunk by two direct hits, with a loss of five men ; and the oiler *Kanawha* was hit and sank later whilst in tow. At 1512 the destroyer *Aaron Ward*, when near Lengo Channel, was attacked by another wave of bombers ; she shot down one aircraft but was sunk with the loss of 27 of her crew by a direct hit and four near misses. This was one of the largest Japanese air attacks of the war in the Guadalcanal area, 50 bombers escorted by 48 fighters being engaged. The force was intercepted by about 60 U.S. fighters which shot down 27 fighters (though the Japanese only admit nine) and 12 bombers, their own losses being seven, all except one pilot being saved. The ships also shot down an undetermined number of the enemy. The Japanese officially claimed to have sunk one cruiser, one destroyer and ten transports. They had arranged to run a supply convoy to their air bases in the southern Solomons under cover of the air attack, leaving Bougainville on 7th April, but the convoy was not sighted, probably because all Allied aircraft were fully engaged in defending the Guadalcanal area.

In April, bases in New Guinea were again heavily attacked, the opportunity being taken to run convoys to Hansa Bay and Wewak as already noticed (Section 89). On the 11th the Australian Minesweeper *Pirie* was damaged in a raid on Oro Bay, New Guinea, though 17 of the 45 enemy raiders were shot down. Next day 50 Japanese medium bombers escorted by a similar number of fighters, attacked the three airfields at Port Moresby, Wards, Berry and Schwimmer : causing considerable damage but losing a high proportion of their numbers. Oro Bay was attacked again on the 14th by 45 aircraft, which were routed by 43 Allied fighters. The airfield and shipping at Milne Bay were raided by 75 aircraft at noon on the same day ; the Dutch s.s. *Van Heemskerck* (2,996 tons) was sunk and the *Van Outhoorn* and the m.s. *Gorgon* were damaged, and two corvettes received slight damage ; but again the enemy lost heavily.

Darwin airfield was attacked on 2nd May, and several of the 32 Spitfires which went up to intercept were lost through trying to outmanœuvre the Japanese in the air, a feat beyond even the highly manœuvrable Spitfires[1] ; and on the 10th Millingimbi, 300 miles east of Darwin, where there was an airfield, was attacked by nine Zero fighters.

At the request of the Australians who considered there was a danger to Australia unless the air forces in the area were reinforced the Americans despatched to the South Pacific 90 bombers and 75 fighters which had been intended for Europe. The Admiralty estimated that by June the total Allied operational air strength in the South and South-West Pacific Areas would be not far short of 4,000 aircraft, or about four times the number that the Japanese

---

[1] *General Kenney Reports*, p. 255.

had or were able to place in the area.[1] The air offensive was now, however, at an end. The attacks on Oro Bay and Milne Bay on the 14th were the last of the large scale daylight attacks on shipping and airfields at the centres of Allied strength in New Guinea, though during May a series of night raids took place on airfields at Dobodura and Wau. The Japanese carrier air groups were already leaving the area. In a fortnight's fighting they had incurred losses amounting to 15 per cent., and in order to preserve them for future operations they were withdrawn to Truk. Their place was taken by the Twenty-first Air Fleet from the Andamans, which on 15th April was transferred from the South-West to the South-East Area Command and incorporated in the Eleventh Air Fleet. It soon became clear, however, that the land-based air forces were unable by themselves to stop the Allied advance. They lost heavily in opposing Admiral Halsey's operations around Munda, and it was decided to reinforce them with the air group of the 2nd Carrier Squadron, the less well trained of the two squadrons which then made up the carrier force. The group was sent to Buin on Bougainville with about 150 aircraft, but in the next four months it was driven back to Rabaul and lost almost all its aircraft and pilots.[2] In July the final struggle for air supremacy over New Guinea and the Solomons opened. The Japanese, however, did not handle their aircraft effectively. They made piecemeal attacks and failed to follow them up. Moreover, they had no rugged heavy bombers like the B–17 (' Fortress ') and B–24 (' Liberator ') that could fight their way to the target and back.

We must follow the Japanese story to its dismal conclusion. At the end of October the air group of the 1st Carrier Squadron was ordered to the South Pacific to reinforce that of the 2nd Squadron. But in opposing the Allied landings on Bougainville in November it lost approximately 30 per cent. of its aircraft in less than a fortnight.[3] By that time there remained only a very few of the splendidly trained pilots of the original carrier force which had rendered possible the conquest of the Far East, and the survivors were withdrawn to Singapore and Japan to form a nucleus for a reconstituted carrier force. But before it was reconstituted, it had to be prematurely committed when the Americans attacked the Marianas in June, 1944.[4] In two days it lost the majority of its half trained pilots and when in October of that year the Combined Fleet was called upon once more to defend the Philippines, the Naval Air Force could muster little more than one hundred pilots to man the aircraft of their carrier fleet. The fighting force which in the winter of 1941–42 had enabled Japan to become master of South-East Asia in a space of four months, had almost ceased to exist.

93

On 18th April, the Commander-in-Chief, Combined Fleet, Admiral Yamamoto, was killed when the aircraft in which he was visiting the Upper Solomons was shot down.[5] The death of this aggressive and experienced commander was a

---

[1] The Admiralty estimate of the Japanese Air strength as about 1,000 aircraft was almost certainly a little too high (*see* Section 91). They probably had not allowed for the Army Air Force strength in the area being as low as it actually was.

[2] The Japanese monthly losses of aircraft throughout the war are given in Appendix Q.

[3] This is the figure given in the U.S.S.B.S. Report *Japanese Air Power*, p. 13. Morison, *U.S. Naval Operations in World War II*, Vol. VI, p. 347 states that 70 per cent. of the aircraft and 45 per cent. of the pilots and crewmen were expended during those two weeks.

[4] These operations will be dealt with in Volume IV of this History.

[5] American Intelligence discovered his intended movements, and realising that his death would be the equivalent of a major victory, they sent out a force to attack the aircraft in which he was flying.

serious loss to the Japanese, for there was no Admiral of his calibre to replace him. His place was taken by Admiral Mineichi Koga, who had been Commander-in-Chief of Yokosuka Naval Station since 1942 but had little experience afloat in the present war.

Admiral Koga succeeded to a fleet damaged but not broken.[1] After the Battle of Midway in June 1942 the defence of the Solomons had been the only cause of serious attrition, and even in that area Admiral Yamamoto, after the Battle of Guadalcanal in November 1942, had adopted a cautious policy as far as the main units of the fleet were concerned. The losses of ships, other than carriers, had been largely made good. Nevertheless, the future had been mortgaged. No more battleships were building, the four sunken 8-inch cruisers were not being replaced, and the number of destroyers on the stocks was less than half the thirty-two that had been lost. Only one of the five carriers sunk had been replaced, and the First Air Fleet had been disbanded. Of its six fleet aircraft carriers and four light fleet carriers there remained four and two respectively. These were formed into two squadrons of a completely reconstituted Third Fleet which then became the carrier fleet and was termed the Striking Force. It was a balanced force, battleship and heavy cruiser components being supplied by withdrawals from the First and Second Fleets respectively. The latter, now termed the Diversion Attack Force, contained only five heavy cruisers.

In the task force organisation which was set up in August 1943 (see Appendix J), the Striking Force and the Diversion Attack Force were normally expected to act together, and in the eyes of the Allies who had no certain knowledge of the depleted state of the aircraft carrier groups they seemed to present a formidable array of strength. Behind them stood six battleships, which were all that remained afloat apart from the two in the Third Fleet ; the seventh, the *Mutsu* was sunk by internal explosion in the Inland Sea on 8th June 1943. These battleships were formed into two forces termed respectively the Main Body and the Battleship Force, each nominally containing one squadron ; but two of the ships, the *Ise* and *Hyuga*, were undergoing conversion to ' battleship-carriers ' by the removal of their two after 14-inch turrets and the fitting of flight decks ; and at least one other battleship was absent, in process of being modernised.

94

In the task force organisation the South-East Area Command received an accession of strength, both surface ship and air. The Eighth Fleet which constituted the striking force in the Command, contained two heavy and two light cruisers, and ten destroyers. It also included the largest single aggregation of naval air strength, namely portions or all of four out of the five air flotillas (21st, 22nd, 24th, 25th and 26th) which at that time constituted the Eleventh Air Fleet. The three latter flotillas were at the headquarters and advanced base of the South-East Area Command at Rabaul. The 21st Flotilla was training in the Marianas, but was available for reinforcements.[2] The 22nd had now returned to the Marshall Islands and was under the operational control of the Commander-in-Chief, Fourth Fleet, whose striking force was composed of three light cruisers. In October 1943, the 24th Flotilla

---

[1] The composition of the Combined Fleet is given in Appendix J.

[2] According to Captain Miyazaki, Senior Staff Officer of the 25th Air Flotilla at Rabaul from April 1943 to April 1944 however the aircraft of 21st Flotilla were transferred to the 25th at the end of April 1943. (Interrogation Nav. No. 97.)

was also transferred to the Marshalls. As Commander, Inner South Seas Command, the Commander-in-Chief Fourth Fleet was responsible for a huge area which included not only the Marshall and Gilbert but also the Marianas and Caroline Islands—in fact, all Micronesia.

The Japanese in March 1943, after the loss of Guadalcanal, had removed the Southern Solomon Islands and Eastern New Guinea from the area to be defended at all costs : only delaying operations were in future to be carried out there. In south-western and southern New Guinea Imperial Headquarters had already, on 25th March 1943 ordered an advance to be made. It never was made however. The Japanese had occupied Mimika (4° 42′ S., 136° 27′ E.), on the south-western side of New Guinea (see *Plan 14*) on 15th December 1942, by some 270 troops brought in the destroyer *Hatsuharu*[1] and the frigate *Tomozuru* : and a fortnight later they established the Headquarters of the 25th Special Naval Base Force to co-ordinate the defence of western New Guinea and control the area. In May 1943, the Japanese garrisons in the Banda Sea–Arafura Sea–Dutch New Guinea area were estimated at a total of some 20,000 troops. As already explained, the Allies continued to hold a base at Merauke (8° 22′ S., 140° 13′ E.) with Australian and Dutch troops, and the Royal Australian Air Force Command kept the area so thoroughly neutralised that it was considered unnecessary to carry out the amphibious operations planned for the purpose of reconquest of south-western New Guinea (see Section 132). The Allies left even Timor alone, save for air assault.

About May, the Japanese drew up a new war plan for the south-west Pacific area, termed the ' Z ' Plan. The operational policy was to establish a defensive front along a perimeter guarding the vital area, and running through the Aleutians, Wake, Marshalls, Gilberts, Nauru, Ocean Island and the Bismarcks, local commands being responsible for countermeasures to hold up, or at least delay attacks on this line. The so-called Mobile Fleet, at first based, as we have seen, on Truk but later withdrawn to Japan, was ready to sail in support of Japanese forces attacked on the perimeter. This force consisted of the Striking Force and the Diversion Attack Force, together with any available battleships. The Japanese were still hoping to bring the United States Fleet to decisive action on their own terms, that is, within range of their land based air forces. Under the new war plan submarines were to keep watch on the movements of the Allied Fleet, whilst seaplanes or land based aircraft were to carry out search and reconnaissance as before.

Complementary to the ' Z ' Plan was the ' Y ' Plan for the defence of the Andamans–Nicobar–Sumatra–Java–Timor line. The operational policy was identical, and if this line were threatened the Mobile Fleet would be moved to the Philippines or Singapore. The local naval forces available to delay Allied attacks on the line were those of the South-West Area Command which had been established to guard the conquered areas in South East Asia, the Netherlands East Indies and the Philippines (see Section 18). They consisted of one heavy and three light cruisers, a few destroyers and submarines and the First, Second and Third Southern Expeditionary ' Fleets ' with headquarters at Surabaya, Manila and Ambon respectively.[2] The land based naval air forces comprised the 23rd Air Flotilla whose headquarters were at Kendari in the Celebes with detachments at Manila and in northern Sumatra. One further

---

[1] Another Japanese account calls her the *Hatsukari Maru*.

[2] The fourth local command was the North-East Area Command which operated the Fifth Fleet (*vide* the chapters on the Aleutians in Volume II of this history). These ' Fleets ' consisted merely of small cruiser-destroyer, local defence, and anti-submarine and escort forces.

small extension of the perimeter was envisaged to take place ' at the opportune time ' ; this was the capture of the Cocos Islands in the south Indian Ocean.[1] It was never put into effect.

95

Before May was out the Japanese began withdrawing their ships from Truk and by June the Combined Fleet was concentrated in home waters. The chief reason for this was no doubt the immobilisation of the aircraft carriers, but other causes combined to operate simultaneously, notably the situation in the north about which there had always been nervousness. The Japanese were well aware that the shortest route to Japan was via the Aleutians, and in the early summer of 1942 a submarine had reconnoitred Seattle in order to discover whether the Americans were preparing there an expedition for the invasion of Japan. The Germans though they did not actually put pressure on Japan were now advocating an attack on Russia, pointing out how timely was the present whilst the U.S.S.R. was engaged in a life and death struggle with Germany. They also drew attention to Russian shipping traffic between the U.S.A. and Vladivostok, alleging that the Russians were receiving munitions by this route. The Japanese replied that the Russian shipping in question was regularly examined and that up to date no contraband had been found. In fact, however, they had given up examining these ships and did not interfere with them in any way, for nothing was further from the thoughts of the Japanese Imperial Staff than to provoke Russia, particularly since they had been forced to withdraw forces from Manchuria and North China in the early part of the year, to strengthen northern New Guinea. The perennial apprehension lest the Russians should lease Siberian air bases to the Allies was aggravated by the visit to Moscow of President Roosevelt's representative, Mr. Davis, a visit which it was thought might be connected with the subject. During June 1943 the Japanese, in an effort to create a favourable atmosphere in which to ask for reassurance that Russian airfields would not be made available to the Americans, agreed to release two Russian ships which had been held up at Otomari in Karafuto on account of their transfer to the U.S. flag after the outbreak of war.[2] However, the agreement of the Russians to extend for another twelve months the Russo-Japanese fishery convention, and thus obviate any excuse for either side to pick a quarrel over the fishing rights, was taken as a sign that the U.S.S.R. too, did not desire any worsening of relations at the moment, and perhaps emboldened the Japanese in September to seize another Russian ship, the *Dvina*, which was carrying chrome to the U.S.A.

96

By August Admiral Koga was forced to enunciate a policy which recognised that Japan was everywhere on the defensive. On the 15th of the month he ended Second Phase Operations (consolidation and strengthening of the defensive perimeter) and began Third Phase Operations.[3] Japan's task was

---

[1] Instruction No. 209 of the Navy Staff Section of the Grand Imperial H.Q. (25th March 1943). Reprinted in *Japanese Studies in World War II*, J.S.29.

[2] Mr. Molotov had already informed the Japanese Ambassador that Russia would do nothing contrary to the Russo Japanese Neutrality Agreement. In July the Japanese asked for a renewed assurance to that effect.

[3] Date based on special intelligence and U.S. *Pacific Fleet and Pacific Ocean Areas Weekly Intelligence*, Vol. 2, No. 20. But Morison in his *History of U.S. Naval Operations in World War II*, Vol. VI, seems to imply that the new operational policy was not actually agreed to by Imperial Headquarters until late in September.

now to defend as much as possible of the areas won at the beginning of the war. In September the Marshall and Gilbert Islands were removed from the area whose retention was vital. Those outlying garrisons were left to defend themselves. The Aleutians had already been given up in July. To defend the vital areas, Admiral Koga established a system of 'interception zones.' These consisted of a number of bases from which local forces would operate to destroy any enemy invasion group. Nine zones were established, ranging from the Kuriles through the Marianas, Solomons and New Guinea, Malay Barrier, to Burma and the Andaman Islands. The centre of each zone was an advanced base having a fleet anchorage with anti-aircraft and anti-submarine defences, and facilities for supply, repairs and communications. Within each zone were groups of bases, each having as its centre an air base. These air bases were to be located within 300 miles of each other if possible. An effort was made to provide defence in depth by reinforcing the perimeter bases with two other lines of bases in rear. All were to be as strongly defended as possible, in order to free the Combined Fleet and the Base Air Forces from the requirements of local defence so that they could engage in mobile operations. This static defensive system suffered from the inherent defect that the forces available to implement it were inadequate. The front held firm on the Indian Ocean until near the end of the war owing to the inability of the Allies to bring against it the weight necessary to rupture it. In the New Guinea–Solomons area it gave way slowly with stubborn resistance. In the Central Pacific the little atolls of Micronesia were insufficiently closely knit for mutual reinforcement and support under the fast-moving conditions of modern warfare. They were overwhelmed as Wake Island was and as Midway would have been if the Americans had been compelled to rely there on static instead of mobile defence.

97

Meanwhile, a threat to the Allied position in the South and South-West Pacific which had never been far from the thoughts of the Commanders, suddenly came into prominence. With the conclusion of the Guadalcanal campaign the Japanese decided to accede to the urging of the Germans to employ their submarines against the Allied shipping in the Pacific. Ribbentrop in conversation with the Japanese Ambassador in March stressed the importance of submarine war, not for the first time. He declared that in 1942 Germany, Italy and Japan had sunk twelve million tons of enemy shipping. The Allies could not increase their shipbuilding capacity sufficiently to make good losses on this scale, and their available tonnage was steadily decreasing. The Germans stated they were convinced that the submarine campaign alone could force the Allies to abandon the war. They placed two or three prototype submarines at the disposal of the Japanese Government; these subsequently arrived in Japan.[1] But Japanese shipyards were not capable of mass production of submarines so complicated as the modern German U-boat; and before long the great advance in anti-submarine research made by the Allies, and the failure of the Japanese to evolve counter-measures, caused under-water warfare by Japan to lose much of its danger, though not until a campaign comparable to the assault on the Cape route in the summer of 1942, had been undertaken in the Southern Pacific. During March 1943 the Japanese established submarine patrols in the Fiji and Samoa areas and there were signs of an intended campaign against Allied shipping in the Southern Pacific. For a few weeks the enemy submarines continued to operate spasmodically as they had been doing

---

[1] Presumably R.O. 500, 501, 502.

since November 1942. Towards the end of April, however, the expected offensive began. On the 24th the s.s. *Kowarra* (2,125 tons) was sunk about 180 miles north of Brisbane, the m.s. *Limerick* (8,724 tons) 200 miles south of Brisbane next day, the American s.s. *Lydia M. Child* (7,176 tons) 100 miles east of Sydney on the 27th, and the s.s. *Wollongbar* (2,239 tons) 150 miles north-east of Sydney two days later. General MacArthur asked for more destroyers to combat the menace off his Australian bases, but they could not be spared on account of the threat in the Fiji–Samoa area, where the .campaign began on 1st May with an unsuccessful attack on the s.s. *Peter Sylvester* near Samoa and the sinking of the American s.s. *Phoebe A. Hearst* (7,176 tons) 150 miles south of Fiji. The s.s. *William Williams* was torpedoed next day in the same area but was successfully towed to Suva. On the 17th the *William K. Vanderbilt* (7,181 tons) was sunk 150 miles west of Viti Levu ; next day the tanker *H. M. Storey* (10,762 tons) which had been routed north of Fiji to avoid the danger area to the southward was torpedoed twice and sunk, 300 miles north-east of Suva ; and on the 23rd the Panamanian tanker *Stanvac Manila* (10,169 tons) was sunk 90 miles south of Numea. In General MacArthur's area a recrudesce of the offensive seemed to be threatened with the sinking on 5th May of the Norwegian s.s. *Fingal* (2,137 tons) 160 miles north of Newcastle but it ended with an attack on one further ship, the s.s. *Ormiston* ; she was torpedoed in convoy—a rare event—on the 12th, 100 miles south of Brisbane, but reached harbour.

At 1815 on the 13th the Australian hospital ship *Centaur*, fully illuminated, was torpedoed in clear weather in 27° 17′ S., 154° 5′ E., about fifty miles east of Brisbane, whilst on her way from Sydney to Cairns, and sank in three minutes. The ship had been officially notified and her details communicated to the Japanese on 25th January. No evidence of the attack was received until nearly thirty-six hours afterwards, when survivors were sighted by aircraft and were picked up by destroyer a few minutes later. No more than one nurse and 55 men were rescued out of a total of 352 on board. The Japanese rejected the Australian protest against the outrage. This attack raised, not for the first time, the question of distinctive marking of hospital ships. The Army and political authorities in Melbourne wished all recognition marks to be removed and hospital ships to be escorted, darkened at night. The Chiefs of Staff both in Britain and the United States decided, however, that it was in Allied interest of humanity that immunity of hospital ships should be maintained, and reprisals avoided which might lead to the Axis abandoning the Conventions.[1] The sinking of the *Centaur* might conceivably have been the act of an irresponsible Commander.[2] It is not known which submarine was responsible for the sinking.

Several of the ships attacked were torpedoed in bright moonlight whilst not zigzagging. There was a shortage of escorts, but evasive routeing was not employed to the fullest extent, and our observer with the Pacific Fleet envisaged further losses in the future unless drastic A/S precautions were insisted upon.[3]

[1] J.S.M. 972 C.O.S. (W) 650, *see* Admiralty Tel. 281134B/June.

[2] The Japanese Imperial General Headquarters issued the following order on 10th January 1942. 'Naturally the rules of international law dealing with hospital ships will be respected. However, it has become known that the enemy (especially Britain and the Netherlands) had resorted in desperation to utilising the immunity of these ships for the escape of important personages. Upon sighting an enemy hospital ship, therefore, an inspection will be made and, if any suspicious persons are aboard, they will be detained. Every effort will be made to uncover and put a stop to illegal actions of this type.' (Ultra-secret Despatch 442) A.T.I.S. No. 39 (Part XII) 18th August 1945.

[3] Observers with U.S. Pacific Fleet : Report I.B. 24 by Commander (A.C.C.) Miers (V.C.), N.I.D. 004884/43.

But after the sinking of *R.O.–107* by the U.S. Submarine Chaser 669 on 28th May in 15° 35′ S., 167° 17′ E., about 180 miles south-east of Numea there was an interval of two months without attacks. The conclusion of operations in the Aleutians at the end of July set free a number of Japanese submarines, and during August a few attacks occurred. Thenceforth, however, the enemy submarines were largely ineffective. With the calls for transport and supply that were being made on them by the Army, the Japanese had not sufficient submarines for sustained offensives.[1] Much of their effort was devoted to reconnaissance : boats seem to have been stationed for this purpose permanently off Hawaii, for example. Much effort, too, was dissipated in raids of little value, such as the bombardments of Canton and Fanning Islands on 22nd March, which necessitated ocean passages of great length during which no attacks on shipping were carried out.

There were always submarines working in the Solomons. The destroyer *O'Bannon* on the night of 4th/5th April sank *R.O.–34* north of the Russell Islands, in 8° 15′ S., 158° 55′ E. In the south Solomons, the night of 22nd/23rd June was marked by a successful attack by *R.O.–103* on a convoy of three ships escorted by two destroyers and a minesweeper. The convoy was proceeding south from Guadalcanal, in 11° 35′ S., 162° 08′ E., zigzagging, with a full moon directly overhead, when at 0445 the auxiliary cargo ships *Aludra* and *Deimos* were hit by torpedoes almost simultaneously. All three escort vessels were equipped with radar, but no contacts were made either before or after the attack, except one doubtful contact about an hour before which through the inexperience of personnel was not developed. The commander of the escort was unable to establish voice radio communication with the ships hit. He made his search on the wrong side of the convoy ; and *R.O.–103* escaped. Both the *Aludra* and the *Deimos* sank.

---

[1] The Japanese Fleet List, 1st August 1943, shows 72 submarines (48 I. class, 24 R.O. class), though of these 2 I. and 2 R.O. class had already been sunk.

CHAPTER XII

Campaign in New Guinea : Advance to Lae

(*See* Plans 14 and 23)

98

FOLLOWING the conclusion of the campaign in Papua Allied forces worked along the coast of New Guinea. In the continued absence of an amphibious force they were still hampered by lack of supply routes and progress was slow. By April 1943 they had reached a point 75 miles north-west of Buna. The enemy meanwhile reinforced his land and air strength along a strong defensive line extending from Rabaul to Hollandia in New Guinea.

The general plan of operations preliminary to the final attack on Rabaul, known as the ' Elkton ' Plan, called for the establishment of a series of air and naval bases along the north coast of New Guinea in order to facilitate the advance ; for the success of Allied airborne reinforcement and supply operations at Buna at the end of 1942, as well as the heavy though sporadic air attacks made by the Japanese, had emphasised the value of complete control of the air. The Allies had agreed at the inter-Allied conference at Casablanca in January 1943 that the American Chiefs of Staff should settle the details of the Pacific operations in accordance with the changing situation and available material. In the final form of the plan, ' Elkton III,' no attempt was made to fix definite dates for the beginning or end of the successive assaults. The campaign was divided into five separate but interdependent operations. The first task was the capture of Lae by a combined drive by an airborne force operating overland through the Markham River Valley and an amphibious force moving along the coast in small craft. The intention, which was not, however, adhered to, was to bypass Salamoa in both attacks, but Finschafen and other bases in the Huon Gulf–Vitiaz Strait area were to be seized by ' coast hopping ' operations. Madang was to be captured by a combined airborne and amphibious assault. The capture by Admiral Halsey's forces in the South Pacific area of the New Georgia group in the central Solomon Islands, was to be the signal for the two commands, South-West and South Pacific, supported by air operations from bases captured in the preceding phases, to make simultaneous airborne and amphibious assaults upon New Britain in the west and Bougainville in the east. The successful accomplishment of these tasks would prepare the way for the capture of Kavieng and the isolation of Rabaul, depriving it of naval support and supply by sea and air. The Allies would have the requisite airfields to gain air superiority in the entire area and would weaken the Japanese land defences by naval and air bombardment. After these preliminary operations were completed, the combined forces would begin the culminating drive upon Rabaul.

Admiral Halsey had sufficient forces for his advances through the Solomons, but each of General MacArthur's operational commands needed reinforcement. It was estimated that the Allied Naval Force in the South-West Pacific Area needed an additional three cruisers, nine destroyers, and four squadrons (flotillas) of motor torpedo boats. Allied air forces needed 1,816 combat and transport aircraft in addition to those already assigned to the Fifth Air Force and the Royal Australian Air Force Command ; while MacArthur's land forces required an additional five divisions. The planners considered that this increase in land, air and naval strength would enable the combined commands to drive the enemy back to Truk in the Carolines and Wewak in New Guinea during 1943. A committee appointed by the Joint Chiefs of Staff examined the plan and reported that the forces set out were the minimum with which the operation could successfully be undertaken. But the American Chiefs of Staff, though they were empowered to settle the details of Pacific operations in so far as their available resources allowed, had no power to alter the allocation of men and material as between the Pacific and the western battle fronts,[1] and the shortage of shipping and of heavy bombardment aircraft together with the priority assigned to the European theatre, set definite limits to the reinforcements that could be sent to the Pacific, where Admiral King personally estimated that no more than 15 per cent. of the total resources of the United Nations were at that time deployed against Japan. It was arranged that the Pacific Fleet should furnish General MacArthur with such naval units as Admiral Nimitz could make available, but the five infantry divisions could not be supplied, and the increase in aircraft was limited to 860 by expunging the heavy bombardment groups for which the General asked. The offensive, consequently, could not be undertaken as planned. The task for 1943 was reduced to the seizure of the Solomon Islands, the north-east coast of New Guinea as far as Madang, and western New Britain. Airfields were to be constructed on Kiriwina and Woodlark Islands in the Solomon Sea, to compensate for the shortage of heavy bombers. These two islands, 115 and 165 miles respectively north and north-east of Milne Bay, provided positions from which medium bombers with fighter cover could attack targets in New Britain and support the operations of the South Pacific forces in the Solomons ; and Admiral Halsey undertook to construct an airfield on Woodlark and to station there a fighter squadron which would operate under the control of General Kenney, Commander Allied Air Forces South-West Pacific. On 29th March, the Joint Chiefs of Staff directed General MacArthur to take charge of these operations ; he thus became responsible for strategical control of the campaign in the South Pacific Area as well as the South-West Pacific. Operations in the Solomon Islands were, however, to be conducted under the direct control of Commander South Pacific Area (Admiral Halsey) subject to general directions from General MacArthur. Admiral Nimitz allocated ships for Halsey's operations (and subsequently for support of the Hollandia Operation, in the South-West Pacific Area) subject only to the rulings of the Joint Chiefs of Staff conveyed to him through Admiral King, directions to General MacArthur being conveyed through General Marshall ; and the Commander South Pacific Area retained his title until the command was broken up more than a year later.[2]

It was intended that after the New Guinea Force captured the Huon Gulf–Vitiaz Strait Area Admiral Halsey should capture New Georgia and push northwards through the Solomons to Bougainville where he could establish airfields and take over the responsibility for neutralising Rabaul. Under the new plan Rabaul was not now to be captured. The Allies did not require to

---

[1] Admiral King who sat on both the Combined and Joint Chiefs of Staff Committees had the power to allocate all new construction to the European and Pacific Theatres.

[2] Based on a summary of the Directive J.C.S. 238/5/D of 28th March 1943 given in *Marine Aviation in the Philippines*, Historical Division, H.Q. U.S. Marine Corps, p. 1.

make use of it as a base, and assault on this tremendous stronghold would be a costly operation. At the Quadrant Conference in Quebec in August 1943, the American Chiefs of Staff reported that neutralisation instead of capture had been decided upon. Before the operation began, however, Admiral Halsey was given permission to advance the date of launching his assault on New Georgia, and the advances in this and the Huon Gulf–Vitiaz Strait began simultaneously at the end of June.

99

The organisation of the South-West Pacific Area Forces for the campaign was complex. The national components were united for training and for administration in so far as matters of broad policy and supply were concerned. The Australian First and Second Armies and the United States Sixth Army were under the control of General Sir Thomas Blamey, Commander-in-Chief of the Australian Army and also, for purposes of training and administration, Commander of the Allied Land Forces South-West Pacific Area. In the field, however, General Blamey controlled only the Australian troops, and not always all of these. For General MacArthur transferred the American components of the Allied Land Forces South-West Pacific Area (Sixth Army) under Lieut.-General W. Krueger, together with the Australian troops detailed for each operation, to a special task force termed the Alamo Force, commanded by General Krueger who was responsible directly to General Headquarters without an intermediate echelon of command. Neither General Blamey nor the Australian Government offered any objection to this arrangement and it worked well. The air forces in the South-West Pacific, known as Allied Air Forces South-West Pacific Area, were commanded under MacArthur by Lieut.-General G. C. Kenney, U.S. Army, Commander Fifth (U.S.) Army Air Force. These Allied Air Forces South-West Pacific Area consisted, in addition to the Fifth Army Air Force, of the Royal Australian Air Force Command and the Royal Netherlands East Indies Air Force. The forward commander was Major-General E. P. Whitehead, U.S. Army, Deputy Commander Allied Air Forces South-West Pacific Area. The naval forces, consisting of the U.S. Seventh Fleet and units of the Royal Australian and Royal Netherlands Navies, were grouped under the title Allied Naval Forces South-West Pacific Area and commanded under MacArthur by Vice-Admiral A. S. Carpender. They were organised in separate task forces as requisite for the various operations.

The transports and landing craft of the VII Amphibious Force[1] concentrated at Townsville (Woodlark Force) and Milne Bay (Kiriwina Force). Reconnaissance of landing beaches and shipping was carried out both by air and submarines. The South-West Pacific Submarine Force based on Australia had been reduced during the first quarter of 1943 to its former establishment of 20 boats, by the withdrawal of certain submarines temporarily transferred to it from the Pacific Fleet at the time of the Japanese threat to Port Moresby in the previous autumn. Of these 20 submarines, however, 12 operated from Brisbane with Task Force 72 (Commodore J. Fife, Jr.), as a component of Admiral Halsey's Third Fleet. The remaining eight were under the operational control of Rear-Admiral R. Christie at Fremantle and were included in the Seventh Fleet.

100

The Japanese Naval Air Force had lost so heavily in opposing Halsey's advance in the Solomons that in July–August the Army Air Force moved to New Guinea. The need had been foreseen, and during the first half of 1943 the

---

[1] For its strength at this date *see* page 138, footnote 1.

Fourth Air Army had been built up in Rabaul. During the previous winter the Japanese had begun to construct a series of airfields along the northern coast of New Guinea at Wewak, Dagua, But, Aitape, Tami, Hollandia, Nubia, and at Manus in the Admiralty Islands, whilst there were advanced staging fields at Madang, Alexishafen (Sek), Lae, Salamoa, Finschafen and Saidor.[1] In August the air route was in full operation and the Fourth Air Army moved from Ambon and Rabaul to New Guinea and became responsible for the area east of longitude 140° E. By the middle of August the airfields at Wewak, the headquarters of the Japanese Fourth Air Army, were crowded with aircraft, many of them flown in and left without pilots. The Japanese believed themselves out of range of any large scale American attack, but just before dawn on 17th August they were taken by surprise when U.S. Fifth Air Force heavy and medium bombers escorted by fighters newly equipped with long range fuel tanks began a series of attacks in strength. The attacks were repeated next day, and when they ended the Japanese losses had aggregated 120 aircraft, almost the entire operational Army air strength in the New Guinea area.[2] Several tons of aircraft fuel, a number of large supply dumps and many of the anti-aircraft defences around Wewak were also destroyed. The set-back to the build-up of air strength in New Guinea was severe, and during the latter part of 1943 and early in the following year the Japanese Army Air Force gave it first priority. The intention was to build it up to 400 aircraft or more, but losses en route from the Philippines were high, as much as 30 per cent. of the aircraft ferried. Moreover, because of the inexperience of ferry pilots, bad maintenance along the route, and the poor condition of the forward fields, many aircraft were unfit for combat when they reached forward areas. Consequently, air strength in New Guinea rarely exceeded 200 aircraft. Owing to maintenance difficulty many aircraft were abandoned which might easily have been repaired in rear areas. Allied submarine and air attacks on convoys to Wewak became increasingly effective, and the Japanese found it more and more difficult to maintain an adequate supply of spare parts. They had no air transport cargo service such as had the Allies, to serve their air forces in an emergency of this nature. Furthermore, the main repair base for New Guinea was at Halmahera, a thousand miles from Wewak. It never functioned adequately ; in order to make engine changes, for example, the Japanese had to send aircraft to Manila or to Malang in Java, each more than 1,500 miles from Wewak. Under these circumstances, few engine changes and none but the simplest repairs were in fact ever carried out. As a result, operational losses were high, serviceability low, and operations involving more than 15 sorties were rare. Fighter and bomber units with an average strength of about 200 aircraft lost nearly 1,000 machines in 1943, whilst air crew losses were 175 per cent. The consequences of this state of affairs became evident during the second phase of the campaign in New Guinea.

101

In order to deceive the Japanese as to the main direction of the forthcoming Allied offensive constant air raids were made on Kupang, Ambon, Timor, Tanimbar and other enemy bases in the Dutch East Indies. Dummy signal traffic in Dutch code was sent via the radio stations at Darwin, Perth and Merauke, the Allied base on the south coast of New Guinea, to give the impression

---

[1] *See* Appendix R and Plan 23. The airfields at Dagua, But, Aitape and Tami are not included in the list in Instruction 280 of Grand Imperial Headquarters, Navy Section, September 1943.

[2] These are the figures given by the Japanese.

that at least a diversionary attack was to be mounted from north-western Australia. It was thought that the opening of a simultaneous advance at three different points would further confuse the enemy. Hard pressed for shipping and having expended more aircraft than they could afford in the unsuccessful attempt to hold Guadalcanal, the Japanese were in no situation to jeopardise their main defensive position in the Bismarcks and New Guinea by reacting in strength to the invasion of the Huon Peninsula.

The initial movement in General MacArthur's area was made by Alamo Force against unoccupied Woodlark and Kiriwina Islands on 23rd and 24th June. The main parties sailed from Townsville (for Woodlark) and Milne Bay (for Kiriwina), arriving a week later. Airfields were quickly completed on both islands. An American fighter squadron from Admiral Halsey's command began operating from Woodlark on 24th July and an Australian fighter squadron from Kiriwina on 18th August, providing escorts for daylight bombing raids on Rabaul. The enemy did not react for a month, and then only by light air raids, for much of his air strength was at that time being used in defence of the Solomons where Admiral Halsey had begun the attack on the New Georgia group on 30th June. U.S. troops of the Sixth Army made an unopposed landing on the same day at Nassau Bay in New Guinea and began a movement up the coast, co-ordinated with an overland march from Wau and Mubo and an advance down the coast by the Australians. Possession of Nassau Bay gave us a valuable advanced base for the supply of Allied troops in Papua by water instead of air or land tracks.

The main landings at Woodlark and Kiriwina Islands and Nassau Bay provided a try-out for the newly formed Amphibious Force of the Seventh Fleet. Unloading was subjected to delays resulting not only from heavy seas but also from incorrect organisation of troops and crews and lack of experience. The Amphibious Force gained valuable experience, however, which later enabled it to launch a series of operations averaging about five weeks between landings for a period of eighteen months. Air cover was furnished by fighters of the Fifth Air Force based on Dobodura and on Goodenough Island which as already related had been occupied in October 1942 for that specific purpose. The Fifth Air Force also carried out anti-submarine escort and defensive reconnaissance.

In order to supply the infantry during their advance along the coastal fringe through heavy jungle a Boat Battalion with 20 landing craft was employed, working from the Natter–Morobe Bay (7° 39′ S., 147° 39′ E.) area, nearly 70 miles from Lae. Supplies were landed on beaches in some cases only a few hundred yards from the front lines, usually at night. This entailed accurate navigation to avoid landing in enemy held territory. Mooring facilities were not to be had within a reasonable distance of the beach ; all boats had to be beached, with bows made fast to the shore and stern anchors out. On many nights surf was as high as 5 to 6 feet, and the boats were consequently held on the beach for as short a time as possible when loading and unloading. The advance of the infantry was so rapid that it was often necessary to land supplies on forward beaches before a reconnaissance could be made.

The Seventh Fleet was responsible for anti-submarine patrols and preventing reinforcements by the Japanese. The destroyers maintained patrols in Huon Gulf to prevent the movement of reinforcements from the north by motor barges, of which, since they were built locally of timber all over the area, the Japanese had a considerable number, though their losses were also considerable. The enemy depended upon them and upon submarines for supplying their garrisons at Lae and Salamoa, the only alternative being overland trails. His merchant ships unloaded their cargoes at Wewak and Rabaul, and supplies were then loaded on barges which made their way along the coast of the Huon Peninsula and New Britain by night. Only a small proportion of the barges reached their destination. For example during the ten days ending 3rd August attacks by South-West Pacific Air Forces and Allied M.T.B.s destroyed or rendered useless nearly 200, a total estimated to have been sufficient to transport a division of troops. A barge supply system that ensured delivery of three barge-loads of provisions daily would suffice to supply normal rations to a Japanese division of 18,500 men.[1]

Supply by submarines began in September. Three to five submarines were employed. Their carrying capacity was 40–50 tons below decks and 20–30 tons on the upper deck. The usual procedure was for the submarine to leave Rabaul and proceed on the surface, hugging the north coast of New Britain. On the second day, the submarine would proceed submerged, only surfacing at night and early dawn to charge batteries. Arrival was timed for sunset on the third day, when the supplies would be transferred to lighters, an operation which it is said was sometimes performed in 20 minutes.

For several days previous to the landings at Lae the Japanese airfields at Wewak, Hansa Bay, Alexishafen, Madang and in New Britain were neutralised by Allied air attacks. In a low-level attack on shipping at Wewak on 2nd September, by 16 medium bombers, the vessels were, for the first and only time in the campaign, found to be protected by barrage balloons. These interfered considerably with the attack, forcing the aircraft to change their entire scheme of approach. Nevertheless they destroyed two cargo ships.[2] The Japanese covering fighter aircraft were all of naval type ; they put up an unexpectedly tough fight, and four American aircraft were lost. Ten of the Japanese fighters were shot down.

Bobdubi, 3 miles south-west of Salamoa, was occupied by the Allies on 11th May and the Japanese in the area withdrew to Salamoa. The operation against Salamoa and Lae entailed an outflanking landing at the mouth of the Bussu River, some 15 miles east of Lae, bypassing Salamoa. Fighters from Wau gave air cover, the Papuan airfields being too far distant. On 4th September, under cover of a smoke screen together with bombardment by ships and aircraft the 9th Australian Division was landed by the 7th Amphibious Force.[3] The force formed up in Milne Bay and staged from Buna, crossing Huon Gulf at night. The landing was made just after dawn, in haze which lent protection from air attacks. The Japanese had anticipated that the landing would be made at Salamoa, and the initial stages were unopposed. During the afternoon the fog over the Solomon Sea cleared somewhat and enemy air attacks began. The aircraft came in over the mountains undetected by the radar guard in the destroyer *Reid*, and before retiring they caused some losses amongst landing craft and the troops on board, though the Japanese losses in the air were also

---

[1] The large type Japanese landing barges were from 38 to 63 feet in length. They could load 15 tons, transport the cargo 300 miles, and unload in the space of five days. In contrast, the 4,000-ton Japanese transport commonly used for amphibious operations would load 4,550 tons, transport it 300 miles and unload in about four days. According to a Japanese document dated September 1942, a large barge loaded to capacity would carry rations for some 6,200 men for one day.

[2] *Hankow Maru* (4,104 tons) and *Nagato Maru* (5,901 tons).

[3] The organisation of the Amphibious Force is given in Appendix G.

extremely heavy. By 12th September, 16,500 troops were ashore, nearly half of whom had been landed on the first day. On 5th September 1,700 U.S. paratroops and Australian gunners carried in 302 aircraft which took off from eight different airfields, made a co-ordinated airborne landing at Nadzab, in rear of Lae, jumping with their 25 pounder guns. The build up of the 7th Australian Division at Nadzab by air drop continued for three days uninterruptedly, under strong fighter protection.

In the operation against Lae a naval bombardment unit which had been raised in the Australian Imperial Force for the control of naval bombardment in amphibious operations, was used for the first time. Shore fire control parties accompanied the assault troops and bombardment liaison officers were employed in the U.S. destroyers which supported the landing. The unit took part in most of the subsequent amphibious operations in the South-West Pacific.

Between 11th and 13th September the Australians captured Salamoa airfield, port and town. The place itself was unimportant, and the principal object of the campaign was to divert troops from Lae and mislead the enemy as to the main objective. The strategy was successful, and the Japanese lost over 4,000 troops and many barges, small craft and much material in unsuccessful attempts to hold a place of little military value. The U.S. Fifth Air Force aided the deception scheme by making heavy air raids on Salamoa, though their main operations were concentrated on the neutralisation of enemy air strength by raids on the major airfields at Wewak and on Hansa Bay and other positions in preparation for the assault on Lae. The capture of the latter place by the Australian 7th and 9th Divisions on 16th September gave the Allies control of Huon Gulf. This enabled them to operate surface ship patrols against the enemy barge traffic between New Britain and New Guinea.

102

Times, Z — 10

In order to attack the Japanese whilst off balance the date for the assault on Finschafen was advanced more than three weeks and took place on 22nd September. The 20th Australian Infantry Brigade of the 9th Division embarked at Lae in landing ships and craft of the 7th Amphibious Force which staged there from Buna, giving the impression of a simple reinforcement operation, which seems to have deceived the Japanese. The expedition sailed from Buna in two detachments, the first just before midnight on D minus 2-day, consisting of six L.S.T.s escorted by the destroyers *Lamson*, *Mugford*, *Drayton*, *Flusser* and the tug *Sonoma*, and the second on the following morning, comprising 16 L.C.I.s led by the *Conyngham* (flag of Rear-Admiral Barbey) and escorted by the *Perkins*, *Smith*, *Reid*, *Mahan*, and *Henley*. The landing was made at 0445, so that the troops would have good light soon after going ashore. Opposition was slight and no great difficulties were encountered despite the fact that photographic coverage of the beaches, which were situated six miles north of Finschafen, was inadequate, whilst a party of scouts landed on the night 11th/12th September from M.T.B.s had been prevented by Japanese activity from obtaining all the supplementary information required. The first enemy air attack was made soon after noon when the last of the L.S.T.s were retiring, but no less than four squadrons of fighter aircraft of the Fifth Air Force—more than a hundred machines—were covering the landing and unloading, and caused enormous losses amongst the Japanese aircraft. The garrison of Finschafen attempted to escape in barges, many of which M.T.B.s sank.[1] The only Allied loss occurred on the following evening. Whilst the destroyers *Reid*, *Smith* and *Henley* of the VIIth Amphibious Force were engaged on anti-submarine operations off Finschafen the *Henley* (Commander C. R. Adams) was torpedoed by a submarine which escaped. She sank in three minutes with the loss of one officer and 14 men.

On the night 19th/20th October, the six U.S. destroyers *Perkins*, *Drayton*, *Mahan*, *Smith*, *Mugford* and *Reid*, whilst engaged in a convoy reinforcement operation at Langemak Bay, just south of Finschafen, were subjected for an hour and a half in bright moonlight to attacks by groups of enemy aircraft estimated to number up to sixty in all. The destroyers made smoke which evidently proved effective; but the enemy were able to conduct the attack with little gunfire to contend with, for the continuous manoeuvring of the destroyers which made large alterations of course to port and starboard under full helm with drastic changes of speed, left them few opportunities to fire their A.A. guns, and they were fortunate to escape unhit. Only the *Perkins* was near missed and had some casualties. One hundred and thirty-five holes were found in the plating of her upper works, caused by a demolition bomb filled with rivets and the like, which her side plating had, however, been strong enough to withstand.

As a result of the foregoing successful operations Allied destroyers passed through Dampier Strait and operated off the north coast of New Guinea for the first time on 28th/29th November.

Saidor, an important Japanese barge centre with airstrips, was now required by the Allies for development as a light naval operating base and an advance air base. It was captured on 2nd January, 1944, by units of the U.S. Sixth Army. The actual landing of 7,000 troops and 3,000 tons of supplies and equipment, covered by bombardment by H.M.A.S. *Arunta* and *Warramunga*, was unopposed. Less than a week previously South Pacific Forces had landed at Cape Gloucester in New Britain. The Saidor landing following immediately caught the Japanese confused and unprepared. Signs of the hasty departure of the Japanese troops gave evidence of the effectiveness of the bombardment. There was no enemy reaction to the landing until 1600 on D-day, when a force of 30 Japanese aircraft made an attack on the landing beaches. This was partially broken up by Allied fighters. The last of the landing craft had cleared the beaches about four hours previously, but some damage and casualties resulted ashore. The Saidor area and airstrips were captured on the day after the initial landing. The effect was to cut off the retreat of the enemy forces moving northward by land from the Huon Peninsula. Attempts to evacuate troops by sea were severely handled by Allied aircraft and light naval forces, whose operations in cutting off supplies were chiefly responsible for the numbers of Japanese found starved to death in the Huon Peninsula. On 14th January the Australians captured Sio, and on 13th February, when they made junction with the 32nd U.S. Division coming from the eastward final occupation of the Huon Peninsula was complete and the first phase of the campaign in New Guinea was at an end.

[1] A short description of the landing is given in *Military Reports of the United Nations*, a publication of the U.S. Military Intelligence Division.

CHAPTER XIII

Capture of New Georgia

(*See* Plans 8, 15, 16, 17, 18, 19)

103

THE capture by General MacArthur's forces of the Huon Gulf–Vitiaz Strait area was to have been the signal for the resumption of the advance in the Solomons with an assault on New Georgia by Admiral Halsey. As already noticed, however, it was finally arranged that the date of the latter operation should be advanced, and it took place simultaneously with the campaign against Lae, at the end of June 1943.

The New Georgia group of islands lies 200 miles north-west of Guadalcanal and extends in a north-westerly-south-easterly direction for 150 miles. Most of the islands are mountainous and are of volcanic origin. Off their coasts, barrier islands and reefs have formed lagoons which in times past were the habitat of a people known throughout Melanesia for their maritime aggressiveness. The first reports of Japanese activity in this area were received in August 1942. Initially, the Japanese made use of numerous hideouts and dispersal anchorages and established staging points in the islands for ferrying troops and supplies to Guadalcanal. Later, after their failure to gain command of the air over Guadalcanal in November 1942, they began to construct the airfield near Munda Point which the Americans tried vainly to neutralise by air and naval bombardment. The enemy's advanced and staging bases at Munda and Vila-Stanmore constituted a serious threat to the American plans for expansion in the Solomons. By the end of February Japanese cargo and troop ships from Rabaul were making the run to the bases not only by night but on occasion in daylight. The airfield facilities were being increased, whilst the occasional M.T.B.s reported to be based on the islands, were a threat to the development by the Americans of an advanced airfield on the Russell Islands, a small group about 30 miles north-west of Guadalcanal which, the Japanese temporary occupation having come to an end, the Allies had occupied on 21st February 1943 as a staging point for the advance to New Georgia. The Americans were bringing in supplies, equipment and personnel nightly to the Russells, installing defences, improving harbours and forming an M.T.B. base. A fighter airstrip on the east end of Banika Island was ready for use by the end of March.

In the hope of interrupting enemy shipping as much as in the expectation of causing any permanent damage Admiral Halsey gave orders for simultaneous bombardments of Vila-Stanmore and Munda early in March. Two task groups, 68.1 and 68.3, were formed under Rear-Admiral A. S. Merrill, consisting of three cruisers and three destroyers for Vila[1] and four destroyers for Munda.[2] The two groups proceeded in company through Lengo Channel (*Plan 12*), separating at 2000 on 5th March at a point seven miles north of Russell Islands. Fighter cover was given during daylight. Both bombardments were to be simultaneous. The three destroyers of the Vila group were to be used only for screening, though under certain conditions two of them, the *Conway* and *Cony*, were to open fire on the north shore of Blackett Strait. At 2230 a coast watcher's report was intercepted that two Japanese light cruisers or destroyers had left Faisi (*Plan 8*) at 1910 and were heading south at high speed. Shortly afterwards, one of the spotting aircraft sighted two enemy cruisers (actually destroyers) heading east by south at 30 knots in 7° 35' S., 156° 50' E., apparently making for Blackett Strait (see *Plan 16*). Admiral Merrill increased speed in order to arrive at the Vila bombardment line about five minutes before zero hour, lest the Munda group should open fire first and alert the enemy in Vella Gulf or Kula Gulf. At 0010 Task Group 68.1 turned to port into Kula Gulf and ran down the east side at 20 knots, keeping as close as possible to the shore where the lively surf decreased the risk of detection of the ships' wakes from the air. The flagship *Montpelier* was followed by the *Cleveland* and the *Denver*. The *Conway* took station 2,000 yards ahead of the flagship and the *Cony* dropped back on the port quarter of the cruisers to guard against motor torpedo boat attack from the many coves that indent the eastern shore of the Gulf. The *Waller* was 6,000 yards ahead, detached from the formation. The night was exceptionally dark, and navigation was entirely by SG radar.

At 0057, when the force was well down the gulf, two ships on a course approximately opposite to the Americans were discovered by radar, and at about 0100, when all ships had contact and were tracking the enemy, the flagship broke wireless silence and ordered the group by voice radio to stand-by to open fire (see *Plan 15*). A minute later, the *Montpelier* opened up with her main battery, followed by the *Cleveland* and *Denver*. There was apparently no doctrine for distribution of fire, and all three cruisers, without pre-arrangement, concentrated on the second ship in column, perhaps because she showed up better on the radar screens. The enemy replied ineffectively. After the *Montpelier's* sixth salvo a fire broke out on board the target vessel and almost simultaneously a huge explosion occurred amidships, caused by the left wing torpedo of a broadside of five fired by the *Waller* just as the cruisers opened fire. As the light silhouetted her, the enemy ship was identified as a destroyer; she broke in two and sank immediately, leaving a glowing mass of wreckage surrounded by flaming oil. The cruisers had already shifted target to the leading enemy ship, which continued on her northerly course, firing spasmodically. She was repeatedly hit, and stopped, guns silent, and she sank soon after 0130. The two enemy ships were the destroyers *Minegumo* and *Murasame*, and the Japanese report that of their entire crews only 49 men survived and swam ashore.

The shore bombardment began in an unforeseen manner while the surface engagement was at its height. The *Denver*, third cruiser in line, had ceased firing on the first Japanese ship and was training her guns on the second, when

---

[1] *Montpelier, Cleveland, Denver, Conway, Waller, Cony.*

[2] *Fletcher, O'Bannon, Nicholas, Radford.*

a battery was seen firing on the formation from a point on the west shore of the Gulf, some five miles north of Vila ; and as the starboard 5-inch battery was not engaged at the time the fire control officer ordered it to open fire on the flashes ashore. At 0118 the cruisers started the turn to a northerly course for the bombarding run. This was carried out between 0124 and 0133, using star shells. The reply from the shore was weak and ineffective. The Munda bombardment was carried out, beginning at 0141. The bombardments had little or no lasting effect. Though the Americans attacked the Munda airstrip repeatedly from dawn on the 6th enemy aircraft were soon operating from it again, and the use of the base by enemy shipping seemed to diminish only slightly, if at all, during the succeeding weeks. Other bombardments undertaken on 15th/16th March and 12th/13th May, gave similar disappointing results.

104

The Japanese continued to reinforce New Georgia and it became apparent to the Americans that they themselves had neither the ships nor the opportunities for the continual skirmishes by which alone they could put a stop to this traffic. Early in May, therefore, the Commander-in-Chief, Pacific, decided to mine the approaches to the staging base at Vila. Accordingly, on the night 6th/7th May a task group consisting of the destroyer *Radford* as guide and the light mine-layers *Preble, Gamble* and *Breeze* steamed up Ferguson Passage and laid a standard three-row minefield in Blackett Strait, 8,400 yards long, mining speed 15 knots, mining interval 12 seconds (100 yards), mining time 17 minutes, being covered whilst thus engaged by Rear-Admiral Ainsworth's task force.[1] Conditions were ideal for the operation, though it was not until the last moment that the *Radford's* radar, upon which the navigation of the force in the restricted waters depended, could be made to function effectively. The night was moonless, with intermittent violent squalls in which visibility fell to zero, a state of affairs which rendered the transit of Ferguson Passage and the close approach to Kolombangara Island hazardous. Though the operation had been thoroughly rehearsed beforehand conditions of visibility were such that a mark for beginning the lay had to be given by the *Radford* on voice radio. As the ships turned to the mining course visibility cleared sufficiently to show that the minelayers were in perfect position. The operation was apparently unobserved by the enemy, who in any case were short of mine sweeping gear, and within 48 hours it bore fruit with the sinking of three Japanese destroyers, the *Kuroshio, Oyashio* and *Kagero* : the two latter being finished off by U.S. Navy land-based bombers.

The Japanese continued to bring in reinforcements to Munda at night, using small transports and barges, occasionally escorted by destroyers and light cruisers, though it was believed that the mining of Blackett Strait forced them to bring these convoys in around the north of Kolombangara Island. It was consequently decided to lay another and more extensive minefield in Kula Gulf, combined with a bombardment of Munda and Vila Stanmore. The operation under the command of Rear-Admiral Ainsworth was timed for the night of 12th/13th May. The bombardment groups consisted of three cruisers and five destroyers for Vila Stanmore,[2] and one cruiser and two destroyers for Munda.[3] The mining group was composed, as before, of the *Radford, Preble,*

---

[1] Cruisers *Honolulu* (flag), *Nashville, St. Louis,* destroyers *O'Bannon, Chevalier, Strong, Taylor.*

[2] *Honolulu* (flag), *Helena, Nashville, Nicholas, O'Bannon, Taylor, Strong, Chevalier.*

[3] *St. Louis, Jenkins, Fletcher.*

Gamble and *Breeze*. Navigation was again by radar. Both bombardments and minelaying began simultaneously at 0100 on the 13th. Two hundred and fifty-five mines were laid. No enemy ships were encountered. Accurate navigation in the Gulf was found to be extremely difficult : at distances of 10 to 15 miles from land positions were in error up to two miles, decreasing to half a mile when within six or eight miles of the shore. During the bombardment an explosion occurred in the gun chamber of No. 3 turret in the *Nashville*; 29 men were killed or seriously injured, two of the three guns were put out of action and the ship had to go to San Francisco for repairs. The results of the bombardment were again disappointing, for the airfield was in use once more within 12 hours. There is no record that any ship was ever sunk in the minefield.[1] The advantages of the operation had been weighed against the difficulty of getting the ships out of the Gulf in the event of opposition, but the Commander-in-Chief, Pacific, subsequently reported that he did not consider a large-scale bombardment involving heavy expenditure of ammunition merely for harassing purposes, with the ships exposed to M.T.B. and submarine attack, was justified, though a minor bombardment to cover the minelaying operation would have been worth while.

105

The British aircraft carrier *Victorious* from the United Kingdom arrived at Numea on 17th May and joined Task Force 14. In consequence of the arrival of this ship and of the battleship *North Carolina* and the departure to reinforce the North Pacific Area, of the *Enterprise, Washington* and *Nashville* and the only three effective 8-inch cruisers, the *Louisville, San Francisco* and *Wichita*, Admiral Halsey's Task Forces were reconstituted on 1st June as follows :—

Task Force 10 :
    Battleships *Massachusetts, Indiana, North Carolina*.
    10th Destroyer Squadron : *Henley, Helm, Bagley, Selfridge, Mugford, Patterson, Ralph Talbot, Stanly.*

Task Force 11 :
    Battleships *Maryland, Colorado.*
    22nd Carrier Division : (escort carriers) *Sangamon, Suwannee, Chenango.*
    15th and 28th Destroyer Divisions : *Lang, Sterett, Stack, Wilson, Conway, Eaton, Converse.*

Task Force 14 :
    Carriers *Saratoga*, H.M.S. *Victorious.*
    Light Cruisers *San Juan, San Diego.*
    6th Destroyer Squadron : *Maury, Craven, Gridley, McCall, Dunlap, Cummings, Case, Fanning.*

Task Force 18 :
    9th Cruiser Division : *Honolulu, Helena, St. Louis*, H.M.N.Z.S. *Leander.*
    21st Destroyer Squadron : *Chevalier, O'Bannon, Strong, Taylor, Nicholas, Fletcher, Radford, Jenkins.*

Task Force 19 :
    12th Cruiser Division : *Montpelier, Denver, Columbia, Cleveland.*
    43rd Destroyer Division : *Waller, Saufley, Philip, Renshaw, Pringle.*

---

[1] *The Offensive Minelaying Campaign against Japan* (U.S. Strategic Bombing Survey), p. 103 states that one merchant ship was sunk and one damaged in the minefield, but the joint Army/Navy Assessment Committee found no ship over 500 G.R.T. was lost in the field and *The War against Japanese Transportation* (U.S. Strategic Bombing Survey) and Japanese Monograph No. 116 show no ship sunk there.

In addition, there were available for escort duties or to reinforce screens when necessary the 23rd Destroyer Division (*Gwin, Woodworth, Buchanan, Farenholt, McCalla*) and the 1st Mining Division (*Preble, Breeze, Gamble*).

The Americans still continued their practice of operating their carriers separately, each with her own close screen. Battleships were included in the screen even when manoeuvring at 25 knots, and in submarine waters, the risk being accepted if air attack was imminent and considered a greater menace than submarine attack.

By the time preparations for the assault on New Georgia were complete the Americans had four fully operational airfields in Guadalcanal and two in the Russell Islands. Both naval and army aircraft in the South Pacific were under the command of a naval commander, Vice-Admiral A. W. Fitch who had taken over from Rear-Admiral McCain on 20th September 1942. Admiral Fitch flew his flag in the seaplane tender *Curtiss*. The command, which was subordinate to Admiral Halsey, included 40 flying boats operating from Espiritu Santo, Santa Cruz, and occasionally Suva, and a similar number of Army long range bombardment aircraft operating from Espiritu Santo.

The operational plan for the invasion of New Georgia envisaged simultaneous landings on 30th June at several points on Rendova Island and at Viru Harbour, Segi Point and Wickham Anchorage on New Georgia Island (see *Plan 16*). The landings on New Georgia were to be made without preliminary bombardment, but support fire was provided for. The main thrust was to come from Rendova. At the first opportunity troops from there were to move across Roviana Lagoon and land east of Munda to capture the airfield in one quick stroke. This movement was to be covered by preliminary landings on Sasavele and Baraulu Islands, which would secure the Onaiavisi entrance to the lagoon. The attack from Rendova was to be accompanied by the seizure of enemy positions in the Bairoko–Enogai area, in order to prevent the Munda garrison from being reinforced from the north. This was to be accomplished by troops from the Russells. As soon as the Munda and the Bairoko–Enogai areas were occupied, preparations were to be made to capture the Vila–Stanmore position on Kolombangara.

Three major task forces were provided (*see* Appendix N). The Amphibious Force, Task Force 31, under Rear-Admiral R. K. Turner, was to carry out the landings. It was subdivided into two groups. The Western, under Admiral Turner's own orders, conducted the operations in the Rendova–Munda area, whilst the Eastern Force was responsible for the landings and subsequent operations at Viru, Segi, and Wickham Anchorage, at the south-east end of the New Georgia group. Task Force 36, a powerful aircraft carrier and battleship force under the direct command of Admiral Halsey, was to cover the operation and furnish fire support. South Pacific Air Force (Task Force 33) under Vice-Admiral A. W. Fitch, rendered the main air support; it conducted reconnaissance and strikes, provided direct air support during and after landings, and furnished liaison and spotting aircraft. Submarines (Task Force 72) were to start an offensive reconnaissance near latitude 1° N. to the northward of the prevailing equatorial weather front, primarily for detection of enemy forces on passage south from Truk. When the enemy became aware of the operations, the submarines were to withdraw to the southward and cover the Buka–New Ireland Channel and the north side of Bougainville.

For four days before the landing, Munda was heavily attacked by naval bombardment aircraft. On the night of 29th/30th June a group of light cruisers and destroyers (Task Group 36.2)[1] under Rear-Admiral A. S. Merrill bombarded the Buin–Shortland area, whilst the minelayers *Preble*, *Gamble* and *Breeze*, led by the *Pringle*, laid 336 mines off Shortland Harbour (on the south-east side of Shortland Island) (*see Plan 8*). This area was 231 miles beyond the most advanced Allied base in the Russell Islands and it seemed almost certain that the task force and minelayers would be detected *en route*. The bombardment and minelaying operations were therefore to be preceded by a diversionary bombardment of the Vila–Stanmore area by two of the destroyers, in the hope of concealing the real object. The weather deteriorated during the night, visibility decreasing almost to zero, and the forces reached their objectives unobserved. Rear-Admiral Merrill after the operation expressed the opinion that simultaneous bombardment and minelaying operations were of little value except in forward enemy-held areas where the Japanese were unable to maintain adequate sweeping services. It is a fact that no Japanese ship was ever lost in this minefield. The effect of the bombardment was merely to alert the enemy to the need of sweeping prior to initiating any ship movements in the area. Higher authority felt, however, that the slow old minelayers which were all that were presently available, must be given the protection of bombardment.

The landing at Segi Point in southern New Georgia was made by the 4th Marine Raider Battalion on 21st June in advance of the main operation as a result of reports that the Japanese were moving into the area. It was unopposed.

At 0230 on 30th June the destroyer *Talbot* and the minesweeper *Zane* landed units of the 43rd Division on Sasavele and Baraulu Islands. The *Zane* ran ashore in the low visibility and heavy rain storms and did not get off until the afternoon when the ships immediately cleared the area and took station astern of the main task group, which had by that time completed the landings at Rendova and was passing through Blanche Channel *en route* to Tulagi.

The main landing in New Georgia took place on 30th June at Rendova Harbour on the north side of the island of that name. Troops from an advance unit[2] landed at dawn to secure the beachhead for the occupation force which followed an hour later. The landing of the first echelon[3] was opposed by machine gun fire from the beach and by the shore batteries in the Munda Point area. The first salvo registered a hit on the destroyer *Gwin*. Seven batteries were put out of action by the destroyers *Buchanan* and *Farenholt*, exchange of fire between shore batteries and destroyers continuing intermittently throughout the day. By 0730 all troops except ship working details had been landed. Within two hours of the initial landing batteries were emplaced on Kokorana Island and were shelling the enemy at Munda. The transports completed unloading by 1500, having twice to get under way owing to the threat of air attack. It was not until cruising formation had been assumed and the force was standing out through Blanche Channel for the return to Guadalcanal, that air attack actually materialised. A group of 24 to 28 Japanese torpedo bombers

---

[1] Light cruisers *Montpelier, Cleveland, Columbia, Denver* ; destroyers *Waller, Renshaw, Saufley, Philip*.

[2] Transports : *Dent, Waters*.

[3] Transports : *McCawley* (flag of Rear-Admiral Turner), *President Jackson, President Adams, President Hayes, Algorab, Libra* ; Screening Unit : *Gwin, Woodworth, Jenkins, Radford* ; Fire Support Unit : *Farenholt, Buchanan, McCalla, Ralph Talbot*.

with fighter escort which had fought its way through the opposition of 16 marine fighters, was sighted coming in over the north-west corner of New Georgia Island. As the attack began all ships opened fire. Ignoring their losses, the bombers pressed home the attack to point of release at 500 yards or less. The *Farenholt* was hit by a torpedo dropped from 300 yards, a distance presumably inside pistol safety range, for the torpedo failed to arm. The *McCalla* avoided three torpedoes, one of which apparently passed under the ship. The transport *McCawley*, flagship of Rear-Admiral Turner, was hit by a torpedo which tore a hole 18 to 20 feet in diameter in her side and she began to settle. In 8 minutes the attack was over. Only two of the enemy aircraft survived the attacks of the protecting fighters and the fire of the ships ; both were shot down by American aircraft during their retirement. About an hour later, the *McCawley* was attacked by a group of 12 to 15 dive bombers. She was unhit, but was already clearly sinking, and was abandoned. At 2023 friendly M.T.B.s, mistaking her for an enemy, sank her with three torpedoes.

The landings in Wickham Anchorage, Vangunu Island, took place at 0345 on the 30th under hazardous conditions in high winds and heavy seas.[1] From the transports, the outline of the beach could scarcely anywhere be discerned, and after one or two boats had been loaded it was discovered that the transports were in the wrong position, and they had to shift berth. The first wave of boats became thrown into confusion, and the troops landed along a stretch of 6 or 7 miles of coast to the west of the designated landing beach. Six boats were lost in the heavy surf. There was no opposition, however, and the landing was completed by 1000. By 3rd July all objectives in the area were taken.

The landing at Viru was delayed until 1st July. The directive provided that the landing force should not go ashore until the enemy guns guarding the entrance to the harbour had been immobilised by the advance unit attacking from the direction of Segi. Enemy resistance delayed the unit, and the transports[2] which arrived off Viru at 0610 on 30th June, were shelled by a shore battery and retired. Orders were given to change the landing place to Segi ; and there the troops landed. The capture of Viru by the advance unit was reported at 1700 on 1st July and additional forces were able to land directly from seaward that night.

The landings at Rice Anchorage in Kula Gulf, on the north coast of New Georgia, were also postponed for 24 hours, and took place on the morning of 5th July. Their object was to prevent the Japanese garrison at Munda from receiving reinforcements from Kolombangara. By that time, the American beachheads east of Munda were firmly established, and preparations were being made to advance on the airfields. The landing force consisted of two battalions of infantry and a Raider Battalion, the transport group being made up of seven destroyer transports[3] and the destroyer *McCalla*, with a mine group[4] and a screening unit.[5] During the night of 4th/5th July, in preparation for these landings, as there was little possibility of surprise, Task Group 36.1 consisting of the cruisers *Honolulu*, *Helena* and *St. Louis* and four destroyers[6] under

---

[1] Composition of force : Minesweeper *Trever* (flag of Read-Admiral G. H. Fort) ; high speed transports : *Schley, McKean, L.C.I.s 24, 233, 333, 334, 335, 336 ;* Landing force : 2 companys 4th Marine Raider Bn.

[2] *Kilty* (S.O., Commander S. Leith), *Crosby*, minesweeper *Hopkins*, one L.C.V. Landing force 1½ companys 103rd Infantry, 20th Construction Bn., Naval Base Units, Battery E (less one platoon), 70th Coast Artillery.

[3] *Dent, Talbot, Waters, McKean, Kilty, Crosby, Schley.*

[4] *Hopkins, Trever*, destroyer *Ralph Talbot.*   [5] *Woodworth, Gwin, Radford.*

[6] *Nicholas, O'Bannon, Strong, Chevalier.*

Rear-Admiral Ainsworth, bombarded enemy positions and gun batteries in the Vila–Stanmore and Bairoko Harbour areas. The enemy replied with four well concealed 4·9-inch guns at Enogai. No ship sustained more than light damage, but the destroyer *Strong* was torpedoed by an unseen antagonist and sank very quickly. Her commanding officer, Commander J. H. Wallings and three-quarters of the crew were saved, blinded by oil fuel and suffering from the concussion of the destroyer's depth charges although these had been set to safe. The weapon that sank the *Strong* was one of the Japanese Mark 93 long range, oxygen fuelled torpedoes[1] fired by a division of destroyers many miles to the northward, standing into the Gulf on a transport mission. This was not known at the time, but the fact that the *Chevalier* and *O'Bannon* remained on the spot during rescue operations and were not hit led the Americans to believe that a two-man submarine may have been responsible. One or two surface contacts had been detected in the Gulf by the bombarding force but the firing ships were employing their radars not for search, but for fire control and station keeping ; it was too close to the land for reliable detection of surface vessels by radar ; the installations moreover as not infrequently happened were affected by gunfire shock in various degrees. The enemy appeared unaware of the presence of the landing force until daylight. At 0559 when 98 per cent. of the troops had been landed and the volume and accuracy of fire of the shore batteries was increasing all transports were ordered to clear the area.

When the attack on New Georgia began, many of the larger Japanese submarines of the Sixth Fleet were in the north, supporting the Aleutian operations. The available boats were despatched to New Georgia to intercept the Allied landings. They were quickly detected. At 1948 on 1st July, during the retirement of the Amphibious Force from Rendova the *Radford*, one of the screening destroyers, made a radar contact at 12,000 yards, and caught *RO–101* on the surface in Blanche Channel, sinking her with gunfire and depth charges. At 0448 on the 11th *I–25* was sunk in a similar manner by the destroyer *Taylor* whilst standing out of Kula Gulf. The enemy submarines achieved only two successes. On 18th July L.S.T. 342 was torpedoed and sunk south of New Georgia whilst proceeding independently, nearly a hundred of her crew and the troops aboard being lost. Two days later, H.M.A.S. *Hobart* operating with the *Australia* and six destroyers (Task Force 74) south-east of San Cristobal was hit aft by a torpedo, but reached Espiritu Santo under her own power.

107

On 4th July the Japanese 22nd Destroyer Division ran reinforcements to Kolombangara undetected by the Allies. A similar operation was ordered for the night of the 5th/6th (*see Plan 17*). On the afternoon of 5th July while Task Group 36.1 (*see* Appendix N) was between Guadalcanal and San Cristobal, returning to a fuelling rendezvous after the bombardment operation of the previous night Admiral Ainsworth received orders to reverse course and proceed northwards to the Kula Gulf area in order to intercept a Japanese force of small high speed ships which was expected to pass through Kula Gulf or Blackett Strait that night with troop reinforcements. The Task Group reversed course and proceeded via Indispensable Strait and close to the southern end of Santa Isabel Island at 29 knots in order to reach the Gulf in time to intercept, picking up the *Radford* and the *Jenkins* in place of the sunken *Strong* and the *Chevalier*, the latter having been damaged whilst going alongside the *Strong* to

---

[1] Details of the torpedo are given on page 54, footnote 1.

take off survivors. The force steamed up the ' Slot ' in night anti-aircraft cruising formation, the cruisers in single line ahead 5 cables apart in the order *Honolulu* (flag), *Helena, St. Louis*, with the destroyers *Nicholas* and *O Bannon* 3,000 yards fine on the ' engaged ' bow of the flagship and the *Radford* and *Jenkins* 2,000 yards on the ' engaged ' quarter of the rear ship. As the Gulf was entered, speed was reduced first to 27 then to 25 knots, to economise fuel. The night was very dark and squally, visibility 1 to 2 miles. No information of the enemy had been received from night reconnaissance aircraft. The task group had orders to retire at 0200 on 6th July if contact with the Japanese had not been made.

The enemy force consisted of ten destroyers under Rear-Admiral T. Akiyama which had come down the Slot from Buin to land troops and supplies at Vila, was in three groups, as follows[1] :—

Support Unit (Rear-Admiral T. Akiyama) :
Niizuki, Suzukaze, Tanikaze.

1st Transport Unit :
Mochizuki, Mikazuki, Hamakaze.

2nd Transport Unit :
Amagiri, Hatsuyuki, Nagatsuki, Satsuki.

The Japanese destroyers were armed with Mark 93 24-inch, 49-knot torpedoes, a fact which was not known to Admiral Ainsworth.[2]

At 0136 while on course 290°, with Visuvisu Point New Georgia, bearing 1440 distant 11 miles the flagship made radar contact with an enemy group on the port beam[3] about 5 miles east of Kolombangara Island, range 26,500 yards. Ordering the destroyers to assume battle formation, which entailed forming into sub-divisions ahead and astern of the cruiser line, the Admiral informed his ships that the action would be fought in accordance with Night Battle Plan 1.[4] This entailed opening fire at ranges between 8,000 and 10,000 yards in full radar control without illuminants. At 0142 the force was turned 60° to port together to close the range, and at 0150 a turn together to starboard placed the formation on a firing course of 292°. The Japanese Admiral had detached the 1st Transport Unit to land its troops at Vila more than an hour earlier whilst running up the Gulf. He was just sending off the 2nd Transport Unit when Admiral Ainsworth turned to port at 0142. The 2nd Transport Unit broke off on a reverse course as ordered but Admiral Akiyama, sighting the American force five minutes later ordered the unit to turn back again to a northerly course (0154) to support him.

Most of the American ships soon had contact on their radars. The flagship's analysis was three ships followed by four slightly larger ships (actually all seven were destroyers) all on the same line of bearing 355°. The distance between ships appeared to be about 600 yards. The interval between groups 6,000 to 8,000 yards, was too great to permit attacking them simultaneously, so Admiral Ainsworth decided to ' blast (the leading) group first, reach ahead,

---

[1] Based on Morison, *History of U.S. Naval Operations in World War II*, Vol. VI, p. 162.

[2] Morison, Vol. VI, p. 196, says : ' Why was everyone in the South Pacific, from Admiral Halsey down, ignorant of this ' long lance ' and its performance ? Japanese destroyers had employed it since the beginning of the war. One is said to have been picked up on Cape Esperance in January or February 1943 and taken apart, and the data sent to Pacific Fleet Intelligence, but nothing except rumour appears to have reached the Fleet—not even Halsey's Staff knew about it.'

[3] The official account (Battle Experience No. 10) says the enemy bore 218°, but the plan shows the bearing to have been about 280°.

[4] *See* Appendix L.

then make a simultaneous turn and get the others on the reverse course.' Admiral Ainsworth's turn back into line ahead at 0150 had put the leading group which was closing at high speed, approximately on the port beam. After this manœuvre the two van destroyers, *Nicholas* and *O'Bannon*, found themselves on the disengaged bow of the flagship and were unable to deliver an early torpedo attack without endangering the cruisers. The rear destroyers had been unable to reach their positions in the battle dispositions before the first turn signal was executed, and the *Jenkins* fouled the range of the *Radford* during the early part of the engagement. The Admiral designated the leading enemy group as the target and waited for reports from the ships that they were ready to open fire, a practice which appears to have been standard in Task Force 18. He waited too long. The Japanese had already fired torpedoes, and when the O.T.C. gave the order to open fire, at 0157, the range was down to approximately 7,000 yards, and the ships, which had maintained a steady course and speed for seven minutes, and continued to do so for a further seven, were approaching an area heavily infested with torpedoes. The Americans poured in very heavy gunfire on the Japanese, concentrating on the *Niizuki* ; and with her steering gear destroyed the enemy ship sank very quickly with heavy loss, including her Captain and Admiral Akiyama.

Since first contact with the enemy, fifty or more high frequency voice transmissions had been made by the Americans. There seems to have been a feeling that in a night action such as this the rapidly changing situation together with the use of slang expressions and code words, constituted sufficient safeguard to prevent the enemy learning anything from the transmissions. The practice resulted however in loss of surprise, and though the Japanese radar failed to give them warning the American voice radio transmissions enabled them to track the force by D/F.[1] The leading enemy group at 0153 began a simultaneous turn to port and the *Suzukaze* and *Tanikaze* fired torpedoes, the *Niizuki* having already been overwhelmed by the American gunfire. The effect of the turn was that they were enfiladed by the guns of the Americans, whose fire, however, like the Japanese reply, achieved no definite result. Of the American destroyers only the *Jenkins* fired torpedoes :[2] all missed. By 0204 all enemy ships visible on the flagship's screen appeared (erroneously) to be stopped or out of action, and Admiral Ainsworth gave the order to turn 16 points to starboard, to attack the rear group. The salvoes of torpedoes fired by the first Japanese group had just begun to arrive.[3] Three struck the *Helena* within the space of 2½ minutes, and one, fortunately blind, the *St. Louis*. A fifth passed the *Honolulu* close aboard. The *Helena* with her bow blown off, turned out of line to port in a sinking condition just as the other cruisers were executing the 16-point turn : in the low visibility and smoke of battle this was not noticed by the flagship until later. Unlike the other cruisers which used flashless propellant and salvo firing, the *Helena*, which had used up her flashless propellant in the previous night's bombardment, used smokeless (full flash) powder and continuous firing.

---

[1] Interrogation No. 75 and *Secret Information Bulletin No. 10, Battle Experience* Series.

[2] ' Insufficient training and excitement of battle combined with the complicated control installation probably accounts for this. The van destroyers were apparently prevented from launching torpedoes due to their position on the disengaged bow of the cruisers.' (*Secret Information Bulletin No. 10*, 52–10.)

[3] ' Captain Cecil of *Helena*, who had heard the rumour (of the Japanese Mark 93 torpedo), warned Admiral Ainsworth, when discussing his battle plan before the Kula Gulf action, against closing to 10,000 yards ; but Ainsworth, with no definite information, and believing that *Strong* had been sunk by a submarine's torpedo, felt he could dismiss the tale.' (Morison, *History of U.S. Naval Operations in World War II*, Vol. VI, p. 196.)

Immediately upon completion of the 16-point turn course was altered to 142° to close the enemy. The *Honolulu* and *St. Louis* continued to fire at the *Suzukaze* and *Tanikaze* as opportunity offered, but the destroyers became dispersed and out of position. The *O'Bannon* sheered off to the north out of formation, fired five torpedoes at 0213 at no discoverable target, and did not regain station until about 0230. The *Nicholas* and *Jenkins* more or less maintained station, but the *Radford*, which had already turned out of line to clear the *Jenkins*, became widely separated from the rest. She launched four torpedoes at the leading enemy group at 0210, following this up by gunfire, before the enemy retired into Kula Gulf.

At 0214 the Americans made a simultaneous turn of 60° to port and took under fire the second enemy group which was then coming up fast on a northerly course, at ranges between 11,000 and 9,000 yards. Their reply fire was light and ineffective, for only the two leading Japanese ships, the *Amagiri* and the *Hatsuyuki*, could see the target, and the rear ships *Nagatsuki* and *Satsuzuki* did not open fire. Three of the four ships turned away to starboard and one, the *Hatsuyuki*, to port.

At 0244 Admiral Ainsworth made a sweep to the north-west as no ships were visible on the radar screens, and between 0240 and 0249 the *Honolulu* and *St. Louis* fired star shells in order to illuminate any possible targets but as none were seen cease firing was ordered at 0250. The *Nicholas* made a radar sweep into the mouth of Vella Gulf and the *Radford* into Kula Gulf, but no enemy were discovered. The two destroyers then proceeded to the rescue of *Helena's* oil-soaked survivors, who were scattered over an area a mile square. They were several times interrupted by the appearance on the radar screens of enemy destroyers coming back into the battle after reloading torpedoes and the 2nd Transport Group returning up the east coast of Kolombangara after landing their troops. On the first two occasions no engagement resulted, but about 0522 the *Nicholas* fired five torpedoes at a range of 7,950 yards at the *Amagiri* which had returned to rescue the *Niizuki's* survivors, and at 0530 the *Radford* fired at the same ship : the four torpedoes fired by the *Radford* straddled the enemy but did not hit. A short gun engagement in which the enemy's fire caused no damage then ensued before the Japanese ship retired. The *Mochizuki* appeared a few minutes later and was engaged in her turn without definite result. She had been delayed in leaving Vila after landing her troops.

Admiral Ainsworth had retired at 0327, but reversed course for a few minutes some three-quarters of an hour later, on the *Radford* reporting her first enemy contact. Daylight was breaking as the final engagement of the *Nicholas* and *Radford* with enemy destroyers came to an end. Taking into account the retirement of the enemy and absence of information as to his strength and whereabouts, together with the possibility of submarines being in the area and the probability of air attack very shortly, the Admiral ordered the two destroyers to retire. The task force returned to Espiritu Santo with 20 to 30 per cent of fuel on board. The cruisers had ammunition sufficient for only ten minutes firing by their main batteries : the *St. Louis* alone had expended 900 rounds of 6-inch. Captain C. P. Cecil and 68 officers and 912 men of the *Helena's* crew, out of 77 officers and 1,110 men, were saved, many of them being subsequently rescued from the shore of Vella Lavella where they had landed and remained in hiding, aided by coast watchers and friendly natives. Admiral Ainsworth's first report stated that at least six enemy ships had been sunk and one beached, subsequently scaled down to two Japanese destroyers sunk and others possibly sunk or damaged. Actually, the only enemy loss apart from the *Niizuki* was the *Nagatsuki* which ran ashore near Vila whilst making for the anchorage to land her troops after the battle. The *Satsuki* attempted in vain to pull her off, and she was destroyed by bombing during the 6th.[1] None of the other enemy destroyers suffered more than slight damage : the *Tanikaze* was hit by a blind shell and the *Hatsuyuki* by two which in spite of being blind knocked out her steering gear and flooded her engine room. The *Amagiri* was hit by four shells, all of which detonated, and had ten men killed.

108

Bombardments in support of the troops were carried out on 8th/9th and 11th/12th July, when cruisers and destroyers fired a total of 3,204 rounds of 6-inch and 6,751 of 5-inch. They damaged the Japanese morale but little else.[2] On 11th July H.M.N.Z.S. *Leander* joined Admiral Ainsworth's task group as a replacement for the *Helena*. That night the group operated as a covering force for a unit of high speed transports engaged in unloading munitions and supplies at Rice Anchorage. During this operation the *Leander* which mounted two quadruple torpedo tubes but carried only eight 6-inch and four 4-inch high angle guns as against the U.S. cruisers' fifteen 6-inch and eight 5-inch H.A./L.A. guns, was employed as a destroyer.

On 12th July it was learned that the Japanese intended to send a fast convoy from Rabaul to land reinforcements at Vila, in Kolombangara Island, and Admiral Halsey instructed Admiral Turner to reinforce Admiral Ainsworth with all available destroyers for a night operation up the Slot. Only six were available. These were from three different squadrons (flotillas) and had never before functioned together as a tactical unit nor had the Commander of Squadron 12, to which three of the destroyers belonged, ever had an opportunity to exercise the ships of his squadron in making an attack. Admiral Ainsworth sailed from Tulagi at 1700, picking up off Santa Isabel Island such of the six reinforcing destroyers as were at sea. His orders were to arrive north of Visuvisu Point at 0100 on the 13th and to retire by 0230 if no contact was made with the enemy. He organised his force for battle as follows :—

Task Force 18 (Rear-Admiral W. L. Ainsworth)
Destroyer Squadron 21 *Nicholas, O'Bannon, Taylor, Jenkins, Radford.*
Cruiser Division 9   *Honolulu* (flag), H.M.N.Z.S. *Leander, St. Louis.*
Destroyer Squadron 12 *Ralph Talbot, Buchanan, Maury, Woodworth, Gwin.*

The force proceeded at 25 knots on a north-westerly course to the northward of New Georgia. The cruisers were in single line ahead, five cables apart, with the destroyers of Squadron 21 spread on a screen 5,000 yards ahead and those of Squadron 12 spread 4,000 yards astern. The visibility was five miles between rain squalls. At 0036 a reconnaissance aircraft reported an enemy force of one cruiser and five destroyers north of Vella Lavella, about 26 miles ahead of the Allied force, heading south-east at high speed. This was the escort of four destroyer-transports carrying 300 troops apiece, under Rear-Admiral S. Izaki, which had sailed from Rabaul on the morning of the 12th, with a force organised as follows :—

Light cruiser   *Jintsu* (flag).
Destroyers   *Mikazuki, Yukikaze, Hamakaze, Kiyonami, Yugure.*
Destroyer-transports *Satusuki, Minazuki, Yunagi, Matsukaze.*

---

[1] Morison, *History of U.S. Naval Operations in World War II*, Vol. VI, pp. 172–175. The Joint Assessment Committee found however that the *Nagatsuki* was sunk by U.S. surface craft.

[2] Cincpac Reprint of Early Reports of Operations in the Pacific Ocean Areas, July 1943, Annex D.

On receipt of this report Admiral Ainsworth ordered the destroyers to form divisions in line ahead and speed was increased to 28 knots (the *Leander's* maximum) course 275°. His battle line at this time is estimated to have extended over a distance of six miles, and the course and speed was maintained until 0107, a period of 31 minutes after the receipt of the aircraft enemy report. During this period some 50 voice transmissions were made. The Japanese discovered the Allied force long before the latter detected the Japanese :—

> ' Since Ainsworth has radar and the enemy has none, he expects to make a surprise attack and is confident that he has. But the Japanese task force is using a new and clever radar-detecting device. By receiving and plotting the electric impulses from the American radar Izaki has determined the presence of Ainsworth's force almost two hours before, and plotted his approach accurately for one hour before the battle joined.'[1]

At 0102 the Commander of the van destroyers reported enemy bearing 309° and a minute later that the enemy were in sight visually. The cruisers, except the *Leander* which had no radar comparable to the American SG, had already obtained radar contact at about 30,000 yards. At 0107 Admiral Ainsworth specified Battle Plan A which entailed opening fire at ranges of 8,000 to 10,000 yards without illuminants. The van destroyers immediately altered course in succession to 305° to close the range for torpedo attack. The enemy's course was 120°, speed estimated as 25 knots, the destroyer *Mikazuki* leading, followed by the *Jintsu*, with the remaining four destroyers in the rear. Two minutes later, Admiral Ainsworth ordered the destroyers to fire torpedoes at discretion. The van destroyers fired their torpedoes between 0111 and 0113, the range of the *Jintsu* from the *Nicholas* being 8,150 yards. The attack was not a co-ordinated one nor was that from the four rear destroyers which fired their torpedoes two minutes later, at a range of some 11,000 yards, from a most difficult position. They were bunched together as the result of two turns to port together executed before they were properly on station in the battle disposition; the *Ralph Talbot's* torpedoes must have narrowly missed the *St. Louis* and the *Radford's* the flagship, whilst torpedoes from the *Buchanan* and *Woodworth* were fired on a course unlikely to hit the enemy. At 0122 three minutes after the order to the destroyers to fire torpedoes and before the torpedoes had time to reach the target Admiral Ainsworth ordered the cruisers to open fire with gun armament, turning them at the same time 30° to port, the range from the flagship to the leading enemy ship having closed to 10,200 yards. Spotting was by the night Catalina which had originally reported the enemy. The *Leander* took as target an enemy ship which had just exposed a searchlight. This was the *Jintsu*. She extinguished the searchlight almost immediately and thereafter the *Leander* continued to fire using radar ranges and, since target bearing indication by radar was inaccurate, hits on enemy ships and his gun flashes as points of aim. The *Honolulu* and *St. Louis* also concentrated on the largest pip on the radar screen, the *Jintsu*. The latter replied, but made no hits before she was stopped and overwhelmed by this concentrated gunfire. She was also hit by one or perhaps two torpedoes after being immobilised.[2] The ship broke in half and sank with the loss of almost all hands, including the Admiral and her captain.

---

[1] Morison, Vol. VI, p. 183.

[2] Morison, *op. cit.*, p. 184 says the three cruisers fired 2,630 rounds of 6-inch at her.

Up to now, the two forces had been passing on opposite courses, and at 0117 Admiral Ainsworth ordered ' 18 Turn ' (16-point turn together) to port, his ships being then theoretically on a line of bearing of 275°, course 245°, though actually not all the ships were in station. It was a bold manœuvre with a force composed of ships with different turning circles which had not trained together. Owing to a voice radio defect the executive for the 16-point turn came through so faintly that the *Leander* and four of the five rear destroyers missed it, and the situation was further complicated by the dense smoke from the American flashless propellant. Collisions were narrowly avoided. The Japanese had turned away at 0108 and fired torpedoes (one minute before Admiral Ainsworth's order to his destroyers) as soon as they had visual contact with the Allied force. The enemy's torpedoes now arrived and one of them struck the *Leander* just after she had steadied on the new course, flooding one of her boiler rooms, rendering a second untenable, causing other damage, and putting the ship out of action. Twenty-eight men were killed. The *Leander* was escorted back to Tulagi by the *Radford* and *Jenkins*, the former of which had engine trouble whilst the latter had become separated from the formation. There now appeared to be only three enemy ships on the radar screen, all of them stopped, but the night Catalina reported four enemy ships steaming north at high speed and the van destroyers were ordered to pursue. Four of them moved out. They completed the sinking of the *Jintsu*, but did not go further. Of this however Admiral Ainsworth was unaware, for he had lost touch with them.

Meanwhile, the Japanese destroyer-transports had retired unseen under the coast of Kolombangara and the four enemy destroyers completed reloading torpedoes and turned back at 0136 to continue the fight. Six minutes later, the two American cruisers and the rear destroyers, which latter were out of position, turned to a north-westerly course to pursue the enemy reported by the reconnaissance aircraft steering north. At 0156 Admiral Ainsworth made contact with the four Japanese destroyers which were now returning and closing rapidly on a course 130°, bearing 284°, range 20,400 yards. Uncertain whether or not they were not his own van destroyers, he spent several minutes in establishing the whereabouts of the latter, and it was not until 0206 that he ordered ships to turn 60° to starboard together and open fire. The Japanese used the delay to good advantage, and the *St. Louis*, *Honolulu* and the destroyer *Gwin* were torpedoed in quick succession before firing a single round. The enemy after firing their torpedoes, retired unhit and the battle ended. The *Gwin* lost two officers and 59 men ; she could not be saved and had later to be scuttled. The *Honolulu* and *St. Louis* made Tulagi under their own steam.

The new Japanese 24-inch torpedo was shown to be a formidable weapon, and the Allies had paid a heavy price for defeating this latest reinforcement attempt. Nevertheless, the two night actions of 5th/6th and 12th/13th July removed the threat to the Allied landings on the north coast of New Georgia. They also deterred the Japanese from continuing to use the Kula Gulf route to supply and reinforce their garrisons at Vila and Munda. During the remainder of the campaign the enemy was reduced to the expedient of sending ships and barges around Vella Lavella to the west of Kolombangara and concealing them in anchorages along the south coast of that island. If Admiral Ainsworth was rash in pursuing with his cruisers at night a group of enemy destroyers which had had time to reload torpedoes and of whose position he was uncertain, at least he had shown that aggressiveness without which battles are seldom won.

The Japanese learned from the battle that radar was essential in a fleet engagement, and they at once began to equip their ships with all speed.

Twelve months later, all ships of destroyer size and larger were equipped with some form of radar, principally early warning radar to detect aircraft, but as late as October 1944 the battleships *Fuso* and *Yamashiro* were sunk in a night action without being able to fire a single shot, having no effective fire control radar. The efficiency of the various types of Japanese equipment was generally lower than the Allied, and difficulty was experienced in training personnel to maintain and operate it.

109

Progress against Munda airfield was slow. On 15th July Major-General O. W. Griswold assumed command ashore in New Georgia, and at the same time Rear-Admiral T. S. Wilkinson relieved Rear-Admiral Turner in command of the South Pacific Amphibious Force, the latter being required to take charge of the amphibious forces in the forthcoming Central Pacific operations. Ten days later the troops began the final assault on the Munda airfield. It was co-ordinated with a bombardment by seven destroyers[1] and the heaviest air bombardment yet seen in the South Pacific, 145 tons of bombs being dropped by 171 bombers in half an hour. By 5th August the enemy were worn down and all organised resistance ceased around Munda airfield.

During the last two weeks of the campaign Allied naval operations were mainly confined to activity by M.T.B.s under Captain E. J. Moran, Commander Motor Torpedo Boat Squadrons South Pacific. Throughout the period M.T.B. patrol groups based on Rendova made almost nightly contacts with the Japanese, forcing them to employ landing barges in preference to the larger destroyer-transports. As at first armed, the M.T.B.s were not well equipped to destroy the Japanese barges : these latter were immune to torpedo attack because of their shallow draft, whilst the M.T.B.s' light guns were ineffective except against personnel ; moreover many of the barges carried heavier arma-ment than the M.T.B.s. Later, 37-mm. guns were mounted in the latter. Nevertheless, some sinkings of barges were achieved. Communication difficulties resulting in a few accidental encounters between M.T.B.s and other surface craft or aircraft caused the Rendova boats to be limited to operations south of 8° S., whilst those based on Lever Harbour, on the north-east side of New Georgia Island, were confined to port when the cruisers went up the Slot. The Japanese were consequently able sometimes to pass shipping through Wilson and Gizo Straits hugging the shore of Vella Lavella, and to cross Vella Gulf to Kolombangara without interference from the M.T.B.s. The latter contributed in no small measure, however, to the success of the operations against Munda, by systematically searching out enemy supply concentrations throughout the New Georgia Islands, and by breaking up attempts at reinforcement.

110

Capture of the Munda airfield by the Americans brought all the Japanese air bases in the Solomons within range of fighters and light bombers. It greatly diminished the usefulness of the Japanese airfield at Vila, across the Kula Gulf. The Japanese continued, however, to reinforce Vila, and on 5th August intelligence came in, that they intended to effect a reinforcement during the night of 6th/7th August, using destroyers and possibly a cruiser. No American

---

[1] *Conway* (S.O.), *Wilson, Taylor, Ellet, Patterson, Maury, Gridley.*

cruisers were available at the moment, and Commander F. Moosbrugger, who had just taken over command of Destroyer Division 12, was ordered to defeat the attempt with six destroyers.[1] Leaving Tulagi at 1230 on the 6th, he was to proceed to Vella Gulf by a route south of the Russell Islands and Rendova so as to arrive at Gizo Strait at 2200 and search the Gulf. If no enemy contacts were made by 0200 on the 7th, he was to return at maximum speed down the Slot, passing north of Kolombangara. M.T.B.s were to operate in the southern part of Kula Gulf. Night reconnaissance aircraft were to co-operate and fighter cover was arranged for the 6th and at dawn on the 7th. Defects limited the speed of one of his destroyers, the *Maury* to 27 knots.

The enemy were reported by aircraft at 1730 on the 6th north of Buka, steering 190° at 15 knots, and it was estimated they would reach Vella Gulf by midnight. The force consisted of the destroyers *Shigure* (S.O., Captain T. Hara),[2] *Hagikaze*, *Arashi* and *Kawakaze*, the last three of which carried troops and supplies.

On emerging from Gizo Strait into Vella Gulf about 2200 the Americans assumed battle formation in a line of division columns in close order, the 15th Division, in the order *Lang, Sterett, Stack*, forming on bearing 150°, distant 4,000 yards from the 12th Division, which was in the order *Dunlap* (S.O.), *Craven, Maury*. Speed was 25 knots. After sweeping the approaches to Blackett Strait the force steered up the west coast to Kolombangara Island. With the setting of the moon at 2228 the night became very dark, with frequent rain squalls. At 2333 the *Dunlap* made contact with the enemy bearing 359°, range 23,900 yards approaching at a speed of 25 knots (Figure 4). At 15,000 yards four enemy ships in column were on the radar screen, and at 2340, when the range was between 4,820 and 4,300 yards the order was given to fire torpedoes. Allowing for delays in execution, this should result in a nearly perfect mean division track angle. Visibility at the time was less than 4,000 yards, and no ships had been sighted by eye. All twenty-four of the 12th Division's torpedoes were away by 2342 and at 2345 the division turned to starboard to haul clear of possible enemy torpedoes. The Japanese had sighted the American force too late to avoid the torpedoes ; as they put their helms over, the silence and blackness of the night—for no gun had yet spoken—were rent by a succession of fiery explosions. The three rear enemy ships, *Hagikase*, *Arashi* and *Kawakaze* were each hit by torpedoes and only the *Shigure* escaped destruction. She fired a salvo of torpedoes but too late to reach the Americans before their turn away, and she then withdrew to the northward under cover of smoke. Moosbrugger, coming round to a southerly course opened fire on the striken ships at 2356. The 15th Destroyer Division had turned to port at 2341, and as the torpedoes of the 12th Division found their targets the destroyers opened fire with their 5-inch guns and added to the havoc : the *Stack* alone fired torpedoes. The first enemy destroyer, the *Kawakaze*, was reported sunk at 2352, the second disappeared at 0010. The 15th Division turned sixteen points to starboard, to keep their guns in action, at 2356 ; and at 0027 after they had fired six torpedoes at the last of the three

---

[1] Task Group 31.2 :
  Destroyer Division Twelve (part) (Commander Moosbrugger) : *Dunlap* (S.O.), *Craven, Maury*.
  Destroyer Division Fifteen (part) (Commander R. W. Simpson) : *Lang* (S.O.), *Sterett, Stack*.

[2] This is the name given in Report No. BIOS/JAP/PR/711. Morison, *op. cit.*, p. 214. says that Captain Kaju Suguira was in command.

Japanese destroyers still afloat and burning furiously, the radar screen showed clear. Commander Moosbrugger having doubled back through south to north-west, made a radar sweep north of the coast of Vella Lavella though without making contact with the *Shigure*. For though Captain Hara had turned back at 0009, after reloading torpedoes, on seeing other of his ships, as he thought, being bombed by aircraft, and disliking what he saw, he retired once more. The 15th Division, meanwhile, had been detailed to pick up Japanese survivors, with which ' the sea was literally covered ' ; but these, one and all, refused to be rescued. Crews and troops alike perished in the sea of flaming oil surrounding the wrecks. The Americans then withdrew down the Slot. They had fought a minor, but classic engagement, with approach under the land to avoid radar and visual detection, withholding of torpedo fire until torpedoes would strike normal to the enemy's hulls, quick turn away from possible torpedo

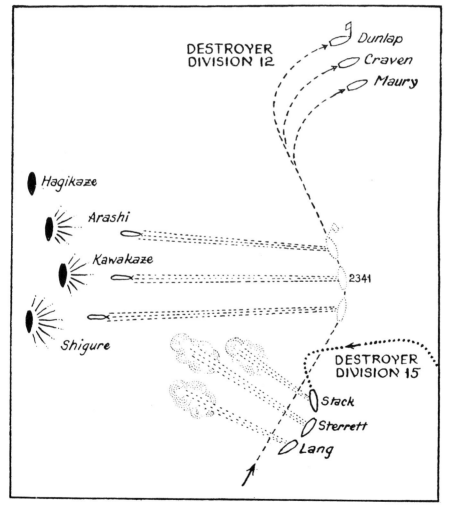

Fig. 4. Battle of Vella Gulf, 6th–7th August 1943

water, and follow-up of torpedoes with gunfire.[1] For the first time, United States destroyers had operated without being attached to a big ship force. For the first time, they had achieved a real success.

111

Consolidation of the Allied position in New Georgia Island was completed on 25th August when Bairoko Harbour, the last enemy stronghold, fell to Allied troops. The Japanese still held three of the main islands in the group, namely, Arundel, Kolombangara, and Vella Lavella, besides lesser islands. Arundel, a small island situated at the junction of Blackett Strait and Kula Gulf, controlled the approaches to both Munda and Vila, the latter being within artillery range from Arundel. It was captured between 27th August and 20th September after considerably stiffer resistance than the Americans had anticipated. The Japanese position about Vila, their principal centre of strength in Kolombangara, was thus neutralised.

After more than twelve months of severe fighting with heavy losses the Allies had conquered only half the Solomon Islands chain. At that rate of progress the Japanese seemed in a fair way to accomplish what they set out to do, namely tire out their opponents. It is true that the Japanese losses at sea and in the air were mounting fast. In the fighting for New Guinea, the Solomons and Bismarcks they had lost two battleships, three heavy and five light cruisers, two carriers and 33 destroyers. In the struggle for air supremacy over the region their naval air forces were being decimated. Recently, too, a new danger had appeared. Deceived by the considerable additions to their merchant fleet through captures during the early months of the war the responsible Japanese authorities had only recently taken into account that their merchant shipping, always the Achilles heel of an island power dependent upon overseas sources of supply, was suffering dangerously from the depredations of American submarines. More than two million tons amounting to nearly one-third of their pre-war fleet, had already been sunk ; and although the future was still hidden from them the following month was to witness a change in the graph mounting of losses. The steady upward curve of the first twenty-two months of war altered in October 1943 to a steep and as events were to prove uncontrollable rise ; whilst the curve of available tonnage, after remaining steady during the early months of the war, had for a year been moving downwards (*see Fig. 5*). In August 1943 the High Command gave orders that all cargo vessels were to be escorted. In November, in an attempt to reduce the losses which threatened to devitalise the country and defeat the war effort the General Escort Command was formed and placed under an officer answerable only to the Emperor himself, whilst in the following month the 901st Air Fleet was organised for the purpose of escorting convoys.[2] These measures had no effect in reducing shipping losses. The desperate resistance ashore in the Solomons, the heavy and irreplaceable losses of destroyers in the nightly attempts at reinforcement, and the sacrifice of the Naval Air Forces, were being nullified by a danger against which the Japanese resources, so meagre in comparison with those of the Allies, had not permitted them adequately to guard, namely the destruction of their shipping fleet.

---

[1] The magnetic exploding device had been inactivated throughout the U.S. Navy. The Americans had been plagued since the beginning of the war by defective torpedoes. Having dealt with deep running, they had now discovered their magnetic exploder to be faulty. The fitting of a reliable one began in the month following this engagement.

[2] The campaign against Japanese shipping will be dealt with in Volume V of this History.

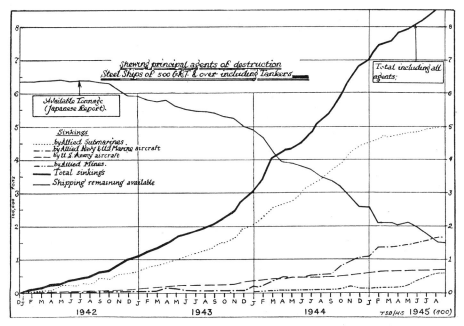

Fig. 5. Japanese Merchant Ship Tonnage Sunk and Remaining Available

At this juncture the Americans introduced a new strategy designed to speed up the conquest of the Solomons. Up to 12th July, Kolombangara had been selected as the next objective after New Georgia Island. On that date, however, when the fall of Munda appeared to be impending and it seemed likely that its airfield could be used to extend the range of Allied fighter cover, Admiral Halsey decided to cancel the earlier plan, by-pass Kolombangara, and proceed to an assault upon the northernmost island, Vella Lavella, where the enemy strength was estimated at no more than 250 men, equipped with light A.A. guns, and concentrated principally on the north-west coast, from which they operated barge supply points. This was the leap-frog strategy the notion of which American naval thought had for some time been actively entertaining. It had already been practised in the Aleutians, where the capture of Attu had been preferred before that of Kiska, the available forces being insufficient to seize more than one of the two islands at a time ; the result was, that Kiska became too expensive to hold, and the Japanese evacuated it. General MacArthur employed the technique in New Guinea when he by-passed Salamoa and landed at Lae on 5th September ; and Admiral Nimitz was preparing to undertake a campaign in the Central Pacific in the course of which the new strategy, in combination with a new operating technique which enabled fleets to remain at sea for many weeks together, was to reach its highest exposition.

112

In July, Admiral Koga began advancing the Combined Fleet from Japan to Truk, and by the end of August the main units, apart from four battleships and two light aircraft carriers, were concentrated at the southern Pacific base. The force was superior in every category of ships to that of the Americans in the South Pacific and especially in 8-inch cruisers, of which the Japanese had ten and the Allies none. Accordingly, during July the new carriers *Lexington*, *Princeton* and *Belleau Wood* were transferred from the Atlantic to the Pacific and Admiral King asked for the return of Task Force 92.4, consisting of the 16-inch battleships *South Dakota* and *Alabama* and six destroyers which were at Scapa. Admiral Nimitz formed a new task force composed of the 16-inch battleship *Washington*, the carriers *Essex* and *Enterprise* and seven destroyers, and retained it at Pearl Harbour as a strategic reserve until the intentions of the Japanese were known, for there were various indications that enemy operations were in contemplation, including the introduction on 5th August of a new naval general cypher. The Americans appreciated the enemy's intentions correctly, however, of avoiding action until there should be an opportunity of dealing with an inferior Allied force.

The distribution of ships at the end of August 1943 was approximately as follows :—

JAPANESE	ALLIED
Home (Japan)	*Home (west coast of U.S.A.)*
2 16-inch battleships	1 fleet carrier (96 aircraft)
2 14-inch battleships	4 escort carriers (107 aircraft)
1 light carrier (36 aircraft[1])	1 8-inch cruiser
1 converted carrier (42 aircraft[1])	About 12 destroyers
1 8-inch cruiser	About 4 submarines
3 light cruisers	
About 20 destroyers	
About 25 submarines	
South Pacific	
2 16-inch battleships	5 16-inch battleships
4 14-inch battleships	1 fleet carrier (96 aircraft)
2 fleet carriers (144 aircraft[1])	4 escort carriers (114 aircraft)
2 converted carriers (84 aircraft[1])	4 6-inch cruisers
10 8-inch cruisers	2 5-inch cruisers
9 light cruisers	About 35 destroyers
About 35 destroyers	About 20 submarines
About 30 submarines[2]	
4 seaplane carriers	
Central Pacific (Hawaii)	
	1 16-inch battleship
	6 fleet and light carriers (396 aircraft)
	1 escort carrier (25 aircraft)
	2 6-inch cruisers
	About 25 destroyers
	About 40 submarines
North Pacific	
	5 14-inch battleships
	6 8-inch cruisers
	4 6-inch cruisers
	About 30 destroyers
	About 12 submarines
South-East Pacific	
	3 6-inch cruisers
	About 6 destroyers
	About 4 submarines

[1] Complement. It is doubtful whether trained pilots were available for all the aircraft.

[2] A few of these worked in the Central Pacific (Hawaiian area).

JAPANESE	ALLIED

Australia

	1 escort carrier (25 aircraft)
	1 8-inch cruiser (R.A.N.)
	1 6-inch cruiser (R.A.N.)
	About 12 destroyers
	About 15 submarines

N.E.I.—Malaya

2 converted carriers (96 aircraft[1])
1 8-inch cruiser
3 light cruisers
About 6 destroyers
About 5 submarines
2 seaplane carriers

Damaged ships not included above

2 converted carriers	1 16-inch battleship
2 8-inch cruisers	2 14-inch battleships
4 light cruisers	2 8-inch cruisers
About 20 destroyers	5 6-inch cruisers (1 R.A.N., 2 R.N.Z.N.)
About 10 submarines	About 20 destroyers
	About 15 submarines

113

D-day for the landing on Vella Lavella was fixed for 15th August. Preliminary reconnaissance established that most of the island was unoccupied by the Japanese, but a scouting party which landed during the night 12th/13th August to mark the channels and beaches to be used by the landing craft found that several hundred partially armed refugees from Kolombangara and survivors from the enemy ships sunk during the night 6th/7th August were at large. Accordingly troops were moved in from Rendova in M.T.B.s after dawn on the 14th, to deal with them. No word of this seems to have reached the ears of the Japanese Command at Vila or Rabaul ; and in spite, also, of the heavy increase in intensity of air attacks on Kahili, Vila, Rekata Bay and other enemy bases during the week preceding the landing, the landing itself came as a surprise. The narrowness of the landing beach selected, at Barakoma, on the south-east coast, a portion of the island unoccupied by the enemy, and the fact that the landing was to take place within 90 miles of Kahili, in south Bougainville, the largest Japanese air base in the Solomons, affected the arrangements for the operation. The expedition was organised in three Transport Groups consisting of seven destroyer transports, twelve L.C.I.s and three L.S.T.s carrying respectively a Marine Battalion, a Regimental Team and a Naval Base Force, escorted by destroyers ; the latter after performing convoy duty to Barakoma, were to form a screen for the landing operations. Rear-Admiral Wilkinson who was in command, flew his flag on board the destroyer *Cony*. The Third Fleet was held in reserve to counter any attack by the Japanese forces at Truk, and M.T.B.s based on Rendova and Lever Harbour screened the expedition to the south, west and north-east of Vella Lavella during the night of 14th/15th August. Shore-based aircraft of the Solomons Air Command, in which Brigadier General N. Twining on 25th July had relieved Rear-Admiral Mitscher, supported the operation from Munda airfield.[2] Whilst loading at Guadalcanal the ships were attacked by aircraft on the 13th, without, however, suffering any damage or being recognised as an expedition in preparation.

---

[1] Complement. It is doubtful whether trained pilots were available for all the aircraft.

[2] Rear-Admiral Mitscher was required to take command of the fast carrier task force.

The three transport groups, each with its screen of destroyers, sailed independently on 14th August, being timed to arrive at Barakoma next day as follows :—

			Leave *Guadalcanal* *14th August*	*Arrive* *Barakoma* *15th August*
Advance Transport Group (7 destroyer transports)	..	..	1600	0610
Second Transport Group (12 L.C.I.s)	..	..	0800	0710
Third Transport Group .. (3 L.S.T.s)	..	..	0300 (15th)	0800

It was hoped thus to avoid undue exposure to air attack by giving each group full use of the beaches and cutting to a minimum the time other groups would be kept awaiting opportunity to unload. Friendly aircraft from Munda were to be overhead by 0605. General MacArthur was asked to support the operation by air attacks on Rabaul, but was unable to comply.[1]

The Advance Transport Group completed its disembarkation by 0715 and sailed 15 minutes later, leaving the *Cony* and *Pringle* to reinforce the screen of the Second Transport Group. The latter arrived at 0715 and began beaching. It was found that the three beaches would accommodate only eight instead of twelve L.C.I.s as had been planned, and unloading was not completed until 0900. The Third Transport Group, which arrived at 0800 as scheduled, had to await the retraction of the L.C.I.s before disembarking its troops, and it did not complete unloading and retire until 1800. The first air attack was detected by the Fighter Director destroyer's radar at 0740. A proportion of the enemy dive bombers got through the fighter screen, but for some reason they ignored the immobile L.C.I.s and slow moving L.S.T.s, concentrating instead on the destroyers. The weather was so clear that aircraft types could be distinguished at 24,000 feet and during the afternoon Venus was visible to the naked eye.[2] Further attacks took place during the day, but no ships were hit and only slight damage from near misses occurred. On the way back to Guadalcanal the Third Transport Group underwent six horizontal bombing attacks between 2034 and 2330, without serious damage. Eight subsequent echelons of reinforcements, reliefs and supplies including the 14th Brigade of the 3rd New Zealand Division, were sent to Vella Lavella by 1st October, a total of 6,505 men and 8,626 tons of equipment and supplies being landed.

114

Japanese Imperial Headquarters had already decided that no further troop reinforcements would be sent to the Central Solomons.[3] Efforts were to be concentrated instead on strengthening the outer defences of Rabaul, especially Bougainville ; and it was not long before the enemy began evacuating his bases and depots on Kolombangara, Choiseul and Santa Isabel. This was perhaps fortunate for the Allies, whose control of the waters was not sufficiently complete

---

[1] Observers with U.S. Pacific Fleet, Report No. 1 B.33. N.I.D. 0050447/43.

[2] *Battle Experience* and Morison, *History of U.S. Naval Operations in World World II,* Vol. VI, p. 231.

[3] Morison, VI, p. 233.

for effective by-passing of Kolombangara. A proportion of the enemy barges got through by hugging the reefs and coasts of the islands by night and fading into the overhanging jungle by day.

Evacuation of the large garrison of Kolombangara, nearly 10,000 men, called for a staging point en route to Bougainville and the Japanese on 17th August sent a barge convoy escorted by destroyers, to establish such a staging point at Horaniu on north-eastern Vella Lavella. On the afternoon of that day, aircraft sighted four destroyers fifty miles west of Buka Passage, between Buka and Bougainville Islands, steering a southerly course, and four American destroyers were sent to intercept them. A brief engagement took place off Horaniu between 0056 and 0121 on the 18th, in which two Japanese destroyers were slightly damaged. They deserted the barges they were escorting and retired after firing torpedoes, none of which hit. The barges scattered and most of them escaped.

The blockade of Kolombangara was maintained by aircraft and M.T.B.s. The latter, in addition to operating by day, patrolled every night unless kept in harbour, whilst destroyers were operating. Aircraft took a heavier toll of enemy barges, however, than M.T.B.s. The Japanese evacuated one position after another; and after the capture of Horaniu by landward advance from Barakoma on 14th September their barges engaged in evacuating Kolombangara staged through Choiseul, destroyers going direct to Rabaul from Tuki Point, in the north of the island. The evacuation was completed during the dark of the moon at the end of September and beginning of October, with the co-operation of aircraft and submarines. The latter were ineffective. They lost one of their number on the night of 30th September/1st October when the destroyer *Eaton* (Commander E. L. Beck) caught *I-20* on the surface and sank her by gunfire in 7° 40' S., 157° 10' E., between Kolombangara and Choiseul.

By 5th October the enemy had been hemmed in the north-west corner of Vella Lavella Island, the last part of the Allied advance being semi-amphibious, the troops and supplies being transported in landing craft from bay to bay in a series of bounds up both the east and west coasts. By the first week in October the Japanese could no longer sustain their barge losses, and they decided to evacuate the few hundred surviving troops on the island during the night 6th/7th. The intention was suspected by Admiral Wilkinson. The three destroyers *Selfridge* (Captain F. R. Walker, S.O.), *Chevalier* and *O'Bannon* (Task Group 31.2) which were south-west of New Georgia returning from patrol of the Slot, were ordered to return and rendezvous with the *Talbot*, *Taylor* and *La Vallette* of Task Group 31.6 ten miles west of Vella Lavella, to intercept an enemy evacuation force composed possibly of nine destroyers accompanied by torpedo boats and submarine chasers, which were expected to be north-west of Vella Lavella at 2230 to embark troops at Marquana Bay about an hour later, after which they would retire in the direction of the Treasury Islands. As Task Group 31.6 was delayed, Captain Walker's three destroyers proceeded alone to intercept, in accordance with orders.

The Japanese force consisted of the destroyers *Fumitsuki*, *Matsukaze* and *Yunagi* and landing craft, employed as transports, with submarine chasers and M.T.B.s escorted by the six destroyers *Akigumo* (flag), *Isokaze*, *Kazagumo*, *Yugumo*, *Shigure* and *Samidare*, Rear-Admiral M. Ijuin being in charge of the operation. Captain Walker's force was illuminated with flares and float lights and reported by enemy aircraft which were in touch almost continuously from sunset onwards. For some reason, the three Japanese destroyers acting as

179

transports returned to Rabaul long before the forces came in contact. The small craft and landing craft continued however to steer for Marquana Bay. At 2231, when about seventy miles north-east of the rendezvous, all three of Captain Walker's destroyers made contact almost simultaneously with two groups of ships on the starboard bow which were approaching one another on opposite courses (*see Plan 19*). The nearer group, 17,800 yards distant, which was closing the Americans, consisted of four of Admiral Ijuin's escorting destroyers (believed by the Americans at the time to be five) whilst the further group comprised his two remaining destroyers, the *Shigure* and *Samidare* (believed by the Americans to be four destroyers) which were steering to resume formation after the retirement of the transports. Task Force 31.6 was an hour's steaming to the southward, out of touch by voice radio, and Captain F. R. Walker proceeded to attack with his three destroyers, although heavily outnumbered and deprived of surprise.[1]

Admiral Ijuin sighted the American destroyers a very few minutes later. He made a wide circle to port and came gradually to a southerly course. The Americans steered to close. At 2251 the larger enemy group, which was then right ahead, distant approximately 10,000 yards, turned sharply to port in line of bearing, course 115°, as if to attack. Captain Walker turned to starboard to engage on the reverse course, since a turn to port to engage on a parallel course would have taken him further from the smaller Japanese group which had not turned at 2251 but was continuing to steer south-westerly. At 2255, when the range was 6,000 yards the three American destroyers fired a half salvo of torpedoes at the enemy who were then bearing 227° from the *Selfridge*, opening fire with their guns a minute and a half later. One torpedo hit the *Yugumo*, the nearest ship in the Japanese formation, which for some reason had circled to port, towards Task Group 31.2 and alone of the enemy had fired torpedoes, the remaining three ships being blanketed. Only one, the *Kazagumo*, opened fire with her guns. The *Yugumo* received most of the American gunfire and soon burst into flames. Meanwhile, since firing torpedoes Captain Walker had been approaching enemy torpedo water, taking a chance in order to keep his guns bearing. At 2301 the *Chevalier* was hit. She swung to starboard, out of control, with her bows blown off as far as the bridge, and the *O'Bannon* blinded by gunfire smoke crashed into her. The *Selfridge* went on alone in chase of the *Shigure* and *Samidare*, engaging them with her guns. These two ships turned to starboard and fired torpedoes at their attacker at about the same time that the *Chevalier* was hit. One or two of their torpedoes hit the *Selfridge* forward. She could still steam, however, and efficient damage control kept her afloat. The *Yugumo* sank about now, helped perhaps by the torpedoes which the *Chevalier* fired at her in order to reduce top weight. Task Group 31.6, steaming at 30 knots, was still nine miles short of the rendezvous at 2300 when the flashes of gunfire were seen to the north. At 2335 Captain Walker ordered two of the ships of the group to search Marquana Bay and to the westward for evacuation craft and cripples. They discovered nothing but Captain Walker's three crippled ships; yet the Japanese successfully completed the evacuation and when the New Zealanders moved forward next morning they found no enemy left. Group 31.6 sank the *Chevalier* which was too badly damaged to be towed, and covered the retirement of the *Selfridge* to Tulagi, where the *O'Bannon* returned independently.

---

[1] With regard to the American estimate of the total enemy force seen on the radar screens as nine ships instead of six it will be remembered they had been informed that the enemy might consist of nine destroyers.

Admiral Ijuin had accomplished his object. He saved a few hundred men though at the cost of a badly needed destroyer. Both antagonists consoled themselves by making extravagant estimates of the enemy's losses in the engagement. To the Americans, maintenance of the spirit of attack was worth the loss of a destroyer or two now that ships were coming faster into service. There was still a shortage of trained men, however.[1]

So ended the campaign for the capture of New Georgia and the lesser islands of the group. It was the prelude to the establishment of an airfield in Bougainville, the final and most difficult operation in the Solomons.

---

[1] On 24th June Commander-in-Chief Pacific informed the Bureau of Personnel that recruits were arriving in the Pacific in insufficient numbers to allow of trained men being drafted to the United States, for new construction, without reducing the fighting efficiency of the ships to a dangerous extent. Though the drafting situation was improving, the Bureau was unable to hold out hope of the Pacific Fleet receiving its full numbers until October.

CHAPTER XIV

The Bougainville Campaign and Final

South Pacific Area Operations

(*See* Plans 8, 14, 20, 21, 24, 29)

115

IN THE Pacific, prior to 1944 much of the attention of the American strategic planners was directed towards the reduction of Truk, the great Japanese base which barred the approach to the Marianas and western Caroline Islands. Rabaul constituted Truk's southern bastion; it was a formidable outwork and a possible sally port for the reconquest of New Georgia and Guadalcanal. To enable fighter aircraft to operate against it in conformity with the decision of the Quadrant Conference in Quebec in August 1943 that it should be neutralised from the air rather than captured General MacArthur considered it essential to develop airfields in Bougainville, the northernmost large island in the Solomons group. Bougainville presented problems which were unique in the Solomons campaign. The Japanese could easily reinforce it from Rabaul by supply and communication routes which were within easy reach of Truk and Kavieng as well as their minor bases at Buka, Kieta and in southern Bougainville and the Shortland Islands. They could support their operations, not only from the air bases in Bougainville itself, but from airfields in New Britain, New Ireland and Truk which were beyond the range of the Allied land-based fighters. Experience had shown that the enemy would fight hard in defence of his airfields. His vulnerability lay in his shortage of shipping and aircraft: on land he was strong and well entrenched, a fact which argued for the seizure of an undeveloped area. Rather than carry out costly operations to gain possession of heavily defended enemy air bases in Bougainville Admiral Halsey, who was to conduct the operations, considered it preferable to seize a more lightly defended area and there build airfields for himself. The defences of Bougainville had been built up until the island was far more strongly held than any other of the Solomon Islands for it was the last remaining barrier between the Allies and Rabaul. The garrison was estimated to number 35,000, and there were large air bases both in the north and south. Despite the fact that a beachhead could be brought under continual attack from these bases the

Commander South Pacific, with General MacArthur's concurrence, decided to seize and hold such a beachhead in an undefended and undeveloped part of the island, rather than attempt to conquer the whole island. The physical characteristics of Bougainville rendered this feasible. Even amongst the South Pacific Area forces themselves, however, some felt misgivings at this bold proceeding.

Bougainville, which with the adjoining islands Buka, Shortlands and the Treasury group formed part of the Australian Mandated Territory of New Guinea, is the largest of the Solomon Islands (see *Plan 29.*) Mountain ranges with heavily afforested slopes form its central backbone. Settlements and plantations were confined to the coastal areas and to the southern plain where alone roads existed. The inhabitants probably did not number more than 40,000. Japanese propaganda had made headway amongst them and they were less well disposed towards the Allies than in the other islands of the Solomons, and in fact many of them assisted the Japanese. The main enemy strength was concentrated in the south where the only good harbour, Tonolei, was situated. Kahili, a large and well developed airfield, lay at the southern tip of the island near Buin ; and Kara, a new strip, seven miles north-west of Kahili. In the south too, there was an airfield at Ballale in the Shortlands and a seaplane station at Faisi. Kieta air base, 28 miles north of Kahili, on the east coast, was non-operational in the autumn of 1943 ; close by, was Kieta seaplane anchorage. At the north tip of Bougainville island was Bonis airstrip, and just across a narrow passage Buka island carried an airstrip. There were disadvantages in attacking any of the three Japanese airfield areas. Buka was too far distant from the American airfields at Munda and Barakoma for fighter aircraft to cover the operation ; reconnaissance in August disclosed that there was insufficient usable beach area in Shortland to permit a landing in force ; and Kahili was too strong to justify attack with the forces available in the South Pacific. After due consideration Admiral Halsey approved a position for the beachhead near Cape Torokina, at the northern end of Empress Augusta Bay, about half-way up the western coast of Bougainville, a locality where the Japanese did not expect a landing to take place. The coast like practically all the coasts of Bougainville with the exception of the south, was very imperfectly surveyed. An aerial photographic survey prior to the operation showed the northern coast-line of Empress Augusta Bay (Torokina Point) to be eight to ten miles out of the position indicated by Hydrographic Office charts, which were only approximations. The bay afforded little shelter and no satisfactory anchorage for larger vessels. The shore was low, swampy and timbered ; the area was almost entirely undeveloped and there were only a few foot trails. But it had the advantage that it formed a natural defensive region of approximately eight miles by six, lightly defended, and so completely cut off from the enemy concentrations in the north and south by mountains, swamps and jungles, that it was estimated it would require ten to twelve weeks for the Japanese to bring artillery to bear against it.

116

East Longitude dates

In order to obtain intelligence about Bougainville recourse was had to ground patrols landed from seaplanes, M.T.B.s and submarines. Towards the end of April 1943 the submarine *Gato* landed 16 coast watchers and Australian intelligence troops on Téop (5° 31′ S., 155° 04′ E.) on the north-east coast (*see Plan 8*).[1] She made a sounding survey of Numa Numa Bay, some ten miles south of Téop, on 25th May. Six months later she landed a reconnaissance party on the east coast. On the west coast, the *Guardfish* landed a surveying party on 31st July and reconnaissance parties on 20th–28th September and 25th–28th October. U.S. submarines of both the Fremantle and Brisbane forces had been carrying out assignments of this nature in connection with the Solomons operations since the beginning of the campaign, as well as minelaying and scouting duties. Practically all amphibious landings were preceded by submarine reconnaissance or by advance scouting parties landed by submarine. During the campaign in the Upper Solomons which was about to begin the principal duty of submarines was the interruption of the enemy's surface operations and the cutting of his Solomons, Bismarcks and eastern New Guinea supply lines. They were also employed to watch with periscope and radar, the open seas south of Truk from positions north of the prevailing region of bad weather, the South Pacific Area Command holding their employment as a distant scouting line to be the most direct manner in which they could support fleet operations. It proved largely ineffective. Before the Bougainville landings were made, five or six submarines were on patrol in the area with orders to watch for and report any Japanese warships which might be standing southward to interfere with the operation. One submarine was stationed directly off Truk, and the remainder were deployed in a scouting line. Despite the fact that the Japanese Combined Fleet sortied in the middle of October and carried out a sweep to the Marshall Islands,[2] whilst the Second Fleet cruisers steamed southward to Rabaul passing through or around the line of submarines, not one of the latter sighted the enemy. It is true that the *Growler* which was nearest to Truk, had been forced by defects to quit her station ; but the Japanese could have steamed out by an alternative pass had the *Growler* been on station and been detected. What the submarines might have accomplished had they been employed solely to attack shipping, is shown by the figures of sinkings. During the New Guinea–Solomons campaign, despite their pre-occupation with other duties, from May to December 1943 inclusive they sank 28 cargo vessels, 12 transports, two oil tankers, and 10 miscellaneous vessels, a total of 52 enemy ships loaded with troops, guns, food, munitions and aviation fuel.

117

Times, Z — 11

As a preliminary to the landing in Empress Augusta Bay Admiral Wilkinson on 27th October invaded and occupied the Treasury Islands with the object of establishing long-range radar and small craft facilities for the protection of the Bougainville convoys and providing an intermediate landing ground from which fighter aircraft could protect the sea supply line. The 6,300 troops employed were mainly New Zealanders (18th Brigade group), carried in two groups of destroyer transports and landing ships and craft escorted by destroyers. For close fire support two L.C.T.s were converted into gunboats equipped with 3-inch guns. The landings were made after short preliminary bombardment by

---

[1] *U.S. Submarine Operations in World War II*, p. 267. Morison, *History of U.S. Naval Operations in World War II*, Vol. VI says that the *Gato* evacuated coast watchers and women and children in *March* 1943.

[2] The sortie was probably the result of the combined air attack and bombardment of Wake Island which was carried out on 5th–6th October by Task Force 14 of the Pacific Fleet as a rehearsal for the offensive about to begin in the Central Pacific. (*See* Volume IV.)

LANDING FROM L.S.T.s EMPRESS AUGUSTA BAY, BOUGAINVILLE, 1ST–2ND NOVEMBER 1943

ADMIRAL SIR GEORGE D'OYLY-LYON WITH CAPTAIN J. A. COLLINS, R.A.N.,
ON BOARD H.M.S. *Shropshire*

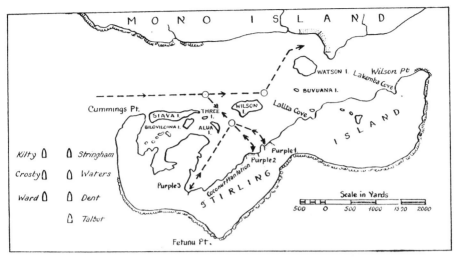

FIG. 6. LANDING ON TREASURY ISLANDS, 27th OCTOBER 1943

destroyers and aircraft at daybreak on 27th October, on the south side of Mono Island and the north side of Stirling Island, which together enclose the area known as Blanche Harbour. There was some resistance by the small Japanese garrison on the north side of the harbour, in dealing with which the gunboats proved of considerable value. One pillbox, the fire of which could not be silenced and threatened to hold up unloading, was dealt with by a resourceful New Zealander who, using the raised blade of his bulldozer as a shield, worked to the blind side of the pillbox and, lowering his blade, ploughed the pillbox and its seven defenders into the ground, tamping it all well down. A minor air attack was made on the landing ships during the early afternoon, but the main enemy reaction did not take place until about 1530, by which time the troops were ashore. A heavily escorted force of some 25 Japanese dive bombers got through the protecting fighters and attacked the destroyers *Philip* and *Cony*. The latter was hit by two bombs and disabled, and had to be towed to Tulagi. But the enemy lost about half their attacking bombers, the *Cony* alone shooting down five.[1]

A diversionary landing for the Treasury and Bougainville operations was also made on Choiseul Island on the night 27th/28th October using two divisions of destroyer transports which had completed unloading at the Treasury Islands that morning. The landing was designed to lead the Japanese to believe that the objective in the northern Solomons would be the east coast of Bougainville ; in this it succeeded. An additional reason for the raid was to disrupt the transfer to Bougainville of Japanese troops evacuated from Kolombangara to Choiseul. The raiders were withdrawn on 4th November.

118

The campaign to neutralise the airfields in the Buin–Shortlands area had been intensified in the middle of October by aircraft of the Northern Solomons Air Command. This Command was constituted on 1st September 1943 as part of Admiral Fitch's land-based South Pacific Air Command at Espiritu Santo,

---

[1] (U.S.) Combat Narrative No. XII, p. 21.

and controlled directly all air operations over the Bougainville beaches working from airfields at Barakoma and Munda under Brigadier-General F. Harris, U.S. Marine Corps.   The Solomon Islands Air Command had been created in February 1943 under Rear-Admiral C. P. Mason who was relieved on 1st April in that year by Rear-Admiral M. A. Mitscher ;   and on 25th July 1943, command of the forces was made over to the U.S. Army, in the person of Brigadier General M. Twining.   During the last half of October 18 attacks were made on Kahili, 17 on Kara, six on Ballale, seven on Buka and two on Kieta ; and before the Empress Augusta Bay landing took place on 1st November Admiral Fitch reported that these southern Bougainville airfields had been rendered inoperative.   In the meantime General Kenney's Fifth Army Air Force in the South-West Pacific Area intensified the heavy air offensive it had mounted against the enemy in mid-August, particularly against Rabaul.   These attacks accomplished less than General Kenney thought at the time, but they somewhat reduced the threat to the landing in Bougainville.[1]

The Buka and Bonis airfields in North Bougainville, which were within reach of naval gunfire from the sea, were bombarded during the night 31st October/1st November by Task Force 39 consisting of four 6-inch cruisers[2] and eight destroyers[3] under Rear-Admiral A. S. Merrill.   This was followed by a shelling of the Shortland area at 0600 on D-day (1st November), after which Task Force 39 proceeded to provide cover for the operations at Empress Augusta Bay.   The navigational hazards in this deep penetration into enemy waters were considerable, for the area was very imperfectly surveyed and contained numerous uncharted reefs and shoals.   The bombardments of Buka and Bonis were carried out in face of harassing tactics by enemy aircraft using machine gun fire and the dropping of flares and lights, though no torpedo or bombing attacks were made.   Reply fire from the shore was spasmodic and inaccurate, and no damage to the bombarding ships occurred.   In the attack on the Shortland area the enemy shore batteries opened heavy fire at 0629, five minutes after sunrise, at a range of 13,000 yards.   However, their fire was inaccurate and the only ship hit was the destroyer *Dyson*, which sustained slight damage.

Meanwhile Rear-Admiral F. C. Sherman with one of the fast carrier task groups of the Fifth Fleet which Admiral Nimitz had detailed to support the landing in Empress Augusta Bay, and consisting of the *Saratoga* and the light carrier *Princeton*, with the A.A. light cruisers *San Diego* and *San Juan* and ten destroyers,[4] had launched before dawn on 1st November an air strike on Buka and Bonis.   This strike was designed to supplement the surface bombardment in rendering those airfields temporarily ineffective during the landing operations and establishment of the landing forces at Empress Augusta Bay. The force sailed from Espiritu Santo on 29th October and made its run at 25 knots arriving at the launching point on the afternoon of the 31st.   During the next two days flight operations were conducted in an area between 65 and

---

[1] Morison, *History of U.S. Naval Operations in World War II*, Vol. VI, p. 288.   The reasons given there for the comparative ineffectiveness of the Fifth Army Air Force against Rabaul in contrast to its remarkable work in New Guinea waters are
    (1) Japanese interception of high quality over Rabaul, their most important base in the south ;
    (2) excellent A.A. defence ;
    (3) the harbour was too narrow for effective skip bombing ;
    (4) too much of the bombing was done from such high levels that it was inaccurate.

[2] *Montpelier* (flag), *Cleveland, Columbia, Denver.*

[3] *Charles F. Ausburne, Dyson, Stanly, Claxton, Spence, Thatcher, Converse, Foote.*

[4] *Lardner, Farenholt, Woodworth, Buchanan, Lansdowne, Grayson, Sterett, Stack, Wilson, Edwards.*

180 miles east of Buka. Admiral Sherman made two strikes on the morning of 1st November and two on the following morning. The first strike of 26 bombers escorted by 18 fighters took off at 0427 in glassy calm with occasional rain squalls. Three aircraft went into the water. Long catapult intervals on board the *Princeton* and the difficulties of forming up in darkness with a low ceiling and no horizon delayed the departure of the groups until an hour and forty minutes after the first launching. By then, the sun had risen and little advantage had been gained to compensate for the difficulties and casualties of a take-off in the dark. A second strike was launched about 0930 on the 1st and a third on 2nd November. Admiral Sherman's force was reconnoitred but not attacked for there were no aircraft left at Buka and Bonis to retaliate though Tokyo claimed to have sunk both the carriers.

119

The northern coast of Empress Augusta Bay (Cape Torokina) being only 235 miles from Rabaul, it was essential to reduce to the minimum the unloading time of the ships carrying out the landing. The eight transports and four cargo ships which were all that were available for sea-going supply in the South Pacific, were employed. They were organised in three divisions and escorted by 11 destroyers, together with minesweepers and minelayers whose duty it was to lay mines off Cape Moltke, 15 miles to the northward of Cape Torokina, to protect the shipping.

TASK ORGANISATION, SOUTH PACIFIC FORCE, NOVEMBER 1943

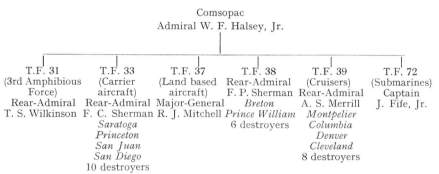

Comsopac
Admiral W. F. Halsey, Jr.

T.F. 31	T.F. 33	T.F. 37	T.F. 38	T.F. 39	T.F. 72
(3rd Amphibious Force)	(Carrier aircraft)	(Land based aircraft)	Rear-Admiral F. P. Sherman	(Cruisers)	(Submarines) Captain
Rear-Admiral T. S. Wilkinson	Rear-Admiral F. C. Sherman	Major-General R. J. Mitchell	*Breton* *Prince William* 6 destroyers	Rear-Admiral A. S. Merrill	J. Fife, Jr.
	Saratoga			*Montpelier*	
	Princeton			*Columbia*	
	San Juan			*Denver*	
	San Diego			*Cleveland*	
	10 destroyers			8 destroyers	

Rear-Admiral T. S. Wilkinson was in control of the operation, Commodore L. F. Reifsneider being in command of the Transport Group.[1] The Landing Force consisted of part of the 3rd Marine Division with a Raider Regiment and other details, a total of 14,321 troops. All elements were to be landed simultaneously, no divisional reserve being provided. Between 7,000 and 8,000 troops were scheduled to land in the first wave. The ships were specially loaded for rapid unloading, the assault transports being loaded only to one half and the assault cargo ships to one quarter capacity. The period 13th to 30th October was devoted to training and rehearsal at Guadalcanal, Efate and Espiritu Santo. Twelve landing beach sites, one for each ship, were selected, giving a frontage of 8,000 yards. Eleven of the beaches were on the mainland north of Cape Torokina, the twelfth being on Puruata, a small island lying off the Cape.

---

[1] The organisation of the expedition is given in Appendix M.

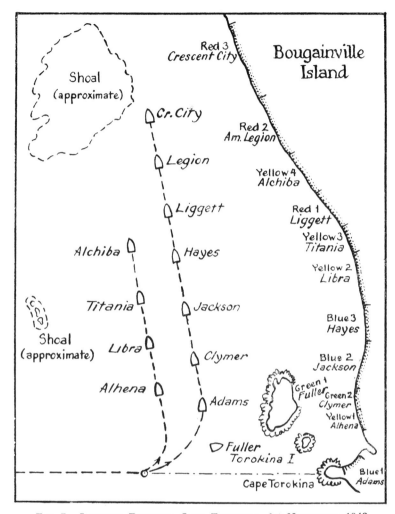

FIG. 7. LANDING BEACHES, CAPE TOROKINA, 1st NOVEMBER 1943

The three transport divisions proceeded separately as a precaution against discovery and were not merged until the forenoon of the day prior to the landing. At 0547 on 1st November the four destroyers of the main fire support group began a bombardment of the well concealed defences. It was without result. These defences covered Cape Torokina and the practicable landing beaches, the bulk being sited to cover the water approaches from the west. They consisted of bunkers and individual rifle pits, the key being one 75 mm. gun mounted on the Torokina peninsula and sited for anti-boat fire. The defence force consisted of no more than 270 men of the Japanese 23rd Infantry, for though the Japanese expected a landing in Bougainville they did not anticipate it would take place in the swampy Empress Augusta Bay area. The bombardment was lifted at 0721 and 31 torpedo-bomber aircraft then bombed and machine gunned the landing beaches for five minutes. The first wave of boats carrying more than half the landing force, began to reach the beach at

0726, four minutes before H-hour. So far, everything had gone with perfect precision ; a few landing craft were sunk or damaged and there were a few casualties. But when the boats reached the beaches trouble began. No hydrographic reconnaissance had been made of the coast and the beaches were found to be too steep for landing craft to ground properly and so narrow that in most places two bulldozers could not pass abreast between jungle and sea. For a mile back of the beaches the land consisted of swamp through which ran two narrow corridors of firm ground. All cargo had consequently to be piled up on the narrow beach, just above high water mark. Surf was found to be bad and caused the loss of 86 landing craft on their first trip. Shoals prevented the stranded boats from being hauled off. It became necessary to discard the three western beaches after the troops had landed, and double up at the next three. Also Beach Blue I could not be held, and the *President Adams* landed her supplies at another beach.

At 0738, after all assault waves had cleared the ships, the presence of enemy aircraft made it necessary for ships to get under way for two hours to evade and repel air attack. Unloading was again interrupted for two hours at 1300 when the formation once more stood to seaward to avoid a large air attack coming in. Both attacks were broken up by the patrol of 32 fighter aircraft stationed over the area from dawn to dusk, and no damage resulted, though one assault transport grounded for several hours. By 1730 eight of the 12 ships were cleared, no less than 40 per cent. of the entire Assault Force (Navy and Army) having been engaged in unloading and running craft. Of the troops alone the total number employed in the shore party was roughly 5,700 or more than one-third of the total embarked. Since the working parties had also to perform combat duties some delay in unloading was inevitable.[1] An enemy task force of four cruisers and six destroyers had been reported at 0750 standing towards Rabaul from the direction of Truk ; and at 1800 the transport group got under way and retired to the south-eastward to avoid attack during the night. The four transports whose unloading was incomplete, left the formation at 2300, intending to return to Cape Torokina at dawn and resume unloading. The news that Admiral Merrill with Task Force 39 was attacking an enemy force some 30 miles west of Cape Torokina delayed their return until it was learnt that the enemy had been defeated and driven back, whereupon the four transports steamed back to the Bay and completed unloading. They sailed for Guadalcanal at 1500, where the remainder of the Assault Force arrived at 2400 on 2nd November.

120

After completion of the Shortlands bombardment on the morning of 1st November Admiral Merrill had orders to remain under way north of Vella Lavella in readiness to intercept and destroy any enemy surface raid on the ships unloading in the Empress Augusta Bay area ; he was to cover their withdrawal, when this took place, from a position approximately 10 miles north-west of the lowering position. His force was subsequently to cover the approach, landing and withdrawal of the shipping of the second and third

---

[1] Each assault transport was required to furnish a complete shore party of some 550 officers and men, of which 120 were for work in the ship, 60 were used as boats' crews, 200 on the beach for unloading, and the remainder for shore party H.Q., pioneer work, as vehicle drivers, dump supervisors, communications and medical personnel, beach party and for work at inland dumps. Each assault cargo ship was supposed to furnish 120 men to work in the holds, 50 as boats crews and 200 for unloading on the beach. Since the cargo ships carried only 350 officers and men it was necessary to make up the difference by drawing men from transports.

echelons of the forces engaged in establishing the Bougainville beachhead, which were due to arrive on 6th and 10th November respectively.   An oil barge for his use had been placed in Hathorn Sound, at the head of Kula Gulf.

Task Force 39 was sighted on its way north to bombard the northern Bougainville airfields.   There were at Rabaul at the time the heavy cruisers *Myoko* and *Haguro*, detached from the striking force of the Combined Fleet at Truk.   At noon on 31st October Vice-Admiral S. Omori was ordered to take these and a screen to intercept.[1]   Owing to bad weather, Omori's reconnaissance aircraft were unable to find the Americans, and the Japanese Admiral returned to Rabaul at 1100 on 1st November.   By that time, news of the landing of the Americans at Cape Torokina had come in, and headquarters instructed him to escort a force of 1,000 troops which were then embarking in five destroyer transports, to make counter landings at Mutupina Point, at the south end of Empress Augusta Bay, and at Torko, 10 miles further down the coast.   Omori sailed at 1700, with the following force :—

Heavy cruisers *Myoko* (flag), *Haguro*.

Destroyers   *Agano* (light cruiser), *Hatsukaze*, *Wakatsuke*, *Naganami*, *Sendai* (light cruiser), *Shigure*, *Shiratsuyu*, *Samidare*.

After reaching St. George's Channel the Admiral was informed that there was a delay in loading the troops.   It was not until 2030 that the five destroyer transports made their rendezvous with him.   He found they were old vessels with a maximum speed of 26 knots, and he ordered them to come on with him at once at the full speed of which they were capable.   Additional delay occurred through making a diversion to avoid an American submarine which was sighted just after leaving St. George's Channel.   At 2120 the force was sighted and attacked by an unknown American aircraft, actually a B–24 (heavy bomber). Since he had been sighted, and in view of the delays that had already occurred and the slow speed of the destroyer transports the Japanese Admiral recommended that the counter-landing should be called off and he should proceed instead to attack the transports which he assumed were still unloading in Empress Augusta Bay.   Rabaul approved this at 0030 on 2nd November.   The five destroyer transports thereupon turned back, and Omori went on at 32 knots, steering for a point south of Sand Island which lies about 10 miles west of Cape Moltke (*Plan 29*).

The Japanese force had been reported, as Admiral Omori correctly assumed, though the *Myoko* and *Haguro* had been mistaken for light cruisers.   Admiral Merrill was ordered to take up a position to protect the landing operation and minelayers engaged in laying a field off Cape Moltke.[2]   He was told that five of the Assault Force ships, with a tug and five destroyers, were returning to Cape Torokina to complete unloading, and that he was to protect them.   Reconnaissance aircraft kept him well informed of the movements of the enemy force.

The order of battle of Task Force 39 as it approached the enemy was as follows :—

Van Destroyers (Destroyer Division 45) :
  Charles F. Ausburne, Dyson, Stanly, Claxton.

Main Body (12th Cruiser Division) :
  Montpelier (flag), *Cleveland, Columbia, Denver.*

---

[1] Heavy cruisers *Myoko* (flag), *Haguro* ; light cruisers *Sendai, Nagara* ; two destroyers.
[2] Two hundred and fifty-five mines were laid in 6° 0′ S., 154° 42′ E.

Rear Destroyers (Destroyer Division 46) :
  Spence, Thatcher, Converse, Foote.

As was so often unavoidable, the force was newly constituted and had never operated together as a unit.

Radar contact with the enemy was made at 0227 2nd November at a range of 35,900 yards (*Plan 20*). At the time, Task Force 39 was on a course 345°,[1] speed 28 knots, the cruisers in open order, the leading destroyer of the 45th Division 6,000 yards ahead of the Flagship, the rear destroyer division (the 46th) which had just joined up after fuelling, distant 3,000 yards from the rear cruiser. The Americans had already been reported, for at 0140 a reconnaissance aircraft launched from the *Haguro* had sighted and reported ' about 50 miles from the beach about half way between Torko and Moltke,' a force consisting of one cruiser and three destroyers (whether Admiral Merrill's force or the minelayers off Cape Moltke is uncertain), and the Japanese steered a south-easterly course to engage.[2] A few minutes later the *Haguro*'s aircraft reported that transports were disembarking troops in Empress Augusta Bay, and Omori thereupon took these as his objective. His force was in cruising disposition, in three columns, the two heavy cruisers in the centre, the *Sendai*'s destroyer division on the left (north) and the *Agano*'s on the right.[3] The *Haguro* had been attacked by an aircraft ten minutes earlier, and a bomb had hit and opened up her side plating, reducing the speed of the formation to 30 knots.

On the American van destroyers (45th Division) reporting that they had a clear picture of the enemy formation Admiral Merrill at 0231 ordered them out to attack with torpedoes, and they altered course to the north-westward to attack the Japanese northern group (the *Sendai* and her three destroyers). The Division fired their torpedoes at 0246 and turned away to avoid enemy torpedoes. One minute earlier the *Sendai* had sighted them broad on the port bow, and after firing 18 torpedoes the Japanese division altered course from 160° to 180°. A few minutes later they turned away and the American torpedoes ran out harmlessly.[4] By this time the Americans had picked up all three enemy groups, but before the radar picture had been sufficiently developed to indicate the enemy's intentions Admiral Merrill who at 0239 had turned to a southerly course ordered the rear destroyers to attack the Japanese southern group. The three leading destroyers of Division 46 accordingly at 0245 turned to a westerly course to reach a position for firing torpedoes. The *Foote*, however, was out of position, for she had misunderstood the signal at 0239 to alter course in succession to 180° and whilst the cruisers executed the 16-point turn already referred to the *Foote* instead of following in succession turned at once to 180° ahead of the other three destroyers in Division 46. Discovering her mistake she tried to rejoin, was hit by a torpedo fired by the *Sendai*'s group and her

---

[1] *Battle Experience* (Secret Information Bulletin No. 14), p. 66/14 says the course was 000°, but the plans show it to have been 345°.

[2] In addition to the U.S. and Japanese reports listed in the Bibliography in this volume the interrogation of Vice-Admiral Omori (U.S.S.B.S. No. 389) will be found useful.

[3] *See* Plan 20.

[4] The Japanese alteration of course from 160° to 180° is not shown on their plan. The Commander-in-Chief U.S. Fleet thought the turn away at 0250 might have been due to loss of surprise through the American radio voice transmissions, of which there were 27 between 0206 and 0232, or through interception by the Japanese of the order by radio voice transmission to Comdesron 23 to attack with torpedoes. The Japanese however do not mention intercepting the American radio voice transmissions.

stern blown off. She had eventually to be towed home. The remaining three destroyers had to manœuvre to avoid their own cruiser's fire, and whilst so doing the *Spence* and *Thatcher* collided, though both were able to continue at 34 knots. The despatch of both destroyer divisions to attack was criticised by the Commander-in-Chief, U.S. Fleet, since it ' left no destroyers to attack on later developments or " targets of opportunity " (a " second group " of enemy ships usually materialises in all actions with the Japanese striking groups).'

On receiving a report that the Japanese northern group had turned away Admiral Merrill ordered the cruisers to open fire on that group and at 0251 turned to starboard to close the range. The enemy quickly replied. The *Sendai* was hit almost immediately, the cruisers concentrating on her as the most conspicuous target on the radar screen. Her rudder jammed and she became unnavigable and thus an easy target. In endeavouring to avoid the American salvoes the destroyers *Samidare* and *Shiratsuyu* were in collision at 0252. The former was also hit three times by a destroyer's gunfire. Both ships hauled out of the battle with their speed reduced to 14 or 15 knots, and made for Rabaul. The Japanese Admiral was still uncertain of the position of his antagonists. Modified aircraft radar sets had been installed in some of his ships, but they were unreliable. Accordingly, the *Myoko* fired starshells. They proved to be faulty, and the *Myoko* came under fire, as did also the destroyer *Hatsukaze*. This ship, in trying to avoid the shells collided at 0307 with the *Myoko* ; she was practically cut in half and sank about daybreak with the loss of her entire crew.

Admiral Merrill, determined to keep his cruisers out of torpedo water, had been doing some complicated manœuvring at 30 knots. If this rendered the enemy's fire inaccurate it evidently had a similar effect on his own. The *Haguro* alone was hit at this time ; she was struck by six shells, four of which failed to burst. The Japanese heavy cruisers' fire, on the other hand, improved after they sighted the enemy for the first time, at 0313. This they did when at a range of over 20,000 yards they at length produced excellent starshell illumination, and Admiral Omori steered to close. The *Denver* was straddled by five successive salvoes and hit by three 8-inch shells, and though all were blind, they holed her, and the cruiser squadron's speed had to be reduced to 25 knots to enable her to keep up. But the Japanese fire was bad for deflection, and no other ship was hit. At 0326, with the range down to 13,000 yards and closing fast, Admiral Merrill turned away under cover of smoke. He was determined to fight the action at ranges which would keep him safe from the Japanese 24-inch heavily loaded long-range torpedo. Three minutes later Admiral Omori also ceased firing and turned away to the westward with the *Agano's* destroyer division. He believed himself to be opposed by at least seven heavy cruisers and twelve destroyers, of which he thought he had sunk at least one heavy cruiser and two destroyers. The *Sendai* was sinking (she was abandoned at 0400 and subsequently sank with the loss of 320 of her crew) ; the damaged *Hatsukaze* was lost to him ; and two others of his destroyers had quitted the scene. The *Myoko* was damaged and the *Haguro's* speed reduced to 26 knots. He felt he had better escape out of reach of attack by dive bombers before daylight.

Admiral Merrill had not permanently retired from the scene, for he held there was always the possibility that one or more of the Japanese ships might penetrate into Empress Augusta Bay and attack the transports. At 0332 he turned again towards the enemy. All his ships except the *Denver* had ceased firing, and the Japanese were definitely retiring. Expecting a heavy air attack at dawn or soon after, he ordered his destroyer leader to collect his two divisions and rendezvous in the position where the *Foote* had been torpedoed. This took a long time, for the two destroyer divisions had become widely separated by their independent and unco-ordinated movements. Destroyer Division 45, after clearing torpedo water, had turned back and about 0349 fired a few rounds at the retreating *Samidare* and *Shiratsuyu* of the northern group whose north-westerly course they paralleled for a time. The *Sendai*, leader of that group, was already immobilised, and the fourth ship, the *Shigure*, had turned south and joined the Japanese cruisers. The three remaining destroyers of Division 46 also chased after the *Samidare* and *Shiratsuyu*, firing a few torpedoes at the *Sendai* as they passed. At 0413 the *Spence* turned out of formation through loss of suction due to a shell hit and at 0510 encountered the damaged *Hatsukaze*, and engaged her as the cruiser squadron had also done a few minutes earlier in passing. Her IFF was not working and she was chased away and fired on by Destroyer Division 45. The latter ultimately discovered their mistake and found and engaged the *Hatsukaze*, sinking her at 0539. The Admiral then repeated his order to retire. By daylight all his ships had rejoined him.

Admiral Merrill reported that the gunfire of his cruisers was ' superb.' It was certainly lavish. They expended 4,591 rounds from their main armaments alone,[1] whilst the destroyers fired a more modest 2,618 rounds and 52 torpedoes. This vast expenditure resulted in sinking two ships, the *Sendai* and the *Hatsukaze*, the latter whilst immobilised through collision damage, and slightly damaging three others, the *Myoko*, *Haguro* and *Samidare*. To what extent the various Japanese collisions may be attributed to the American shell fire or to poor handling respectively, cannot be determined. The Admiral reported that the great majority of the Japanese salvoes were just ahead for deflection and he believed this to have been due to the enemy using the round figure of 30 instead of 28 knots for their estimate of his speed. Admiral Merrill himself avoided speeds which were multiples of five, the tendency to estimate by eye in multiples of five being a human frailty, and avoidance consequently likely to cause the enemy to make an incorrect estimate.

On the way back to Treasury Islands Task Force 39 was attacked about 0800 on the 2nd by a large force of Japanese aircraft of the 1st Carrier Squadron which had arrived at Rabaul on the previous day. The task force was in two groups at the time. Ten miles north of the main group, the *Claxton* was towing the *Foote* at slow speed, escorted by the *Charles Ausburne* and *Thatcher*. The enemy aircraft disregarded this group and made for the main body. This was formed in circular anti-aircraft disposition, with the destroyers on a 5,000-yard circle. Speed was increased to the *Denver*'s maximum of 25 knots, and course was altered to 140°, the approximate direction from which the air cover was expected to arrive. The main air cover was delayed by bad weather, but a mixed force of 16 U.S. naval, marine, army, and New Zealand fighters began to arrive just before the enemy aircraft came in sight from the cruisers. The enemy strike was estimated to total 60 to 70 aircraft, made up largely of dive bombers with some high level bombers, covered by fighters. All the ships' 5-inch batteries opened up at 14,000 yards range. These guns were capable of a very high rate of fire, and Admiral Merrill had paid great attention to A.A. gunnery training ; and the formation manœuvred and used its guns to such good effect that many of the enemy aircraft were shot down, whilst the only

---

[1] The *Columbia* also fired 680 and the *Denver* 25 rounds of 5-inch.

ship hit was the *Montpelier* which was slightly damaged by two small bombs.[1] The attack, which began at 0805, was all over in seven minutes. Task Force 39 was not further molested, probably because Rabaul, from which the enemy came, was under heavy attack by the Fifth Air Force at the time.

The Japanese during the night 6th/7th November, using barges, made one small secret landing by less than 600 men on the right flank of the beachhead, not far from Puruata Island. This was soon discovered and the landing party destroyed or dispersed; for without command of the sea and air the enemy were unable to reinforce it. It seems, too, that they did not take the American landing very seriously, believing that the Marines were merely staging at Empress Augusta Bay, on the way to attack Buka. Between 6th and 13th November the Americans landed four more echelons, totalling nearly 20,000 men, and began the construction of airfields. The Japanese carrier air groups were still shore-based at Rabaul, and attacks were made on the Allied convoy escorts, the *Birmingham* being hit by three bombs on 8th November and the *Denver* torpedoed during the night 12th/13th, though both ships reached harbour safely. In the final echelon the destroyer transport *McKean* was sunk by air torpedo on 17th November, with the loss of 52 embarked Marines and three officers and 61 of her crew.

121

On 5th-6th October a powerful American fast carrier force carried out a raid on Wake Island, as a rehearsal for the operations in preparation in the Central Pacific. In the belief that some point on the perimeter was about to be attacked, Admiral Koga with the Combined Fleet—three carriers, six battleships and eight heavy cruisers—made a sweep to the eastward as far as Eniwetok in the north-western Marshall Islands. The Marshall and Gilbert Islands had by now been eliminated from the vital areas to be protected by the Japanese fleet, but Admiral Koga's object was to bring any American forces met with to action within reach of Japanese land-based air power. This was in accordance with the ' Z ' Operation Plan formulated in May, which was still valid. No American forces were met with and the Combined Fleet returned to Truk on 26th October. After this there was to be no further opportunity for a fleet action under air conditions favourable to the Japanese. Admiral Koga was compelled to despatch his only trained air groups to suffer destruction in the Bismarcks. On 3rd November, the news of the American landing at Empress Augusta Bay having come in, Vice-Admiral Kurita, Commander-in-Chief, Second Fleet, took the 4th, 7th and 8th Cruiser Squadrons, consisting of the 8-inch cruisers *Atago* (flagship), *Takao, Maya, Chokai, Suzuya, Mogami* and *Chikuma*, with destroyers and a fleet train, down from Truk to Rabaul to destroy the amphibious force in Empress Augusta Bay. They were sighted north of Mussau Island (*Plan 14*) on the 4th. Heavy bombardment aircraft attacked damaging two of the tankers, which turned back, escorted by the *Chokai*. In the belief that the Japanese intended an attack on the Empress Augusta Bay invasion forces Admiral Halsey, having no heavy ships in his force at the time, for all had been

---

[1] Ammunition expenditure by the cruisers during the attack was as follows :—

			6-inch	5-inch	40-mm.	20-mm.
Montpelier	..	..	47	305	1,250	4,662
Cleveland	..	..	0	230	294	942
Columbia	..	..	0	329	1,974	2,013
Denver	..	..	0	140	745	1,044
			47	1,004	4,763	8,661

detailed for the Central Pacific offensive which was on the point of opening, ordered an immediate carrier-based air strike on the Japanese cruisers, which by then had arrived at Rabaul. At the moment, Rear-Admiral F. C. Sherman's fast carrier Task Group 38 (*Saratoga* and *Princeton*), which had carried out the pre-invasion air strike on Buka-Bonis, was fuelling south of Guadalcanal. They made a fast run to a point about 7° S., 154° 30′ E., 235 miles south-east of Rabaul.[1] Arriving at 0900 on 5th November, they at once began launching a strike of every available aircraft, 23 torpedo bombers and 22 dive bombers, escorted by 52 fighters. Aircraft of Task Force 33 (Solomons Air Force) from Barakoma gave the carriers fighter cover during approach and retirement. The Japanese were taken by surprise, for though Admiral Sherman's force had been sighted by aircraft en route to the launching position the carriers had been mistaken for cruisers or transports. When the attack came in soon after 1100 some of the enemy ships were fuelling or preparing to fuel in Simpson Harbour. The harbour was heavily defended by anti-aircraft guns, but the attacking American bombers and torpedo aircraft flew in formation through the curtain of fire whilst the 70 Japanese fighters which were in the air declined to fly through their own flak and stayed outside to be attacked by the American fighters. The dive bombers attacked first, followed immediately by the torpedo aircraft. Bomb hits or near misses damaged the *Maya*, *Takao*, *Atago* and *Mogami* and the light cruiser *Agano*. The *Noshiro* was torpedoed, and the destroyer *Wakatsuki* was holed. The destroyer *Fujinami* was hit by a torpedo which failed to explode. All the damaged ships except the *Maya* were able to withdraw from Rabaul under their own steam. But they never returned. Japanese heavy cruisers were seen no more at Rabaul. The Americans lost five bombers and five fighters; seven pilots and eight crewmen were killed or missing. About an hour later, 27 heavy bombers of General MacArthur's Army Air Force, finding no aircraft at the airfield, bombed the town and wharves of Rabaul.

A second carrier-based air strike on Rabaul was arranged for 11th November, the earliest date by which an additional carrier group could be made available to increase the weight of the attack. The strike was to be in continuation of the operations which South-West Pacific air forces had been conducting for the neutralisation of the Japanese base at Rabaul and designed to cause as much damage as possible to warships and merchant shipping in harbour. Rear-Admiral A. E. Montgomery's group consisting of the new fleet carrier *Essex* with a complement of 91 aircraft, the *Bunker Hill* with 75 and the light carrier *Independence* with 33 aircraft carried out the strike.[2] All bombers were armed with 1,000-lb. bombs. Nine destroyers furnished a screen and cover was provided by Admiral Merrill's cruiser and destroyer force which was supporting the Empress Augusta Bay landing.[3] The combat air patrol was reinforced by 36 naval fighter aircraft from New Georgia which used the carriers' decks for

---

[1] It is not known why a position so far distant from Rabaul was chosen unless it was that no surface cover for the carriers was available to protect them against the heavy cruisers at Rabaul. No detailed report of the raid has been seen, and this brief account is based on Morison's *History of U.S. Naval Operations in World War II*, Vol. VI, pp. 324–328, *The Campaigns of the Pacific War*, and the interrogation of Captain Tishiki, Senior Staff Officer of Vice-Admiral Kurita, Commander-in-Chief 2nd Fleet (U.S.S.B.S. No. 396).

[2] The *Bunker Hill*, together with other carriers and cruisers, had been engaged recently in transporting personnel and stores from the west coast of U.S.A. to Hawaii. On one trip she carried 500 officers, 5,160 other ranks, 166 aircraft and 200 tons of stores.

[3] The only detailed report on this strike which is available is that of Commander R. M. Smeeton, R N., who was stationed on board the *Essex* as observer with the U.S. Pacific Fleet. (M.056426/44.) A brief account is in *Operations in Pacific Ocean Areas—November, 1943*.

landing.   The launching points were about **225** miles from Rabaul.[1]   This, though closer than the attack of 5th November, was nevertheless near the limit of the effective operating range of the Dauntless single-engine bombers of which the *Essex* launched 28, but it was determined by the necessity of being within reach of surface cover at dawn.   The strikes were timed to be over Rabaul at the following times :—

0800	*Saratoga* and *Princeton* groups.
0930	*Essex, Bunker Hill* and *Independence* groups.
0945	Naval heavy bombers (Liberators).
1100	U.S.A.A.F. (from New Guinea).

The fleet carriers launched about 80–84 aircraft apiece and the light carriers 25–32, making a total of some 290 aircraft of which a few remained for A/S patrols and to relieve the shore based protective fighters.   Many enemy fighters were encountered, for the neutralising air attacks which General MacArthur had been asked to make on the Rabaul airfields on 9th and 10th November had been badly reduced in weight by the weather.   The *Saratoga* had one lift out of action, which delayed launching, whilst Admiral Montgomery's group was half an hour early, so that both forces arrived over the target at about the same time.   By 0920 the attack was completed.   The light cruiser *Agano* and the destroyer *Naganami* were badly damaged by torpedoes, the destroyer *Suzunami* was sunk by bombing, and three other ships were slightly damaged. A second strike by Admiral Montgomery's group was prevented by enemy air attacks which developed from about 1400 onwards.   At the time, including the shore based fighters, some 90 fighter aircraft were over the three carriers.   The latter were in a new formation, in a single group forming a triangle on the 2,000 yard circle, with the nine destroyers spaced evenly on the 4,000 yard circle.   The Japanese attacks, with the exception of the first which was made by about 25 bombers, were unco-ordinated.   Moreover, the enemy torpedo bombers failed to use the excellent cloud cover which existed at 6,000 feet ; they flew in from the horizon low down and the Japanese fighters failed to come down to sea level to assist them.   The losses of enemy aircraft and pilots on that day were very heavy.   They brought to an end the period during which the carrier air forces were land based.   After two years of war the flower of the Japanese naval air force had been destroyed.   The Americans saw to it that no time was given it to recover.

The events of that day were destined to have their effect on the great operation which Admiral Nimitz was preparing to launch in the Central Pacific. Until then, the operation of carriers within range of strong land based air forces had been considered a big risk.   Admiral Montgomery's carriers had just repulsed successfully an attack by the best of those forces still remaining to the Japanese.   The action demonstrated the improvement that had taken place during the past twelve months both in the fighter aircraft and the anti-aircraft armament of the ships ;   and it resulted during the remainder of the war in the bold employment of carriers the effect of which played so great a part in carrying the Allies to the gates of Japan.

122

In the belief that their northern Bougainville airfields were the ultimate objective of the troops at Empress Augusta Bay the Japanese continued to reinforce Buka–Bonis.   They arranged that during the night 24th/25th November

---

[1] *Operations in the Pacific Ocean Areas—November 1943.*

the destroyers *Amagiri*, *Yugiri* and *Uzaki* should land troops at Buka screened the new destroyers *Orami* and *Makinami*. American Intelligence had wind of an apparent intention by the Japanese to evacuate certain technical personnel, and dispositions were made to intercept with destroyers and M.T.B.s. Nine of the latter were stationed near Buka Passage, where three of them had contact soon after midnight with the *Orami* and *Makinami* which were patrolling the western end of Buka Channel during the landing of the troops and were mistaken by the M.T.B.s for American destroyers of Squadron 23 which had also been sent up with orders to get athwart the Buka–Rabaul route.[1]

The American squadron was constituted as follows :—

Destroyer Division 45 :

Charles F. Ausburne (Captain A. A. Burke), *Claxton*, *Dyson*.

Destroyer Division 46 :

Converse, *Spence*.

At 0141 on 25th November, the American force was in 5° 20′ N., 153° 45′ E., about half way between Buka Passage and St. George's Channel, steering north, Division 45 leading, with Division 46 in position 225°, 5,000 yards distant, when radar contact was made with enemy ships 11 miles to the eastward.[2] These were the *Orami* (Captain K. Kagawa) and *Makinami* which were steering a westerly course at 24 knots, followed at a distance of 13,000 yards by the three transport destroyers in column. The latter had completed the landing and evacuation of personnel and were now hurrying to catch up with the screen. Four minutes after making contact Captain Burke altered course to starboard towards the enemy ; and at 0156, with the enemy bearing 069°, distant 5,500 to 6,000 yards, the three ships of his division each fired a half salvo of five torpedoes, and immediately turned eight points to starboard increasing speed to 30 knots to clear possible enemy torpedo water. The Japanese sighted the Americans too late to avoid the torpedoes. Both destroyers were hit and sunk, the *Makinami* being finished off by the guns of the 46th Division. Just before the torpedoes hit, the *Charles F. Ausburne* had radar contact with the three destroyers of the Japanese transport group. These turned to a northerly course, pursued by the *Ausburne*, *Claxton* and *Dyson* at their best speed. The Americans altered course at 0215 thereby unconsciously avoiding the enemy's torpedoes which exploded harmlessly close astern. At 0222 the range from the leader, the *Ausburne*, which had worked up to more than 32 knots, was 7,600 yards and the division opened fire on all three targets. The enemy fanned out and returned the fire, but the American ships remained unhit. The *Amagiri* and *Uzuki* drew out of range after about half an hour and the *Claxton* and *Dyson* concentrated on the *Yugiri* which the *Ausburne* was engaging. The *Yugiri* took a great deal of punishment before she sank at 0328, without having made a hit on her adversaries. At this juncture the 46th Division came within radar range and the squadron reformed and stood to the westward at high speed, hoping to pick up the two remaining enemy destroyers ; but at 0404, when 33 miles from Cape St. George and with daylight barely two hours away, the search was abandoned and course set for Tulagi. Fighter cover reached the ships at 0651, but no air attack developed, and harbour was reached without further incident.

---

[1] It is not known why the M.T.B.s were not kept out of the way of the destroyers as usual.
[2] *See Plan 21.*

This was the last attempt made by the Japanese to run re-inforcements and supplies to Bougainville by destroyers. Henceforth the waters of the upper Solomons were untenable for such surface craft : indeed, three months later, destroyers were even forced to quit Rabaul itself.

123

In order to blockade the ports of southern and northern Bougainville the Americans carried out against them a co-ordinated mining campaign by surface craft and aircraft. During November 1943 the three old South Pacific minelayers laid three minefields in Bougainville Strait at the south end of the island and one off the west end of Shortland Island. During May 1944 two fields were laid off Buka in the north. Naval and Marine craft had mined Kahili and Buin harbours at the south end of Bougainville as long ago as March 1943. This field was replenished in the following May when Faisi harbour (Shortland Islands) was also mined. Subsequent aircraft minelaying operations included the mining of Buka Pass in November 1943 and again during May of the following year, and Rabaul harbour in February 1944. The campaign was supported by the planting from landing craft of a few acoustic mines in various rivers along the west coast of Bougainville in order to eliminate Japanese barge traffic and to isolate enemy units. The minelayers suffered no casualties during the operations but it was otherwise with the aircraft minelayers. In 121 successful sorties they lost a total of 13 aircraft, rather more than 10 per cent., though nearly half of these occurred in the mining of Simpson Harbour, Rabaul, in February 1944, when six of the aircraft taking part were shot down or crashed into the mountains after the pilots were blinded by the searchlights. The operation was ill-conceived. The types of mines and aircraft available were both unsuitable for the place and purpose.[1]

The mining of Buka Passage by aircraft on 16th and 17th November occurred after the Japanese had withdrawn shipping from the area on account of losses from enemy aircraft which sank two ships in October and two in November. The Americans believed that the southern Bougainville minefields ' eventually provided a complete blockade of the only available anchorages.'[2] Since the Japanese were short of minesweeping gear this may well be correct but no ship was ever sunk in those minefields until the submarine *RO.100* met her end a year later (25th November 1944).

124

The final operations in Admiral Halsey's area were designed to complete the encirclement of Rabaul towards which, in the west, General MacArthur, too, was making steady progress. The operations, in contrast to those of the past sixteen months, were nearly bloodless.

Though the Japanese had during the summer removed the Bismarck Archipelago from the areas whose defence was vital to Japan, and by the early winter had reduced their naval forces in the region to the minimum number of destroyers and submarines required for supplying their troops they had no intention of abandoning their bases at Rabaul and Kavieng. The latter, situated at the northern end of New Ireland, was used as a staging point for aircraft and troop re-inforcements for Rabaul, and acquired additional importance

---

[1] *The Offensive Minelaying Campaign against Japan*, p. 103. It is there stated that the Shortland fields accounted for two Japanese submarines and a merchant vessel during the Bougainville campaign, but this is incorrect.

[2] The same.

as a ferry barge transfer and assembly point when Allied air attacks rendered it no longer safe to risk ships larger than destroyers in Simpson Harbour. Advantage was taken of the immobilisation of the carriers during the period whilst their air groups were being reconstituted after the withdrawal of the survivors from Rabaul, to form the three heavy cruisers which normally worked with them, into a special force based on Truk, which was available for re-inforcements operations. The new battleship *Yamato* was to have been used for the same purpose, but was torpedoed and damaged by the submarine *Skate* off Truk on Christmas Day, and her run had to be postponed. On that day Rear-Admiral Sherman with a fast carrier group consisting of the *Bunker Hill* and *Monterey* with six destroyers, made an air attack on Kavieng, launching his aircraft in the dark. Few ships were found in the harbour and only the cargo vessel *Tenryu Maru* was sunk. The force was attacked by aircraft that night, but suffered no damage. The Japanese managed to carry out some successful re-inforcing operations of New Guinea and the Bismarcks with destroyers. On 1st January 1944 Admiral Sherman's carrier aircraft attacked the light cruisers *Oyodo* and *Noshiro* and destroyers outside Kavieng whilst engaged on such an operation, but the Japanese had powerful fighter protection and suffered little damage. On the 4th Sherman attacked two destroyers similarly engaged at Kavieng, again without decisive result.

Early in January 1944 Admiral Halsey, to use his own words, ' decided to do something useful '[1] with his forces pending the assault on Kavieng which was not due to take place for at least three months. He chose the occupation of the Green Islands (*Plan 8*). This group of coral atolls lies 55 miles east of East Cape, New Ireland, and the terrain was believed to be suitable for the construction of airfields. A landing there would be within range of fighter cover from Torokina where the Americans had already formed fighter and bomber air strips ; and though airfields on Green Islands would not permit direct shore-based fighter cover for aircraft whilst bombing Kavieng, 235 miles away, they would be sufficiently close to enable dive bombers to be escorted to the target by fighters. The final neutralisation of Rabaul would be facilitated by the establishment of another base, nearer than Torokina ; and furthermore, the establishment of a M.T.B. base in the islands would permit of patrols along the east coast of Buka and off the eastern entrance to Buka Passage as well as in St. George's Channel and the waters adjacent to Rabaul. Buka would be cut off from all but submarine traffic. There were indications that the Japanese were using the Green Islands as a staging point for barge traffic from New Ireland to Buka. As hydrographic, terrain and enemy intelligence were all incomplete, on 31st January, 300 troops of the 30th New Zealand Battalion and U.S. naval specialists carried in three destroyer transports made a reconnaissance in force. During the withdrawal two of the escorting destroyers, *Guest* and *Hudson*, sank the Japanese submarine *I–171* in 5° 37' S., 154° 14' E., 30 miles west of Buka Passage.

On account of the proximity of the Japanese air bases at Rabaul and Kavieng Admiral Halsey whilst detailing two cruiser task forces (T.F.38 and 39) of the Third Fleet to support the operation for the occupation of the Green Islands decided that it should be carried out by evasion. D-day was 15th February. Rear-Admiral T. S. Wilkinson, Commander Task Force 31 (III Amphibious Force) was in charge. On account of the shallow water only light draft vessels were used, and a measure of the strength which the Americans had now built up in the South Pacific is shown by the number of

---

[1] Morison, *History of U.S. Naval Operations in World War II*, Vol. VI, p. 413.

destroyers employed, namely 17 with the four transport units, in addition to eight destroyer transports, with two squadrons for screening. The 3rd New Zealand Division (less one brigade group) under Major-General Barraclough furnished the landing force. Though the landing was unopposed, the operation was not carried out bloodlessly. The attack group was heckled and bombed by aircraft throughout the night 14th/15th February, without suffering any damage ; but at dusk Task Force 38 covering the forces to the westward was subjected to a heavy dive bombing attack in which the cruiser *St. Louis* was damaged.

With the occupation of the Green Islands, the campaign in the Solomons was complete for strategic purposes. One final operation was carried out, completing the part of the South Pacific Area forces in forming the ring of airfields to neutralise the Japanese air bases on Rabaul, Truk, Palau and Yap. This was the landing on Emirau Islands (*Plan 14*), which Admiral Wilkinson carried out on 20th March under cover of bombardment of Kavieng by four battleships of the Pacific Fleet.[1] From the time of departure of the Attack Group from Guadalcanal on 17th March no opposition whatever was encountered.

The only organised Japanese forces remaining in the Solomons were in Bougainville and Buka. These were capable of delivering vicious counter attacks, as the Australians found when at the beginning of October 1944 they took over from the American troops the conduct of the remaining operations in the Solomons. But the Japanese had abandoned hope of re-conquest of the islands, or indeed of doing anything more than rescuing by submarine such key personnel as from time to time they were able.

---

[1] *New Mexico, Mississippi, Tennessee, Idaho.*

CHAPTER XV

Campaign in New Guinea, Final Phase

(*See* Plans 8, 14, 23)

125

THE advance of the Allies in New Guinea and the invasion of New Georgia compelled the Japanese to revise their plans. The perimeter was to be strengthened by completing operational bases and re-inforcing the defences of strategic points in the Netherlands East Indies, Caroline and Marianas Islands. The defences of the Philippines were to be strengthened. All this work was to be finished by the spring of 1944. If the situation permitted, an offensive campaign was to be instituted after midsummer of that year, but the Japanese had not yet decided where to counter-attack. On 30th September 1943 Imperial Navy Headquarters had issued Instruction No. 280, under which the Navy was to concert with the Army the necessary measures for defence and for a counter-attack at a point on the southern perimeter between the eastern part of the Netherlands East Indies–New Guinea area and the central Pacific.[1] But in the last months of 1943 the strategical situation had greatly changed. The region ranging from western New Guinea through Timor and the lesser Sunda Islands to the Celebes, hitherto regarded as of secondary importance, now became part of the main Japanese defensive line. The essence of the defence plan for this sector was the establishment of air bases, whilst Kaoe Bay, in Halmahera, was to be equipped as a rear base.[2] The Japanese had already

---

[1] See *Japanese Studies in World War II*, J.S.29, Document No. 34444. The Japanese (or the translators) term this area ' North Australia.'

[2] Presumably Navy–Army–Air base, such as Rabaul.

completed 84 airstrips or airfields in the area, whilst a further 30 were in various stages of construction ; all were to be ready by the spring of 1944.[1] Construction units were despatched rapidly to the localities concerned, but before the airfields in western New Guinea were completed General MacArthur overran the region.

During the Southern Operations in the early part of 1942 the Japanese had drafted the 23rd and later the 21st Air Regiment into northern Melanesia (New Guinea, the Bismarcks and Bougainville). These were absorbed into the South-East Area Command when the latter was formed in June 1942, and operated thenceforth under naval direction. Until the Allied attack on Guadalcanal forced the enemy to transfer air forces from the South-West to the South-East Area the Japanese made frequent raids on Port Darwin, Port Moresby, Townsville, and other targets. As part of an operation to extend the occupation of the islands in the Arafura Sea the South-West Area Commander, Admiral Takahashi ordered an offensive to be carried out against Port Darwin for a week beginning on 25th July. The 23rd Air Regiment made night attacks on the 25th/26th and 26th/27th ; and on the 30th, 26 bombers escorted by a similar number of fighters made a daylight attack. Very little damage was caused in these raids, whilst a further offensive ordered in the early autumn was barely noticed at Darwin. Though the Japanese troops in the South-West Area were continually reinforced, the power of the perimeter for offence and defence steadily declined as the enemy air forces became weakened through attrition caused by Allied air attacks. After the summer of 1943 air supremacy over the isolated islands in the Arafura Sea and Timor areas was in the hands of the Allies, and Kendari, Makasar and Balik Papan became targets of attack which increased in strength day by day.

126

The Allied leaders decided at the Inter-allied Conference at Quebec in August 1943 (the ' Quadrant ' Conference) that in the first instance eastern New Guinea should be seized or neutralised as far west as Wewak. The Admiralty Islands and the Bismarck Archipelago were necessarily included in General MacArthur's directive since he could not safely leave the airfields of Manus and Kavieng on his flank and rear even though the Manus fields were inactive at that time. He was to establish advanced naval anchorages at both Manus and Kavieng where there were large harbours. Subsequently, his forces were to advance along the north coast of New Guinea as far as the Vogelkop Peninsula. Each step westward was to be closely supported by air power based on new or existing airfields : in fact, the general scheme of manoeuvre envisaged the advance of the land-based bomber line westward along New Guinea to the Philippines by successive occupation of the minimum bases required, employing the principle of ' leap-frogging ' which was to result in so great a saving of time.[2] Whilst General MacArthur worked westward along the New Guinea coast as outlined above, Admiral Nimitz's Pacific Ocean Area forces, when ready to take the offensive, were to make their thrust through the Japanese mandated islands of the central Pacific. The latter operation was to begin in November 1943 with the capture of a base in the Gilbert Islands, a British Colony which the Japanese had occupied a few days after the outbreak of war.

---

[1] *See* Appendix R and Plan 23.
[2] The outline plan was known as ' Reno.'

Before beginning operations to the west of the Huon Peninsula where he then stood, General MacArthur wished to obtain control of the Vitiaz and Dampier Straits, between New Guinea and New Britain, for which purpose he considered it necessary to capture and develop the western end of New Britain where the Japanese had an emergency airstrip near Cape Gloucester, which they were improving. New Britain, at the extreme north-east end of which Rabaul is situated, is a mountainous, heavily afforested island nearly 300 miles long. There were no roads, except in the neighbourhood of Rabaul; and the only means of communication between Rabaul and garrisons in other parts of the island was by sea, air or footpath.

The first intention was to make two landings; the first at Gasmata and a subsequent landing with the same amphibious shipping at Cape Gloucester. But Gasmata was found to be too strongly held, and accordingly Arawe, half way to Cape Gloucester, was substituted. The military situation in New Guinea did not permit General MacArthur to begin operations until the end of November 1943. On the 26th of that month Vice-Admiral T. C. Kinkaid succeeded Vice-Admiral Carpender in command of the Seventh Fleet; he began preliminary operations three days later with the bombardment of Gasmata, on the south coast of the island, by a group of warships which included the Australian destroyers *Arunta* and *Warramunga*. In order to avoid putting the Japanese on the alert air preparation for the landing at Arawe was delayed until D — 1 Day, when the Fifth Air Force dropped 433 tons of bombs on the place. The naval expedition was commanded by Rear-Admiral Barbey with his flag in the destroyer *Conyngham*. The landing was planned to be carried out on 15th December by the 112th U.S. Cavalry Regiment (dismounted) which was transported from Buna in the transport *Westralia*, the L.S.D. *Carter Hall*, and the destroyer transports *Humphreys* and *Sands* of the Amphibious Force (Task Force 76). The transports were escorted by the destroyers *Shaw*, *Drayton*, *Mugford* and *Bagley*, and the expedition was covered by Rear-Admiral Crutchley's Task Force 74, consisting of the *Australia* (flag), *Shropshire*, *Warramunga*, *Arunta* and the U.S. destroyers *Helm* and *Ralph Talbot*. M.T.B.s guarded the western approaches to the Vitiaz and Dampier Straits. Five destroyers, the *Reid*, *Smith*, *Lamson*, *Flusser* and *Mahan*, covered the landing with gunfire. The carriers of the Pacific Fleet were not available, being engaged on the offensive in the Central Pacific which began on 20th November, and accordingly the Fifth Air Force provided cover on D-day. It could not do so subsequently on account of strategic bombing commitments, accordingly two A/A batteries and a searchlight battery accompanied the troops. The plan called for two subsidiary landings in darkness an hour before the main landing, each by 150 men in 15 rubber boats from the destroyer transports. Of these two landings, that on Pilelo Island which covered the entrance to the harbour was successful, but a landing on a beach ten miles east of Arawe was repulsed; none of the rubber boats succeeded in reaching the beach and casualties amounted to half the force.[1] The main landing at the harbour, took place in daylight from amphibious tractors after 15 minutes' destroyer bombardment supplemented by rockets fired from two amphibious trucks (DUKW.s), this being the

---

[1] Morison, *History of U.S. Naval Operations in World War II*, Vol. VI, pp. 374–5, says 'an American party of amphibious scouts in looking over that beach on 10th December had caused the Japanese to suspect that a landing would take place right there.' But Commander-in-Chief U.S. Fleet (Cominch P–001, p. 1–24) states 'There was no indication that the party was detected, while the beach was the only practicable one known for many miles east of Cape Merkus.'

first occasion of the use in the Pacific of these trucks for rocket firing. The landing vehicles were launched in moonlight at 0500 at a point about five miles from the beach, an hour and a half being allowed for the approach. Events proved that a five-mile run was too far for the DUKW.s. Delays and confusion occurred during the movement, the timing broke down, and the naval bombardment was not co-ordinated to the situation ; but fortunately the landing was only lightly opposed, and the objective was secured in accordance with the plan. The enemy air reaction was immediate. Within three hours a force of Japanese naval aircraft from Rabaul managed to elude the American fighter cover and attacked the ships. By that time, the transports and supporting destroyers had withdrawn into an area of cloudy weather, and only beaching craft and the Headquarters Ship were attacked, no damage being done. The first follow-up convoy on the 18th was almost continuously attacked from the air whilst approaching, landing, and retiring. Air cover having been withdrawn, the beaching craft had to rely on their A/A armaments. One coastal transport was sunk and several other vessels damaged. Next day the air raids slackened off, as it became apparent to the Japanese that the landing at Arawe was not to be followed by an advance from the beachhead. General MacArthur had intended to establish an M.T.B. base at Arawe, but the location was strategically unsuitable, and the Navy made no use of it.

128

Whilst the South-West Pacific Air Forces carried out preparatory bombardments of New Britain during December the troops and amphibious craft for the landings at Cape Gloucester began to concentrate at Milne Bay, Oro Bay and Goodenough. The necessary survey work was carried out and charts for the landings were prepared by the Australian Naval Survey Service. Parties landed secretly during September and November had already reconnoitred the beaches and obtained intelligence of the enemy. The persistent raids on Cape Gloucester combined with its strategic location at the west end of New Britain guarding Vitiaz Strait and the line of communication between Rabaul and New Guinea marked it clearly for the Japanese as the next Allied objective. Up to then, their destroyers had been making regular runs from Rabaul with reinforcements and supplies for transhipment in barges from Garove in the Vitu Islands. By December, however, there were no destroyers to spare for the work and the burden fell entirely on the barges. The losses of the latter had become increasingly heavy as the Allies pushed their bases closer to Dampier Strait, in spite of efforts at camouflage, concealment and dispersion by day and the confining of movement exclusively to the dark hours. The result was, that by the time General MacArthur was ready to assault Cape Gloucester the garrison which was estimated to number 5,000 to 7,500 men (the higher figure being actually the correct one), were on half rations. They were, however, well supplied with ammunition.

The Allies carried out their planning under difficulties. Representatives of the Sixth Army, First Marine Division, Fifth Air Force and Seventh Amphibious Force, all of whom were concerned, had their various headquarters at Goodenough Island, Cape Sudest, Dobodura[1] and Milne Bay. The landing

---

[1] Owing to frequent interruption of radio communication between Port Moresby and Dobodura the Americans in May 1943 ran a telegraph line over the 150 miles of razorback ridges, gorges and jungle of the Owen Stanley mountains. The work was completed in a month by 250 natives, 100 American and 100 Australian signal troops.

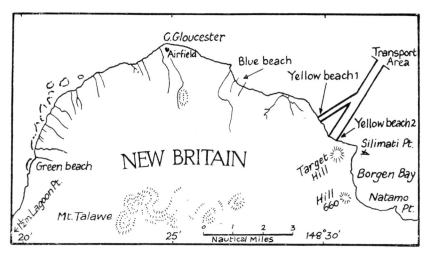

FIG. 8. CAPE GLOUCESTER, 20th DECEMBER 1943–18th JANUARY 1944

force consisted of the First Marine Division with artillery, air warning detachments and aviation engineers. For covering and supporting the landing Task Force 74 under Rear-Admiral Crutchley was reinforced by the U.S. cruisers *Phoenix* (flagship of Rear-Admiral R. S. Berkey, Second-in-Command Task Force 74) and *Nashville,* and the U.S. destroyers *Bush, Ammen, Mullany* and *Bache.*

The landing was carried out at 0730 on 26th December, after the approaches to the beaches through the reefs had been swept and buoyed. The assault groups, consisting of two combat teams of the 1st Marine Division which after evacuation from Guadalcanal had been rehabilitated in Australia, were transported as follows and landed on two beaches east of Cape Gloucester :—

9 assault transports	1,300 troops 4 waves of L.C.P.(R)s to each beach.	H to H + 15 min.
14 L.C.I.s	2,800 troops 2 waves (6 L.C.I.s) to Beach 1. 3 waves (8 L.C.I.s) to Beach 2.	H + 20 to H + 40 min.
7 L.S.T.s	3,500 troops, vehicles, guns and equipment 1,050 D.W. tons.	H + 40 min. to H + 5 hours
7 L.S.T.s	3,350 troops, vehicles, guns and equipment 1,050 D.W. tons.	1400 to 1800 D-day

A small subsidiary landing was also made at Tauali, on the west side of the Cape Gloucester peninsula. The landings were preceded by L.C.I.s firing rockets, and were covered and supported by bombardment by Task Force 74 whilst the Fifth Air Force dropped 400 tons of bombs on the beaches. The troops were able everywhere to land without opposition, a result considered to be due partly to the naval and air bombardment which preceded the landing, for abandoned guns, rifles and documents were found near all the beaches.[1] Moreover, the beaches chosen were the only ones on that part of the coast which were not defended by pill boxes and trenches. There was no enemy naval reaction to the landings and air reaction was tardy. Expecting that the landing was a diversion for reinforcement of Arawe the Japanese attacked that place first. At 0800 on D-day the *Shropshire*, which was fighter director ship for the area, detected a large enemy air raid and vectored fighters out to meet it. The Japanese dropped their bombs at Arawe and retired. Early in the afternoon, however, 20 medium bombers escorted by 50 to 60 fighters attacked the invasion forces at Cape Gloucester. Ten aircraft succeeded in penetrating the Fifth Air Force fighter cover. They sank the destroyer *Brownson* with the loss of 108 of her crew, severely damaged the *Shaw* and slightly damaged the *Lamson*, *Mugford*, *L.S.T. 66* and coastal transport *A.P.C. 15*. The Japanese made a further attack at dusk by 18 aircraft all of which were shot down before causing any damage. After this, Japanese air opposition was confined to small harassing night raids and diminished rapidly, ceasing altogether three days after the landings. In all, 24,000 men were landed by D + 14-day. The enemy concentrated their defence round the airstrips, and when these were captured on 30th December effective resistance ceased.

129

The Cape Gloucester campaign affords an excellent illustration of the enemy's logistic problems in his South-east Area Command, and his difficulties in coping with those problems. The invasion of western New Britain began at a time when the established superiority of Allied air power was making it difficult or even impossible for him to keep open his shipping lanes to Rabaul. The last substantial reinforcement to reach New Britain before the landings of the Americans had been the 17th Division in October 1943. By the end of November, except for an occasional light cruiser, all warships larger than destroyers were withdrawn from Rabaul. Supply convoys coming from China, or from Truk via Kavieng, or from Palau via the Admiralty Islands, were being increasingly subjected not only to submarine, but also to air attack, and were suffering heavy losses. Troops numbering up to 150,000 in Bougainville, New Britain and New Ireland could not live off the land despite the development of agriculture by special units, but had to be supplied with fish and rice and other staple foods. Stores could be built up in the Rabaul area, but they were continually being expended or destroyed by bombing, and required replenishment ; fuel, munitions, clothing and equipment were expended equally with food. As already described, rather than commit his warships and merchant vessels outside the main sea lanes, the enemy had since 1942 developed a highly complex network of supply and communication by means of small craft, principally barges operated by the Shipping Engineers of the Army. But with the Allied landings and the establishment of bases in Bougainville and on the Huon Peninsula of New Guinea, his small craft shipping activity was hit hard by aircraft and motor torpedo boats operating from those bases. By the end of November 1943 the Allies had 700 M.T.B.s in the South-west and South Pacific, and the Japanese supply problem was becoming acute, particularly in such areas as western New Britain. The three Army Divisions, 38th, 6th and 17th, based in New Britain, and the three, 20th, 41st and 51st, fighting in

---

[1] ' The whole defence area had been so thoroughly saturated in a long and persistent bombardment that the word ' gloucesterize ' came into usage in the South-West Pacific as ' coventrize ' had in England.' *The Army Air Forces in World War*, Vol. IV, p. xvii.

New Guinea, were both operationally controlled from the headquarters of General Matsuda's Eighth Area Army in Rabaul.[1] The Allied establishment of an operational base at Finschafen and the seizure of Cape Gloucester drove a wedge between these two main groups, and made control of the New Guinea forces from Rabaul no more than nominal. Circumstances militated almost as strongly against Japanese transportation by land as by sea. Supplies conveyed to Borgen Bay (east of Cape Gloucester) by barge and stored in dumps, had to be distributed thence amongst the units disposed throughout the area. Beginning in July 1943, certain trails had been improved into roads for motor transport, though as M.T. roads they left much to be desired and there was, in any case, little motor transport available. The denseness of the vegetation protected them from aerial observation. The landing of the First Marine Division witnessed the beginning of a series of conditions adverse to the Japanese which by 20th January 1944 became unbearable and compelled them to evacuate the Cape Gloucester area. The beach-head secured by the Allies in the course of the first day contained a barge landing and all the supply dumps on which the troops in the area depended, and it dominated the main barge hideout on the western shore of Borgen Bay and the road leading inland from there. The last attempt to run barges in to Borgen Bay under fire was made on 10th January. The Marines seized and used the captured food, tentage and clothing. The terrible weather conditions of a north-west monsoon in full blast made a quagmire of the enemy's roads, over which he had not only to march on foot but to manhandle all guns, arms and supplies. Under the circumstances little could be carried. ' Hunger, under-nourishment, positive starvation, malaria, diarrhœa, foot rot, skin disease, and all the rest brought a large proportion of the Emperor's troops to a condition of physical weakness, emaciation and inability even to walk.'[2] Nevertheless, there is no evidence that their willingness to fight was impaired.

Early in March 1944 the Allies landed at Gasmata in the south and the Willaumez Peninsula on the north coast. They captured Talasea and moved to Cape Hoskins, where they occupied the airfield on 5th May. Most of the enemy had withdrawn to the Gazelle Peninsula, at the extreme north-east end of New Britain, where the Japanese hoped to maintain them by sending bare necessities by risky destroyer runs and submarines from Palau. The remainder of New Britain was in Allied hands.

Rabaul and Kavieng were now useless to the Japanese. After November 1943, responsibility for keeping these bases neutralised had passed to the Thirteenth Air Force together with the Naval and Marine and Royal New Zealand Air Force air units of Rear-Admiral M. A. Mitscher's Air Solomons Command, which as we have noticed was a component of Vice-Admiral A. W. Fitch's South Pacific Air Command operating from the Solomons airfields. Both bases had been and continued to be subjected to air attack, and between 17th and 29th February 1944 Destroyer Squadrons 12, 22, 23 and 45 made a total of six sweeps in the Bismarcks, on three of which they bombarded both Rabaul and Kavieng with impunity. The damage they caused was not significant, for the raids were rather in the nature of demonstrations, though on 22nd February the 23rd Squadron intercepted and sank the minelayer *Natsushima*, the naval tug *Nagaura*, and the small cargo vessel *Kyosei Maru*. Later, battleships bombarded both the Bismarcks' bases. About 21st February 1944, after devastating raids on Truk by the carriers of the Third Fleet during

---

[1] General Matsuda relieved General Iwasa in July 1943.
[2] C.C.O.R.s Bulletin No. 56.

which two light cruisers, four destroyers and 52,000 tons of tankers were sunk[1] and its usefulness as a naval base was destroyed the Japanese withdrew all their aircraft from Rabaul and concentrated them at Truk ; and on 12th March General MacArthur received from the Joint Chiefs of Staff directions to isolate the Rabaul–Kavieng area with minimum forces and leave these once powerful bases to their fate. Their maintenance in a state of neutralisation was carried out with the assistance of the Third Fleet carrier aircraft. It remained a major task, but sea and air power had rendered them impotent and saved the Allies from the necessity of undertaking one of the most costly operations of war, assault from the sea on a huge and strong fortress.

130

The directive of the Joint Chiefs of Staff to General MacArthur for implementing the decisions of the Quadrant Conference had specified Hansa Bay (between Madang and Wewak), Manus in the Admiralty Islands, and Kavieng in New Ireland as the first objectives of the South-west Pacific Forces. General MacArthur's plan (Reno III) had been based upon his assumption that on the conclusion of the operations in the Solomons and Bismarcks all Admiral Nimitz's mobile air, ground and naval forces in the South Pacific Area would be transferred to the South-west Pacific Command. Actually however the Joint Chiefs of Staff had given first priority for allotment of fresh forces and the new equipment now coming off the production lines to Admiral Nimitz, since the operations planned to begin in the Central Pacific towards the end of the year seemed to promise a greater possibility of rapid advance towards Japan and her vital lines of communication in the south and east and a greater chance of bringing the Japanese Combined Fleet to action, than advance through New Guinea, the Netherlands East Indies and Philippines. As a result General MacArthur had insufficient amphibious equipment in the South-west Pacific Area to carry out all three of the operations of Reno III simultaneously. He decided that the seizure of the Admiralty Islands should be his first object.

The Admiralty Islands offered the potentialities of a great advanced base. They contain the vast landlocked Sea Eagle harbour and ample space on the largest island, Manus, for military installations (*see Figure* 9). The Japanese had annexed the group in March 1942 and had constructed airfields on Manus and Los Negros Islands ; but they made little subsequent use of the airfields, and whilst garrisoning the islands, had not constructed any formidable defences against either landings or air attacks. On 23rd February the daily air reconnaissance report indicated that the Japanese might be withdrawing their troops from Los Negros back to the adjacent island, Manus. Preparatory to the assault on Manus, the Fifth Air Force had for the past fortnight been bombing Los Negros where the enemy had an airstrip at Momote. The airfield installations had been destroyed, the fuel supplies burned, and most of the anti-aircraft defences put out of action. Following the report of the 23rd February General MacArthur next day ordered an immediate reconnaissance in force of Los Negros, his intention being that the troops should remain in occupation if the area was found to be inadequately defended.

A thousand troops of the 1st Cavalry Division were detailed to carry out the operation. On 29th February they were conveyed the 430 miles from Buna

---

[1] These raids will be dealt with in Volume IV of this Staff History.

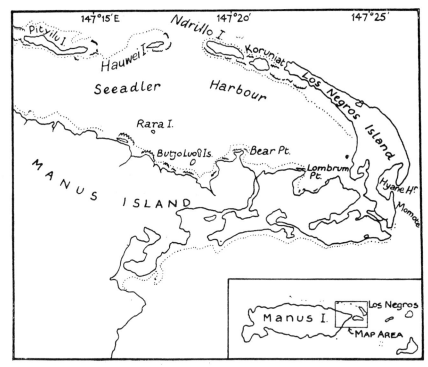

FIG. 9. MANUS AND LOS NEGROS

under crowded conditions, in three destroyer transports and nine destroyers,[1] covered by Rear-Admiral Berkey with the cruisers *Phoenix*, and *Nashville*, and destroyers *Beale, Bache, Daly,* and *Hutchins*. This force was also to support the assault by bombardment, for a last minute report from Alamo Scouts landed on the 27th left it in doubt as to the extent of opposition to be expected to a landing and indeed the garrison of the island was subsequently estimated to have been more than 4,000. Admiral Nimitz transferred a force which included five 14-inch battleships from the Central to the South Pacific to cover the landings in the Admiralty Islands and to bombard Kavieng. In the expectation that the entrances to Seeadler (Sea Eagle) Harbour, which is formed by the bight of Los Negros and Manus Islands, would be mined, a landing beach was selected in the small Hyane Harbour, on the east side of Los Negros, the entrance to which is very narrow. The landing was fixed for 0815. Bad weather dislocated the arrangements for air bombardment, but the ships continued their shelling past the scheduled time. The troops in the first wave of landing craft got ashore without opposition, but subsequent waves were subjected to heavy crossfire from both sides of the harbour when entering and several boats were sunk. The conformation of the harbour rendered support by ships' gunfire difficult, but a blinding tropical rainstorm which broke over the scene screened the latter part of the landing, and by 10 o'clock the airstrip was captured and a defensive perimeter established. Six hours after the landing General MacArthur, who was present as an observer, went ashore and ordered the force to hold what was

---

[1] These are the numbers given in Cominch P.004, *Amphibious Operations, January–March 1944*. The destroyer transports carried an average of 170 troops apiece and the destroyers 57.

taken. The destroyers *Bush* and *Stockton* were left to support the troops, and the remainder of the ships sailed away. During the next two days determined Japanese counter attacks and attempts at infiltration were repulsed ; but for some reason the enemy did not employ his air forces based in New Guinea. On the third day reinforcements began to arrive in six L.S.T.s screened by the destroyers *Warramunga* (R.A.N.), *Ammen* and *Mullany* and minesweepers *Hamilton* and *Long*.[1] With the combat troops came more than 500 of the 40th Naval Construction Battalion (' Seabees '), to rebuild the air-base and render the island habitable.

The minesweepers *Hamilton* and *Long* were sent to sweep the entrance into Sea Eagle Harbour, but were driven off by the Japanese coastal guns on Hauwei Island. On D + 4 day, therefore, Task Force 74, consisting of the *Shropshire* (flag), *Phoenix*, *Nashville* and four destroyers[2] returned to the area to destroy the guns. The ships fired **77** rounds of 8-inch. The Japanese withheld their fire, and it was impossible to establish whether this modest expenditure of ammunition achieved any result. On 7th March the task force bombarded Ndrillo Island, at the entrance to Sea Eagle Harbour. The destroyer *Nicholson* was then sent to draw the fire of the batteries, after which the *Phoenix* and *Nashville*, accompanied by bombers of the Fifth Air Force, bombarded them before the area was swept for mines whilst the troops crossed the narrow strait from Los Negros to Manus. Organised resistance in the Admiralty Islands ended on 11th April, and after a month of jungle fighting under difficult weather conditions mopping up on Manus was completed. Allied troops landed on Pityilu Island on 30th March, after preliminary bombardment by destroyers, M.T.B.s and aircraft. Other small islands were occupied without opposition. The absence of enemy air intervention during this period attested to the degree of neutralisation of enemy air bases which had been achieved throughout New Guinea and the Bismarcks.

The capture of the Admiralty Islands completed the ring of air bases surrounding Rabaul and virtually sealed off the whole of New Britain and prevented it from receiving reinforcements and supplies. All the waters between Truk and New Guinea were now within air range, and in Sea Eagle Harbour the South-west Pacific Forces had a fleet anchorage for use in the invasion of the Philippines. Within a few months the Americans formed a naval base at Manus, capable of servicing and supplying a fleet on a scale equivalent to that of a Royal Dockyard. It was intended that the Pacific Fleet should operate from Manus, and Admiral Nimitz consequently recommended that it should be taken over by the South Pacific Forces. General MacArthur opposed this suggestion and again proposed that the forces of the South Pacific, other than those required for local defence and the operation of the necessary bases, should be transferred to his South-west Pacific Area. The Joint Chiefs of Staff decided that the South Pacific Command should be broken up and the principal fighting forces divided between the South-west and Central Pacific. The naval base at Espiritu Santo was closed and its facilities moved forward in part to the Admiralty Islands and in part to Kwajalein in the Marshall Islands which Central Pacific forces had captured at the beginning of February 1944. The Third Fleet, apart from some units needed to make good deficiencies in the Seventh Fleet,[3] with the 1st Marine Corps and most of the naval air forces of

---

[1] The L.S.T.s were Nos. *171, 454, 458, 466, 22, 202.*

[2] *Daly, Hutchins, Beale, Bache.*

[3] On 1st May 1944 the Allied Forces in the South-West Pacific Area (Seventh Fleet) consisted of 3—14-inch battleships, 11 escort carriers (300 aircraft), 2—8-inch cruisers, 4—6-inch cruisers, 40 destroyers and 30 submarines.

the South Pacific were transferred to the Central Pacific Command. The Army and Army Air Forces were allocated to General MacArthur. This caused the latter to reorganise his Command. The Thirteenth Air Force was to be given to him, and he established the Far East Air Force under General Kenney to direct its operations and those of the Fifth Air Force. He formed two army forces, the New Guinea Force and the XIV Corps, the latter being responsible for defence of the air and naval bases in the Solomons–New Britain–Emirau.

131

In New Guinea, Madang, and Sek (Alexis) harbour, 8 miles north of Madang, were occupied by Australian and U.S. troops, with little opposition, between 24th and 26th April 1944. The Joint Chiefs of Staff on 12th March had cancelled the assault on Kavieng (*cf.* Section 130), and at General MacArthur's suggestion, it was decided to by-pass Hansa Bay, the third of the three objectives specified by the Joint Chiefs of Staff in the plan ' Reno III,' and jump 300 miles to Hollandia on Humboldt Bay in Dutch New Guinea where there was a sheltered but undeveloped harbour.[1] Admiral Nimitz's fast carrier forces were to support the operation. The Japanese had apparently given up hope of holding anything in the South-west Pacific except Rabaul, Kavieng, and the part of New Guinea west of Wewak. Initially, the latter had been made a major base into which the enemy drafted the best of their Army Air Force as they had done with their Naval Air Force at Rabaul. Destructive air attacks on 17th and 18th August had caused them to shift from Wewak to Hollandia, which at that date was out of range of American fighter aircraft so that Allied bombers had to proceed unescorted. As the Japanese naval air forces were worn down in the Solomons and Bismarcks the enemy, withdrawing forces even from South-east Asia, had drafted army air units into New Guinea and built up air strength at Hollandia to succeed Wewak. Hollandia was now the principal enemy rear supply base in New Guinea and had an estimated garrison of 14,000 troops. The airfield area which was about 12 miles west of Humboldt, contained three large airfields, Hollandia, Cyclops and Sentani.

There were still large numbers of troops in the Wewak area, and during March the Americans discovered that the Japanese intended to try to run in a convoy of reinforcements and supplies about the 18th or 19th of the month. On 17th and 18th March destroyers bombarded Wewak, and on the night of the 17th/18th two American heavy bombers, equipped with a newly developed radar bomb sight, made an armed reconnaissance of the waters between Hollandia and Wewak. In the early hours of the morning they detected and attacked a convoy of eight vessels about 60 miles north-east of Hollandia, heading south-east. The attack was continued next morning by a group of heavy bombardment aircraft. Two cargo ships, the *Yakumo Maru* and the *Taiei Maru,* and two submarine chasers, *Nos. 47* and *49* were sunk. The enemy made no further attempts to reinforce Wewak by sea.

Air preparation for the landing at Hollandia began on 30th March when the fast carriers of the Pacific Fleet struck Palau, Yap and Woleai (West Carolines) repeating the raids on 1st April. Air attacks on the three airfields at Hollandia also began on 30th March. Fifty-eight new U.S. long range fighter aircraft had arrived in the South-West Pacific Area, and General Kenney fitted others with extra fuel tanks which enabled them to escort his heavy bombers all the way to

---

[1] This plan was called Reno IV.

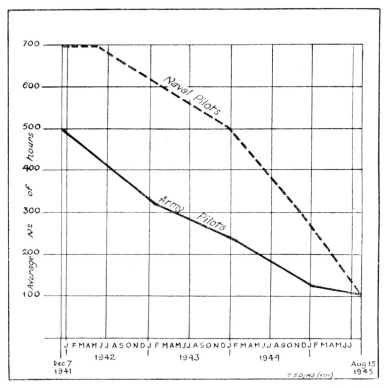

Fig. 10. Decrease in Japanese Pilot Flying Experience, 1941–1945

Hollandia and remain over the target for an hour. Six days of devastating air attacks by the Fifth Air Force followed. One hundred and twenty Japanese aircraft were destroyed[1] and the remainder of the 288 aircraft at Hollandia were disabled,[2] whilst over 2,000 men of the ground crews and service troops were killed. By 6th April the Hollandia air base had been ruined. The effect on the Japanese Army Air Force of these attacks on Hollandia coming after the devastation of Wewak in the previous September during the preparations for the assault on Lae, and on top of the losses incurred through feeding in reinforcements piecemeal over a period of nearly two years, was both immediate and lasting. The Japanese Army Air Force was disorganised to a point from which it never recovered. Even though the available aircraft strength remained high, the pilot quality was gone.[3] More than 95 per cent. of its experienced pilots with between 300 and 600 hours flying time had been lost, and it is reported that the general level of experience was reduced to 30 per cent. of that

[1] *Japanese Air Power*, U.S. Strategic Bombing Survey, p. 15. This was the figure admitted by the Japanese.

[2] *Employment of Forces under the South-west Pacific Command*, U.S. Strategic Bombing Survey, p. 34.

[3] 'The Army's effort to bolster up the defence of the southern islands resulted in the loss of at least 30 per cent. of the total available Army Air Strength.' *War Organisation of Japan*, Advanced Echelon Pacific Air Command U.S. Army, 25th January 1946, A.P.O. 925 S.502 (N.I.D. 2168/46).

212

on the outbreak of war.[1] The result was not immediately apparent, but was seen later when attacks by the Fifth Air Force in the Halmaheras and by carrier task forces operating in the western Pacific and Netherlands East Indies met with little or no effective air resistance. The Japanese Army Air Force had the numbers, but never again the quality and thus in desperation was driven ultimately to adopt suicide tactics.

132

The part of the Royal Australian Air Force Command in the preparations for the assault on Hollandia consisted in attacking Japanese air bases in the Arafura Sea and near Geelvink Bay, the great bight between the mainland of New Guinea and the Vogelkop Peninsula. Part of southern New Guinea was in the hands of the Allies, who had a base at Merauke, but the Japanese had for some time past been attempting to extend their hold eastward and construct airfields as laid down in the revised operational plan of 30th September 1943, to complete the line of air defence extending from Malaya to the Solomon Islands which they had begun in 1942.[2] On 31st January 1944 Australian and Dutch troops repulsed an attempted Japanese landing near the mouth of the Eilanden Revier (approx. 6° S., 138° E.), about 300 miles south-east of enemy-held Kaukenau (4° 42' S., 136° 27' E.).

Operating from airfields in north-western Australia the Australians conducted long-range bombing and minelaying raids on enemy held areas in the Netherlands East Indies and the lands bordering on the Arafura, Banda and Timor Seas, strikes which entailed round trips of up to 2,500 miles. One-fifth of their effort was devoted to minelaying, which began on 22nd April 1943, 422 mines being laid in 18 areas between that date and April 1944.[3]

Though the Chief of the Air Staff, Melbourne, greatly overestimated the damage caused to Japanese shipping, there can be little doubt that in the conditions prevailing, namely harbours suitable for mining and a shortage of minesweeping equipment in the Japanese Navy, minelaying did achieve results which could not have been obtained with the same effort by bombing of land targets.[4] Though part of the Royal Australian Air Force effort was devoted to bombing and reconnaissance the principal duty which claimed two-fifths of all sorties was convoy escort. Altogether the Royal Australian Air Forces neutralised the eastern Netherlands East Indies and south-west New Guinea so effectively that the amphibious assaults and airborne attacks planned to take place in those regions were rendered unnecessary. Domination by air saved the Allies both effort and loss of life.

---

[1] *Air Campaigns of the Pacific War*, U.S. Strategic Bombing Survey, p. 24.

[2] *See* Plan 23 and Appendix R.

[3] Details of the entire minelaying campaign until its conclusion in July 1945 will be given in Volume V of this history.

[4] *Minelaying Operations in the S.W. Pacific by the R.A.A.F., April 1943–April 1944.* (M.058049/44.) The Australians claimed the known casualties in that period as 13 ships sunk and 11 damaged and stated : ' To have done as much damage to the enemy's war supplies by bombing, would have required the full-time employment of about 20 squadrons.' But as far as can be discovered the actual number of ships sunk was only seven (*Mie Maru* 24th July 1943, *Yusho Maru* 5th September 1943, *Minesweeper No. 16* 11th September 1943, *Seikai Maru* 16th September 1943, *Ryuosan Maru* 4th November 1943, *Tsukushi* 4th November 1943, *Amagiri* (destroyer) 23rd April 1944). There were 230 effective sorties, equivalent to the full time employment of half a squadron during the twelve months under review. Three aircraft were lost on these operations.

The intention of the Hollandia operation (Operation ' Reckless ') was to land Allied forces for the capture of Hollandia and Aitape and the airfields in their neighbourhood with the specific object of establishing heavy bomber bases for preliminary bombardment of the Palau Islands and the neutralisation of western New Guinea and Halmahera. A successful outcome of the operation would also give the Allies small harbours from which to attack the many enemy airfields, shipping lanes and bases much further to the west and north-west. It would isolate the Japanese forces at Wewak and Madang from support, in the same way that those at Kavieng, Rabaul and the northern Solomons had been isolated.[1] This was the largest operation and the longest amphibious move yet undertaken by the South-West Pacific Area forces. The objective was 985 miles from the principal staging area, Goodenough, in north-east Papua, and 481 miles from the advanced staging point of the expedition at Cape Cretin, south of Finschafen. The operation called for landings on the coast and penetration through dense jungle, swamp and rugged mountains. Information was obtained by aerial photographs and from the few available former inhabitants of the area, and was secured by patrols landed from naval craft. But little was known of the condition of the beaches and the nature of the terrain. Maps, where they existed at all, showed little detail. The plan had to be such that it could be adjusted to meet unexpected developments.

The forces employed in the operation were organised from Central, South and South-West Pacific Commands.[2] The VII Amphibious Force under Rear-Admiral D. E. Barbey was organised as Task Force 77 consisting of three attack groups for the assault of three beaches, at Tanah Merah Bay just west of Hollandia, Humboldt Bay in which Hollandia was situated, and Aitape 100 miles to the east of Hollandia. Besides transporting and landing the troops and supplies Task Force 77 was to furnish escort on passage and close support for the landings. First and Second Reinforcement Groups were to follow up the initial landings, and a Floating Reserve was provided. In all, over 200 vessels and nearly 80,000 Army and Air Force persons took part. The Aitape area, where the enemy had an air base at Tadji which the Fifth Air Force required for fighters, had, like Hollandia, been ' softened up' by the Royal Australian Air Force and the airstrips there and at Wewak were reported on 21st April (D — 1 day) to have been rendered unserviceable. The weather was bad during the ten days previous to the landings, and in a strike on Tadji on the 16th by the Far East Air Force 33 pilots and 31 aircraft were lost.

Task Force 77 was given air and anti-submarine escort and close support for the Aitape landing by Escort Carrier Task Force 78 under Rear-Admiral R. E. Davison, consisting of eight escort carriers lent from the Pacific Ocean Area, with Admiral Crutchley's two cruisers the *Australia* and *Shropshire*, and three under Admiral Berkey, with attendant destroyers (Task Forces 74 and 75 respectively). The escort carriers under Admiral Davison were to remain for eight days after the landing if the Fifth Air Force did not establish an airfield earlier.

A criterion of the huge size to which the U.S. Pacific Fleet had now been built up is afforded by Task Force 58, a fast carrier task force from the Central

---

[1] The isolation of Wewak was maintained by mining. On 19th–20th June the British fleet minelayer *Ariadne* which had been lent to the U.S. Fleet and was attached to Task Force 75, laid 146 mines off Wewak, operating from Manus. These mines had been embarked in the United Kingdom on 19th January ; they were carried 21,343 miles before being laid. On 1st September the *Ariadne* mined Wewak harbour again.

[2] *See* Appendix O.

Pacific under Rear-Admiral M. A. Mitscher which covered the expedition from the north and north-west and gave air support to the landings in Humboldt Bay and at Tanah Merah. It consisted of 12 carriers, 6 battleships, 14 cruisers and 50 destroyers. Admiral Nimitz stipulated however that the Japanese airfields at Hollandia should be rendered inoperable before the fast carriers came within range of attack. It was arranged that Task Force 58 should make a series of raids on the Carolines air bases before arriving off Hollandia, and the carriers were also to carry out air strikes on Wakde and Sarmi, in north-west New Guinea. Admiral Mitscher's aircraft were to provide for search, scouting, reconnaissance and photo reconnaissance. His force was, further, organised to be ready if necessary to fight a main battleship action with carrier-based air support, and to destroy enemy surface vessels located in harbours along the coast which might endeavour to escape to the westward. The U.S. Fifth Fleet operating from the Marshall Islands provided cover for the operation.[1] Seven Allied submarines were stationed to the north-west of the Hollandia area between Palau and Halmahera from D — 6 day, to intercept enemy vessels going to the area.

Rear-Admiral Barbey, who commanded the Attack Force, was in control until the landing forces were established ashore when the control passed to the Landing Force Commander at a time to be agreed by the commander of each attack group and Landing Force Commander at each beach. At each objective each commander of an attack group controlled the fighter cover aircraft in his area through a fighter director ship, he also controlled support aircraft through the Aircraft Controller in his flagship, until an Aircraft Controller ashore took over, who in turn was under the direction of the Commander of the Landing Force.

The troops (Sixth Army and Alamo Force) to be landed at each beach were as follows :—

Tanah Merah Bay	10,500	Follow-up convoys	11,000
Humboldt Bay	8,364	Follow-up convoys	5,000
Aitape	6,296	Follow-up convoys	3,800

These numbers included a very large proportion of Engineers for work on the difficult terrain over which the forces would have to move and rehabilitation of the airfields as well as the establishment on shore of the forces. The enemy strength in the Hollandia area was estimated at 14,000 to 16,000, half of this total being service troops. The naval forces in New Guinea at that date consisted of the Ninth Fleet under Vice-Admiral Y. Endo. This fleet had been formed at Wewak on 15th November 1943, for operations along the coast of New Guinea, and it consisted of only one or two destroyers, two or three mine-sweepers, and a coast defence vessel. The nearest Japanese tactical force was the Second Fleet at Palau, part of the Combined Fleet, which consisted of one 16-inch battleship, one converted carrier, six 8-inch cruisers and one light cruiser with destroyers. The Japanese had however no intention of using the Combined Fleet to oppose invasions in New Guinea, but were relying on the land-based air forces for this duty.[2] After the loss of the Admiralty Islands the Japanese moved the 23rd Air Flotilla under Rear-Admiral Y. Ito from Kendari to Davao, in the expectation of carrier-based air attacks on Palau and the Philippines, and in April when the intention of the Allies to advance along the New Guinea coast became evident it was transferred to Sorong at the west end of the Vogelkop Peninsula, where there was a large newly completed airfield.

---

[1] The composition of the Fifth Fleet is given in Section 136.
[2] Interrogation of Capt. T. Ohmae, I.J.N.

The strength of the flotilla was then at its nadir, for it comprised no more than 57 aircraft. These were reinforced up to a strength of 180, and 70 Fourth Air Army aircraft were sent from Manila and placed under the Admiral Ito's command. Close east of Sorong was Samate, where the 4th Air Army had forces. But both army and naval air forces suffered from shortage of spare parts and poor maintenance which greatly reduced their effectiveness.[1]

134

Task Force 58 sailed from Majuro in the Marshall Islands on 13th April to a rendezvous north of New Ireland where it refuelled. Enemy aircraft sighted the force on the 19th and 20th, but no attack took place. During the following day Admiral Mitscher's aircraft joined in the pre-invasion air bombardment of Hollandia and Wakde. The assault convoy was believed to have been sighted on the 19th whilst on passage to the objective, but again no attack developed. It took the route through Vitiaz Strait to the Admiralty Islands, then west, finally turning south to the landing beaches. This, whilst longer than the direct route, would it was hoped give less chance of early detection and prevent the Japanese from definitely determining the objective. Actually, strategic surprise was successfully achieved.

Tanah Merah Bay was found to be undefended. The assault troops landed on the morning of 22nd April after the ships had fired 2,100 rounds of 8-inch, 5-inch and 4·7-inch without eliciting any reply. Two hours were allowed for the transports to put landing craft into the water, load the troops and form up the assault waves. In spite of the ample time the interval between leading waves widened, and the assault elements might not have been built up sufficiently rapidly had opposition been encountered. When two battalions of infantry and a battery of artillery of the 24th Division had landed it was decided that the landing place was unsuitable as there were insufficient dispersal areas and roads. Accordingly, the landing was switched to Humboldt Bay. But most of the food for the Division had already been landed and it was found impossible to re-embark it. Owing to this and to what happened to the supplies of the 41st Division at Humboldt Bay, the entire air effort of the Fifth Air Force for the next week was confined to flying in food and ammunition to the troops in the Hollandia area.

At Humboldt Bay, serious opposition had been anticipated. Accordingly, aircraft from the escort carriers covered the landing from 30 minutes before to 60 minutes after H-hour (the hour of landing) and three light cruisers and six destroyers carried out a bombardment at daylight previous to the landing. The troops went ashore covered by a rocket barrage. There were no defences and no opposition was encountered, for, unusually, most of the Japanese in the place either retreated precipitately or surrendered. Unfortunately, air bombardment on D − 1 day set on fire Japanese supply dumps, and in the evening of D + 1 day a hostile aircraft, using the fires as aiming mark, dropped a stick of bombs and started a series of conflagrations which spread to the American supplies. The entire day's unloading of food and ammunition went up in smoke.

The 41st Division landed one regiment at Aitape. The boats beached in error east of the scheduled spot, the coast line being featureless and visibility poor. There was no opposition, however, and they found a good track and a

---

[1] Interrogation of Capt. H. Komoto, I.J.N., attached to Staff of 23rd Air Flotilla, June 1943–July 1944.

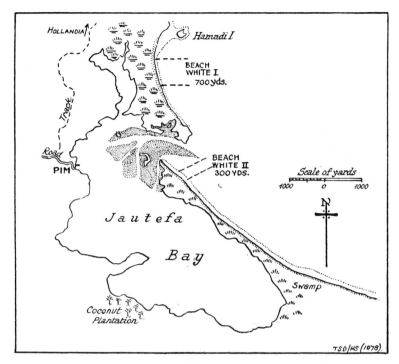

FIG. 11. THE HUMBOLDT BAY AREA

good road leading to the Japanese base. The prepared defences of the base were found abandoned and the place was captured with little effort. The landing strip was rapidly repaired and two squadrons of Australian fighter aircraft moved in to support the troops and assist in covering shipping between Tadji and Hollandia.

The carriers of Task Force 58 had arrived off the coast at daybreak on 22nd April, to support the landings. They found few worthwhile targets, but shot down a considerable number of fighter aircraft which went up to oppose them. Since there was nothing for them to do, they withdrew that afternoon. The troops ashore quickly advanced inland, and by the 26th had captured the three airfields, which shortly afterwards took the place of those at Port Moresby and the Dobodura area.

The Japanese lost over 1,800 killed and nearly 400 prisoners, an unusually high number. The Allies set free 621 prisoners of the Japanese, 462 of whom were British Indians. The occupation of Hollandia cut off approximately 50,000 Japanese in the eastern half of New Guinea. Evacuation by sea was not possible, whilst further supplies were almost completely cut off. The Japanese Ninth Fleet was dispersed and the ships drafted to other fleets between 25th March and 5th May 1944.

135

The airfields at Hollandia were limited in size and were found to be suitable only for fighters and light bombers. By 17th May these types were operating from them. Pre-assault air attacks on Wakde and Biak (Schouten Islands) had already begun ; for when the limitations of the Hollandia airfields were known General MacArthur at once decided to move 130 miles to the westward and seize the island of Wakde, where the Japanese had an airstrip, and the area around Maffin Bay. His object in this movement was to obtain airfields from which to cover his further movement into the Geelvink Bay region in June and subsequent operations in the Vogelkop Peninsula. Reconnaissance showed, however, that the construction of airfields in the Maffin Bay area would probably call for considerable engineering effort. Accordingly, a move to Biak was planned, to provide the additional airfields which the Far East Air Force would shortly need. The coral formation of Biak Island would facilitate the rapid construction of airfields for an advance to Morotai in Halmahera, which was to be the final objective of General MacArthur's forces before the advance to the Philippines. There were already three landing strips on Biak, for with the mounting Allied offensive in New Guinea early in 1944 the Japanese had vigorously developed the possibilities of the island. But attrition had hit their air forces so hard that their Order of Battle, Air in the New Guinea–Bismarcks area showed now no more than 130 army and navy land-based aircraft.

The timing of the Wakde Operation ('Straightline') depended upon the establishment of adequate supporting air forces in the recently captured Hollandia area. The landing was fixed for 17th May. The expedition was mounted from Aitape and Hollandia, and involved a coastwise movement westward. The garrison of Wakde Island was estimated at 500, and the Maffin-Sarmi area was believed to contain about 5,500 troops and two airfields, though immediately before the operation there were indications that this force was being reinforced by troops who escaped overland from Hollandia. Owing to the possibility of encountering strong defences, direct assault on Wakde was discarded in favour of capture from a beach-head seized on the mainland. The landing force consisted of one U.S. Regimental Combat Team reinforced, a total of 9,700 troops. The Naval Attack Group (Task Group 77.2) was under the command of Captain A. G. Noble.[1] Cover and support for the landing were furnished by Rear-Admiral Crutchley's Task Force 74 and Rear-Admiral Berkey's Task Force 75, a total of two heavy and three light cruisers, 20 destroyers and three destroyer escorts. It was not possible to carry out a prior rehearsal owing to the commitments of craft and a change of plan at a late stage. The assault troops were some who had, however, recently carried out a landing operation. The approach of the expedition was uneventful and undetected. After an initial bombardment the landing of over 7,000 troops was carried out on 17th May on the mainland at Sarmi within artillery range of Wakde Island. No opposition was encountered on the beach and only about 20 Japanese were killed during the day. Wakde Island was kept under bombardment from 0605 on D-day to 0850 on D + 1 day, about 1,000 tons of bombs per square mile being dropped on it.[2] Troops from the Sarmi beach-head landed at 0903 in face of nothing worse than scattered rifle and automatic fire,

---

[1] H.Q. Ship .. .. 1 destroyer.
Transport Group .. .. .. 2 transports, attack.
L.S.T. Group .. .. 7 L.S.T.s.
L.C.I. Group .. .. 12 L.C.I.s.
Bombardment and Protective Group *Australia, Shropshire, Phoenix, Nashville, Boise,* 20 destroyers, 3 destroyer escorts.
Special Service Group .. .. 3 rocket L.C.I.s, 2 rocket submarine chasers, 2 control submarine chasers, 2 tugs.
Beachmaster unit .. .. .. 3 officers, 17 O.R.
Reinforcement Group .. .. 8 L.S.T.s, 4 destroyers, 3 destroyer escorts.

[2] *General Kenney Reports,* p. 520.

which however caused a number of casualties both ashore and in the landing craft. Resistance ceased 36 hours after the landing. Nearly 800 dead were counted, and one prisoner was taken.

136

The capture of Wakde Island and the rapid repair of the airfield for operational use by fighter aircraft ensured adequate fighter aircraft cover and thus established the primary condition considered necessary for a successful operation to capture Biak Island. Prior to the early part of 1944 the Japanese had evidently not realised the potential airfield possibilities of Biak. The mounting Allied offensive caused a change in their attitude and construction of airfields on the island was vigorously undertaken. On 27th May, when the Allies carried out the assault, 21 enemy airfields existed in the Geelvink Bay, Vogelkop and Halmahera area, all within range of Biak (*see Plan 23*). The enemy had never maintained large air forces in these areas and although the capture of Hollandia caused him to expedite new construction, the Fifth Air Force heavy bomber strikes from New Guinea and northern Australia prevented any large air reinforcement prior to the operation.

Biak Island, the largest of the Schouten Group, lies in the mouth of Geelvink Bay. An elevated coral escarpment averaging over a mile wide and from 50 to 150 feet high fringes the coast, rising abruptly from the water in some places. At Bosnik, the area selected for the landing, on the south shore of the island, this coastal cliff was about 500 yards from the beach and 100 feet high. The entire southern coast is fringed by a wide coral reef drying at low tide. Deep water exists generally off this reef but in some places a barrier reef lies further off shore. The conditions were such as to make the proposed landing (Operation ' Horlicks ') the most difficult yet attempted in the South-West Pacific area. There was no clear indication as to whether the Japanese intended to fight for Biak. The garrison was estimated at 4,500 : actually the Japanese commander, Colonel Kuzume, had at his disposal 9,842 troops, of which only the 222nd Infantry Regiment (3,000) and the 19th Naval Guard Division (450) were combatant troops. It was subsequently found that the defence of the island afforded an excellent example of the weakness and strength of Japanese defensive tactics. Full advantage had been taken of the natural features of the ground, but these had not been integrated into a well co-ordinated defensive position by the use of obstacles, mines, cleared fields of fire, and constructed fortified areas. Some A/A and naval guns had been emplaced.

The main strength of the Japanese Combined Fleet at this time was at Tawi Tawi in the Sulu Archipelago, with small detachments at Davao and Waigeo Island between Halmahera and New Guinea. When concentrated the Fleet consisted of the following :—

Three 16-inch battleships (*Yamato, Musashi, Nagato*).

Three 14-inch battleships (*Fuso, Haruna, Kongo*).

Three fleet carriers (*Taiho, Zuikaku, Shokaku*) (222 aircraft).

Six converted carriers (*Hiyo, Junyo, Ryuho, Chitose, Chiyoda, Zuiho*) (252 aircraft).

Twelve 8-inch cruisers (*Atago, Takao, Maya, Chokai, Haguro, Myoko, Kumano, Suzuya, Mogami, Tone, Chikuma, Aoba*).

Four light cruisers (*Oi, Natori, Kinu, Yahagi*).

Thirty-five destroyers.

The efficiency of the aircraft pilots was low, and insufficient were available to man all the carrier aircraft.

The Fleet was under the command of Admiral Soemu Toyoda, who had been appointed on 3rd May in succession to Admiral Koga killed on 30th March whilst flying from Palau to Davao.

The Seventh Fleet commanded by Vice-Admiral T. C. Kinkaid contained, in addition to the Amphibious Force (Task Force 77) an Escort Carrier Force (Task Force 78) under Rear-Admiral R. E. Davison, of eight escort carriers and 17 destroyers, together with Admiral Crutchley's and Admiral Berkey's covering forces (Task Forces 74 and 75) with a total of two Australian and three U.S. cruisers, and two Australian and eight U.S. destroyers.

The nearest Allied force was the American Fifth Fleet. This was advancing on the Marianas from the Marshall Islands which had been cleared of the enemy in April. It was a formidable armada consisting of six 16-inch and seven 14-inch battleships ; 15 fleet carriers and 12 escort carriers, with a total complement of 1,175 aircraft ; ten 8-inch and ten light cruisers ; 100 destroyers and 75 submarines.

The expedition to Biak (Operation 'Horlicks') was under Rear-Admiral W. M. Fechteler, who flew his flag in a destroyer leader. The Naval attack force, designated Task Force 77 consisted of five transports, 24 L.C.I.s, eight L.S.T.s and a similar number of L.C.T.s carrying a total of 12,000 troops.[1] Fifty-three tracked landing vehicles and 25 amphibious trucks were carried to overcome the difficulties of the reef. The convoy was escorted by Admiral Crutchley's and Admiral Berkey's task forces.

137

Z-day, the day fixed for the landing was ten days after the landing at Wakde, namely 27th May, and H-hour, the hour of landing, at 0715 in order to confine the approach to darkness whilst allowing as long as possible for unloading. The convoy left Hollandia at 1800 on Z — 2 day and followed a course parallel to and out of sight of Dutch New Guinea. The approach to Biak Island was made from the north-east in order to avoid islands in Japen Strait and to keep outside land observation as long as possible. A circular screen of destroyers guarded the convoy, with radar guardships further out. The cruiser covering forces remained with the formation during daylight and took up covering dispositions to the west and north-west at night. The enemy failed to discover the expedition and surprise was complete.

Admiral Crutchley's and Admiral Berkey's task forces reinforced to a total of two 8-inch and three 6-inch cruisers, 21 destroyers and three rocket L.C.I.s carried out the preliminary bombardment. Sixty-two B.24 (heavy bombardment) aircraft were also to have been used to cover the beaches and airfield areas, but on account of the weather only 22 arrived to take part. The bombardment, which continued until three minutes before the landing, was intense and well timed, though owing to the overcast there was insufficient light to begin shooting at the scheduled hour of 0630. It was compressed into as short a time as possible since time to complete unloading was an important consideration. The policy of landing at a point where serious opposition appeared unlikely was justified. The landing area was found to be very lightly defended, and apart from a little sniping, opposition except in the east ceased within half an hour of landing. One Allied destroyer was damaged by a shell hit. No carrier-borne aircraft were employed in the operation to cover and support the landing, reliance being placed entirely on land-based aircraft to provide continuous

---

[1] *See* Appendix P.

fighter cover over the convoy and landing area throughout Z — 1 and Z-days between 0715 and 1700 hours. This might have resulted in a serious situation, for on Z day the weather prevented fighter cover from arriving until 1100. Fortunately, the first Japanese air attack did not take place until 1640, when a small raid of some 12 aircraft approached. Part of it was intercepted by the fighter cover, but two fighters and four bombers flew in low over the escarpment without warning and attacked the L.S.T.s. They caused little damage, and all four bombers were shot down.

For more than a month after the Allied landing on Biak the enemy resisted stubbornly and major battles took place, whilst the attacks of the Japanese air forces grew in strength and determination. The Mokmer airstrip was taken on 7th June, but it was not until the 20th that the Japanese airfields of Sorido and Borskoe, 5 miles to the west of Mokmer, were occupied. An air base, soon to become one of the most important in the South-West Pacific area and the Headquarters of the Fifth Air Force, was set up by 21st June on the unihabited island of Owi, just to the south of Biak.[1] Biak held out until 2nd July.

138

A Japanese message intercepted at that date indicated that the enemy intended to stand fast in Halmahera and at Sorong in the extreme west of New Guinea. Manokwari and Biak were only to be held 'as long as possible.' On 6th May the American submarine *Gurnard* (Lieut.-Commander C. H. Andrews) intercepted off Menado (Celebes) a convoy of ten ships heavily loaded with troop reinforcements from Manila which were due at Manokwari on the 10th, and sank three ships, the *Tenshinzan Maru, Taijima Maru* and *Aden Maru.* The Japanese diverted the remainder of the convoy to Kau Bay, Halmahera. A reinforcement of Halmahera from the southern Philippines took place about a fortnight later. The convoy, consisting of some nine transports with five escorts, was attacked on the night of the 22nd/23rd May by U.S. submarines and the *Ray* (Commander B. J. Harrel) sank the *Tenpei Maru* north of Talaur Eilanden in 5° 43' N., 127° 37' E., whilst the *Cero* (Commander D. C. White) next day sank the *Taijun Maru* north of Halmahera, in 2° 38' N., 128° 08' E. The Japanese at the end of May withdrew the outer defence line to the Marianas–Palau and Sumatra–Java–Timor–Western New Guinea, and moved the battle fleet to Singapore (the 'A' Operations Plan). This defensive perimeter they continued to reinforce, and they arranged for six convoys, comprising in all 131 ships, to sail from Japan during June, for the Netherlands East Indies and Malaya.

The Japanese knew that the capture and development of Biak by the Allies would introduce a direct air threat to Halmahera and the Philippines, and they regarded the U.S. landing more seriously than any other recent setback in the south-west Pacific. Imperial Headquarters described it as 'the first enemy penetration of our inner defence line,' and the Japanese made every effort to prevent the Americans from securing the airfields. Almost daily from 1st June onward fighters and bombers from the 23rd Flotilla at Sorong and the 4th Air Army at Samate appeared over Biak. Immediately the Commander-in-Chief Japanese Combined Fleet received a report of the landing he ordered an

---

[1] General Kenney relates that the natives stated the place was tabu, but the Americans considered this 'just another silly native custom.' In about ten days the troops began to develop scrub typhus and the aid of the doctors had to be invoked to discover some solution with which clothing could be impregnated to repel the almost microscopic mites that carried the infection.

amphibious (*syn.* Commando) brigade to be sent to reinforce the island. This was known as the ' Kon ' operation. Part of the brigade, some 2,500 troops, who were in Mindanao (Philippines), embarked in the 8-inch cruiser *Aoba,* the light cruiser *Kinu* and destroyers, with some minelayers and transports, and sailed from Davao for New Guinea on 2nd June under the command of Rear-Admiral M. Shimanouchi in the *Kinu.* A covering force consisting of the 14-inch battleship *Fuso,* the 8-inch cruisers *Haguro* and *Myoko* and seven destroyers sailed from Davao at the same time.[1] These forces were sighted several times on 3rd June by U.S. submarines and aircraft. Three Liberators (B–24 heavy bombers) attacked them next day and sank the tank landing ship *Transport No. 128* in 4° 0′ N., 129° 45′ E. Believing that an American carrier force was near Geelvink Bay, the Japanese changed the plans for the expedition. The covering force reversed course and returned to Davao, whilst the assault force with the troops went on to Waigeo Island, between New Guinea and Halmahera, where they arrived on the 5th. The Allies discovered the convoy there next day, and 15 Liberators made an attack, but sank no ships. Weather at that time caused a good deal of interference with air operations, and before the expedition could be attacked again it made a fresh start for Biak, using only the fast ships, which slipped out of the anchorage at midnight on 7th/8th June. The destroyers *Shikinami, Uranami* and *Shigure* each carried as many troops as could be packed on board. They were screened by the *Harusame, Shiratsuyu* and *Samidare* and supported by the light cruisers *Kinu* and *Aoba,* whilst the 23rd Air Flotilla provided air cover. This flotilla, being controlled by the First Air Fleet, was under the direction of the Commander-in-Chief, Combined Fleet. At noon on the 8th ten medium bombers escorted by eight fighters picked up the force off Manokwari moving east along the north coast of the Vogelkop Peninsula covered by six fighters. Making a low level attack, they sank the *Harusame* and slightly damaged others of the destroyers. Two of the bombers were lost. The remainder of the hostile force continued to steer eastward.

It was known by South-West Pacific Area Headquarters on 5th June that the Japanese were about to make an attempt to reinforce Biak. The date of the landing was uncertain, but it was known to be timed to take place between 2100 and 2300, and the landing points were also known to the Allies. Admiral Crutchley's and Admiral Berkey's cruiser forces had been covering Biak. Admiral Kinkaid combined them in a single force under Admiral Crutchley, consisting of the cruisers *Australia* (flag), *Phoenix* (flag of Rear-Admiral Berkey) and *Boise* and 14 destroyers.[2] As soon as the news of the enemy force north of Biak was received Admiral Crutchley sailed from Humboldt Bay to attack it. At 2200 on the 8th a reconnaissance aircraft detected five Japanese destroyers north-west of Biak ; the sixth the *Harusame,* had been sunk by bombing that afternoon. Admiral Crutchley's ships made radar contact about 2320 at a range of 23,400 yards. The Japanese reversed course when sighted, and a running fight at high speed ensued, during which only the U.S. destroyers were able to gain firing range. The exchange of fire at long range resulted in no important damage to either side, and after some three hours Admiral Crutchley had to abandon the chase in order to get within range of friendly fighter cover by daylight ; the enemy consequently escaped to the westward, landing their troops at Sorong in lieu of Biak.

---

[1] This was the force detailed, but it is uncertain whether any changes were made before sailing.

[2] *Hutchins, Daly, Beale, Bache, Trathen, Abner Read, Mullany, Ammen, Fletcher, Radford, Jenkins, La Vallette,* H.M.A.S. *Arunta,* H.M.A.S. *Warramunga.*

The Japanese planned a third attempt at landing troops, reinforcing Admiral Shimanouchi's squadron for that purpose with the two 18-inch battleships *Musashi* and *Yamato*, the heavy cruisers *Myoko* and *Haguro*, a light cruiser and three destroyers, the intention being to land the troops at all costs, regardless of losses. These ships sailed on 10th June from Tawi Tawi, where the Combined Fleet was lying, to Batjan Anchorage, Halmahera (Moluccas). Against a force of such strength Admiral Crutchley would have been powerless. However, on 13th June the operation was suddenly cancelled. A direct threat to the Japanese Empire was materialising and Biak had to be sacrificed. The preliminary air and ship bombardment, minesweeping and beach preparation for a landing on Saipan by Central Pacific Forces had begun. The order to prepare to put into effect the ' A ' Plan for the defence of the Marianas was issued and the Japanese forces engaged in the ' Kon ' Operation were ordered north.

139

The Americans rapidly established a main air base on Biak Island, but air to air warning, and light naval facilities were needed somewhat in advance of this, and on 15th June orders were given to seize Numfor Island. This island lies in Geelvink Bay, between Biak and Manokwari on the Vogelkop Peninsula. At Manokwari, 50 miles distant, the Japanese had an air base. Though no more than 15 miles in diameter Numfor Island contained three airfields. The garrison on the island was estimated at 3,000 Japanese, but proved to be somewhat less. In order to eliminate air opposition to the landing the Fifth Air Force carried out a continuous offensive prior to D day against all enemy airfields within striking distance. The Japanese began withdrawing their air forces northward in the middle of June, to defend the Marianas[1] and by the time the Allies landed on Numfor Island there remained no aircraft at Sorong and Samate. The Japanese no longer attempted air reinforcement of New Guinea.

The 158th U.S. Infantry Regiment (reinforced), with engineers, a total of 7,000 men, were detailed to make the assault landing. The attack force under Rear-Admiral W. M. Fechteler comprised 19 destroyers, 28 landing craft, 16 tank landing ships, patrol vessels and tugs. Amongst the 135 small craft and amphibians[2] were 53 D.U.K.W.s. The expedition was given cover and close support by Admiral Berkey's and Admiral Crutchley's cruiser and destroyer force, in which on 13th June Commodore J. A. Collins, R.A.N., had relieved Admiral Crutchley. Two scout companies visited the island prior to the landing, but were detected by the enemy, and withdrew without obtaining much information. Good photographic interpretation resulted however in the selection of a safe landing point. Landing conditions necessitated a frontal assault on a known defended locality across a wide reef, and were expected to be the worst encountered in the New Guinea campaign. Ideal weather was considered essential.

The troops sailed from Finschafen and from Toem, on the mainland opposite Wakde Island. In order to achieve surprise, the expedition was routed to Biak Island to give the appearance of being a reinforcement convoy for that place and left Biak at dusk on 1st July. To counteract the strong opposition which

---

[1] The 23rd Flotilla was withdrawn to Palau and the 4th Air Army to the Celebes and Halmaheras.

[2] 40 L.C.M., 40 L.V.T. (carried in the L.S.T.), 53 D.U.K.W.s (in L.C.M. and L.S.T.) and one L.C.V. (?) and one L.C.S. at L.S.T. davits.

was expected, bombardment was increased to approximately two and a half times that theoretically considered necessary to neutralise a lightly defended area. This naval gunfire support involved a total of

8-inch	300 rounds
6-inch	1,200 rounds
5-inch	
4·7-inch	} 10,000 rounds
4·5-inch rocket	800 rounds

The bombardment, with cruiser aircraft spotting, covered a period of 80 minutes from 0640 to H-hour (0800) on 2nd July and was supplemented by bombing by 17 heavy bombers (B.24's) superimposed on the naval gunfire. This resulted in a complete absence of opposition to the landing, and no hostile reaction occurred for an hour. Using the tide effectively, L.V.T.s and D.U.K.W.s manned by army personnel carried out the assault landing over the reef with success, the assault waves being commanded by experienced naval officers. Artillery and six medium tanks in L.C.T.s, the reserve battalion in L.C.I.s, and the shore battalion in L.C.M.s and L.C.T.s, all disembarked at the reef edge at half ebb-tide, the earliest of them finding 3 feet of water shoaling rapidly to 1 foot. Heavy infantry equipment was floated ashore in rubber boats. Close naval fire support after the landing was provided by rocket L.C.I.s using rockets and 40-mm. guns, and by destroyers. Coloured smoke was used ashore to mark the progress of forward troops. Navy, Army and Air Force all used an identical map.[1]

On 30th July a reinforced regimental combat team of the U.S. 6th Infantry Division landed in the Cape Sansapor area of the Vogelkop Peninsula (Operation 'Globetrotter') without naval or air bombardment; for though there were some 18,000 Japanese troops in western New Guinea they were concentrated at Manokwari, Babo and Sorong. Secondary landings were made on Middleburg Island, and two days later Amsterdam Island was occupied in order to set up an M.T.B. base there. M.T.B.s went on patrol from the future base that same evening.

140

The Japanese employed the submarines of the 7th Flotilla to co-operate in the 'Kon' Operation for the reinforcement of Biak. The Americans suspected that a force of five enemy submarines was operating on a patrol line on the Equator north-east of the Admiralty Islands in the latter part of May, and they sent there a task force consisting of the escort carrier *Hoggatt Bay* and four destroyer escorts, the *England, George, Raby* and *Spangler*, to carry out anti-submarine operations. Remarkable success soon attended their efforts. The *England* alone sank five submarines single handed and one with assistance, between 19th and 29th May. Coming from the sinking of *I–16* on the 19th north of the Solomons and *R–106* on the 21st north-west of New Ireland, on 22nd May she had radar contact on a surfaced submarine. The *England* obtained three hits in a hedgehog attack in 1° 40′ N., 150° 31′ E. and though it was not known at the time, the submarine, *RO–104* was sunk. At 0600 on the 23rd contact was made by radar with another surfaced submarine. After five unsuccessful hedgehog attacks the *England* obtained eight to ten hits in another attack, followed by violent underwater explosions after further depth-charge attacks which brought up oil and debris. Although only considered probably sunk, the enemy, *RO–116* was actually sunk, the position being 0° 53′ N., 149° 14′ E.

---

[1] Apparently for the first time.

Submarines were attacked by the group on both the night of the 24th/25th and on the morning of the 25th, but without lethal results. On the night of the 25th/26th, however, the *Raby* and *England* made radar contact and the latter successfully sank *RO–108* by hedgehog attack at 250 feet in 0° 32′ S., 148° 35′ E. Finally, on 29th May the *England, George, Raby, Hazlewood* and *McCord* sank *RO–105* in 0° 47′ N., 149° 56′ E. The destroyer escorts were relieved on 2nd June by four destroyers from Seeadler Harbour, Manus, to continue the operations. The enemy submarines left soon after, however, to co-operate in the defence of the Marianas.[1] None of them had accomplished anything.

141

General MacArthur had no need to undertake any further amphibious operations in New Guinea. He had neutralised the island as a base for enemy operations and secured for the Allies bases for an advance to the Philippines. There was much fighting still to be done, however, for large numbers of Japanese troops remained in the island. On 1st October 1944 Australian troops took over from the Americans the task of clearing the enemy out of New Guinea, simultaneously with the Solomon Islands and Bismarck Archipelago. General MacArthur was able to report :

> The enemy garrisons which have been bypassed in the Solomons and New Guinea represent no menace to current or future operations. Their capacity for organised offensive effort has passed. The various processes of attrition will eventually account for their final disposition. The actual time of their destruction is of little or no importance and their influence as a contributing factor to the war is already negligible. The actual process of their immediate destruction by assault methods would unquestionably involve heavy loss of life without adequate compensating strategic advantages.[2]

The most decisive development of the campaign had been the Allied domination of the air. The Japanese lost freedom of movement and the ability to supply and reinforce their garrisons because the Allies were able to concentrate greater air strength in contested areas, thus overwhelming the air cover intended to protect Japanese movements. This same control of the air by the Allies gained for them freedom of movement. Their naval forces demonstrated their capacity to lend the necessary support to all amphibious operations which they undertook and as events shortly proved, to defeat the Japanese at sea wherever they might choose to give battle.

The outstanding characteristic of the Japanese war machine at that date was its lack of balance. The armies of the enemy were relatively unaffected, although some highly trained naval landing parties and other front line troops had been lost ; but his naval strength no longer sufficed to protect his outposts ; and whilst he was still willing to commit the Combined Fleet in defence of regions vital to the security of the home islands, his lack of carrier based air forces limited the *venue* of a successful encounter to the area covered by his land based aircraft. His air arm could no longer effectively support his ground troops or protect his long lines of communication with regions of which he was

---

[1] This will be dealt with in Volume IV of this Staff History.

[2] Quoted in Biennial Report of the Chief of Staff of the U.S. Army, 1 July 1943 to 30th June 1945.

still in undisputed possession.   The unremitting pressure of Allied submarines, aided during the past twelve months by aircraft, had cost the Japanese half their merchant fleet.   No shipping route was safe from attack.   No ship in or out of harbour was safe south of Japan.   The effect of the restriction of imports through shipping shortage was being reflected in a decline of output of many industries producing essential war materials.   Though the public were kept in ignorance of the true facts there were not wanting in Japan serious students of the war who knew that the country was facing defeat.

APPENDIX A

Operation Stream-Line-Jane: Forces Engaged

(Rear-Admiral W. G. Tennant and Major-General R. G. Sturges, R.M., Joint Commanders)

NAVAL

Cruisers	*Birmingham* (S.O. Force M. and G.O.C.)
	Dauntless
	Gambia
	Caradoc
A.A. ship, ex Light Cruiser	*Heemskerck*
Battleship	*Warspite* (for Operation ' Jane ' only)
Carrier	*Illustrious*
Monitor	*Erebus*
H.Q. ship	*Albatross*
Fast minelayer	*Manxman* (Captain R. K. Dickson)
Destroyers	H.M.A.S. *Napier* (Captain S. H. T. Arliss, Commodore (D) for ' Jane ' and ' Tamper ')
1st Division	H.M.N.S. *Van Galen*
(Carrier screen)	H.M.N.S. *Tjerk Hiddes*
2nd Division	
3rd Submarine (A/S)	*Norman*
	Nizam
4th Submarine	*Foxhound*
	Hotspur
3rd Division	*Arrow*
5th Submarine (special)	*Blackmore*
6th Submarine	*Active*
	Inconstant
4th Division	
(Battleship screen)	*Fortune*
	Nepal
Minesweepers	*Cromer*
14th M/S Flotilla	*Cromarty*
	Romney
	Freezia
A/S whalers	*Sigfar*
	Lurcher
	Mastiff
Netlayer	*Brittany* (for Operation ' Stream ' only)
Merchant ships	
Assault ships	*Empire Pride* (8 L.C.A.)
29th Brigade	*Dunera* (6 L.C.A.)
' Stream ' and ' Jane '	*Dilwara* (6 L.C.A.)
M/T ship	*Ocean Viking* (2 L.C.A.)
Personnel ships	
(22nd Brigade)	*Empire Woodlark* (1 L.C.M.)
	Abosso
	Khedive-Ismail
	Llandaff Castle
M/T ships	
(22nd Brigade)	*Ocean Vesper* (2 L.C.M.)
	Empire Squire (2 L.C.M.)
	Delius (2 L.C.M.)
	Wanderer

MAINTENANCE CONVOY

M/T ships	*Gascony* (4 L.C.M.) (and for assault on ' Stream ' and ' Jane ')
	Adviser (2 L.C.S.), *Charlton Hall* (2 L.C.M.), *Ross*
Personnel ship	*Empire Trooper*
Oilers	*British Energy, Easedale, Eaglesdale, Doryssa*
Petrol ship	*Kola*
Hospital ships	*Vasna, Dorsetshire*

AIR

	JANE	STREAM
Ship-borne-Swordfish	18 T.B.R.	18
Fulmar	6 F	6
Martlet	21 F	21
Walrus	8 Amphibious boat R/C	6

Long range reconnaissance Catalina

(*a*) Landbased (at Majunga)

S.A.A.F.	Maryland 5
	Beaufort up to 8 B
	Lysander 5 Coopn.
Naval	Albacore 6 T.B.R.
	Fulmar 6 F

(*b*) Long range reconnaissance

R.A.F.	Catalina 6

Landings at Guadalcanal — (Operation 'Watchtower')

ORGANISATION OF ALLIED NAVAL AND AIR FORCES

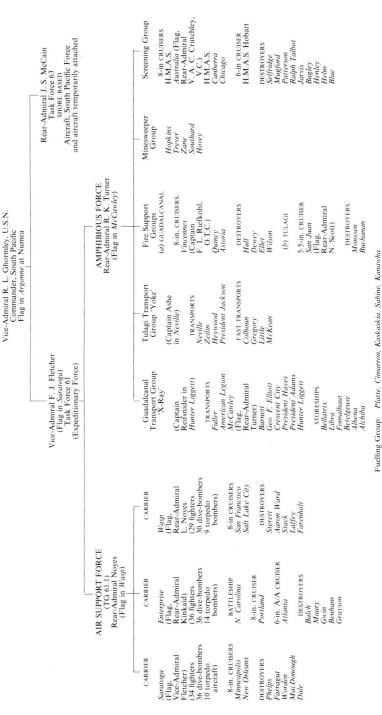

Vice-Admiral R. L. Ghormley, U.S.N.
Commander, South Pacific
Flag in *Argonne* at Numea

Vice-Admiral F. J. Fletcher
(Flag in *Saratoga*)
Task Force 61
(Expeditionary Force)

Rear-Admiral J. S. McCain
Task Force 63
SHORE BASED
Aircraft, South Pacific Force
and aircraft temporarily attached

AIR SUPPORT FORCE
(TG 61.1)
Rear-Admiral Noyes
(Flag in *Wasp*)

AMPHIBIOUS FORCE
Rear-Admiral R. K. Turner
(Flag in *McCawley*)

AIR SUPPORT FORCE

CARRIER
Saratoga
(Flag,
Vice-Admiral
Fletcher)
(34 fighters
36 dive-bombers
10 torpedo
aircraft)
8-in CRUISERS
Minneapolis
New Orleans
DESTROYERS
Phelps
Farragut
Worden
MacDonough
Dale

CARRIER
Enterprise
(Flag,
Rear-Admiral
Kinkaid)
(36 fighters
36 dive-bombers
14 torpedo
bombers)
BATTLESHIP
N. Carolina
8-in. CRUISER
Portland
6-in. A/A CRUISER
Atlanta
DESTROYERS
Balch
Maury
Gwin
Benham
Grayson

CARRIER
Wasp
(Flag,
Rear-Admiral
L. Noyes)
(29 fighters
30 dive-bombers
9 torpedo
bombers)
8-in CRUISERS
San Francisco
Salt Lake City
DESTROYERS
Sterett
Aaron Ward
Stack
Laffey
Farenholt

AMPHIBIOUS FORCE

Guadalcanal
Transport Group
'X-Ray'
(Captain
Reifsnider in
Hunter Liggett)
TRANSPORTS
Fuller
American Legion
McCawley
(Flag,
Rear-Admiral
Turner)
Barnett
Geo. F. Elliott
Crescent City
President Hayes
President Adams
Hunter Liggett
STORESHIPS
Bellatrix
Libra
Fomalhaut
Betelgeuse
Alhena
Alchiba

Tulagi Transport
Group 'Yoke'
(Captain Ashe
in *Neville*)
TRANSPORTS
Neville
Zeilin
Heywood
President Jackson
FAST TRANSPORTS
Colhoun
Gregory
Little
McKean

Fire Support
Groups
(a) GUADALCANAL
8-in. CRUISERS
Vincennes
(Captain
F. L. Riefkohl.
O.T.C.)
Quincy
Astoria
DESTROYERS
Hull
Dewey
Ellet
Wilson
(b) TULAGI
5-5-in. CRUISER
San Juan
(Flag,
Rear-Admiral
N. Scott)
DESTROYERS
Monssen
Buchanan

Minesweeper
Group
Hopkins
Trever
Zane
Southard
Hovey

Screening Group
8-in CRUISERS
H.M.A.S.
Australia (Flag,
Rear-Admiral
V. A. C. Crutchley,
V.C.)
H.M.A.S.
Canberra
Chicago
6-in CRUISER
H.M.A.S. *Hobart*
DESTROYERS
Selfridge
Mugford
Patterson
Ralph Talbot
Jarvis
Bagley
Henley
Helm
Blue

Fuelling Group: *Platte, Cimarron, Kaskaskia, Sabine, Kanawha*

Battle of Eastern Solomons

24th August ·1942

ORGANISATION OF JAPANESE NAVAL AND AIR FORCES

(Based on Morison, *U.S. Naval Operations in World War II*, Vol. V, pp. 84–85)
Admiral I. Yamamoto, C.-in-C. Combined Fleet, in *Yamato* with screen

(operating near Truk)

ADVANCE FORCE

(Vice-Admiral Kondo)

MAIN BODY

4th C.S. (8-inch)	*Atago, Maya, Takao*
5th C.S. (8-inch)	*Myoko, Haguro*
Destroyers	*Yura* (light cruiser) (Rear-Admiral T. Takama)
	Asagumo, Yamagumo, Kuroshio, Oyashio, Hayashio

SUPPORT GROUP

	Mutsu (battleship) (S.O.)
Destroyers	*Murasame, Harusame, Samidare*

SEAPLANE GROUP

	Chitose
Destroyer	*Natsugumo*

OCCUPATION FORCE

(Vice-Admiral G. Mikawa)

Light cruiser	*Jintsu* (Flag, Rear-Admiral R. Tanaka)
Destroyers	*Suzukaze, Umikaze, Uzuki*
Transport unit	*Kinryo Maru*
	(Auxiliary cruiser) carrying five Yokosuka Landing Force Patrol Boats Nos. 1, 2, 34, 35*, carrying 2nd Echelon Ichiki Detachment

BOMBARDMENT FORCE

Destroyers	*Isokaze, Kawakaze, Kagero, Mutsuki, Yayoi*

COVERING GROUP

	Chokai (8-inch cruiser) (Flag of Vice-Admiral Mikawa)
6th C.S. (Rear-Admiral Goto)	*Aoba* (8-inch), *Kinugasa* (8-inch), *Furutaka* (8-inch)

SUBMARINE GROUP

I–121, I–125, RO–54

* Converted old destroyers.

STRIKING FORCE

(Vice-Admiral Nagumo)

Carriers	*Shokaku*[1] (Flag, C.-in-C.), *Zuikaku*[2]
Destroyers	*Akigumo, Yugumo, Makigumo, Kazagumo, Shikinami, Uranami*

ADVANCE FORCE

(Rear-Admiral H. Abe)

Battleship Division 2	*Hiyei, Kirishima*
7th C.S.	*Suzuya, Kumano, Chikuma*
10th D.F.	*Nagara* (light cruiser)
Destroyers	*Akizuki, Hatsukaze, Maikaze, Nowaki, Tanikaze, Yukikaze*

---

[1] 26 fighters, 14 bombers, 18 torpedo, 1 scout observation aircraft.

[2] 27 fighters, 27 bombers, 18 torpedo aircraft.

DETACHED FORCE
(Rear-Admiral T. Hara)

Light carrier	*Ryujo*
8-inch cruiser	*Tone* (Flag, Rear-Admiral Hara)
Destroyers	*Amatsukaze, Tokitsukaze*

LAND-BASED-AIR FORCE
(Vice-Admiral N. Tsukahara, C.-in-C. Eleventh Air Fleet)
About 100 operational aircraft

ADVANCE EXPEDITIONARY FORCE

Submarines   *I–9, I–11, I–15, I–17, I–19, I–26, I–31, I–174, I–175*

APPENDIX D

Battle of Eastern Solomons

ORGANISATION OF ALLIED NAVAL FORCES

TASK FORCE 61
(Vice-Admiral F. J. Fletcher)
(Flag in *Saratoga*)

TASK FORCE 11	TASK FORCE 16
Carrier :	Carrier :
Saratoga	*Enterprise*
(Flag, Vice-Admiral Fletcher)	(Flag, Rear-Admiral Kinkaid)
Cruisers :	Battleship :
Minneapolis	*North Carolina*
(Flag, Rear-Admiral Wright)	
New Orleans	Cruiser :
H.M.A.S. *Australia*	*Portland*
(Flag, Rear-Admiral Crutchley, V.C.)	(Flag, Rear-Admiral Tisdale)
Light Cruiser :	A.A. Cruiser :
H.M.A.S. *Hobart*	*Atlanta*
Destroyers :	Destroyers :
Phelps	*Balch*
(Captain Brewer,	(Captain Sauer, S.O. 6th Squadron)
S.O. 1st Destroyer Squadron)	
Farragut	*Maury*
(Commander McInerney,	*Benham*
S.O. 2nd Destroyer Division)	*Ellet*
Worden	*Grayson*
MacDonough	(Commander Holcomb,
Dale	S.O. 22nd Division)
	Monssen

U.S. Plans and Dispositions in South Pacific Area 30th October 1942

From : B.A.D. Washington

To :   Admiralty

Message 1519Z/27th October

Date :   27.10.42
Recd. : 1702

3.

Personal for 1st Sea Lord.

Following received by C.-in-C. U.S. Fleet from C.-in-C. Pacific Fleet and brought over to me by one of his staff. Begins—Halsey has requested reinforcements by one or more carriers of British Eastern Fleet. In view of urgent and immediate need for every possible increase, particularly of Carriers, I recommend this idea be explored to utmost. Ends.

2. U.S. landing forces now in Guadalcanal hope to hold. Landing ground is still in use and they have local air supremacy. Result depends upon prevention of any large reinforcements reaching the island and supply of own forces. This depends on command of sea and this issue is being fought out now by surface forces. It will be largely dependent upon carriers.

3. Results in most recent actions were received in Navy Department yesterday and are as follows :

     (a) Japanese Forces. A/C Carrier *Shokaku* and A/C Carrier *Zuikaku* are out of action one having received three 1,000-pound bomb hits and the other two 500-pound bomb hits. In addition one of them has received one torpedo hit. This leaves the auxiliary Carrier *Hitaka* and *Hayataka* only operating in the area.

     (b) U.S. Forces. A/C Carrier *Hornet* is sunk. A/C Carrier *Enterprise* is damaged but still operating at about 50 per cent efficiency with one elevator out of action. A/C Carrier *Saratoga* should rejoin fleet latter half of November when A/C Carrier *Enterprise* most probably returns to Pearl Harbour.

4. They ask for immediate equipping of H.M.S. *Illustrious*. U.S. planes are available but presumably *Illustrious* would sail with full complement and be prepared to take S.B.D.s on deck stowage as replacements.

5. This is a real cry for immediate help.   1519Z/27

To :   B.A.D. Washington

From : Admiralty

Personal from 1st Sea Lord.

Message 0110A/28th October

Date :   28.10.42

Your 1519Z/27 raises issues of the gravest importance concerning the ultimate command of the sea, and before we can appreciate the situation it is essential that we should have information on the following points :—

     A. Disposition, giving names of effective U.S. capital ships.

     B. Which U.S. ships are in the South-West Pacific area.

     C. What reinforcement it is intended to send to the South-West Pacific area.

     D. What new U.S. Carriers will come into service in 1942 and the first half of 1943.

     E. The state in detail of Japanese Capital Ships and Carriers.

     F. U.S. policy regarding the South-West Pacific area.

     G. How was *Hornet* sunk and where did the action in which she was sunk take place.

     H. As you are aware every British Carrier with the exception of *Indomitable* and *Illustrious* are employed in Torch and the former is under repair.

     J. Though the Japanese may have only two auxiliary Carriers in the South-West Pacific area at the present time they can according to our estimate send three and possibly four more there before *Illustrious* could reach the area.

K. If the South-West Pacific area is fed with weak reinforcements at intervals the United Nations capital ship and carrier strength will be liable to suffer further attrition and we may have the command of the sea wrested from us.

L. Please inform Admiral King that we are most anxious to help but in view of the grave issues which are at stake it is essential that we should have a clear picture of the situation.   0110A/28

From : B.A.D. Washington   Message 2155Z/30th October

To :   Admiralty   Date : 31.10.42
                                                  Recd. : 0333
543.

Personal for 1st Sea Lord.

My 2141 30th *

(A) Effective battleships in addition to those on Task Forces are as follows :

U.S. B/S *Colorado*, U.S. B/S *Maryland*, U.S. B/S *New Mexico*, U.S. B/S *Mississippi*, all at Pearl Harbour.

(B) Three Task Forces :

(1) U.S. B/S *South Dakota*, U.S. A/C Carrier *Enterprise* (damaged), one heavy and one light cruiser, seven destroyers.

(2) Two heavy and three light cruisers, ten destroyers. U.S. A/C Carrier *Hornet* was in this force.

(3) U.S. B/S *Washington*. One heavy one light cruiser. Six destroyers.

(C) (1) U.S. B/S *Indiana* one light cruiser and four destroyers leave Atlantic coast early November.

(2) U.S. B/S *North Carolina*, U.S. A/C Carrier *Saratoga*, both having received torpedo hits complete repair at Pearl Harbour early November and with three heavy and one light cruiser and about eight destroyers should arrive in the area the beginning of December.

(D) U.S. A/C Carriers *Essex*, *Lexington*, *Independence*, and possibly *Princeton*.

(E) (1) 12 battleships in service. Three or four of which one is damaged, are operating to southward from Truk. Remainder in home waters.

(2) Three fleet carriers of which two damaged, *vide* my 1519 27th. Other is *Zuiho* whose characteristics are unknown.

(3) It seems clearly established that following are sunk Japanese A/C carrier *Akagi*. Japanese A/C carriers *Kaga*, *Hiryu*, *Soryu*, *Ryujo* and *Shoho*

(F) No information.

(G) Usual long range carriers versus carrier action. She was in company with Force mentioned in B (2) above about 100 miles north of Santa Cruz in recent action.

(J) U.S. estimate that only three or possibly four Japanese carriers could be operating in South-West Pacific by first December. These include *Hitaka* and *Hayataka* each carrying 58 aircraft and *Zuiho*.   2155Z/30

---

* This message is not necessary to an understanding of the situation.

From : B.A.D. Washington   Message 1751Z/6th November

To :   Admiralty   Date :   6.11.42

                                        Recd. : 2300

824. Personal for 1st Sea Lord.

My 2155/30th. Following information has now been received in writing from Admiral King.

- A. As in my 2155/30th.
- B. 5 Task Forces mentioned. Three as in former signal and in addition, (S/ms 24 escort) —two light cruisers, five destroyers.
- C. (1) As in my 2155/30th.
   (2) Date advanced to " about 22nd November ".
- D. As in my 2155/30th.
- E. As in my 2155/30th.
- F. General policy is to hold line of communications from U.S. to Australia. With this end in view, strong garrison established Pearl Harbour, Samoa, Fiji, New Caledonia. To give depth to this line, Wallis Funafuti, Efate, Espiritu Santo occupied. Airfields have been constructed in each occupied position and appropriately manned. Line threatened by Japanese activities at Guadalcanal which were countered by U.S. occupation in August. Present situation in Guadalcanal occupied by 24,000 troops. Espiritu Santo 5,000, New Caledonia 24,000. Reinforcement planned, 25,000 from New Zealand (of which 13,000 are New Zealand troops) plus one Infantry Division from U.S. Troops to be used to occupy Ndeni and to reinforce Guadalcanal whose sea approaches and land areas are in dispute. In New Guinea area Japanese have been driven back beyond Kokoda. Operations are now under way to occupy north-east coast. It is the intention of U.S. to consolidate their position in Guadalcanal and New Guinea and to then prepare to seize and occupy Rabaul. By such limited offensive protection will be given to lines of communication to Australia and freedom of action will be denied Japanese forces.
- G. U.S. Aircraft Carrier *Hornet* was badly damaged by two air attacks (bombs and torpedoes) in action north of Ndeni on 26th October. Vessel later sunk by U.S. Forces.
- J. It is estimated that Japanese have available for Service the *Hitaka* and *Hayataka* (58 planes each) plus *Zuiho* capacity unknown. In addition there are the small converted carriers *Otaka* ex *Kasuga Maru*, *Unyo* ex *Yawata Maru* and *Chuyo*. These small converted carriers have, in general, been used for ' Plane ferrying trips ', and are not believed efficient for combatant use. In same class U.S. is now operating converted carriers *Long Island, Nassau, Copahee, Altameba* in the Pacific.
- K. Reinforcements are utmost that can be spared from over-riding commitments of ' special operations '. Alternative seems to be the giving of the enemy quite a free hand.

2. Have just received acknowledgment from Admiral Boyd of receipt of my signal sent on 3rd November.   1751Z/6

From : B.A.D. Washington   Message 0321Z/7th November

To :   Admiralty   Date :   7.11.42

                                        Recd :   0517

856. Your 1210 6th. My 1751 6th. Cancel paragraph B and substitute—' In addition to three task forces mentioned in my 2155 30th there are also operating 24 repetition, 24 submarines and on escort duty two light cruisers and five destroyers.'   0321Z/7

APPENDIX F

Bismarck Sea Operation 2nd/4th March 1943

ORGANISATION OF JAPANESE CONVOY
(Rear Admiral M. Kimura)

SHIP AND TRANSPORT	NO.	TONS	SPEED (knots)	18th ARMY H.Q.	DIV. H.Q.	115 INFANTRY REG.	14 FD. ARTY. REG.	51 ENGR. REG. (less 1 Coy.)	DIV. SIGS.	3rd FIELD HOSPITAL	NADA UNIT (BUTM)	H.E. 1 (?)	WATER PURIFYING UNIT	21st IND. MXD. BDE. ARTY.	50th FD. A/A BN. (less 1 Coy.)	8th SHIPPING ENGR. REG.	3rd DEBARKATION UNIT	15th IND. ENGR. (including airfield Bn.)	ARMY SIGS.	TOTAL	Remarks
							51 Div.									*Attached Units*					
Shinai Maru	324	3,793	8.5	2	7	488		225	30		100	50		50	80	50	50		32	1,052	
Teiyo Maru	842	6,869	10	21	7	828	134	206	38		5		25	99	96	150	176			1,923	
Aiyo Maru	947	2,746	9	2				50		102	150					50	50			252	
Kyokusei Maru	776	5,493	10		27	500	81							97	96	70	150		18	1,203	
Oigawa Maru	480	6,493	10	56	67	389	159				10			100	90	150	150	50	20	1,324	
Taimei Maru	967	2,883	10							50	5					100	100			200	
Nojima Maru	—	7,189	—				Commodore of Convoy's ship (Captain K. Matsumoto) carried the naval landing force															
Kembu Maru	—	953	—																		
TOTALS		36,419		83	172	2,205	374	481	68	152	270	50	25	346	362	570	676	50	70	5,954	
Shirayuki (Flag)		1,700	34					6								23				29	Cdr. Escort Force (Rear-Admiral Kimura)
Arashio		1,500	34	50		62		6	9							23				150	
Asashio		1,500	34		21	63	20	6	18							22				150	To rescue A/C and wrecked ships
Asagumo		1,500	34					6								23				29	
Yukikaze		1,500	34	44	40	63		6	19							22				150	Carrying Lt.-Gen. Nakano—Cdr. 51st Div.
Tokitsukaze		1,500	34		24	46	22	6	9							23				150	Carrying Lt.-Gen. Adachi—G.C.O. 18th Army
Uranami		1,700	34		18	84	8	9	9							24				150	} Guide of Transports
Shikinami		1,700	34			82		9	9							24				150	
		12,600		94	103	400	50	54	73							184				958	
TOTAL		49,019		177	275	2,605	424	535	141	152	270	50	25	346	362	754	676	50	70	6,912	

APPENDIX F — *continued*

Bismarck Sea Operation 2nd/4th March 1943

ORGANISATION OF JAPANESE CONVOY
(Rear Admiral M. Kimura)

Equipment

Ship	Convoy No.	M.L.C. Large	Collapsible Boats	Rowing Boats	A/A	15-in. Howitzer	Bn. Gun	Mountain Gun	Light Mortar	M/G	10 Cannon	Field Guns	Regt. Guns	TIA (?) Gun	Carts	Trucks	Motor Cars	Passenger Vehicles	Trailers	Rear Car	Tractors	Unsinkable Drums	Fuel Drums	Fuel cu. metres	Gasoline cu. metres	Ammunition cu. metres	Aircraft Material cu. metres	Air Provisions cu. metres	Personal Property cu. metres
		Landing Craft			Guns										Vehicles										Same ?				
Shinai	1	6	15	6	3				3	1	1		1	1	5	1					1	100					500		
Teiyo	2	5	15	6											23	5				1	1	500				500		500	500
Aiyo	3	4	10	8																									
Kyokusei	4	8			3	2	2	2	4	7	2	2			26	12	2	1				500	350	500					
Oigawa	5	11			3	3	2	2		2						5		1	2			300							
Taimei	6						1															200							
Nojima	7																												
Kembu	X																								300				
TOTAL		34	40	20	9	5	5	4	7	10	3	2			54	23	2	2	2	1	2	1,600	350	500	300	500	500	500	500

Taimei: Reported as a collier. There is evidence elsewhere that she was previously probably used as an M.L.C. Carrier

Kembu: Sea Truck. Used for fast transport of urgent materials—in this case aircraft fuel

Note.—The destroyers carried a total of 14 small M.L.C.s and 54 collapsible boats.

VII Amphibious Force, Lae Operation, September 1943

(Rear-Admiral D. E. Barbey)

Headquarters Group 76.1
Destroyers *Conyngham* (Flag of R. A. Barbey).

Flusser.
High Speed Transport Group 76.2
Brooks, Gilmer, Sands, Humphreys.
L.S.T. Group 76.3
13 L.S.T.s.
L.C.I. Group 76.4
20 L.C.I.s.
L.C.T. Group 76.5
1 Coastal Transport.
14 L.C.T.s.
Destroyer Group 76.6
Perkins, Smith, Mahan, Lamson, Mugford, Drayton.
Coastal Transport Group 76.7
14 Coastal Transports.
9 L.C.T.s.
2 Submarine Chasers.
Service Group 76.8
Rigel (Destroyer Tender).
Sonoma (Ocean Tug)
3 L.S.T.s.
10 Submarine Chasers.
5 Motor Minesweepers.
1 Oil Barge.

Organisation of Forces at Battle of Guadalcanal

13th—15th November 1942

(1) ALLIED

(*a*) Cruiser Action, night 12th–13th November.
Task Group 67.4 (Rear-Admiral D. J. Callaghan).

Heavy cruisers	*San Francisco* (Flag), *Portland.*
Light Cruisers	*Helena,* Juneau* (A/A),* *Atlanta* (A/A)* (Flag of Rear-Admiral N. Scott).
Destroyers	*Aaron Ward, Barton,* Monssen,* Fletcher, Cushing,* Laffey,* Sterett, O'Bannon.*

(*b*) Air Action, 14th November.
Task Force 16 (Rear-Admiral T. C. Kinkaid).

Carrier	*Enterprise* (Flag).
Heavy cruisers	*Northampton, Pensacola.*
Light cruiser	*San Diego.*
Destroyers	*Clark, Anderson, Hughes, Morris, Russell Mustin, Gwin, Preston.*

Aircraft from Henderson Field, Guadalcanal.

*Ships so marked were sunk. The *Helena* was torpedoed and sunk during retirement.

(c) Battleship Action, night 14th–15th November.

Task Force 64 (Rear-Admiral W. A. Lee)

Battleships   *Washington* (Flag), *South Dakota*
Destroyers   *Walke,* Benham,* Gwin, Preston.**

(2) JAPANESE

(a) Cruiser Action, night 12th–13th November.

Raiding Group (Vice-Admiral H. Abe)

11th Battleship Division *Hiyei,* Kirishima.*
10th D.F.   *Nagara* (light cruiser) (Rear-Admiral S. Kimura), *Amatsukaze, Tokitsukaze, Hatsukaze, Terutsuki, Akatsuki,* Inazuma, Ikazuchi, Yukikaze.*
Sweeping Unit (destroyers) *Asagumo* (S.O.), *Murasame, Samidare, Yudachi,* Harusame.*
Patrol Unit (destroyers) *Shigure, Shiratsuyu, Yugure.*

(b) Air Action, 14th November.

Bombardment Unit (Vice-Admiral G. Mikawa)

Heavy cruisers *Chokai, Kinugasa,* Suzuya, Maya.*
Light cruiser *Isudzu*
Destroyers *Tenryu* (light cruiser), *Makigumo, Yugumo, Kazagumo, Michisio, Asashio, Arashio.*

Transport Unit (Rear-Admiral R. Tanaka)

Escort destroyers *Hayashio* (Flag), *Oyashio, Kuroshio, Kagero, Umikaze, Kawakaze, Suzukaze, Takanami, Makinami, Naganami, Mochizuki, Amagiri.*
Cargo and Passenger/Cargo Vessels *Arizona M.,* Brisbane M.,* Kumagawa M.,* Kinugawa M.,* Sado M.,* Hirokawa M.,* Nagara M.,* Yamaura M.,* Nako M.,* Yamatsuki M.,* Canberra M.,* Shinanogawa M.**

(c) Battleship Action, night 14th–15th November.

Emergency Bombardment Group (Vice-Admiral N. Kondo)

Battleship *Kirishima**
Heavy cruisers *Atago* (Flag of Vice-Admiral N. Kondo, O.T.C.), *Takao.*
Destroyers *Nagara* (light cruiser) (Rear-Admiral S. Kimura), *Terutsuki, Shirayuki, Hatsuzuki, Asagumo, Samidare, Ikazuchi, Sendai* (light cruiser) (Rear-Admiral S. Hashimoto), *Uranami, Shikinami, Inazuma, Ayanami.**

* Ships so marked were sunk.

APPENDIX J

Organisation of the Japanese Combined Fleet, 1st July 1943

The major components were as follows :—

ADMINISTRATIVE TITLE	PRINCIPAL COMPOSITION	TACTICAL TITLE
First Fleet	Battleships	Battleship Force
Second Fleet	Cruisers	Diversion Attack Force
Third Fleet	Carriers	Striking Force
Fourth Fleet	Mandates Area	Inner South Seas Force
Fifth Fleet	Surface forces of North-east Area Fleet	Northern Force
Sixth Fleet	Submarines	Advance Expeditionary Force

Eighth Fleet	Surface forces of South-east Area Fleet	Outer South Seas Forces
North-east Area Fleet	Northern Area	North-east Area Force
South-east Area Fleet	New Guinea — Solomons Area	South-east Area Force
South-west Area Fleet	Philippines—Malaya—NEI Area	South-west Area Force
First Southern Expeditionary Fleet	Malaya Area	Malaya Force
Second Southern Expeditionary Fleet	Dutch East Indies Area	East Indies Force
Third Southern Expeditionary Fleet	Philippines Area	Philippines Force
Eleventh Air Fleet	Shore-based air in Mandates and South-east Area	First Base Air Force
Twelfth Air Fleet	Shore-based air in Northern Area	Second Base Air Force

The principal administrative changes since the outbreak of the war had consisted of the following :—

(1) The South-east Area Command and its subsidiary, the Eighth Fleet, were established to command the newly won areas in New Guinea, New Britain, New Ireland and the Solomons.

(2) The South-west Area Command and its subsidiaries, the Southern Expeditionary Fleets, were established to command the newly won areas in South-east Asia, Dutch East Indies and the Philippines.

(3) The First Air Fleet was disbanded and the Third Fleet became the carrier force. Units of the old Third Fleet were turned over to the South-west Area Fleet.

COMBINED FLEET

Musashi (battleship) (Flag)

FIRST FLEET

1st B.S.
Yamato
Mutsu   (Sunk by explosion in Inland Sea, July 1943)

2nd B.S.
Nagato
Fuso
Yamashiro
Ise ⎫ (Undergoing conversion to battleship-aircraft carrier. Did not rejoin fleet
Hyuga ⎭   until July 1944)

11th D.F.
Tatsuta (light cruiser)

6th Division
Ikazuchi
Inazuma
Hibiki
Wakatsuki
Kasumi
Attached : *Noshiro* (light cruiser)

SECOND FLEET

4th C.S.
Atago
Takao
Maya

5th C.S.
Myoko
Haguro

2nd D.F.
Jintsu (light cruiser)   (Sunk 13th July 1943 : replaced by *Noshiro*)

24th Division
Umikaze
Kawakaze
Suzukaze

31st Division
Kiyonami
Makinami
Onami
Naganami

4th D.F.
Nagara (light cruiser)

27th Division
Samidare
Shigure
Yugure (Sunk 20th July 1943)
Shiratsuyu
Ariake

THIRD FLEET

1st Carrier Squadron
Zuikaku
Shokaku
Zuiho

2nd Carrier Squadron
Junyo
Hiyo
Ryuho

3rd B.S.
Kongo
Haruna

7th C.S. (heavy cruisers)
Suzuya
Kumano
Mogami

8th C.S. (heavy cruisers)
Tone
Chikuma

10th D.F.
Agano (light cruiser)

4th Division
Nowaki
Maikaze
Hagikaze
Arashi

10th Division
Akigumo
Yugumo
Kazagumo

16th Division
Yukikaze
Hatsukaze
Amatsukaze

17th Division
Isokaze
Hamakaze
Urakaze
Tanikaze

61st Division
Suzutsuki
Hatsuzuki

Training Forces
Kanoya (Air Group)
Tsukuba (Air Group)
Hosho (light carrier)
Yukaze (destroyer)
Oyodo (light cruiser)

FOURTH FLEET

Kashima (light cruiser) (Flag)

14th C.S.
Isudzu
Naka

FIFTH FLEET (under North-east Area Command)

Nachi (heavy cruiser) (Flag)

21st C.S. (light cruisers)
Tama
Kiso

1st D.F.
Abukuma (light cruiser)

21st Division
Hatsuharu
Hatsushimo
Wakaba

9th Division
Asagumo
Usugumo
Shirakumo

Submarines

Div. 7
I–2
I–3
I–6

I–7 (Sunk 21st June 1943)

SIXTH FLEET

Katori (light cruiser) (Flag)

1st S/M.F.
    I–17 (Flag)
    Heinan Maru (tender)

        Div. 2
          I–19
          I–25
          I–26

        Div. 15
          I–32
          I–34
          I–35
          I–36
          I–38

3rd S/M.F.
    I–11 (Flag)
    Yasukuni Maru (tender)

        Div. 12
          I–168
          I–169
          I–171
          I–174
          I–175
          I–176

        Div. 22
          I–177
          I–178
          I–180

8th S/M.F.
    Hie Maru (tender)

        Div. 1
          I–16
          I–20
          I–21
          I–24 (sunk 27th July)

        Div. 14
          I–27
          I–29
          I–37

        Attached
        I–8
        I–10

EIGHTH FLEET (under South-east Area Command)

Chokai (heavy cruiser) (Flag)

6th C.S.
    Aoba (heavy cruiser)
    Yubari (light cruiser)
    Sendai (light cruiser)

11th Destroyer Division
    Yugiri
    Hatsuyuki
    Amagiri

22nd Destroyer Division
    Satzuki
    Minazuki
    Fumizuki
    Nagatsuki

30th Destroyer Division
    Mikazuki
    Mochizuki
    Uzuki

SOUTH-WEST AREA FORCES

Ashigara (heavy cruiser) (Flag)

16th C.S.
    Kinu
    Oi
    Kitagami
    Kuma

19th Destroyer Division
    Isonami
    Uranami
    Shikinami
    Kashii (light cruiser)

Submarines
    Div. 30
        I–162
        I–166

Air Flotilla 23
First Southern Expeditionary Fleet (H.Q. Singapore)
Second Southern Expeditionary Fleet (H.Q. Surabaya)
Third Southern Expeditionary Fleet (H.Q. Manila)
(Commander-in-Chief South-west Area Fleet was concurrently Commander-in-Chief Second
  Southern Expeditionary Fleet)

North-east Area Forces

Fifth Fleet
Twelfth Air Fleet

South-east Area Forces

Eighth Fleet
Eleventh Air Fleet
7th S/M.F.
  Nine submarines

  (Commander-in-Chief South-east Area Fleet was concurrently Commander-in-Chief
    Eleventh Air Fleet)

Eleventh Air Fleet

Air Flotilla 21   Air Flotilla 25
Air Flotilla 22   Air Flotilla 26
Destroyers
  Akikaze
  Tachikaze

Attached Forces

Unyo (escort carrier)   7th Destroyer Division
Chuyo (escort carrier)   *Akebono*
Otaka (escort carrier)   *Ushio*
                                       Sazanami

In addition to the above forces, about 20 destroyers were regularly assigned to district forces and escort fleets, and were therefore not immediately available for fleet duty. Their numbers were steadily being reduced by submarine attack. A number of new destroyers were training in the Empire and do not appear in the organisation table.

Only 43 submarines are shown in this table. Perhaps 15 more were on training and guard duty in the Empire.

Task Forces

In August 1943 the following principal task forces were formed from the basic fleet organisation.

Main Body (Commander-in-Chief Third Fleet)

1st B.S. (4 battleships)

Striking Force (Commander-in-Chief Third Fleet)

1st Carrier Squadron (2 fleet carriers, 1 light fleet carrier)
2nd Carrier Squadron (less air groups) (2 fleet carriers, 1 light fleet carrier)
3rd B.S.
  Kumano (8-inch cruiser)
  Mogami (8-inch cruiser)
8th C.S. (2 8-inch cruisers)
10th D.F. (part) (1 light cruiser, 12 destroyers)

Battleship Force (Commander-in-Chief First Fleet)

2nd B.S. (4 battleships—only one available)

Diversion Attack Force (Commander-in-Chief Second Fleet)

4th C.S. (3 8-inch cruisers)
5th C.S. (2 8-inch cruisers)
2nd D.F. (1 light cruiser, 6 destroyers)
4th D.F. (part) (1 light cruiser, 2 destroyers)

South-east Area Force (Commander-in-Chief Eleventh Air Fleet)

Eleventh Air Fleet
7th S/M.F.
8th Fleet (2 8-inch cruisers, 2 light cruisers, 10 destroyers)
7th C.S. (part) (1 8-inch cruiser)
17th Destroyer Division (part) (2 destroyers)
27th Destroyer Division (3 destroyers)
Sazanami (destroyer)
5 submarines from Sixth Fleet

240

APPENDIX K

Organisation of the Allied Forces in New Guinea

(16th November 1942—23rd January 1943)

ADVANCED GENERAL HEADQUARTERS
General Douglas MacArthur
|
New Guinea Force
General Sir Thomas Blamey
(Lt.-Gen. E. F. Herring*)
|
Advanced New Guinea Force
Lt.-Gen. E. F. Herring
(Lt. R. L. Eichelberger*)
|

AUSTRALIAN UNITS	U.S. UNITS
Headquarters, Australian 7th Division	Headquarters, U.S. I Corps
Major-Gen. G. A. Vasey	Lt.-Gen. R. L. Eichelberger
Australian 2/7 Cavalry Regiment	
Australian 2/6 Armoured Regiment	Infantry
	32nd Division
Infantry	126th Infantry Regimental Combat Team
Australian 14th Infantry Bde. (attached)	127th Infantry Regimental Combat Team
Australian 16th Infantry Bde. (attached)	128th Infantry Regimental Combat Team
Australian 18th Infantry Bde.	41st Division
Australian 21st Infantry Bde.	163rd Infantry Regimental Combat Team
Australian 25th Infantry Bde.	
Australian 30th Infantry Bde. (attached)	
Australian 2/6 Independent Company	

Artillery
  One battery, Australian 2/1 Field
    Regiment (attached)
  One troop, Australian 2/5 Field Regiment
  One troop, Australian 13th Field Regiment
    (attached)
  Australian 1st Mountain Battery (attached)

---

* After the fall of Buna Mission General MacArthur and General Blamey returned to their headquarters in Australia. Then General Herring commanded the New Guinea Force and General Eichelberger commanded the Advanced New Guinea Force.

Battle Plans

By Rear-Admiral W. L. Ainsworth

In general, the fundamental principle that our force remain concentrated in order to bring its full strength against the enemy shall be observed in all cases where no extended search for the enemy is indicated. The fundamental principle of surprise shall be exploited to the fullest extent.

Assumptions

(*a*) That the enemy forces, both light forces and his heavy ships, may be equipped with radar.

(*b*) That enemy cruisers carry torpedoes, a menace which should not be accepted unnecessarily.

We may assume that the enemy as yet possesses no radar comparable to our SG Position Plotting Indicator which, used in conjunction with the DRT as prescribed for this Task Force, gives us an incomparable instrument for plotting and tracking the enemy at night.

To exploit our assumed superiority in Position Plotting and Fire Control Instruments to the fullest extent, the following general doctrine is established. *First :* That we should endeavour to obtain initial superiority of fire by opening fire first and at ranges beyond sight contact. *Second :* That the approach should be conducted to allow maximum opportunity to track the enemy while attaining a favourable position for opening gunfire and launching torpedoes.

Night Battle Plan " A "

To open fire beyond the maximum range of visibility but at medium ranges of 8,000–10,000 yards, remaining completely dark. Batteries to open in full radar control and rely on their ability to hit the enemy with our first or early salvoes, spotting by tracer control, and by radar on the splashes. Use rocking ladders in order to ensure certain hits on the enemy ships. Use flashless powder.

Night Battle Plan " B "

This plan involves the use of star shell and initial illumination of the enemy. Basic plan involves opening fire with flashless powder with 5-inch/38 batteries to place as many star shells as possible over the enemy. This Battle Plan is adapated to opening fire at ranges not exceeding 13,000 yards.

As the first star shell flare is observed all 6-inch batteries open fire in full radar control shifting to partial radar control (*i.e.* use the optical director if and when necessary). Under this Battle Plan we expect to obtain sufficient illumination for the first salvos to allow them to be spotted visually to the target.

Seizure of Empress Augusta Bay—Task Force Organisation

Rear-Admiral S. Wilkinson

1st Echelon ('Main Body, Northern Force')

Transport Group (Commodore L. F. Reifsnider)

Transport Division A
President Jackson
President Adams
President Hayes
George Clymer (Flag of Rear-Admiral Wilkinson)

Destroyers
Anthony[1]
Wadsworth[1]
Terry
Braine
Sigourney[1]
Renshaw

Transport Division B
American Legion
Fuller
Crescent City
Hunter Liggett

Destroyers
Fullam
Bennett
Guest
Hudson
Conway

Transport Group C
Transport Division C
Alhena
Alchiba
Libra
Titania

Minesweeper Group
Hopkins
Hovey
Dorsey
Southard
Conflict
Advent
Daring
Adroit
Y.M.S. 96
Y.M.S. 197
Y.M.S. 238
Y.M.S. 243

3rd Marine Division (reinforced) (less 21st Regimental Combat Team and other troops reserved for later echelons)

---

[1] These ships formed the main fire support group.

Summary of Operation Orders and Organisation of Allied Forces for Invasion of New Georgia

(i) OBJECT

The operation order stated that the forces involved would :—

(a) Seize and hold a position in the Wickham Anchorage area and establish there a staging point for small craft.

(b) Seize and hold Segi and commence construction in that vicinity of an airfield for fighter aircraft.

(c) Seize and hold Viru and establish at that locality a staging point for small craft.

(d) Seize and hold Rendova and build up a strong force thereon.

(e) Establish operating facilities in and operate M.T.B.s from the Rendova–Viru area.

(f) At the first favourable opportunity, and on orders from Comsopac, capture in succession Munda, Vila and other enemy positions in New Georgia and destroy enemy garrisons.

(ii) FORCES INVOLVED AND THEIR EMPLOYMENT

(a) *Naval forces*

TITLE	COMPOSITION	EMPLOYMENT

Task Group 36.1	*Honolulu*
	Helena
	St. Louis
	H.M.N.Z.S. *Leander**
	(Capt. C. A. L.
	Mansergh, D.S.C.)
	Desdiv 41
	  Nicholas
	  Strong
	  O'Bannon
	  Chevalier
		To leave Espiritu Santo 28th June for point B (13° 10′ S., 156° 20′ E.), arriving at 0700 on 30th. To cover landing operations.

Task Group 36.2	*Montpelier*
	Cleveland
	Columbia
	Denver
	Minelayers
	  Preble
	  Gamble
	  Breese
	Desdiv 43
	  Waller
	  Saufley
	  Philip
	  Renshaw
	  Pringle
		To leave Efate on 27th June for Tulagi and fuel on 29th. *Montpelier, Cleveland, Pringle* and the three destroyer minelayers to reach the Shortland area in early morning of 30th, lay a 3-row minefield near Munia Island, destroy surface craft, and bombard Ballale, Alu, Poporang, Faisi and eastern end of Shortland Island. Operation to be assisted by strikes by shore-based aircraft, which would also afford cover. (*Columbia, Denver* and Desdiv 43 operated in a covering position in the Coral Sea).

Task Group 36.3	*Saratoga*
	H.M.S. *Victorious*
	(Capt. L. D.
	Mackintosh)
	Massachussetts
	Indiana
	North Carolina
	San Juan
	San Diego
	Desron 6
	  Maury
	  Gridley
	  McCall
	  Craven
	  Fanning
	  Dunlap
	  Cummings
	  Case
	Desron 4 (part)
	  Selfridge
	  Stanly
	  Claxton
	  Dyson
	  Converse
		To leave Numea on 27th June for point D (16° S., 159° E.) arriving at 0600 local on 30th. To operate in southern half of area D (circle of 100 miles radius, centre point D) until otherwise ordered. To cover landing operations

Task Group 36.4	*Maryland* *Colorado* Assigned destroyers	To remain at Efate at two hours' notice.

Task Group 36.5	*Chenango*
	Suwannee
	Sangamon
	Conway
	Desdiv 15
	  Lang
	  Stack
	  Sterett
	  Wilson
	Desdiv 44
	  Conway
	  Eaton
		One carrier to cover convoys, south-east of San Cristobal. The others to remain Efate, at two hours' notice, and send aircraft to Guadalcanal, to arrive on 27th

* Added on 11th July to replace *Helena*.

TITLE	COMPOSITION	EMPLOYMENT
Task Force 72	Submarines	To start an offensive reconnaissance along the vicinity of lat. 1° north to the northward of the prevailing equatorial weather front, primarily for detection of enemy forces on passage south from Truk. When the enemy became aware of our operations, to withdraw to the southward and cover the Buka New Ireland channel and the north side of Bougainville Strait

(b) Air forces

TITLE	COMPOSITION		EMPLOYMENT
Task Force 33	Aircraft based on Solomons, E-Santo, Fiji, etc. Following were available in first two named :—		To carry out reconnaissance east of 155°E. and north-east of line Buka Passage–New Ireland, with a permissible overlap of 1° westward. Water areas southwest of Solomons east of 155° E. and northward of 9° S. to be covered. To support and assist forces engaged in the New Georgia operations. To neutralise enemy air forces. To destroy air forces. To destroy enemy surface forces. Operations to start about D minus 5 day.
	Solomons		
	Fighters	290	
	Torpedo planes	75	
	Dive bombers	94	
	Medium bombers	35	
	Heavy bombers	72	
	Patrol planes	18	
	Miscellaneous (scout observation, etc.)	42	
	Espiritu Santo		
	Fighters	40	
	Torpedo planes	36	
	Dive bombers	36	
	Medium bombers	10	
	Heavy bombers	43	
	Patrol planes	35	
	Miscellaneous	18	

(c) Amphibious Force (Task Force 31)

TITLE	COMPOSITION	EMPLOYMENT
Task Group 31.1 (Western Force)	Transport Div. 2 plus 2 others (6 transports) 5 high speed transports of Transport Div. 12, Transport Div. 22 of 3 H.S. transports (assigned to Eastern Force for initial landing). L.S.T. Flotilla 5 (12 L.S.T.s of which 2 were assigned to Eastern Force for initial landing).	To land the Western Landing Force of the New Georgia Occupation Force.
Task Group 31.2	Destroyers *Farenholt* *Buchanan* *McCalla* *Ralph Talbot* *Gwin* *Woodworth* *Radford* *Jenkins*	To screen transports.
Service Unit	*Vireo* *Rail* 2 barges	

245

Task Group 31.3	*Hopkins* *Trever* *Zane* L.C.T. Flotilla 5 (29 L.C.T.s) L.C.T. Flotilla 6 (12 L.C.T.s) A.P.C. Flotilla 5 (15 coastal transports) L.C.I. Flotilla 5 (26 L.C.I.s)	To land Eastern Landing Force of New Georgia Occupation Force.
Russell Is. M.T.B. Sqn.	12 M.T.B.s	
New Georgia Occupation Force Western Landing Force	43rd Infantry Div.(less 103rd Combat Team) 1st Infantry Bn. of 103rd C.T. 9th Defense Bn. 136th F.A. Bn. (155 mm. How.) Company O, 4th Raider Bn. Company 1st Bn. 1st Fiji Infantry. Service Units	To land on Rendova 30th June. Base in Tulagi. The howitzers to bombard Munda airfield. Troops from Rendova to attack Munda in due course
Eastern Landing Force	103rd C.T. (less 1st Infantry Bn., 2nd Bn. 70th C.A. (A.A.)) 4th Raider Bn. (less Company O) Service Units	To land at Viru Harbour, Segi Point and Wickam Anchorage areas, on 30th June. Base in Russell Islands and Tulagi.
Reserve Force	2 Bn. 1st Mne. Raider Regt.	
Naval Base Force	24th Construction Bn.	To land on Rendova on 30th June
Rendova Naval Base Group	Naval Base Units	
Viru Naval Base Group	Half Company 20th C Bn. Naval Base Units	To land at Viru on 30th June
Wickham Naval Base Group	Half 20th C Bn. (less Half Company) Naval Base Units	To land at Wickham on 30th June
Segi Naval Base Group	Acorn 7 (Mobile Airfield Unit) Naval Base Units	To land at Segi on 30th June
New Georgia M.T.B. Squadron	12 M.T.B.s	
New Georgia Air Force	Aircraft assigned	
Assault Flotillas	Boats from pool 18 L.C.I.s	

(*d*) *General Reserve*

The 37th Division, less two combat teams, in Guadalcanal, was to be in general reserve at five day's notice and was given the title of Task Group 36.6.

(*e*) *Reserve M.T.B.s*

Twelve M.T.B.s (T.G. 31.4) were in reserve at Tulagi.

(iii) MISCELLANEOUS NOTES

L.S.T.s and L.C.T.s were to move forward with reinforcements on D plus one, two and three days.

Preparatory ships' gunfire was not planned, but ships were to be prepared to provide 'called' and counter-battery fire.

Stores were to be landed as follows :—

    (*a*) Initially.—30 days' supplies, 3 units of fire, except A.A. units and the groups at Wickham, Viru and Segi, which would have 5 units.

    (*b*) As soon as possible.—5 units of fire, 60 days' supplies.

246

Organisation of Task Forces for Hollandia Operation

TASK FORCE 58
(Rear-Admiral M. A. Mitscher)

TASK GROUP 58.1	TASK GROUP 58.2	TASK GROUP 58.3	TASK GROUP 50.17
CARRIERS	CARRIERS	CARRIERS	
Hornet[1]	*Bunker Hill*[1]	*Enterprise*[1]	12 Oilers
Belleau Wood[2]	*Yorktown*[1]	*Lexington*[1]	10 Destroyers
Cowpens[2]	*Monterey*[2]	*Princeton*[2]	Destroyer escorts as
Bataan[2]	*Cabot*[2]	*Langley*[2]	arranged
CRUDIV 13	BATDIV 7	BATDIV 8	
Santa Fé	*Iowa*	*Massachusetts*	
Mobile	*New Jersey*	*North Carolina*	
Biloxi			
Oakland (A.A.)	CRUISERS	BATDIV 9	
San Juan (A.A.)	*Boston*	*South Dakota*	
	Baltimore	*Alabama*	
	Wichita		
	San Francisco	CRUISERS	
	Minneapolis	*Louisville*	
	New Orleans	*Canberra*	
18 destroyers	17 destroyers	15 destroyers	

The force was also organised for alternate contingencies as follows :—

OPERATION PLAN 1	*or*	OPERATION PLAN 2
For battle with enemy main forces		For destruction of Naval forces and shipping inshore or for bombarding as directed

TASK GROUP 58.6		TASK GROUP 58.6
MAIN BODY	CARRIER T.G. 58.1	MAIN BODY
BATTLE LINE	TO SUPPLY AIR SUPPORT	Batdivs 7, 8, 9
Batdivs 7, 8, 9	*Belleau Wood*	14 destroyers
7 destroyers	*Cowpens*	
	Bataan	*Detached Wing* to pursue and destroy escaping enemy units when directed
	Oakland	
	San Juan	
RIGHT FLANK		Batdiv 7
3 heavy cruisers	10 destroyers	9 destroyers
3 destroyers		
CENTRE		
4 heavy cruisers		
3 light cruisers		
9 destroyers		
LEFT FLANK		
2 heavy cruisers		
3 destroyers		

7th AMPHIBIOUS FORCE
TASK FORCE 77
(Rear-Admiral D. E. Barbey)

TASK GROUP 77.1	TASK GROUP 77.2	TASK GROUP 77.3
Western Attack Group	Central Attack Group	Eastern Attack Group
To transport and land elements on RED beaches in TANAHMERA BAY and support landings by gunfire	at WHITE beaches in HUMBOLDT BAY	at BLUE Beaches at AITAPE

---

[1] Fleet carrier.   [2] Light carrier.

Task Group 77.1	Task Group 77.2	Task Group 77.3
Swanson (destroyer)	*Reid* (destroyer)	*La Valette* (destroyer)
Flag of Rear-Admiral Barbey, Commander of Attack Force	Flag of Rear-Admiral Fechteler	

Task Group 77.1	Task Group 77.2	Task Group 77.3
3 attack transports ⎫ 1 landing ship, dock ⎬ Transports 1 cargo ship ⎭	1 attack transport ⎫ 1 landing ship, dock ⎬ Transports 5 high speed transports ⎭	9 high speed transports ⎫ 1 landing ship, dock ⎬ Transports 1 cargo ship ⎭
15 L.C.I.	16 L.C.I.	7 L.S.T.
7 L.S.T.	7 L.S.T.	5 destroyers
6 destroyers	7 destroyers	2 fast minesweepers
2 submarine chasers	2 fast minesweepers	1 special service vessel
1 ocean-going tug	2 submarine chasers	2 motor minesweepers
2 motor minesweepers	2 L.C.I. (special service vessels)	1 ocean-going tug
	2 motor minesweepers	4 submarine chasers
	1 ocean-going tug	

1st Reinforcement Group
Task Group 77.4

Western Unit Task Unit 77.4.1	Central Unit Task Unit 77.4.2	Eastern Unit Task Unit 77.4.3
1 cargo ship (attack)	5 L.S.T.	6 L.S.T.
7 L.S.T.	2 destroyers	1 cargo ship
2 destroyers	1 frigate	2 destroyers
1 frigate		2 frigates

2nd Reinforcement Group
Task Group 77.5

Western Unit Task Unit 77.5.1	Central Unit	Floating Reserve Task Group 77.6
2 attack transports	5 L.S.T.	2 attack transports
7 L.S.T.	2 destroyers	1 cargo ship, attack
2 destroyers		(To load reserves and await orders at Cape Cretin by D-day)
2 frigates		

TASK FORCE 78
(ESCORT CARRIER FORCE)
(Rear-Admiral R. E. Davison)

Task Group 78.1 (Cardiv 22) (Rear-Admiral V. H. Ragsdale)
> *Sangamon*
> *Suwannee*
> *Chenango*
> *Santee*
> 8 destroyers

Task Group 78.2 (Cardiv 24) (Rear-Admiral R. E. Davison)
> *Natoma Bay*
> *Coral Sea*
> *Corregidor*
> *Manila Bay*
> 9 destroyers

Covering Force " A ", Task Force 74 (Rear-Admiral V. A. C. Crutchley)
> H.M.A.S. *Australia* (Flag) (Captain H. B. Farncomb)
> H.M.A.S. *Shropshire* (Captain J. A. Collins)
> H.M.A.S. *Warramunga* (Captain E. F. V. Dechaineux)
> H.M.A.S. *Arunta* (Commander A. E. Buchanan)
> U.S. destroyers *Ammen, Mullany*

Covering Force " B ", Task Force 75 (Rear-Admiral R. S. Berkey)
> Light cruisers
> > *Phoenix*
> > *Nashville*
> > *Boise*
> 6 destroyers

Assault on Biak (Operation 'Horlicks'): Organisation of Task Force 77

H.Q. SHIP (Rear-Admiral W. M. Fechteler)
    1 destroyer leader

COVERING FORCE " A " (Rear-Admiral V. A. C. Crutchley)
    H.M.A.S. *Australia* (Flag) (Captain E. F. V. Dechaineux)
    H.M.A.S. *Shropshire* (Captain J. A. Collins)
    H.M.A.S. *Warramunga* (Commander N. A. Mackinnon)
    H.M.A.S. *Arunta* (Commander A. E. Buchanan)
    2 U.S. destroyers

COVERING FORCE " B " (Rear-Admiral R. S. Berkey)
    Phoenix
    Boise
    Nashville
    6 U.S. destroyers

FIRE SUPPORT AND PROTECTIVE GROUPS

11 destroyers	
Transport Unit ⎫	5 high speed (destroyer) transports
L.C.I. Unit ⎬[1]	24 L.C.I.s
L.S.T. Unit ⎭	8 L.S.T.s, 8 L.C.T.s (Mark V)
Special	4 submarine chasers (3 control, 1 rocket)
Service Unit[2]	3 L.C.I.s (rocket)
	1 ocean-going tug
	1 L.C.I. (two naval combat demolition units)
Beach Party[2]	3 officers, 17 ratings
1st Reinforcement Group[2]	3 L.S.T.s, 3 destroyers, 2 destroyer escorts
2nd Reinforcement Group[2]	7 L.S.T.s, 3 destroyers, 2 frigates

---

[1] Carrying a total of 12,000 toops, 53 tracked landing vehicles, 25 amphibious trucks, 280 engineer and other vehicles and guns, etc., 2,400 tons (approx.) D.W. of bulk stores and equipment.

[2] Not included in the Z-day Convoy.

APPENDIX Q

Japanese Naval Aircraft Losses, December 1941–August 1945

(*Japanese Air Power*, U.S. Strategic Bombing Survey (Pacific))

Years are fiscal (April–March)

Aircraft type		1941					1942												
		[1] Dec	[2] Jan	[3] Feb	[4] Mar	Total	[5] Apr	[6] May	[7] June	[8] July	[9] Aug	[10] Sept	[11] Oct	[12] Nov	[13] Dec	[14] Jan	[15] Feb	Mar	Total
Fighter	Combat	44	35	31	26	136	36	57	137	103	104	36	120	84	48	47	25	25	822
	Operations	32	34	38	60	164	35	47	70	95	61	54	57	66	70	64	73	76	768
Torpedo and dive bombers	Combat	19	11	15	8	53	19	90	189	49	23	13	103	58	10	7	38	32	631
	Operations	24	23	26	20	93	10	8	12	11	12	8	12	12	10	9	15	12	131
Medium bombers	Combat	25	11	40	5	81	11	21	9	42	46	24	25	30	18	23	21	21	291
	Operations	18	21	25	37	101	14	16	18	10	16	14	13	17	15	13	16	12	174
	Combat															1			1
Reconnaissance	Operations														0				0
	Combat	0	0	0	0	0	3	0	2	1	2	1	1	3	1	1	3	2	20
Transports	Operations	4	5	5	6	20	2	2	4	3	3	4	4	3	4	3	3	2	37
	Combat	2	15	13	13	43	6	38	11	34	32	39	39	26	7	10	13	20	275
Float planes	Operations	11	9	15	15	50	10	13	14	17	17	14	17	13	12	13	16	14	170
	Combat	1	0	0	1	2	1	1	2	0	11	0	0	1	0	0	2	2	20
Flying boats	Operations	5	5	6	4	20	2	1	0	4	2	2	2	2	0	3	4	3	25
	Combat	0	0	0	0	0	0	0	0	0	0	0	0	0	0	0	2	2	4
Trainers	Operations	18	21	27	26	92	24	20	21	22	27	27	30	30	30	36	34	39	340
Total		91	72	99	53	315	76	207	350	229	218	113	288	202	84	89	104	104	2,064
		112	118	142	168	540	97	107	139	162	138	123	135	143	141	141	161	158	1,645

1941

[1] Malaya, Philippines, Hawaii.
[2] Malaya, Philippines.
[3] Java, Singapore.
[4] Ceylon, Surabaya, Batavia
[5] Port Darwin, Bataan.

1942

[6] Darwin, Coral Sea.
[7] Midway, Aleutians.
[8] Attack on Port Headland.
[9] Guadalcanal, First and Second Phase Solomons.
[10] Guadalcanal operataions
[11] South Pacific Naval Battle.
[12] Third Phase Solomons.
[13] First Phase Rennel.
[14] Off S. Isabel, Second Phase Rennell.
[15] Attack on Oro Bay.

Aircraft type		1943												
		[16] Apr	May	[17] June	[18] July	[19] Aug	[20] Sept	[21] Oct	[22] Nov	[23] Dec	[24] Jan	Feb	Mar	Total
Fighter	Combat	65	40	73	93	108	134	112	149	124	80	102	90	1,170
	Operations	95	101	114	132	113	125	184	155	130	183	154	187	1,673
Torpedo and dive bombers	Combat	13	23	26	30	30	60	40	70	25	10	22	18	367
	Operations	15	25	41	48	71	82	26	81	77	86	121	81	824
Medium bombers	Combat	8	26	28	20	15	30	24	52	20	23	40	20	306
	Operations	27	36	57	51	51	41	78	58	64	81	53	66	663
	Combat				1	0	0	1	0	0	0	0	0	2
Reconnaissance	Operations				3	2	0	3	2	0	0	0	0	10
	Combat	4	1	0	2	3	2	2	4	3	2	2	0	25
Transports	Operations	3	2	3	4	1	4	3	4	3	4	5	3	39
	Combat	15	25	9	15	17	16	12	15	5	8	15	12	164
Float planes	Operations	19	21	17	32	24	22	36	32	32	27	32	34	328
	Combat	2	0	1	2	2	3	1	3	1	0	4	0	19
Flying boats	Operations	3	0	5	5	4	5	4	3	5	5	5	5	49
	Combat	1	3	1	0	0	0	0	0	0	0	0	0	5
Trainers	Operations	30	45	50	40	33	60	55	61	67	72	80	97	690
Total		108	118	138	163	175	245	192	293	178	123	185	140	2,058
		192	230	287	315	229	339	459	396	378	458	450	473	4,276

1943

[16] New Guinea, Oro Bay, Florida Islands.
[17] Air Battle off Lunga
[18] Kula Gulf, Kolombangara, Rendova.
[19] Defence of Munda, Vella Levella battles.
[20] Attacks on Rabaul..
[21] Attacks on Rabaul.
[22] First to fourth attack on Gilberts, Rabaul and Bougainville air battles.
[23] Attack on Marshalls, sixth air battle at Bougainville.
[24] Landings on Kwajalein; attacks on Marshalls.

APPENDIX Q — *continued*

Aircraft type		Apr.	May	June[25]	July[26]	Aug.	Sept.[27]	Oct.[28]	Nov.[29]	Dec.[30]	Jan.	Feb.	Mar.[31]	Total	Apr.[32]	May	June[33]	July	Aug.	Total	Grand Total
		1944													**1945**						
Fighter	Combat	50	60	370	46	34	70	210	295	110	95	85	148	1,573	335	175	140	180	160	990	4,691
	Operations	123	206	165	86	190	220	275	297	340	230	200	245	2,577	260	220	230	320	400	1,430	6,612
Torpedo and dive bombers	Combat	20	60	220	20	40	30	120	100	50	20	33	80	793	105	35	81	40	50	311	2,155
	Operations	72	190	105	131	135	104	80	160	115	95	100	70	1,357	95	100	110	120	200	625	3,030
Medium bombers	Combat	25	25	98	25	14	44	91	80	44	26	24	49	545	40	30	45	60	50	225	1,448
	Operations	85	70	44	75	70	80	60	72	80	90	77	88	891	75	50	90	90	110	415	2,244
Reconnaissance	Combat	2	5	12	4	4	6	19	16	8	7	5	9	97	18	13	8	11	15	65	165
	Operations	3	6	8	9	6	8	9	8	6	8	6	7	84	11	16	14	15	29	85	179
Transports	Combat	4	8	5	4	6	3	14	10	16	7	8	9	94	12	11	14	7	8	52	191
	Operations	8	8	9	10	7	8	7	4	6	5	5	7	84	7	6	7	10	10	40	220
Float planes	Combat	15	32	70	15	20	21	35	76	25	28	15	22	374	20	24	35	56	64	199	1,055
	Operations	16	67	28	32	31	47	59	47	27	32	58	52	496	76	76	80	90	89	411	1,455
Flying boats	Combat	2	7	14	1	2	4	8	9	3	1	2	4	57	4	3	4	7	8	26	124
	Operations	3	5	5	2	3	8	5	5	3	3	2	4	48	9	8	10	11	10	48	190
Trainers	Combat	0	0	0	0	0	0	25	15	10	7	15	50	122	80	60	70	120	80	410	541
	Operations	70	80	85	82	100	100	110	105	87	100	95	124	1,138	110	100	110	140	100	560	2,820
Total		118	197	789	115	120	178	522	601	266	191	187	371	3,655	614	351	397	481	435	2,278	10,370
		380	632	449	427	542	575	605	698	664	563	543	597	6,675	643	576	651	796	948	3,614	16,750

1944

[25] Saipan operations.
[26] Attack by China-based planes; Tinian landing.
[27] Landings on Peleliu and Morotai..
[28] Air battles of Taiwan.
[29] Defence of Leyte, battle of Philippines.
[30] Defence of Philippines.
[31] Defence of Okinawa and Iwo Jima. Attack on homeland by Task Force.

1945

[32] Defence of Okinawa.
[33] Losses to B-29s and shipboard planes.

Source: Furnished by
J.N.A.F.

APPENDIX R

Japanese Airfields on the Southern Perimeter

September 1943

(*see also* Plan 23)

(Instruction 280 of Grand Imperial Headquarters, Navy Section)

JAPANESE STUDIES IN WORLD WAR II—No. 29
(New Guinea Area)

Note.—* indicates an exact Romaji transliteration of the original Kana

Bases				Present Situation	Usage
HOLLANDIA ..	..	1st ..	..	Nearly completed	General
HOLLANDIA ..	..	2nd ..	..	Newly completed	Army
WAKDE	..	.. ..	..	Nearly completed	Navy
SARMI ..	..	1st, 2nd	..	Newly completed	Army
NUBOAI* (Nubia)	..	.. ..	..	Newly completed	Army
SERUIBIAK* ..	..	1st, 2nd	..	Newly completed	Army
NABIRE	..	1st ..	..	Nearly completed	Navy
NABIRE	..	2nd ..	..	Newly completed	Army
MUMI* (Moemi)	..	1st, 2nd	..	Newly completed	Army
LAKE AMAROE	..	1st–5th	..	Newly completed	Navy
SORONG	..	1st, 2nd	..	Newly completed	Navy
SORONG	..	3rd–5th	..	Newly completed	Army
MANOKWARI	..	1st–5th	..	Newly completed	Army
FAKFAK	..	1st, 2nd	..	Newly completed	Army
BABO ..	..	.. ..	..	Nearly completed	Navy
KAI ..	..	.. ..	..	Under construction	Army
RINKATTO* (? Lingat on Tanimbar Island)				Under construction	Army
LIANG ..	..	.. ..	..	Under construction	Army
HARUKU*	..	.. ..	..	Under construction	Army
AMAHAI	..	.. ..	..	Under construction	Army
BURA* ..	..	.. ..	..	Newly completed	Army
WAHAI	..	.. ..	..	Newly completed	Army
KAOE ..	..	1st, 2nd	..	Newly completed	Navy
GARERA (? Galela) ..	..	..	..	Newly completed	Army
WASHIRE* (? Washile Bay)..	..	..	Newly completed	Army
SHAIRORO* (? Djailolo)	..	..	..	Newly completed	Army
RABUHA* (? Labuha)	..	..	..	Newly completed	Army
KOEPANG	..	.. ..	..	Nearly completed	Navy
KOEPANG	..	2nd, 3rd	..	Nearly completed	Navy
ATAPOEPOE ..	..	.. ..	..	Nearly completed	Navy
DILI ..	..	.. ..	..	Nearly completed	Navy
ABISU* ..	..	.. ..	..	Nearly completed	Army
RAUTEN (Lauten)—East, West	..	..	Nearly completed	Army
MATOWA*	..	1st ..	..	Nearly completed	Navy
MATOWA*	..	2nd ..	..	Newly completed	Navy
NAMIKA*	..	1st ..	..	Nearly completed	Navy
NAMIKA*	..	2nd ..	..	Newly completed	Navy
WAIBEM*	..	1st–3rd	..	Newly completed	Army
? NUNHORU*	..	.. ..	..	Newly completed	Army

Bases						Present Situation	Usage
SAGA* ..	..	..	..	..	..	Under construction	Army
SAGA* ..	..	..	1st–3rd		..	Newly completed	Navy

(HAIMAHERA, CERAM and other isolated islands)

ARU ..	..	..	1st, 2nd		..	Newly completed	Navy
KEI ..	..	..	1st, 2nd		..	Newly completed	Navy
TANIMBAR ..	..	1st, 2nd			..	Newly completed	Navy
AMBOINA	..	..	1st	..	..	Nearly completed	Navy
AMBOINA	..	..	2nd	..	..	Newly completed	Navy
BURA* ..	..	..	..	..	..	Nearly completed	Navy
NAMLEA	..	..	1st	..	..	Nearly completed	General
NAMLEA	..	..	2nd	..	..	Newly completed	Army
ARU(SHIYA)*	..	..	..		..	Under construction	Army
ARU(SHIYA)*	..	1st, 2nd			..	Newly completed	Army
HARIRURI ..	..	..	..		..	Newly completed	Army
KOEPANG—West	..	..	..		..	Newly completed	Army
WAINGAPPU*	..	..	..		..	Nearly completed	Navy
SUMBA	..	..	1st, 2nd, 3rd, 4th			Newly completed	Navy
BISU ..	..	..	1st	..	..	Nearly completed	Navy
BISU ..	..	..	2nd	..	..	Newly completed	Navy
NAMBASSAR*	..	1st	..		..	Nearly completed	Navy
NAMBASSAR*	..	2nd	..		..	Newly completed	Navy
RAMBAN* (? Rambang)	..	..		..	Nearly completed	Navy
MALUMERA* (? Maumere) ..	..		..	Nearly completed	Army
BABI* (Baoebaoe)	..	..	..		..	Nearly completed	Army
KANDARI	..	..	..	..	..	Nearly completed	Navy
KANDARI	..	..	2nd, 3rd, 4th, 5th			Newly completed	Navy
ANPESSIA* (? Ambesia)	1st, 2nd, 3rd		..	Newly completed	Navy
POMARA* (? Pomelaa)	1st, 2nd		..	Newly completed	Navy
MAKASAR	..	..	..	..	..	Nearly completed	Navy
RAIKAN*	..	..	..	..	..	Newly completed	Navy
MASAMBA	..	..	..	..	..	Newly completed	Navy
MACASSAR	..	..	1st, 2nd, 3rd		..	Newly completed	Army
PINLAN*	..	..	1st, 2nd		..	Newly completed	Army
MUNA*	..	..	1st, 2nd, 3rd		..	Newly completed	Army
GORONTARO	..	1st, 2nd		..	Newly completed	Army
MENADO	..	..	1st, 2nd		..	Newly completed	Army
BALU* ..	..	..	1st, 2nd		..	Newly completed	Army

APPENDIX S

'Checkmate Procedure'

1. A system known as 'Checkmate' is in force in East Indies and South Atlantic Stations for the purpose of supplementing existing merchant shipping information signals and recognition procedure to enable warships to obtain quick corroboration from shore plots of bona fides of suspicious merchant ships.

2. System is intended for occasions when (a) recognition procedure proves inconclusive; (b) boarding is impracticable; (c) there is no strong objection to use of W/T. (It is considered that there are few occasions when risk of breaking W/T silence overrides the paramount importance of ensuring that a raider or blockade runner does not escape.)

3. An organisation has now been set up in Admiralty to deal with 'Checkmate' signals from any part of the world, and Commander-in-Chief E.F. and Commander-in-Chief S.A. will be requested to bring their existing systems into line with the following.

4. On encountering a merchant ship about whose identity any doubt exists warships should make a 'Checkmate' message as follows :—

    (a) Message is to be addressed to Admiralty and Commander-in-Chief or F.O.I.C. of area concerned using plain language procedure.

    (b) Message to bear indication of priority 'Emergency' and to be in the form : (1) the word 'Check'; (2) signal letters, if these have been ascertained; (3) alleged name of merchant ship; and (4) the position (indicated by means of lettered co-ordinates).

    All in plain language.

    Example : GZZ vXPT – O. – T – Z – HJ OI 'Check'
    GKND TUSCAN STAR KLBT 2427 T.O.O. 172317Z.

5. Warships are to use their sea call sign from S.P. 02396 series.

6. Admiralty and/or Commander-in-Chief or F.O.I.C. concerned receiving message will reply with word 'Mate' followed by 'Yes', 'No' or 'Doubtful', all in plain language, using same sea call sign as in 5 above. The term 'Yes' will indicate that ship could be in reported position, 'No' that it is impossible for ship to be in reported position and 'Doubtful' that doubt exists as to whether ship could be in reported position and further investigation is desirable.

7. It is the intention that Admiralty should normally reply to all such messages but Commander-in-Chief or F.O.I.C. addressed should reply to 'Checkmate' messages provided they are in possession of reliable information to enable them to do so before Admiralty can. Such replies should be repeated to Admiralty. Similarly, Admiralty will repeat replies to Commander-in-Chief or F.O.I.C. addressed.

Admiralty 241910 B May 1943

U.S. Ships Engaged in the Pacific

August 1942—July 1944

Showing Types

Aaron Ward	Destroyer	*Foote*	Destroyer
Abner Read	Destroyer	*Formalhaut*	Naval cargo ship
Albacore	Submarine	*Gamble*	Minelayer
Alchiba	Cargo auxiliary	*Gato*	Submarine
Alhena	Naval cargo ship	*George*	Destroyer escort
Amberjack	Submarine	*Greyback*	Submarine
Ammen	Destroyer	*Gregory*	Destroyer transport
Anderson	Destroyer	*Growler*	Submarine
Argonaut	Submarine	*Guardfish*	Submarine
Astoria	Cruiser (6-inch)	*Guest*	Destroyer
Atlanta	A.A. cruiser	*Gurnard*	Submarine
Bache	Destroyer	*Gwin*	Destroyer
Bagley	Destroyer	*Hamilton*	Minesweeper
Barton	Destroyer	*Hazlewood*	Destroyer
Beale	Destroyer	*Helena*	Cruiser (6-inch)
Belleau Wood	Light carrier	*Helm*	Destroyer
Benham	Destroyer	*Henley*	Destroyer
Birmingham	Cruiser (6-inch)	*Henry T. Allen*	Attack transport
Blue	Destroyer	*Herm*	Destroyer
Boise	Cruiser (6-inch)	*Hilo*	M.T.B. tender
Breeze	Minelayer	*Hoggatt Bay*	Escort carrier
Brownson	Destroyer	*Holland*	Submarine depot ship
Buchanan	Destroyer	*Honolulu*	Cruiser (6-inch)
Bunker Hill	Aircraft carrier	*Hornet*	Aircraft carrier
Bush	Destroyer	*Hudson*	Destroyer
California	Battleship	*Hughes*	Destroyer
Cero	Submarine	*Humphreys*	Destroyer transport
Charles F. Ausburne	Destroyer	*Hutchins*	Destroyer
Chenango	Escort carrier	*Idaho*	Battleship
Chester	Cruiser (8-inch)	*Indiana*	Battleship
Chevalier	Destroyer	*Jarvis*	Destroyer
Chicago	Cruiser (8-inch)	*Jenkins*	Destroyer
Clark	Destroyer	*Juneau*	Cruiser (6-inch)
Claxton	Destroyer	*Kilty*	Destroyer transport
Cleveland	Cruiser (6-inch)	*La Vallette*	Destroyer
Colhoun	Destroyer transport	*Laffey*	Destroyer
Colorado	Battleship	*Lamson*	Destroyer
Columbia	Cruiser (6-inch)	*Lang*	Destroyer
Converse	Destroyer	*Lardner*	Destroyer
Conway	Destroyer	*Lexington*	Aircraft carrier
Cony	Destroyer	*Little*	Destroyer transport
Conyngham	Destroyer	*Long*	Minesweeper
Craven	Destroyer	*Long Island*	Escort carrier
Curtiss	Seaplane tender	*Louisville*	Cruiser (8-inch)
Cushing	Destroyer	*McCalla*	Destroyer
De Haven	Destroyer	*McCawley*	Transport
Denver	Cruiser (6-inch)	*McCord*	Destroyer
Drayton	Destroyer	*MacDonough*	Destroyer
Duncan	Destroyer	*McFarland*	Seaplane tender
Dunlap	Destroyer	*McKean*	Destroyer transport
Dyson	Destroyer	*Macomb*	Destroyer
Eaton	Destroyer	*Maryland*	Battleship
England	Destroyer escort	*Maury*	Destroyer
Enterprise	Aircraft carrier	*Meade*	Destroyer
Essex	Aircraft carrier	*Meredith*	Destroyer
Farenholt	Destroyer	*Minneapolis*	Cruiser (8-inch)
Fletcher	Destroyer	*Mississippi*	Battleship
Flusser	Destroyer	*Monssen*	Destroyer

Monterey	Aircraft carrier	*St. Louis*	Cruiser (6-inch)
Montgomery	Minelayer	*Salt Lake City*	Cruiser (8-inch)
Montpelier	Cruiser (6-inch)	*Sands*	Destroyer transport
Morris	Destroyer	*Santee*	Escort carrier
Mugford	Destroyer	*Saratoga*	Aircraft carrier
Mullany	Destroyer	*Saufley*	Destroyer
Mustin	Destroyer	*Seadragon*	Submarine
Nashville	Cruiser (6-inch)	*Selfridge*	Destroyer
Nautilus	Submarine	*Seminole*	Tug
New Mexico	Battleship	*Shaw*	Destroyer
New Orleans	Cruiser (8-inch)	*Smith*	Destroyer
Nicholas	Destroyer	*South Dakota*	Battleship
North Carolina	Battleship	*Southard*	Minesweeper
Northampton	Cruiser (8-inch)	*Spangler*	Destroyer escort
O'Bannon	Destroyer	*Spence*	Destroyer
O'Brien	Destroyer	*Stack*	Destroyer
Patterson	Destroyer	*Stanly*	Destroyer
Pensacola	Cruiser (8-inch)	*Sterett*	Destroyer
Perkins	Destroyer	*Stockton*	Destroyer
Philip	Destroyer	*Strong*	Destroyer
Phoenix	Cruiser (6-inch)	*Suwannee*	Escort carrier
Porter	Destroyer	*Talbot*	Destroyer transport
Portland	Cruiser (8-inch)	*Tangier*	Submarine tender
Preble	Minelayer	*Tautog*	Submarine
Preston	Destroyer	*Taylor*	Destroyer
Princeton	Light carrier	*Tennessee*	Battleship
Pringle	Destroyer	*Thatcher*	Destroyer
Quincy	Cruiser (8-inch)	*Tracy*	Minelayer
Raby	Destroyer escort	*Trathen*	Destroyer
Radford	Destroyer	*Trever*	Minelayer
Ralph Talbot	Destroyer	*Vincennes*	Cruiser (6-inch)
Ray	Submarine	*Vireo*	Destroyer
Reid	Destroyer	*Walke*	Destroyer
Renshaw	Destroyer	*Waller*	Destroyer
Rigel	Destroyer tender	*Washington*	Battleship
Russell	Destroyer	*Wasp*	Aircraft carrier
S–38	Submarine	*Wichita*	Cruiser (8-inch)
S–44	Submarine	*Wilson*	Destroyer
San Diego	Cruiser (6-inch)	*Woodworth*	Destroyer
San Francisco	Cruiser (8-inch)	*Zane*	Minesweeper
San Juan	Cruiser (6-inch)	*Zeilin*	Attack cargo ship

Bibliography

The most important sources of which general use has been made are as follows :—

OFFICIAL

Naval War Diary. Historical Section, Naval Staff.

War Vessels and Naval Aircraft, British Commonwealth of Nations, C.B. 01815B *Series.*

Particulars of U.S. War and Auxiliary Vessels, C.B. 01815 (U) *Series.*

Particulars of Foreign War Vessels, C.B. 01815 *Series.*

Pink List. Operations Division, Naval Staff, Admiralty.

Intelligence Reports and Summaries by Section 4, Naval Intelligence Division, Naval Staff. [These are now filed in the Historical Section.]

Station War Diaries
    East Indies, January to 18th June 1942. Record Office Case 7397.
    Eastern Fleet, October, November, December 1942. T.S.D. 4414/42, 4421/42, 4424/42. 1943 Record Office Case 7590.
    Ceylon 1943, Record Office Case 7693.
    Royal Indian Navy 1942, Record Office Case 7396.

Reports of Observers with U.S. Pacific Fleet—
    Bulletin No. 4–42, dated 5th March 1942. N.I.D. 02139/42.
    Reports, April 1942. N.I.D. 03050/42.
    Bulletin Nos. 16, 17, dated 16th January and 1st February 1943. N.I.D. 001385/43.
    Bulletin No. 24, dated 9th June 1943. N.I.D. 004884/43.
    Bulletin No. 25, for period 1st–15th June 1943. N.I.D. 004912/43.
    Bulletin No. 26, dated 1st July 1943. N.I.D. 0050226/43.
    Bulletin No. 29, dated 16th August 1943. N.I.D. 0050220/43.

Report on the Composition and Activities of the U.S. Submarine Force, U.S. Pacific Fleet, by Commander A. C. C. Miers. U.S./P/SM 2 (Admiral (S) No. SM. 04094/844).

Pacific Islands. Vol. IV, Western Pacific. Naval Intelligence Division, B.R. 519C.

German, Italian and Japanese U-boat Casualties during the War. Particulars of Destruction, June 1946.

Reports on Australian activities from March 1942 to May 1943, when the series was apparently discontinued, are contained in the following papers :—
    M.04702/42, M.05106/42, M.07597/42, M.08987/42, M.051664/42, M.014360/42, M.052255/42, M.0259/43, M.01377/43, M.02475/43, M.03843/43, M.05081/43, M.06432/43.

Official History of New Zealand in the Second World War, 1939–45. The Pacific. O. A. Gillespie. War History Branch Department of Internal Affairs, Wellington, New Zealand.

A Report to the Secretary of the United States Navy by Admiral Ernest J. King, U.S.N., Commander-in-Chief U.S. Fleet and Chief of Naval Operations. Covering Combat Operations up to 1st March 1944. U.S. Government Publication.

Biennial Report of the Chief of Staff of the United States Army to the Secretary of War. 1st July 1941 to 30th June 1943. U.S. Government Publication.

The Campaigns of the Pacific War. United States Strategic Bombing Survey. U.S. Government Printing Office, Washington, 1946.

[U.S.] Information Bulletin No. 22, *Anti-Aircraft Action Summary, July to December 1942.* H.Q. of Commander-in-Chief U.S. Fleet.

Japanese Naval and Merchant Shipping Losses during World War II by all Causes. Prepared by the Joint Army–Navy Assessment Committee, Navexos P–468. U.S. Government Publication, 1947.

Employment of Forces under the South-west Pacific Command. U.S. Strategic Bombing Survey. February 1947.

Operations in the Pacific Ocean Areas. Monthly Reports by the Commander-in-Chief, U.S. Pacific Fleet and Pacific Ocean Areas. A16–3/FF12.

Japanese Air Power. United States Strategic Bombing Survey. July 1946.

The Offensive Mine-Laying Campaign Against Japan. U.S. Strategic Bombing Survey. 1st November 1946.

Reprint of CinCpac Reports of Actions and Campaigns, February 1942 to February 1943. U.S. Pacific Fleet and Pacific Ocean Areas, H.Q. of Commander-in-Chief A16–3/F12, Serial 034372.

   U.S. Pacific Fleet and Pacific Ocean Areas, *February 1943 to August 1943,* A16–3/F12, Serial 034373.

Amphibious Operations. August–December 1943. Cominch P–001 and January–March 1944 (excluding Marshall Islands Operations), Cominch P.004. M.05734/44.

JAPANESE

Interrogation of Japanese Officials. Vols. I, II. U.S. Strategic Bombing Survey. U.S. Government Publication, n.d.

Ship and Related Targets, *Japanese Submarine Operations.* U.S. Naval Technical Mission to Japan, S–17.

The Imperial Japanese Navy in World War II. Japanese Monograph No. 116. Prepared by Military History Section, Special Staff, General Headquarters, Far East Command, February 1952.

Naval Operations in the Southern Area, 1942–1945. Japanese Studies World War II, JS–29. Historical Section, Far East Command of U.S. Navy.

Historical Reports, Naval Operations. G.H.Q., S.C.A.P. Report No. BIOS/JAP/PR/711.

War Diary of the Sixth Fleet for 1942. Department of the Navy: Office of Nava Records and History, Washington D.C. W.D.C., 160628.

Summary of Major Japanese Submarine Operations furnished by the Minister of the Imperial Japanese Navy. Liaison Committee (Tokyo) for the Japanese Army and Navy. N.D. No. 434.

UNOFFICAL

The Royal Australian Navy. F. M. McGuire. Oxford University Press, Melbourne, n.d.

New Zealand at War. K. R. Hancock, A. H. and A. W. Reed, Wellington, New Zealand, n.d.

The Army Air Forces in World War II, Vols. I, IV. Ed. W. J. Craven, J. L. Cate· Office of Air Force History, U.S. Air Force. University of Chicago Press, 1948· (Based on official records.)

History of United States Naval Operations in World War II. S. E. Morison. Little, Brown & Co., Boston, 1949.
   Vol. IV. *Coral Sea, Midway, and Submarine Actions.*
   Vol. V. *The Struggle for Guadalcanal, August 1942 to February 1943.*
   Vol. VI. *Breaking the Bismarcks Barrier, 22nd July 1942 to May 1944.*
   Note.—Though written in a popular style this account is based on official records.

United States Submarine Operations in World War II. T. Roscoe. Written for the Bureau of Naval Personnel. United States Naval Institute, Annapolis, Maryland, n.d. (1949).

U.S. Naval Logistics in the Second World War. By D. S. Ballantyne. Princeton University Press, 1947.

CHAPTER I
OFFICIAL

Naval Staff History Battle Summary No. 16, *Naval Operations at the Capture of Diego Suarez (Operation ' Ironclad '), May 1942.* B.R. 1736 (9).

Monthly Report of A/S Warfare Eastern Area, March-August 1942. C.B. 04199/42 Series.

JAPANESE

Japanese Military and Naval Intelligence Division. U.S. Strategic Bombing Survey (Pacific). N.I.D. 5108/46.

CHAPTER II
OFFICIAL

Attacks carried out against Enemy Submarines by Local A/S Forces in Australian Waters. M.015723/42.

Japanese Midget Submarines' Attack on Sydney Harbour, 31st May to 1st June 1942. A.C.B. 0220.

CHAPTER III

OFFICIAL

The *Naval War Diary* (Hist. Sect. N.S.) has been extensively used in compiling this chapter.

Combined Chiefs of Staff Papers, ' Arcadia ' Report, Serial WW1 (Final).

Bougainville Island—Report by Lieutenant W. J. Read, R.A.N.V.R., on Coast-Watching Activity. N.I.D. 04421/44.

Lieut.-Commander I. Pryce-Jones, R.A.N.R.—Report on Coast-Watching in the Solomons. N.I.D. 04375/44.

The Australian Army at War. Published for the Australian Army Staff by H.M.S.O., London, 1944.

UNOFFICIAL

The Coast Watchers. (Commander E. Feldt (O.B.E., R.A.N.).) Oxford University Press (1947).

CHAPTER IV

OFFICIAL

Eastern Fleet, R. of P. of Force ' A ' for period 1st July to 18th August 1942. M.011510/42.

Eastern Fleet, R. of P. for the period August and September 1942. M.014626/42.

Operation ' Streamline Jane '—Report. M.014590/42.

G.H.Q., S.C.A.P. Historical Reports, Naval Operations, No. B.I.O.S./J.A.P./P.R./711. M.012309/42. Record Office Case No. 7911 (Loss of *Voyager* and *Armidale*).

Solomon Islands Campaign—Makin Island Diversion. CinCpac File Pac–90–Wb. A16–3/MAKIN. Serial 03064. 20th October 1942. M.052182/42.

Operation ' Acquisition '. T.S.D. 5886/41.

Operation ' Countenance '. M.019350/41.

Dutch report on resistance in Timor. Historische Sectie Marinestaf.

CHAPTERS V, VI, VII, VIII

OFFICIAL

Naval Staff History Battle Summary No. 21, *Naval Operations in the Campaign for Guadalcanal, August 1942 to February 1943.* B.R. 1736 (14/49).

> *Note.*—In addition to the sources used in preparing the above Battle Summary the following have been examined :
> Record Office Case No. 8644. This contains a number of reports on the Battle of Guadalcanal (13th–15th November). (Japanese) *Report of Sea Battle of San Island, 8th August 1942.* Historical Reports, Naval Operations, No. B.I.O.S./J.A.P./P.R./711. H.M.S.O., London.

Battle of Santa Cruz Islands, 12th October 1942. T.S.D. 6678/43.

Preliminary Report of Action 12th–13th November 1942. T.S.D. 6629/43.

Report by Commander-in-Chief Pacific Fleet on Torpedoing of ' Saratoga,' ' Wasp ' and ' North Carolina,' 31st October 1942. T.S.D. 6092/43.

Official Report of the Torpedoing of U.S.S. ' Saratoga,' ' Wasp ' and ' North Carolina.' M.052330/42.

U.S. Naval Action in Gilbert Islands (U.S.S. ' Lamson ' Report). M.052523/43, M.052626/43 (Raid on Japanese Patrol Line).

U.S.S. ' Enterprise '—Action Report 13th–14th November 1942. M.053021/43.

Action Report of Task Force 63 for 10th–16th November 1942. M.053037/43.

U.S. Navy Action Reports, Pacific Area. M.053066/43, M.052928/43.

Japanese Air Attacks off Rennell Island, 30th January 1943. M.053038/43 (Sinking of *Chicago*).

Operations in the Pacific Ocean Areas, April 1943 (Commander-in-Chief Pac. 00889. 29th June 1943). M.054268/43.

Operations of T.F. 18 in Solomon Islands Area, 1st–7th April 1943. (C.T.F. 18, Serial 0104, 17th April 1943). M.054262/43.

Report on Air Attack by Japanese Planes, Solomon Islands Area, 7th April, 1943. M.054263/43.

Amphibious Operations During the Period August to December 1943 (Vella Lavella, Treasury Island, Bougainville).

United States Army in World War II—Guadalcanal : The First Offensive. J. Miller, Jr., Historical Division, Department of the Army, Washington, D.C., 1949.

The Guadalcanal Campaign. Major J. L. Zimmerman, U.S.M.C.R. Historical Division Headquarters, U.S. Marine Corps, 1949.

[*U.S.*] *Battle Experience.* Secret Information Bulletins. H.Q. of Commander-in-Chief.
No. 1, December 1941 to June 1942.
No. 2, August and September 1942.
No. 3, October 1942.
No. 4, November 1942.
No. 5, December 1942 to January 1943.
No. 6, January–February 1943.
No. 7, March 1943.
No. 8, May–July 1943.

CHAPTER IX
OFFICIAL

Reports of A/S Warfare, East Indies Station. C.B. 04199/42 Series.

German–Japanese Blockade Running. M.052737/43.

Commander-in-Chief, Eastern Fleet, War Diary.
November 1942. T.S.D.
December 1942. T.S.D. 4424/42.

U.S. Interrogation Report on ' Kota Nopan ' and ' Speybank ' N.I.D. 04368/43.

Operation ' Thwart '—Report. M.056402/44.

German documents.
PG/70704–5 M.S. *Doggerbank,* War Diary, 17th December 1941 to 12th May 1942.
32156 ISKL Teil C. 1943. *Cruiser Warfare in Foreign Waters, January 1943 to October 1944.*
34190 ISKL IK. *Etappenorganisation der Kriegsmarine, October 1942 to April 1943.*

German Naval Forces in the Far East. N.I.D. 3879/46.

Blockade Runners between Japan and France. M.051053/42.

Weekly Intelligence Report. Raider Supplements No. 2, No. 3.

Japanese Submarine Operations. N.I.D. 1845/46.

Atrocities Carried out by Japanese Submarines. N.I.D. 0799/46.

Blockade Running to and from Japan (Admiral Groos's Report). Report No. BIOS/JAP/PR/1608.

CHAPTERS X, XII, XV
OFFICIAL

U.S. Air Operations in Eastern Pacific, May 1945. M.054267/43.

Lae Island Operation, September 1943—Summary of Provisional Boat Battalion Activities. M.06328/44.

The Australian Naval Bombardment Group (A.I.F.)—Short History and Appreciation of. M.1510/46.

Cape Gloucester, New Britain—Report on Bombardment, 26th December 1943. M.03807/44. (In R.O. Case WHS 9538.)

H.M.A.S. ' Shropshire '—Bombardment of Hauwei Island, 4th and 7th March 1944. M.07279/44. (In R.O. Case WHS 9538.)

Amphibious Operations in North New Guinea. N.I.D. 03796/44. (Deals with the ' Hollandia ' Operation.)

Papuan Campaign : the Buna–Sanananda Operation, 16th November 1942 to 23rd January 1943. Military Intelligence Division, War Department, Washington, D.C.

C.O.H.Q. Bulletins.
Y/30 *Operation ' Reckless '.* T.S.D. (Misc.) 3692/44.
Y/40 *Noemfoor Island Operation.* T.S.D. (Misc.) 4588/44.

C.C.O.R. Bulletins.
46 *Report on the Operations of the 1st Corps at Hollandia, April 1944.* M.08893/44.
53 *Operation ' Horlicks ' : Capture of Biak Island, Dutch New Guinea.* M.09190/44. (In R.O. Case WHS 9538.)
54 *Operation ' Straitline ' : Capture of Wakde Island, Dutch New Guinea.* M.09191/44. (In R.O. Case WHS 9538.)
56 *Cape Gloucester Operation—Functioning of Intelligence.* M.09396/44.
66 *Biak Island, Part I—The Defence of Biak. Part II—Japanese Cave Defences on Biak.* M.012351/44.

Minelaying Operations in the South-West Pacific by the R.A.A.F., April 1943 to April 1944. M.058049/44.

Amphibious Operations During the Period August to December 1943 (Lae, Finschafen, Arawe, Cape Gloucester) Cominch. P–001—*During the Period January to March 1944* (Saidor, Admiralty Island). P–004 (U.S. Fleet, H.Q. of Commander-in-Chief). M.05734/44.

H.M.S. ' Ariadne,' Report of Minelaying Carried out off Wewak on Night of 19th/20th June 1944. M.08365/44.

JAPANESE

Report on the Battle of the Bismarck Sea (Military Intelligence Section, G.H.Q., S.C.A.P.). Report No. BIOS/JAP/PR/695.

A.T.I.S., *South West Pacific Area, No. 7*—Parts I, II (Details of the Bismarck Operation translated from Japanese sources.)

The Kon Operation for the Reinforcement of Biak. Japanese Monograph No. 91.

UNOFFICIAL

Battle Report : The End of an Empire. Prepared from official sources by Captain W. Karig, U.S.N.R. Rinehart & Co., Inc., New York and Toronto. 1948.

General Kenney Reports. By George C. Kenney. Duell, Sloan and Pearce, New York, n.d. (General Kenney assumed command of the Allied Air Forces in the South Pacific in August 1942.)

> *Note.*—Both the above books, though inaccurate on points of detail, provide useful background information. Morison, *History of U.S. Naval Operations in World War II*, Vol. VI, p. 288, referring to General Kenney's figures says : ' Never . . . have such exorbitant claims been made with so little basis in fact.'

CHAPTER XI

German–Japanese Relations from 1936 to 1945. Report No. BIOS/JAP/PR/392. H.M.S.O., London.

CHAPTER XIII, XIV

OFFICIAL

Engagement off Kula Gulf, 5th–6th July 1943. (Contains reports of Commander Task Group 36.1 (Commander Task Force 18), U.S.S. *St. Louis*, and Commander Destroyer Squadron 21). M.054516/43. Ditto (U.S.S. *Ralph Talbot*). M.054513/43.

Bombardment of Vila-Stanmore Area, Kolombangara Island, 15th–16th March, 1943. M.053406/43, M.053361/43.

U.S. Action Report, 30th June 1943—Rendova Island. M.054146/43.

Bougainville and the Northern Solomons. By Major J. N. Rentz, U.S.M.C.R., H.Q. U.S. Marine Corps, 1948.

Report of Proceedings from Commander 3rd Amphibious Force. M.055090/43.

U.S. Action reports :—
> *4th–5th July 1943, Rice Anchorage, Kula Gulf* (U.S.S. *Ralph Talbot*). M.054145/43.
> *29th–30th June 1943, Vila Stanmore, Kolombangara Island, Shortland Island.* (U.S.S. *Waller*). M.054514/43.
> *4th–5th July, Vila Stanmore and Bairoko Harbour Bombardments* (C.T.G. 36.1). M.054515/43.
> *12th–13th July, Battle of Kolombangara* (C.T.G. 36.1. Contains also *Leander's* Report). M.054513/43.
> *Night 6th/7th August 1943, Kula/Vella Gulf.* M.054520/43.

Rabaul—Attack by U.S. Forces, 11th November 1943. (Report by Commander R. M. Smeeton, R.N., on board U.S.S. *Essex*). M.056426/44.

U.S. Battle Experience Series, Secret Information Bulletins :—
> No. 10. *Naval Operations, Solomon Islands Area, 30th June to 12th July, 1943.*
> No. 11. *Naval Operations, Solomon Islands Area, 12th July to 10th August 1943.*
> No. 12. *Solomon Islands and Alaskan Areas, July–October 1943.*
> No. 14. *Naval Operations, South and South-West Pacific Ocean Areas, 6th October to 2nd November 1943.*

Amphibious Operations—Period January–March 1944. (Green Island, Emirau.) *Cominch P–004.* M.05734/44.

Operations in Solomon Islands. C.C.O.R. 40. M.06613/44.

Lessons learned from Joint Operations in New Georgia and Bougainville. C.C.O.R. 51. M.08898/44.

Landing at Cape Gloucester. C.C.O.R. 46. M.09396/44.

JAPANESE

Report on Proceedings at Rabaul and Bougainville and Naval Engagements of Kula Bay and Kolombanga, G.H.Q., S.C.A.P., Report No. BIOS/JAP/PR/710. H.M.S.O., London.

Report on the Naval Battle of Empress Augusta Bay. G.H.Q., S.C.A.P., Report No. BIOS/JAP/PR/694. H.M.S.O., London.

Vice-Admiral Samejima's Observations. A.T.I.S., S.C.A.P., Report No. BIOS/JAP/PR/599. H.M.S.O., London.

Historical Reports of Naval Operations. G.H.Q., S.C.A.P., Report No. BIOS/JAP/PR/711. H.M.S.O., London.

Index

References are to pages

' A ' Plan, 221, 223.

A/S vessels, *see* Escorts.

Aaron Ward, U.S.S., 80 ; in Battle of Guadalcanal, 82, 83 ; sunk, 141.

Abadan. Oil refinery captured, 22.

Abdiel, H.M.S., 8.

Abe, Rear-Admiral H. In Battle of E. Solomons, 57, 59.

Abercrombie, Commander L. A., U.S.N. Raids Japanese patrol line, 72.

Abner Read, U.S.S., 222 *n.*

Achilles, H.M.N.Z.S., In S.W. Pacific, 38, 39 ; in Guadalcanal operations, 93, 97 *n*, 98.

Active, H.M.S. Sinks *Monge*, 5 ; in Force F, 8 *n.*

Adelaide, H.M.A.S., 13 ; sinks *Ramses*, 113.

Aden. Reconnoitred by *I–10*, 7 ; fears for shipping route to, 10 ; submarine raid on Gulf, 11, 20–22 ; excluded from E.I. Station, 20 ; convoys, 21, 120, 122.

Aden Maru, 221.

Admiralty Islands (*see also* Lorungau, Manus), 131 ; seized, 208–210.

Advance Expeditionary Force. In Battle of E. Solomons, 58 ; in evacuation of Guadalcanal, 99.

Agano. In Battle of Empress Augusta Bay, 190–192 ; damaged at Rabaul, 195.

Agulhas Bank and Cape. Mines laid off, 108, 112.

Aikoku Maru. Works as raider and supply ship, 6, 8, 10, 11.

Ainsworth, Rear-Admiral W. L. In Solomons operations, 97.

Air. Protection of shipping by (*see also* Catalinas, Convoy Policy), 8, 10, 11, 19, 21, 22, 115–121 ; Division of Indian Ocean into areas, 120 ; importance of in New Guinea, 127 ; domination of N.E.I. and S.W. New Guinea by, 213.

    Army, Fourth (Japanese), 128, 152 (at Wewak) ; 216, 221, 223 *n.*

    Commands. Solomons, 185, 186, 207 ; South Pacific, 185.

    Cover. Value of to convoys, 121 *n.*

Air Fleets.

    First (Japanese). Disbanded, 143.

    Eleventh (Japanese). At Rabaul, 32, 58, 75, 140 ; 21st Air Fleet incorporated in, 142 ; composition of, 143.

    Twenty-first (Japanese), 142.

    901st (Japanese), 174.

Air Flotillas.

    21st. In Marianas, 143.

    22nd. Moved to Bismarcks, 140 ; in Eleventh Air Fleet, 143.

    23rd. At Kendari, 144 ; moved to Davao, 215, 216 ; in New Guinea, 221 ; in ' Kon ' Operation, 222 ; withdrawn to Palau, 223 *n.*

    24th. In Eleventh Air Fleet, 143.

    25th. In Eleventh Air Fleet, 32, 143 ; at Rabaul, 41 ; operations of, 44, 45, 54, 60, 61, 139, 140 ; reinforced, 139, 140.

    26th. Moved to Bismarcks, 32 ; requires reinforcement, 139 ; in Eleventh Air Fleet, 143.

Air Forces.

    Australian. Neutralize S.W. New Guinea, 125, 144, 213 ; strength, 127 ; in S.W. Pacific Area, 151 ; attacks Rabaul, 196 ; in assault on Hollandia, 213, 214.

    Far Eastern. Established, 211.

    Fifth (U.S.). In S.W. Pacific Area, 127, 151, 153, 155, 186 (attacks on Rabaul), 203–205, (New Britain landings), 208 (Admiralty Islands landing), 211, 212, (attacks Hollandia), 214, 216, 219–223 (Biak operation) ; supply carrying by, 216.

Ammen, U.S.S. In Cape Gloucester operation, 205 ; in Admiralty Islands operations, 210 ; in Biak operation, 222 *n*.

Ammunition. Failures of, 15, 51 ; Expenditure of, 45, 97, 167, 193, 194 *n* (A/A).

Amphibian tractors, 45.

Amphibious Force.
        III U.S., 138.
        V U.S., 138.
        VII U.S., 138, 139.

Amphibious trucks, *see* DUKWs.

Amsterdam Island. Occupied, 224.

Andamans. Diversion by Eastern Fleet in, 23, 24.

Anderson, U.S.S. In Battle of S. Cruz, 75 *n*, 78, 84 *n*.

Anna Knudsen, 120.

Annelise Essberger, 111 *n* ; scuttled, 113.

Anshun. Sunk, 129.

Anthony, H.M.S. At capture of Diego Suarez, 5 ; 8 *n*.

Anti-aircraft fire, U.S., 45, 61, 71, 79, 98 (proximity-influence fuze), 193.

Antsirana. Captured, 5.

Anzac Force, 126.

Aoba. In Battle of Savo Island, 47, 48, 50–52 ; in Battle of Cape Espérance, 67, 69 ; in ' Kon ' operation, 219, 222.

Appleleaf, R.F.A., 24 *n*.

Aquitania, s.s., 115.

Arafura Sea, 202, 213.

Arashi, 75 *n*, 95 ; in Battle of Vella Gulf, 172.

Arashio, 135.

Arawe. Allied landing, 203, 204.

Arbuthnot, Admiral Sir Geoffrey, C.-in-C. East Indies, 8.

Arcadia Conference, 12, 31.

Argonaut, U.S.S. In raid on Makin, 17, 18.

Ariadne, H.M.S. Minelaying by, 214 *n*.

Arizona Maru, 85 *n*.

Arliss, Captain S. H. T. In Operation ' Stab ', 23 *n* ; in Operation Stream-Line-Jane, 27.

Armidale, H.M.A.S. Sunk, 19.

Army, Eighth (Japanese), 126 ; Seventeenth (Japanese), 32, 129 ; Sixth (U.S.), 151.

Arthur Cavanagh, H.M.S., 22 *n*.

Arundel Island, 111.

Arunta, H.M.A.S. Withdraws guerillas from Timor, 19, 38 ; sinks *RO 33*, 129 ; lands troops on Goodenough Island, 131 ; in attack on Saidor, 156 ; bombards Gasmata, 203 ; in Biak operation, 222 *n*.

Asagiri. Sunk, 56.

Asagumo, 67 *n* ; in Battle of Guadalcanal, 87.

Asashio, 131, 135.

Ascania, H.M.N.Z.S., 38 *n*.

Ashigara, 24.

Assault, H.M.A.S., 138.

Aster, H.M.S., 24 *n*.

Astoria, U.S.S. In Battle of Savo Island, 48, 50, 52, 53 (sunk).

Atago. In Battle of S. Cruz, 75 ; in Battle of Guadalcanal, 86, 88 ; damaged, 195, 219.

Athene, H.M.S. Sent to Pacific, 74.

Atlanta, U.S.S. In Battle of E. Solomons, 60 ; in T.F. 61, 62 *n* ; in Battle of S. Cruz, 75 ; convoy escort, 80 ; in Battle of Guadalcanal, 82, 83 (sunk).

Atrocities by Japanese, 122, 129 *n*.

Auckland. South Pacific Area base, 31.

Augsburg, 110 *n*.

Auricula, H.M.S. Sunk, 4.

Aust, s.s., 113.

Berry Airfield, 141.

Betelgeuse, s.s., 55, 80.

Beveziers. Sunk, 4.

Biak, 217 ; operation against, 218–225.

Birmingham, H.M.S., 20 ; in Operation Stab, 23 ; in Operations Stream-Line-Jane, 26, 28.

Birmingham, U.S.S., 194.

Bismarck Archipelago. Removed from Japanese vital defensive area, 198.

Blackett Strait. Mining of, 159, 160.

Blackheath, 24 *n*.

Blair, Port. Japanese flying boat base, 24 ; submarine base, 107.

Blamey, General Sir Thomas. Commander Allied Land Forces, S.W.P.A., 130 ; C.-in-C. Australian Army, 151.

Blanche Harbour, 185.

Blockade running. *See also* Submarines, Japanese, supply running by. By German ships, 110–115 ; by *U.178*, 117 ; by Italian submarines, 117, 118.

Blue, U.S.S. In Battle of Savo Island, 48, 49 ; sunk, 56.

Bode, Captain H. D., 49, 51.

Bogota, s.s., 111 *n*.

Boise, U.S.S., 63 *n* ; in Battle of C. Espérance, 67–69 ; in Wakde operation, 218 *n* ; in Biak operation, 222.

Bombardments. Effect disappointing, 159, 160, 168.

Bombay. Convoys, 120 ; 122.

Bonis. Airstrip, 183 ; bombarded and bombed, 186 ; 187.

Bonn, s.s., 109.

Bora Bora, 31.

Borgen Bay, Japanese supply base, 207.

Bosnik, 219.

Bostock, Air Vice-Marshal W. D., Commander R.A.A.F., 127.

Bougainville. Airfield to be established in, 150 ; to be strengthened, 178 ; campaign in, 182–194.

Bougainville, French A.M.C., 4.

Boyd, Rear-Admiral D. W. In Operation Ironclad, 2 ; in Operation Stab, 23 *n*.

Brake, s.s., 113 *n*, 114 *n*, 120.

Breeze, H.M.N.Z.S., 96.

Breiviken, s.s., 118 *n*.

Bremerhaven, s.s., 110 *n*.

Bridson, Lieut.-Commander G., R.N.Z.V.R., 96.

Brisbane. S.W. Pacific Area base, 31, 184.

Brisbane Maru, 85 *n*.

British Genius, s.s., 21.

British Loyalty, s.s., 7.

British Purpose, s.s., 121.

British Venture, s.s., 117.

Broome, H.M.A.S., 133.

Broomdale, R.F.A., 24 *n*.

Brownson, U.S.S., 206.

Buchanan, U.S.S. In Operation Watchtower, 48 ; in Battle of C. Espérance, 67, 68 ; in New Georgia landings, 162 ; in Battle of Kolombangara, 168, 169.

Buin. Japanese base, 32.

Buka. Japanese base, 32, 93.

Buna. Occupied by Japanese, 32 ; supplied by submarines, 95 ; operations against, 126, 128, 131–133, 149.

Bunker Hill, U.S.S. Attacks Rabaul, 195, 196 ; and Kavieng, 199.

Burgenland, s.s., 111 *n*, 112 *n*, 113 *n*.

Burke, Captain A. A., 197.

Diego Suarez. Capture of, 1–5.

Diversion Attack Force, 143.

Djarkarta (*see* Jakarta).

Dobodura, 133 ; air attacks on airfields at, 142 ; telegraph line laid to, 204.

Doggerbank, 112.

Dommes, Commander W., 118.

Dorsetshire. Hospital ship, 8.

Dragon, H.M.S., 8 *n*, 10.

Drayton, U.S.S. In Battle of Tassafaronga, 90, 91 ; 97 *n* ; in capture of Finschafen, 155 ; in convoy reinforcement operation, 156.

Dresden, s.s., 112.

D.U.K.W.s. Employment of, 204, 223, 224.

' Dumbo ' (aircraft), 94 *n*.

Duncan, H.M.S., 8 *n*.

Duncan, U.S.S., 67–69.

Dunlap, U.S.S., 172, 173.

Durban. Reconnoitred by *I–30*, 7 ; convoy base, 120, 122.

Dutch (*see* Netherlands).

Dvina, s.s., 145.

Dyson, U.S.S., 186 ; in Battle of Empress Augusta Bay, 190 ; in Battle of C. St. George, 197.

Eagle, H.M.S., 111.

East Indies Station. Boundary moved, 20.

Eaton, U.S.S., 179.

Edgar Allan Poe, s.s., 65.

Efate. U.S. base, 31, 43, 58, 101.

Eilanden Revier. Enemy landing, 213.

Elbe, s.s., 111.

' Elkton ' Plans, 149, 150.

Elsa Essberger, 111 *n*, 112, 113.

Elysia, s.s., 6–8.

Emerald, H.M.S., 8 *n* ; on patrol, 10, 11.

Emirau Island. Allied landing, 200 ; defence of, 211.

Empire Gull, s.s., 107.

Empire Pride, s.s., 27.

Empress Augusta Bay. Allied landing place, 183, 184, 186 ; the landing, 187–190 ; Japanese landing, 194.

Endo, Vice-Admiral Y., 215.

Engadine, H.M.S. Sent to Pacific, 74.

England, U.S.S. Sinks 5 submarines, 224, 225.

Enogai, 164.

Enterprise, H.M.S. On escort duty, 20 ; in Operation Demcat, 106.

Enterprise, U.S.S. In T.F. 16, 34 ; in Operation Watchtower, 40, 44, 45 ; in Battle of E. Solomons, 58–62 ; damage control, 61 ; under repair, 72 ; in Battle of S. Cruz, 73, 75–78 ; in Battle of Guadalcanal, 81, 84–86 ; 89, 100 *n*, covers *Chicago*, 102 ; sent to N. Pacific, 160 ; returns to S. Pacific, 176.

Eoribawa Ridge, 129.

Erebus, H.M.S. In Operation Stream, 26.

Ericsson, s.s., 44.

Ermland, s.s., 111 *n*.

Erskine Phelps. Oil hulk, 141.

Fleet—*contd.*

>Seventh (U.S.), 126 ; task organization, 139 ; responsibilities, 153 ; composition, 1st May 1944, 210 *n.*

>Sixth (Japanese), 16.

>Third (U.S.). Formed, 138 ; raid on Truk, 207, 208.

>Third (Japanese). Reconstituted, 143.

>United States. Numbered system introduced, 138.

Fletcher, Vice-Admiral F. J. In Operation Watchtower, 39, 40, 46, 49, 53 (fails to order attack on enemy) ; in Battle of E. Solomons, 58–60 ; misses opportunity, 62.

Fletcher, U.S.S. In reinforcement of Guadalcanal, 80 ; in Battle of Guadalcanal, 82, 83 ; in Battle of Tassafaronga, 90, 91 ; sinks *RO–102*, 96 ; in operations against Munda, 97 ; in New Georgia operations, 158 *n*, 159 *n* ; in Biak operation, 222 *n.*

Florida Island, 44.

Flusser, U.S.S., 155, 203.

Flynn, Captain C. W., 53.

Foote, U.S.S., 191–193.

Force.

>' A.' Arrives at Ceylon, 10 ; makes demonstration in Bay of Bengal, 20, 23 ; covers convoy ' Pamphlet,' 115.

>Alamo, 151, 215.

>Anzac, 126.

>' F,' 1, 8 *n.*

>' H,' 1.

>' M,' 26.

Formalhaut, U.S.S., 56.

Formidable, H.M.S. In Madagascar operations, 2 ; in Force ' A,' 10 *n* ; in Operation Stab, 19, 20, 23, 25 ; proceeds home, 26.

Fort, Rear-Admiral G. H., 163 *n.*

Foxhound, H.M.S., 10.

Fremantle Submarine base, 184.

Fritillary, H.M.S., 106.

Frobisher, H.M.S., 8 *n* ; searches for raiders, 10 ; escorts convoy A.P. 1, 21.

Fubuki, 67, 69.

Fujinami, 195.

Fukudome, Vice-Admiral S., 18 *n.*

Fulda, s.s., 110 *n.*

Fumitsuki, 179.

Furutaka. In Battle of Savo Island, 47, 50–53 ; in Battle of C. Espérance, 67, 69.

Fusiyama, s.s., 111 *n.*

Fuso, 219 ; in Kon operation, 222.

G. S. Livanos, s.s., 15.

Gale, H.M.N.Z.S., 96.

Gambia, H.M.N.Z.S., 10 *n* ; in Home Waters, 20 ; in Operation Stream, 26 ; in Operation Sleuth, 114 ; in convoy ' Pamphlet,' 115.

Gamble, U.S.S. Sinks *I–123*, 55 ; in mining operations, 159–162.

Garove. Japanese supply centre, 204.

Gasmata. Japanese base, 32, 124 ; airfield, 134 ; Allied landing cancelled, 203 ; Allied landing, 207.

Gato, U.S.S., 183, 184.

Gavutu Island, 43, 44.

Gazcon, s.s., 21.

Gazelle Peninsula, 207.

Geelong, H.M.A.S., 14.

Geelvink Bay. Japanese air base, 213, 218, 219.

General Escort Command (Japanese), 174.

Halsey, Vice-Admiral W. F., Jr. Commander S. Pacific, 72–100 *pass*, 150, 151, 157–200 *pass* ; asks for British carriers, 73 ; promoted Admiral, 100 ; becomes C.-in-C. Third Fleet, 138 ; placed under General MacArthur, 149, 150 ; in New Georgia operations, 158–181 *pass* ; in Bougainville operation, 182–187 *pass*; occupies Green Is., 199, 200.

Hamakaze. In Battle of S. Cruz, 75 *n* ; in evacuation of Guadalcanal, 103 ; in New Guinea operations, 129.

Hamilton, U.S.S., 210.

Hankow Maru, 154 *n*.

Hansa Bay. Japanese convoy base, 136, 137, 141 ; by-passed, 211.

Hara, Rear-Admiral T., 57.

Haresfield, s.s., 22.

Harmon, Major-General M. F. Commanding General, S. Pacific, 55.

Harris, Brigadier-General F., 186.

Haruna. Bombards Henderson Field, 71 ; at Battle of S. Cruz, 75 ; in Battle of Guadalcanal, 85 ; in evacuation of Guadalcanal, 102 *n* ; 219.

Harusame. Sunk, 222.

Hashimoto, Rear-Admiral S., 87.

Hatsuharu, 144.

Hatsukari Maru, 144 *n*.

Hatsukaze. In Battle of S. Cruz, 75 *n* ; in evacuation of Guadalcanal, 94 ; in Bougainville operation, 190, 192, 193.

Hatsuyuki. In Solomons, 56, 67 (Battle of C. Espérance), 165–168 (Battle of Kula Gulf).

Hauraki, m.s., 6.

Havelland, s.s., 111 *n*.

Havenstein, s.s., 111 *n*.

Hawaii. Japanese submarines off, 148.

Hawkins, H.M.S., 20.

Hyakutake, Lieut.-General H., 129.

Hayashio, 75 *n*, 131.

Hayataka (*see Junyo*).

Hazlewood, U.S.S., 225.

Heemskerck, R. Neth. N.S. Escorts Convoy W.S. 19P, 20 ; in Operation Stab, 23 ; sinks *Ramses*, 113 ; escorts convoy ' Pamphlet,' 115.

Helena, U.S.S. In Battle of C. Espérance, 67–69 ; in Battle of S. Cruz, 75 ; in Battle of Guadalcanal, 80, 82, 83 ; sinks *RO–102*, 96 ; in operations against Munda, 97, 98, 159 *n* ; in T.F. 18, 160 ; in New Georgia operations, 163 ; in Battle of Kula Gulf, 165–167.

Helfrich, Vice-Admiral C. E. L., 23.

Hellville. Captured, 27.

Helm, U.S.S. In Battle of Savo Island, 48, 50, 52, 53 *n* ; in supply of Guadalcanal, 56 ; in Arawe landing, 203.

Henderson Field. Discovered, 31 ; first U.S. aircraft fly in, 56 ; defence of, 57 ; attacked by aircraft, 59 ; bombarded, 71 ; short of aircraft fuel, 71, 79 ; out of action, 74.

Henley, U.S.S. In Battle of Savo Island, 53 *n* ; in supply of Guadalcanal, 56 ; in New Guinea operations, 129, 155, 156 (sunk).

Henry T. Allen, U.S.S., 138.

Herborg, 108.

Herm, U.S.S., 129.

Hermes, H.M.S., 2.

Hermione, H.M.S. In Operation Ironclad, 2, 4, 5.

Hero, H.M.S., 21.

Hikokawa Maru, 86 *n*.

Hilo, U.S.S., 132.

Himalaya, s.s., 113.

Hiravati, H.M.I.S., 120.

Hitaka (*see Hiyo*).

Hitler. Views on Madagascar, 6.

Isonami, 131.

Isudzu. In 2nd Southern Expeditionary Fleet, 24 *n* ; at Battle of S. Cruz, 75 ; in Battle of Guadalcanal, 84, 85.

Italy. Effect of armistice, 117.

Ito, Rear-Admiral Y., 215.

Itsukushima, 132.

Ivato air base, 2.

Iwasa, General, 207 *n*.

Izaki, Rear-Admiral S., 168.

Jakarta (Tandjong Priok (Batavia)), 109 ; Japanese and German submarine base, 119.

Jalabala, s.s. Sunk, 121.

Japan. Buys German ships, 110 ; offers submarine base to Germans, 118 ; lack of Army-Navy co-operation, 129 ; draws up new war plans, 144 ; nervous of Russia, 145 ; task now defensive, 146 ; attitude to International Law, 147 *n* ; puts Plan ' A ' in operation, 223 ; state of in October 1944, 225, 226.

Jarvis, U.S.S. Torpedoed, 45 ; sunk, 50, 54.

Jask, 107.

Jenkins, U.S.S. In New Georgia operations, 159 *n* ; in Battle of Kula Gulf, 164–167 ; in Battle of Kolombangara, 168, 170 ; in Biak operation, 222 *n*.

Jintsu. In Battle of E. Solomons, 57, 62 ; in Battle of Kolombangara, 168-170.

John Adams, s.s., 12.

Jumna, H.M.I.S., 24 *n*.

Juneau, U.S.S. In T.F. 17, 66, 75 *n* ; in reinforcement of Guadalcanal, 80 ; in Battle of Guadalcanal, 82, 83, 88.

Junyo, 31 *n* ; attacks U.S. supply line, 72 ; in Battle of S. Cruz, 75 ; in Battle of Guadalcanal, 85 ; in New Guinea operations, 132.

K–9, 14.

Kagero, 75 *n* ; sunk, 104.

Kahili. Japanese base, 32, 177, 186 ; airfield, 183 ; harbour mined, 198.

Kako. In Battle of Savo Island, 47, 50, 51 ; sunk, 53.

Kalgoorlie, H.M.A.S., 19.

Kalingo, s.s., 96.

Kanawha, s.s., 141.

Kanimbla, H.M.A.S. In midget attack on Sydney, 15 ; in Operation Countenance, 22 ; 38 ; in VII Amphibious Force, 138.

Kaoe Bay. Japanese base, 201.

Kara airstrip, 183, 186.

Karagola, s.s., 106.

Karin, s.s., 112, 113.

Kashii, 106.

Kasuga Maru, 105 *n*.

Katoomba, s.s., 16, 131.

Kaukenau, 213.

Kavieng. Japanese base, 32, 136, 198 ; 124 ; to be captured, 149, 202 ; air strike on, 199 ; bombarded, 207, 209 ; to be isolated, 208.

Kawabe, Lieut.-General, 104 *n*.

Kawakaze. Sinks *Blue*, 56.

Kazegumo, 75, 179.

Keifuku Maru, 134 *n*.

Kembu Maru, 135.

Kendari. Air base, 144, 202, 215.

Kenney, Major-General C. G. Commander Allied Air Forces S.W. Pacific, 39, 41, 127, 150 ; introduces skip-bombing, 135 ; Commander Fifth Air Force, 151, 186.

INDEX

Kenya, H.M.S., 114.

Khorramshahr, 22.

Kieta. Japanese base, 32, 182 ; air base, 41 ; to be seized, 124 ; attacked, 186.

Kilindini. Eastern Fleet base, 1, 115 ; convoys, 120, 122.

Kilty, U.S.S., 163 *n*.

Kimura, Rear-Admiral S., 87, 135.

Kinai Maru, 129.

King, Admiral E. J. C.-in-C. U.S. Fleet and CNO., 17 ; asks for diversion by Eastern Fleet, 17, 19 ; initiates attack on Solomon Islands, 34 ; remarks on unity of command, 47 *n* ; powers of, 150 *n* ; asks for return of T.F. 92.4, 176.

Kinkaid, Rear-Admiral T. C. In Battle of S. Cruz, 75, 76 (directive to) ; in Battle of Guadalcanal, 84 ; Commander North Pacific, 90 ; operation orders by, 90 ; Commander Seventh Fleet, 139, 203, 220 ; in Biak operation, 222.

Kinryu Maru, 57, 62.

Kinu. In 2nd Southern Expeditionary Fleet, 24 ; in Combined Fleet, 219 ; in Kon operation, 222.

Kinugasa. In Battle of Savo Island, 47, 50-52 ; in Battle of C. Espérance, 67-69 ; in Battle of Guadalcanal, 84, 85.

Kinugawa Maru, 86 *n*.

Kirishima. In Battle of S. Cruz, 75 ; in Battle of Guadalcanal, 86, 88.

Kiriwina Island, 150 ; occupied, 153.

Kitts, Captain W. A., 92.

Kiwi, H.M.N.Z.S., 96.

Kiyonami, 168.

Koga, Admiral Mineichi. Becomes C.-in-C. Combined Fleet, 143 ; enunciates defensive policy, 145 ; establishes ' interception zones,' 146 ; sends air groups to Bismarcks, 194 ; killed, 220.

Kokoda, 128, 130.

Kokopo, 134.

Kolombangara Island. Occupied by Japanese, 93, 174 ; airfield discovered, 98 ; source of Japanese reinforcements, 163 ; reinforced, 164, 165, 168 ; to be by-passed, 175 ; evacuated, 178-181.

Kondo, Vice-Admiral N. Commander Second Fleet, 58, 75 ; in Battle of Guadalcanal, 87, 88.

Kongo. Bombards Henderson Field, 71 ; in Battle of S. Cruz, 75 ; in Battle of Guadalcanal, 85.

Kota Nopan, s.s., 112.

Kowarra, s.s., 147.

Kukum, 75.

Kula Gulf. Engagement in, 157-159 ; mined, 159, 160 ; Battle of, 164-168.

Kulmerland, s.s., 111 *n*, 112.

Kumac. Airfield, 31.

Kumagawa Maru, 86 *n*.

Kumano, 75, 219.

Kumusi River. Japanese landing, 131.

Kupang, 152.

Kurita, Vice-Admiral T. At Battle of S. Cruz, 75 ; in Battle of Guadalcanal, 85 ; takes cruiser force to Rabaul, 194.

Kuroshio, 75 *n* ; sunk, 159.

Kuru, H.M.A.S., 19.

Kusaka, Vice-Admiral J. C.-in-C. Eleventh Air Fleet, 75, 93.

Kuttabull, H.M.A.S., 14.

Kuzume, Colonel, 219.

Kwajalein, 210.

Kyokusei Maru, 136.

Kyosei Maru, 207.

Kyushu Maru, 71.

279

L.S.T.s. At capture of Diego Suarez, 5.

L.S.T. 66, 206.

L.S.T. 342, 164.

La Vallette, U.S.S. In Solomons operations, 100 *n*, 102 ; in Battle of Vella Lavella, 179 ; in Biak operations, 222 *n*.

Lae. Captured by Japanese, 32 ; air, advanced, and main base, 42, 131, 133, 134, 152 ; recaptured, 149, 154, 155.

Laffey, U.S.S. In Battle of C. Espérance, 67, 68 ; in reinforcement of Guadalcanal, 80 ; in Battle of Guadalcanal, 82, 83, 88.

Laforey, H.M.S., 10 *n*.

Lamson, U.S.S. Raids Japanese patrol line, 72 ; in Battle of Tassafaronga, 90, 91 ; in landing of 25th Division, 97 *n* ; in attack on Finschafen, 155 ; in Arawe landing, 203, 206.

Landing craft. Shortage of, 125, 130, 133, 138 ; become available, 126.

Lang, U.S.S., 172.

Lardner, U.S.S. In T.G. 62.4, 80 ; in Battle of Tassafaronga, 90, 91.

Lauriana, H.M.A.S., 14.

Lawrence, H.M.I.S., 22 *n*.

Layton, Admiral Sir Geoffrey, 53.

Le Héros (French submarine), 5.

Le Triomphant (French cruiser), 38.

Leander, H.M.N.Z.S. Covers reinforcements, to Fiji, 39, and to Guadalcanal, 63 *n*, 93 *n* ; in Battle of Kolombangara, 168–170.

Leap-frog strategy, 202.

Leary, Vice-Admiral H. F. Commands MacArthur's naval forces, 38 ; with reserve force at Nandi, 100 ; relieved, 139.

Lee, Rear-Admiral W. A., Jr. CTF64, 65 ; covers Guadalcanal convoy, 67 ; in Battle of S. Cruz, 75, 79 ; in Battle of Guadalcanal, 84, 86–88 ; in landing of 25th Division, 97.

Léopard (French cruiser). Recaptures Réunion, 28, 29.

Lesser Sunda Islands, 201.

Leuthen (ex *Nankin*), 108.

Lever Harbour. Allied base, 171, 177.

Lexington, U.S.S., 176.

Liberators (*see* B–24s).

Libra, s.s., 80.

Lightning, H.M.S., 10 *n*.

Lilac, H.M.S., 22 *n*.

Limerick, m.s., 147.

Lismore, H.M.S., 106.

Little, U.S.S., 56.

Lockwood, Rear-Admiral C. A., Jr. Commander Submarines S.W. Pacific, 39, 41, 42, 70 *n*.

Long, U.S.S., 210.

Long Island, U.S.S., 57.

Lookout, H.M.S., 10 *n*.

Lookouts. Failures of, 50 *n*, 65.

Lorungau (*see also* Manus), 124 ; Japanese base, 131, 132.

Los Negros Island, 208–210.

Losmer, s.s., 107.

Louise Moller, s.s., 107.

Louisville, U.S.S. Arrives in S. Pacific, 93 *n* ; in T.F. 67, 97 *n* ; in T.F. 18, 99 *n* ; leaves Pacific, 160.

Lydia M. Child, s.s., 147.

Nagato, 219.

Nagato Maru, 154 *n.*

Nagatsuki, 165, 167, 168.

Nagaura, 207.

Nagumo, Vice-Admiral C. In reinforcement of Guadalcanal, 57 ; in Carrier Striking Force at Battle of S. Cruz, 75–79.

Nako Maru, 85 *n.*

Nandi, 89, 100.

Nankai Maru, 129.

Nankin, s.s., 108.

Napier, H.M.S. In Force ' A,' 23 ; in Operation Line, 27 ; in Operation Rose, 28.

Narbada, s.s., 12.

Nashville, U.S.S. Reinforces S. Pacific, 93 *n* ; in relief of 1st Marine Division, 97 ; bombards Vila-Stanmore, 98 ; in mining operation, 159 *n* ; damaged and leaves for N. Pacific, 160 ; in C. Gloucester landing, 205 ; in Admiralty Islands operation, 209, 210 ; in Wakde operation, 218 *n.*

Nassau Bay, U.S. landing, 153.

Natori. In 2nd Southern Expeditionary Fleet, 24 ; reinforces Hollandia, 132 ; 219.

Natsugumo, 67 *n*, 69.

Natsushima, 207.

Natter, 153.

Nautilus, U.S.S. In raid on Makin, 17.

Navajo, U.S.S., 101.

Naval Landing Forces (Japanese), 57.

Naval power. Effect of lack of in New Guinea, 126.

Ndrillo Island, 210.

Nelson, Cape. Allied base, 132.

Nelson, H.M.S., 20.

Nepal, H.M.S., 114.

Netherlands. Work of Navy, 14, 19, 20, 23, 24 ; and Army, 125, 144, 213 ; and aircraft, 127 ; merchant ships, 130, 133.

Netherlands East Indies. Reinforced by Japanese, 92, 201 ; aircraft transferred to Bismarcks, 136, 202 ; air supremacy in Allied hands, 202.

New Britain. To be attacked, 149 ; described, 203 ; invasion of, 203–208 ; garrison short of food, 205–207 ; effect on capture of Manus, 210.

New Caledonia. On Allied line of communications, 31 ; coast watchers in, 58.

New Georgia. Outpost for Rabaul, 93 ; operations against, 149, 150, 161–164, 174 ; described, 157 ; reinforced by Japanese, 159.

New Guinea. Japanese occupation, 32 ; Allied plans for recapture, 34 ; more important to Japanese than Solomons, 57 ; strengthened by Japanese, 92, 211 ; reconquest of, 124–136, 149–156, 201–219 *pass* ; south-western neutralized, 125, 144 ; importance of air power in, 127 ; Japanese Army Air Force in, 128 ; both Allies and Japanese short of food, 133 ; reinforced from Solomons, 137 ; eastern abandoned, 144 ; maps inadequate, 214.

New Hebrides. On Allied line of communications, 31 ; Allied base, 43.

New Ireland (*see also* Kavieng). Allied plans, 124 ; Japanese hold north part, 198, 199.

New Mexico, U.S.S., 93.

New Orleans, U.S.S. In Battle of E. Solomons, 60 ; in T.F. 61, 62 *n* ; sent to Espiritu Santo, 89 ; in Battle of Tassafaronga, 90–92.

New Zealand (*see also* H.M.N.Z. ships' names). Security of essential, 31 ; employment of her forces, 38, 39, 41, 178, 184, 199, 200, 207 (R.N.Z.A.F.).

Newcastle, H.M.S., 20 ; in Operation Thwart, 114 ; in Operation Player, 118.

Nichiryu Maru, 134.

Nicholas, U.S.S. In Guadalcanal operations, 97 *n*, 98, 99 *n* ; in New Georgia operations, 158 *n*, 159 *n*, 160, 163 *n*, 165–167 (Battle of Kula Gulf), 168, 169(Battle of Kolombangara).

Nieuw Amsterdam, s.s., 115.

Rhakotis, 109, 111 *n*, 112.

Rice Anchorage. Landing, 163.

Richards, Lieut.-Commander D. H., R.A.N.R. (S), 19.

Riefkohl, Captain F. L., U.S.N., 48, 49, 51, 52.

Rigel, U.S.S., 138 *n*.

' Ringbolt,' 89.

Rio de Janeiro Maru, 24.

Rio Grande, s.s., 111 *n*, 112, 113 *n*.

Robert Bacon, s.s., 118 *n*.

Roberts, Lieut.-Commander D. G., 78.

Rockets, 203–205, 216, 224.

Rodney, H.M.S., 20.

Romney, H.M.S., 22.

Roosevelt, President F. D., 72.

Rossbach, s.s., 112 *n*.

Rotherham, H.M.S., 114.

Rover, H.M.S., 105.

Royal Sovereign, H.M.S., 20.

Russell Islands. Occupied by Japanese, 92 ; occupied by Allies, 157 ; airfields, 161.

Russell, U.S.S., 75 *n*, 84 *n*.

Russia. Supplies sent to, 22 ; Japanese relations with, 145.

Ryuho, 219.

Ryujo, 31 *n* ; in Battle of E. Solomons, 57, 59–61.

Ryuosan Maru, 213 *n*.

S-38, 47.

S-44. Sinks *Kako*, 53.

SC-1 radar, 90.

S.C.-669, 148.

SG radar, 91.

Saarland, s.s., 110 *n*.

Sabang, 23, 25, 118.

Sado Maru, 85 *n*.

Saidor. Airfield, 152 ; captured, 156.

Saigon, 112.

San Diego, U.S.S. In T.F. 61, 62 *n* ; in Guadalcanal operations, 66, 75 *n*, 84 ; at Numea, 89 ; in Bougainville operations, 186.

San Francisco, U.S.S. In Battle of E. Solomons, 59 ; in T.F. 61, 62 *n* ; in Battle of C. Espérance, 67, 68 ; in Battle of S. Cruz, 75 ; on convoy escort, 80 ; in Battle of Guadalcanal, 82, 83.

San Juan, U.S.S. In Guadalcanal operations, 48, 59, 75, 88, 89, 98 ; in Bougainville operations, 186, 187.

St. Louis, U.S.S. In operations against Munda, 98, and New Georgia, 159 *n* ; in T.F. 18, 160 ; in Battle of Kula Gulf, 165–167, and Kolombangara, 168–170 ; damaged, 200.

Salamoa. Barge centre, 131 ; by-passed, 154 ; captured, 155.

Salt Lake City, U.S.S. In Battle of E. Solomons, 59 ; in T.F. 61, 62 *n* ; in Battle of C. Espérance, 67–69.

Samate, 216, 221.

Samidare, 75 *n*, 87 *n* ; in Battle of Vella Lavella, 179, 180 ; in Kon operation, 222.

Samoa, 31, 36 *n* ; Japanese submarine patrols off, 146.

Samuel Heintzelman, s.s., 110 *n*.

Sanananda, 133.

Valiant, H.M.S. Working up, 20 ; in Eastern Fleet, 73.

Van Galen, R. Neth. N.S. In Operation Stab, 23 ; in Operation Rose, 28.

Van Heemskerck, s.s., 141.

Van Outhoorn, s.s., 141.

Vandegrift, Major-General A. A. In Operation Watchtower, 37, 45, 46, 49 ; in Guadalcanal operations, 57, 89, 97.

Vangunu Island, 163.

Vella Lavella Island, 164 ; occupied, 177, 178.

Vendetta, H.M.A.S., 38.

Vichy French merchant ships. Blockade running by, 28.

Victorious, H.M.S. Sent to Pacific, 74 ; joins T.F. 14, 160.

Vila Airfield, 98 ; bombarded, 162, 164, 177 ; Japanese reinforce, 165.

Vincennes, U.S.S. In Battle of Savo Island, 48, 50, 52, 53.

Vireo, U.S.S., 71.

Viru Harbour, 161, 163.

Viti (Fijian ship), 38.

Vitu Islands, 204.

Viviana, H.M.S., 116.

Voice radio. U.S. used by Japanese for tracking, 166 ; U.S. employment of, 166, 169 (excessive use of), 170 (failure of), 191 (excessive use of).

Voyager, H.M.A.S., loss of, 19, 38.

W/T (*see also* Radio). Deception, 23, 25, 152, 153.

Waigeo Island, 222.

Wakde. Operations against, 217–219.

Wake Island. Raid on, 194.

Walke, U.S.S., 84, 87, 88.

Walker, Captain F. R., 179, 180.

Waller, U.S.S., 158, 162 *n*.

Wallings, Commander J. H., 164.

Wanigela, 130.

Wards airfield, 141.

Warramunga, H.M.A.S. At Saidor landing, 156 ; in New Britain operations, 203 ; in Admiralty Islands operations, 210 ; in Biak operation, 222 *n*.

Warspite, H.M.S., 19 ; in Operation Stab, 23 ; in Operation Jane, 26, 27, 73 *n* ; in dock, 106 ; sent to Mediterranean, 115.

Washington Conference (' Arcadia '), 12, 31.

Washington, U.S.S. In Guadalcanal operations, 67, 75 ; in Battle of Guadalcanal, 81, 84, 86 *n*, 87, 88 ; 89 ; leaves for N. Pacific, 160 ; in Strategic reserve, 176.

Wasp, U.S.S. In Operation Watchtower, 40, 43–45, 53 ; in Battle of E. Solomons, 58, 59, 62 ; torpedoed, 63, 64, 65.

Waters, U.S.S., 162 *n*, 163 *n*.

Wau, 133 ; attacked, 134, 142.

Wavell, Field-Marshal, 28.

Weather (*see also* Henderson Field). Effect on air operations, 67, 85.

Wellen, s.s., 13.

Wenniker, Admiral, 119.

Weserland, s.s., 112 *n*, 113 *n*.

Westralia, H.M.A.S., 38 ; in VII Amphibious Force, 138 ; in Arawe landing, 203.

Wewak. Japanese landings, 92, 132 ; to be secured, 124 ; Japanese airfields, 127, 152, (Japanese surprised at) ; supply base, 136, 137, 141 ; major base, 211 ; base of Ninth Fleet, 215.

Whyalla, H.M.A.S., 133.

Wichita, U.S.S. In Guadalcanal operations, 93 *n*, 99 *n*, 100 *n* ; leaves for N. Pacific, 160.

Wickham Anchorage, 163.

Wilkinson, Rear-Admiral T. S., Commander III Amphibious Force, 138 ; Commander S. Pacific Amphibious Force, 171 ; in Vella Lavella occupation, 177, and Battle, 179 ; in Bougainville operation, 187 ; occupies Green Islands, 199.

Willaumez Peninsula, 207.

William Dawes, s.s., 16.

William K. Vanderbilt, s.s., 147.

William Williams, s.s., 147.

Wilson, U.S.S. In Battle of Savo Island, 48, 50, 52, 53 *n*.

Winnetou, s.s., 111 *n*.

Woleai, 211.

Wollongbar, s.s., 147.

Woodlark Island. Occupied, 150, 153.

Woodworth, U.S.S., 162 *n*.

Wright, Rear Admiral. In Battle of Tassafaronga, 90, 91.

Y Plan, 144.

Y P-284, 74.

Yae Maru, 105 *n*.

Yahagi, 219.

Yakumo Maru, 211.

Yamada, Rear-Admiral S., 32.

Yamagumo, 67 *n*.

Yamamoto, Admiral I. C.-in-C. Combined Fleet, 58 ; killed, 142, 143.

Yamato. At Truk, 58 ; covers Guadalcanal evacuation, 102 *n*.

Yamatsuki Maru, 86 *n*.

Yamaura Maru, 86 *n*.

Yamazato Maru, 105 *n*.

Yandra, H.M.A.S., 14.

Yap, 211.

Yarroma, H.M.A.S. In midget attack on Sydney, 14, 15.

Yasukawa Maru, 131.

Yayoi, 129.

Young, Captain C., 83.

Ysabel Island, 93.

Yubari. In Battle of Savo Island, 47, 50, 52.

Yudachi. In Guadalcanal operations, 56, 75 *n*, 83 (sunk).

Yugiri. In supply of Guadalcanal, 56 ; in Battle of C. St. George, 197.

Yukikaze, 75 *n*.

Yunagi. In Battle of Savo Island, 47, 50, 51.

Yura, 74.

Yvensang, s.s., 24 *n*.

Z Plan, 144.

Zane, U.S.S. In Solomons operations, 74, 162.

Zanzibar. Reconnoitred by *I-30*, 7.

Zeilin, U.S.S., 80.

Zenyo Maru, 105 *n*.

Zuiho, 31 *n* ; at Battle of S. Cruz, 75, 76.

Zuikaku, 31 *n* ; in Battle of E. Solomons, 57, 59 ; in Battle of S. Cruz, 75, 77 ; 219.

Printed in the United Kingdom for HMSO
Dd 0296898 C15 1/95 9091